Voyages Into Eternity

Voyages Into Eternity

Memoirs of the Miller Family
From 1812 to 1995

Ian Alexander Miller

The Pentland Press Limited
Edinburgh • Cambridge • Durham • USA

First published in 1997 by
The Pentland Press Ltd.
1 Hutton Close
South Church
Bishop Auckland
Durham

British Library Cataloguing in Publication Data.
A Catalogue record for this book is available
from the British Library.

ISBN 1 85821 446 7

Typeset by CBS, Felixstowe, Suffolk
Printed and bound by Antony Rowe Ltd., Chippenham

To my wife, Jane Foster Malcolm Miller,
our daughters, Lynn Anne and Janice Elaine
and to our grandchildren.

CONTENTS

LIST OF ILLUSTRATIONS

PREFACE

The Auld Laird Miller, born in a remote village in Scotland in the year 1812, lived and died amongst his peers, and his memory is already obscured by the mists of time. His sons and his grandsons, each according to his destiny, remained or dispersed to distant lands. They now have sons and grandsons looking to the future, but as each grows older, perhaps glancing back into the past. Yet the Auld Laird himself could stand upon the bones of 500 years of ancestors, buried within the ancient churchyard of St Michael's, consecrated in the year 1200 AD. Great tombstones bear silent record of the Millers back to the sixteenth century. Beyond these dates the older, weatherbeaten stones lie flat upon the ground, and are too well-worn to permit the reading of their inscriptions. This book records the life of one of the Auld Laird's grandsons, Ian Alexander Miller, born on 10 January 1918, and describes how his brief voyage upon the sea of life fitted within these 200 years.

FOREWORD

This is a wonderful book of historic fact with personal glimpses into an extraordinary life of adventure and discovery. Ian Miller's journey takes us from a remote village in Scotland, through the dark days of the Second World War, to countries we have read about only in travel brochures. Finally, he allows us the rare privilege of looking into the heart and soul of the writer.

It is truly a challenge for any biographer to blend together historical reality, personal experiences, profiles of many countries and their people, and still produce an enjoyable and readable manuscript. Ian Miller has accomplished this.

Having an advanced glimpse of the book has allowed me a new perspective on someone I thought I had known very well for almost four decades. However, 'Voyages Into Eternity' has taken me beyond the personal relationship I have enjoyed with the Miller family for so many years.

It is a privilege and an honour for me to present this foreword to 'Voyages Into Eternity'. This is a book which will surely live on, long after its characters. It is a book to read at one's leisure; and above all, it is a book to kindle the spirit of adventure in all of us.

MARY COOK
Broadcast Journalist

PART I

CHAPTER I

THE FARMHOUSE

The Farmhouse, Linlithgow Bridge, by Linlithgow, Scotland was a birthplace about which one could develop a great sense of pride. There was I, Ian Alexander Miller, born on 10 January 1918, the seventh child and fourth son of William Miller, farmer. My father was a gentle person, wise in his own way, a regular churchgoer, a good father, and according to my mother, a devoted husband. He was not an ambitious man, he was content to be well-respected and he was always happy to be referred to by the villagers as the Laird. The title really belonged to his father, my grandfather, also William Miller, and always referred to as the Auld Laird. This was because, in his prime, he had owned everything around him, the village, the farms, and even the pub, or so it was said.

He, William Miller senior, was born on 10 August 1812, the year that Napoleon was beating at the gates of Moscow. He was just three years old when the battle of Waterloo was fought and won by the Duke of Wellington. From tales told by old men in the village, I was able to piece together a picture in my mind of my grandfather, by now long-deceased, as a great man of many talents, and a man who dominated the local scene. There were farms all around in the old days, and mostly occupied by Millers, or Bowies, or Alexanders and all of whom seemed to be full cousins to my father. They visited us, mostly in winter, when it was too dark and too cold to work. They were entertained in the parlour, with a roaring fire, and the whisky running like water. Being allowed to peek only now and again left the impression that they were all very mysterious people, and in the flickering light from oil lamps, they looked a little fearsome, and more preoccupied with the dogs than with small children.

I was constantly in awe of these relatives who arrived and departed in a highly-polished trap drawn by a real high-stepping horse. The Farmhouse in those days, the nineteen twenties, was about a mile away from the market town and county seat, Linlithgow, and as a consequence lay beyond the scope of electric power and sewage services. As a result, we had a massive stone house with attached stables and byres, an enormous garden, an outhouse, a midden, oil lamps, and a water pump operated by hand. However, we did have chickens

3

and ducks, and delightful families of pigs, cows, horses, cats, dogs, and all of them had pet names. Above all, we had my mother, Belle, or Ezybelle as my father was wont to call her, and in many ways she was quite unique.

Miss Belle was a McDiarmid, one of five sisters, all of whom were school teachers, and they were daughters of Donald McDiarmid, the postmaster at Linlithgow. They are reported to have been exceedingly handsome ladies in their youth and all of them appeared to have made good marriages. There were times, however, when I can remember my mother saying they had all married into money except her. Nevertheless what Miss Belle lacked in money she made up for in character. She was a noted driving force throughout the area, had a keen interest in everything that went on, and in particular, in politics. She was a dedicated conservative and she devoted much of her time harassing Emmanuel Shinwell, our local Member of Parliament. During election times, she would rise at five in the morning just to remove all of the Labour Party posters, some of which had to be scrubbed from the telegraph poles.

Music and singing were her passions. She had a very powerful contralto voice, regularly sang in the church choir, and oftentimes taught piano. She was convinced that we should all be musically inclined but she was very disappointed to discover that only her eldest son had an ear for music, and that for jazz. Earl Fatha Hines, the great American jazz pianist was his favourite. Later on my brother garnered a great reputation locally with his jazz band, the 'Blue Dominoes'. Even as the seventh child, I was compelled to take piano lessons from the church organist, James Fleming. I regret to say that despite my persistent studies of Bach, Schumann, and other great composers, the real skills at the piano eluded me.

There were times in the village when we had organized entertainment in Chalmers Hall, a great hall gifted to the village by the paper-mill barons. My mother was always invited to sing and play the piano. I can clearly remember her rendering of the 'Bonnie Wells O' Wearie', and I can see the tears of emotion running down my father's cheeks. There was always boisterous applause and Miss Belle would accept all the adoration very graciously.

I admired my mother greatly. She was already more than forty years old when I was born, and my father over fifty, so, as a small boy, I looked upon my parents as old. I depended upon my big sisters for everything, and I acquired a great deal of respect for age. On special occasions, particularly funerals, my father would wear a long black coat with a velvet collar, a top hat and he carried a cane. My mother was usually decked out in great floral headdress, and in the latest of fashion. It was all very awe-inspiring to a small boy. On the other hand, my sisters, both big girls, prepared great meals with all kinds of pies, and cakes, and stuff, but they never hesitated to reach out and cuff my ears whether I deserved it or not. I do remember how, immediately after school, I was directed to the back garden by the rain barrels where a bucket of potatoes stood waiting, first to be scrubbed into one bucket, then peeled into another.

Nevertheless, the big decisions, the important events in our lives, were always dictated by my mother. Most of the stories about my mother and about the family in general were told to me by my sister Jean. She is four years older than I am, but in one's youth, four years seemed like a lifetime. The earliest story involving me always remains in my mind. It appeared that my father, being the eldest son, waited a few years after the Auld Laird expired before seriously courting a bride. Thereafter, he had a long wait before the family home was vacated by his widowed mother. When he did finally marry, he and his bride were compelled to set up house in Park Cottage, a large, two-storey house, about a quarter of a mile from the farm. His mother, the widow, Jane Stewart, continued to live in The Farmhouse with her three younger, unmarried sons, none of whom appeared to be very keen on work. This situation continued for many long years during which there were almost continuous court appeals against the Auld Laird's last will and testament.

Despite his already advanced years, as a bridegroom the Auld Laird had fathered six children, with his bride Jane Stewart. The last son, Alexander, was born when his father was seventy years old. The eldest child Annie, was born in 1868 and she married John Crawford, son of a local farmer. They moved to a farm in England, near Colchester, and raised a large family. Then came William, the eldest son, and my father. He was followed by Robert in 1872, James in 1874, Barbara in 1878 who died in infancy, and lastly Alexander who was born in 1882. None of my father's brothers had children.

In his early thirties, Robert took off for Canada along with another farmer's son, one of the Browns of Bonnytown. They returned for the Great War, which they managed to survive, then promptly took off again for New Zealand. Robert was never heard of for thirty years, then he suddenly reappeared. James became a prominent banker, and lived in a great mansion house in Paisley, near Glasgow. Alexander, better known as Sandy, spent the greater part of his life at John Brown's shipyards, in Glasgow, where they built the largest and the most luxurious liners ever to sail the seven seas. Robert returned from New Zealand still a bachelor. Sandy lived in Glasgow, and is reported to have made an honest woman out of his housekeeper, very late in life. They had no family and old Robert simply moved in with them.

In the late 1940s my sister Jean and I paid a visit to Aunt Mary, Sandy's wife, as she had expressed a desire to see us. A short time thereafter, Uncle Robert died, and he left his belongings to Sandy. Soon afterwards, both Sandy and Mary succumbed to the harsh Scottish winter, and the combined belongings were left to brother James who survived till 1959. I was told that James, like his brother Sandy, made an honest woman out of his housekeeper, Jennie Steele, and they devoted their declining years together to counting their 'bawbees', as my grandfather often said. It did appear, in retrospect, that James had indeed saved his money, and he did the honourable thing when he died at eighty-five. He left his widow life-rented, as they say in Scotland, and upon her death, the 'Miller Trust' as it was called, was bequeathed to St Michael's Church. I can remember how this infuriated my eldest brother, Willie, who had assumed that all would come to him, being the eldest son.

The bequest is reported to have amounted to 18,000 pounds which was, in those days, a hefty sum of money. However, all the old property around the village that James had acquired had to go to brother Willie, in accordance with Scottish Law. On many an occasion, he managed to dispose of some dirty old house, and thereafter hosted a celebration. By this time he had become the town historian, and he used to regale all his cronies in the 'Cricketer's Arms' with all the juicy stories about the prominent citizenry. He became quite bitter in recalling how the widow, Jane Stewart, hung on to the old farmhouse, and was quite enraged about how our Uncle James tried to stay on, claiming the property as his, when our grandmother died in 1916.

There was no love lost between my mother and her brother-in-law, James, in fact she hated him with a passion for as long as I can remember. Indeed she waited for two years after my grandmother died before she decided to take the law into her own hands. It is said that, although several months pregnant with me, thoroughly sick of the courthouse appeals from brother James, she marched down to The Farmhouse, put her foot through the front window, climbed in, and unlocked all the doors. The remaining brothers were expelled forthwith, and we, including me, took up residence in the family home. This was always looked upon by the villagers as Belle's finest hour. An old lady, Mag Adams, the village midwife, always treated me with the greatest respect. She claimed that I was the Auld Laird come home to roost.

The old house was typical of the Scottish farmhouse design, big and square, with a front garden, and a large front door which was rarely used. Entrance was made by a side door, leading into the area adjacent to the main house, containing the milk-house, the wash-house, extensive storage space, and a near-vertical staircase leading to the loft, which really lay above the milk-house and extended over the stables. In this loft there were three built-in double beds, each with appropriate 'donkey's breakfast' type mattress, solid wood walls, and a large skylight. My three older brothers resided therein, just as their uncles and great-uncles had done before them. They liked it, they were able to sneak out unnoticed and more importantly, to sneak back in at any hour of the night. Despite the insect life that must have joined them, and that there was no light except when the moon shone in, I always envied my brothers their lot in life. Instead, I was always compelled to share my grandfather's room upstairs, in the main house.

My maternal grandfather, Donald McDiarmid, a widower about this time, sold his home 'Lynwood', in Linlithgow, and decided to come and live with us. It always seemed strange to me that he had four other daughters, all of whom were wealthy, and all of whom made a great charade of offering a place in their home at any time, yet he preferred the 'Brig', as he called it, and he felt comfortable with Belle, and with his son-in-law Will. They never spoke much but they seemed to understand one another, and they had a great respect for each other. My grandfather assumed full responsibility for the garden, almost an acre in extent, full of apple trees, berry bushes, and vegetables of all kinds. Laird Will would smoke his pipe, lean over the hawthorn hedge and happily gossip with any passer-by. Everyone admired the garden where each cabbage, each potato, each cauliflower, was placed in its appropriate spot with the ultimate in precision. Weeds simply would not dare to appear. Donald McDiarmid would not permit it.

Although I say it myself, and there are times when I look back in shame at some of the things I did, I was the apple of his eye. He was inordinately proud of his special grandson, the one with the yellow curls, he used to say. He always carried a thick, blackthorn walking-stick, and at times there was an air of the army sergeant about him. I was marched off to church each Sunday, for both morning and evening services. Each way was a full mile, and in summer or winter, I wore heavy boots with real hobnails in them. Old Donal, as everyone called him, had always been a hobbyist shoemaker, and had his own last, leather apron and the necessary tools. I am sure that my feet suffered as a consequence, and I most certainly had the heaviest, hobnailed, tackety boots that were ever produced.

Nevertheless I loved my grandfather Donal dearly. I envied him his great white beard, and the shock of white hair. He and I were constantly on the trail of old castles, monuments, cathedrals, Roman ruins, churches and all other places of historical interest. We rode the omnibus or the train each Saturday on a different adventure. Before returning home we stopped at some café and ate a meat pie washed down with great mugs of hot tea. I was always ravenous and I loved meat pies. He was an elder in the Kirk, and he always held the Minister in high regard. He and I would sit in the Miller pew, occupied by successive generations, and this in the 700-year-old Church of St Michael's, our parish church of Linlithgow.

The village of Linlithgow Bridge was one mile west from the church, and so named because of a massive stone, but badly-skewed bridge reaching over the valley of the River Avon. This bridge allowed passage into Stirlingshire, and on to the 'Trossachs', and the glorious highlands of Scotland. Just as the skewed bridge reached into Stirlingshire, the road divided suddenly into three different routes. Immediately upon crossing the bridge a traveller found himself staring at the main door of a big, old pub, the 'Black Bull', better known as 'Battison's', and herein lies the source of many a humorous, and many a vulgar story about the Auld Laird. The bar is still essentially the same today as it was in his heyday, except for the addition of electric light, running water, and dreadfully loud music. As a young man, say in the 1840s, this inn must have been the main source of local social life and entertainment. Instead of cars and motorcycles, there were high-stepping horses and buggies, and I suspect lots of dogs. In those days the main customers were farmers and farmhands, the railroad men, and shepherds with their dogs.

About this time the Edinburgh to Glasgow railroad was under construction, and it was necessary to carry the railroad over the valley of the River Avon on a great viaduct. The railroad was completed in 1841, and the viaduct, hundreds of feet high in the centre, had twenty-three massive arches. It is recorded that the original Burke, of the duo Burke and Hare, the body-snatchers, worked on this very viaduct. His partner in crime, Hare, was also a labourer, working on the Union Canal. The years of railroad construction must have been very profitable for the local inn.

It is difficult to imagine the grimy interior of that old public house in the middle of a Scottish winter. It was probably crowded with bearded men in damp tweeds, with wet dogs fighting to get close to a blazing fire. The eerie light from colza oil lamps reflected from the many brass spittoons, perched amongst the sawdust spread upon a dirt floor, must have cast a ghostly shadow or two over the faces of these country folk. It is said that benches and tables were provided in those days, and whisky and ale were but pennies a glass. Venturing out into the blackness of a wet night to relieve oneself must have induced much sobering thought. Nevertheless, socialize they did, every man well acquainted with his neighbour, and every man willing to share with those in need. Here the old clan spirit prevailed where every man was equal and presumably the first amongst equals was the Auld Laird.

It is not for me to suggest that William Miller, the senior, was something of a rake, but it is well-known and documented that he did not marry until he was fifty-four years old. It is said that, because of his reputation, he was jilted by his pretty sweetheart who married the publican instead. They had one child, a daughter. Rumour had it that the Auld Laird was fond of the child, and on occasions in the pub, he rocked her cradle with his foot whilst indulging himself with the best of the Scottish brew. The locals were reported to have suggested on many occasions, 'Some day you might marry her, Laird,' and indeed, twenty years later he did. She was christened Jane Douglas Stewart and he married her at twenty-two when he was fifty-four years old. They produced four sons and two daughters. He died on 12 July 1896 at the age of eighty-four. His widow survived until 10 July 1916.

The details of their births and deaths are recorded in a large 'John Brown' bible, presented to the good Laird in 1837. It is also on record that as a wedding gift to his bride he had a brand new second storey built upon his house, in the year 1866. Despite the more modern second storey on this house, with its enormously thick walls, they neglected to dig out the dirt floors on the ground floor. I can clearly remember when this was done by a local contractor about 1932. As a consequence, as it stands now, the house could last for centuries. Whilst the house could last, the farm could not. The land has been developed and the fancy houses around are now occupied by DINKs, as my sister describes them – Double Income No Kids people who commute to Glasgow and Edinburgh in their BMWs. With the explosive rise of the technologists much that was truly of old Scotland has been lost forever.

With the Royal Palace at Linlithgow, and the Royal Charter awarded to the town in the year 1389, it is easy to understand why there are written records available within the town hall, going back for hundreds of years. The records of births, marriages and deaths are easily verifiable by spending a day in the churchyard. There are also many interesting, historical incidents handed down through family records. Local folklore has it that the Millers have farmed the same land for 700 years, through some sort of land grant from the Earl of Lennox. Each time they dig foundations for more houses, more relics are recovered to substantiate the folklore.

Even the skew bridge has been straightened and widened for more lanes of traffic. While the ancient pub remains, but expanded and now the 'Bridge Inn', the surrounding fields and the River Avon have changed. In those early days the river was dammed and diverted to feed a giant paper mill. The paper produced there was sent off to London, to be used in the glossy, illustrated periodicals so popular with the gentry. The feedstuff used in the mill was esparto grass from Egypt. It was brought to the port of Leith by ship, then great bales of these reeds from the mouth of the River Nile were hauled on giant trailers pulled by a massive steam engine all the way to the mill. Even at full speed we could run alongside and torment the driver and his fireman. The 'Steamer', as we called it, had to make a sharp right turn at the top of the hill above the skew bridge to get to the mill. I have some peculiar memories of that hill.

When I was scarcely four years old, a friend of my father presented me with the most beautiful wheelbarrow I had ever seen. It was painted bright green, and on both sides, in bright yellow paint, were the words 'Ian Alexander Miller'. I was really proud of the barrow, and as a consequence plagued the life out of my older brother, Bobby, to wheel me around in it. Master Bobby finally rebelled. He pushed me to the very top of the steep hill leading down to the river, and with a final burst of energy, sent me hurtling down the hill. At the bottom the barrow hit a boulder and I somersaulted into the river just above the dam. A young woman from a cottage backing on to the river became the local hero of the day. She dived into the river from the bridge and rescued a very chastened, small boy. Master Bobby went missing for several days, coming and going through the skylight in the loft, no doubt.

In 1925, Donald McDiarmid received the Imperial Service Medal, a medal given only to those who devoted their entire lives to serving the Government and serving it well. It must have been a proud day for him. By that time the main roads had been surfaced with tarmacadam and great omnibuses, with solid rubber tyres, roamed the roads between Edinburgh, Linlithgow, Stirling and Glasgow. It was something of a climb to get into the charabanc because the chassis was built in its entirety over the tops of the large wheels. As children we looked upon the drivers of these vehicles as though they had come in from outer space. Those were the days when my grandfather and I became best friends. He would tell me stories about his life and of course about how things were in the days of the Auld Laird's youth. My grandfather McDiarmid was born in 1846, but he could remember some of the old men in the town who had fought at the battle of Waterloo. His stories kept me absolutely enthralled for years.

In order to become Linlithgow's postmaster he had spent many long years as a postman, and in those days the mail distribution was a great deal different from how it is today. Bearing in mind that the educated were in the minority, and communication through the written word was limited to those who could afford it, I could readily understand his stories. With Linlithgow as the county seat, the bulk of the mail was an exchange between the gentry who lived in great houses spread widely apart amongst the hills and dales. Farmers and railroad seniors might qualify too, as massive works were underway in the building of bridges, viaducts, aqueducts and embankments for railroad expansion. As a mailman he carried a huge leather satchel slung over his shoulder, stuffed full of letters, newspapers and glossy magazines for distribution to the big houses and farms spread throughout the county. He walked as many as thirty-five miles a day in summer and winter. I often wondered why he didn't have a horse, but with a horse he was compelled to stick to the right of way, whereas on foot he could cut through fields and forests to best suit the selected route of the day.

His wife, my maternal grandmother, had died before I was born. She had owned a china shop in the town, and as a result, all five daughters received their wedding china from the shop. Oddly enough, my mother's beautiful, yellow china teaset was never used to serve tea, and it remains on display to this day, nearly one hundred years later. There were occasions when my grandfather took me to visit the Hendersons. There were several old ladies who patted my head but I never managed to place any of them on the family tree. I always simply supposed them to be more relatives on my grandfather's side. My grandmother was named Black but I never met any of her kin. I think she was the last of her line.

At the tender age of five I was attending the public school, about half a mile from The Farmhouse, and this was the school where my mother and her sisters had been teachers. It was a massive stone building and run with an iron hand by the schoolmaster, Mr Charles Forbes. My older brothers had already moved on but I still had three older sisters who shepherded me around like broody hens. However, on our way to and fro home they told me many amusing stories about the romance between my father and my mother. This was the sort of thing that excited young girls in those days, no doubt. According to them, my mother was a very young pupil teacher at Linlithgow Public School, and she was a very handsome young woman with beautiful auburn hair. My father, the young laird from Linlithgow Bridge Farm, about ten years her senior, came courting.

My sisters claimed that on many occasions my father passed the school with a huge horse and a high cart loaded to the gunwales with manure and placidly smoking his pipe. Miss Belle would rush out of her classroom and down to the iron railings by the main road to claim his attention and engage him in animated conversation. These little adventures caused a great stir in the school and Mr Forbes would threaten reprisals. Donald McDiarmid often marched up to the school with his great hawthorn walking stick and took him to task.

This kind of romantic adventure fascinated me as a small boy, and on my way to school I used to pass a funny old house called the Cellars, where several odd Irishmen lived. They had smaller carts, hauled by the mangiest looking mules you ever saw. The carts were coated with the foulest smelling dirt because their job was to empty the local outhouses and clean out the middens. They arrived at all hours with mule and cart, and a shovel to rake the midden clean. They then climbed back aboard the filthy old cart and the mule would meander along to the next client whilst old McGraw was busy lighting his pipe, usually a clay pipe with the stem bitten down to the last inch. It amused me to wonder if the McGraws did their courting by horse and cart as my father had done. I never did catch sight of any Mrs McGraw, or any little McGraws for that matter. Perhaps, under the circumstances, romance had passed them by.

My schooldays were carefree and my Saturday adventures with my grandfather made my life exciting. School holidays were fabulous too. There were lots of children in the village and lots of playgrounds available. Also, having wealthy relatives, I had lots of hand-me-downs, and lots of the best sports gear, like soccer balls, cricket sets, boxing gloves etc. I was the cock of the walk, my father would say, and all the kids depended on me to produce the gear for the games. In addition, there were lots of great mansions around with broad estates and plenty of fruit trees to be raided. The great River Avon provided a veritable jungle and a series of swimming holes fit for kings. The Union Canal crossed the Carriber Glen on a great aqueduct with fifteen or twenty stone arches and hundreds of feet hight. We swam in the canal the length of the aqueduct, in the most dubious-looking water, but we survived and we enjoyed it. For a shortcut home we trespassed upon Sheriff McConachie's estate, and trembled with suppressed excitement until we ran clear. The good sheriff sat in judgement in the County Courthouse, in wig and gown, and he was a most impressive gentleman.

Later in life, as a member of an academy class, I visited the courthouse to witness the procedure, in preparation for an essay. The case at hand was in reference to two local ladies who had been hauled into court for having created a disturbance of the peace, a serious business in those days. The lady in the defendant's box was asked by the Justice, 'How did this disturbance commence?' The lady pointed to the other one and replied, 'She called me an H, your worship.' Sheriff McConachie removed his pince-nez, straightened his wig, then looked down upon the clerk of the court and said in stern tones, 'Please inform the lady that whore is spelled with a W.' He impressed me tremendously. He had a habit of sentencing errant young fellows to fifteen strokes of the birch, a most unpleasant experience.

At the age of nine I had a most unfortunate but very serious accident at the school. I was being chased by a school friend when I tripped on a projecting water toby, and I measured my length towards the sandstone wall of the schoolhouse. All went black for several months, and I lay behind curtains in the sick children's hospital in Edinburgh for what seemed like ages. The skull was punctured, badly damaged, and full of crud from the sandstone wall. At that time, prior to the introduction of antibiotics, recovery was always in doubt. Nevertheless, with the help of the good doctors and a strong, healthy body, I survived, but with a shaven head for months and months. I was compelled to wear what folks called a 'paddy hat', made out of grey flannel. Eventually, the humps and bumps repaired themselves, and the yellow curls grew back thicker than ever.

During the entire process my mother had conducted a running battle with every available member of the Education Authority and with the school. Meanwhile she determined that I would never set foot in that playground again.

I was marched off to a fee-paying school, Linlithgow Academy, under the rectorship of Mr Beveridge, a grand old man of learning. The school had its beginnings in his youth, and with his stewardship as Rector, the school became well-known and considered to be an institute of higher learning. It later became the Secondary School for the entire community, the fee-paying was terminated and the enrolment increased by leaps and bounds. Sports were a big thing with the Academy, and we participated in leagues and tournaments in soccer, cricket, tennis etc. We had hordes of girls at the Academy although I scarcely knew why I was interested in them at that time. Realization came later in life.

Nevertheless, having three older sisters made me wonder about girls and I pondered upon whether or not they were really needed. However, I had a summer friend in the village, one Barney Mcintyre, who had about a dozen gorgeous sisters and they all lived in a butt and ben. He contributed much to my education about the sexes. In those days the opportunity for social contact with the opposite sex was almost nil, unless one considered chaperoned birthday parties or dull school dances. However the older ones managed to generate all kinds of excitement about local dances held in smiddys, or blacksmith's shops. These were of great interest to me although I was never considered old enough to go. My eldest brother, older by thirteen years, had a dance band. They called themselves the 'Blue Dominoes', and their signature tune was 'Bye Bye Blackbird'. The only place where they could practice, much to my grandfather's chagrin and to my delight, was in the upstairs drawing room. I used to sit on the staircase absolutely enraptured. I would picture myself as the orchestra leader while Painter Downie did a solo on his trumpet with brother Willie thumping on the piano. There were seven members in the band, and they all sounded fantastic to me.

Hot music and ballroom dancing were but a small part of their social life. The real excitement seemed to be in the casino, conducted in a stable workshop by brother Donald. Weird country bumpkins appeared from all over the county to compete at card games, pitch and toss, and everything else that involved betting. They arrived on old motorcycles that were belt-driven and terribly smelly, but I envied them all the excitement nevertheless. Despite these activities, most of which were conducted in the middle of the night, Master Donald managed to excel at school. He went on to become an outstanding student at Herriott Watt College in Edinburgh. Later, he went to work at Scottish Oils at Philpstoun where our Uncle Robert Crichton was Managing Director. They never did get along together and Donald disappeared for some considerable time but later reappeared from Aberdeen with a wife and children. He was always known as Big Don and I was Wee Don; it was a cross I had to bear.

As a boy, Master Donald was reputed to be a real bad rascal by most of the villagers, yet he was always well-liked. Even so, my mother always made excuses for him. 'The boy is just a bit wild, Will,' she would say to my father. Some of his adventures reported to me scarcely bear repetition. It was widely recognized, however, that he was the local genius with all things mechanical and electrical. He had the enviable reputation of being able to make almost anything work. He always rode ancient motorcycles, the older the better, or peculiar automobiles that no one else could possibly coax into life. Our yard was constantly full of locals requiring Donald's assistance. To irritate all of us, he would ride around on a ridiculous penny-farthing bicycle where he sat perched upon the top of an enormous wheel, and pedalled directly. Seeing him disappear down the hill towards the skew bridge always drove my mother and sisters into hysterics. As far as I can gather, he never did change much, even in later life.

I will always remember one incident where I watched a group of my brother's gambler friends playing cards in the stable workshop. Meanwhile, my father and friends fed sulphur and molasses to a huge dying horse in the stable next door. Despite, or perhaps because of their efforts, the old horse died. Getting the corpse out of the stable, and onto a low-slung wagon, then off to the glue works, was a very complex task involving chains, ropes and tackles, and much shouting and bawling. I remember standing to one side, holding on to my dog, a springer spaniel, and feeling absolutely devastated. The gamblers continued on with their game, but to me the death of that old horse signalled the end of the farm. From that year on, steel houses, brick two-storey houses, were springing up all around us, and it was also the beginning of bad times. It seemed that funerals were much more frequent as Ritchie & Sons, Joiners and Undertakers, were regularly seen wearing their tile hats.

Funerals were indeed a solemn occasion. About 1927, my older sister Helen, or Nellie as we all called her, was stricken with rheumatic fever, and in those days there was very little medical assistance available. Neither the doctor nor the chemist had much beyond iodine, cascara sagrada, castor oil, permanganate of potash, friar's balsam and calomine lotion. All one could do was provide tender loving care, hot drinks and warmth. I always felt assured that any sick people I knew died in relative comfort and in the bosom of their family. In addition, of course, we had our faith. My grandfather held my hand whilst we watched my sister's breathing become more laboured, then finally cease. Neighbours rushed in to help, my mother and other sisters returned from town where they were arranging for some kind of cage to keep the weight of the bedclothes off Helen's fevered body.

The old house was hushed and dark, a reminder of generations of Millers, brought into the world with high hopes, christened with holy water, but carried out by successive generations with solemn mien, and buried in the churchyard of the old kirk. The body was laid out in state in the parlour, all the blinds in the house were drawn and we spoke in whispers. My mother sat beside the coffin for hours, nursing her grief. Some years earlier she had lost another girl child, Margaret, scarcely two years old, of what they called convulsions. Relatives appeared from all corners of the country to attend the funeral.

Being young I recovered from the grief very quickly. As always, I was very observant and watched all the relatives and friends, the undertakers and the minister, during the ceremony. It reminded me then of a funeral several years prior to this one. My Uncle Robert Forrester, a lawyer, had died in Broxburn, a small town about eight miles away. This was a very solemn occasion and required the presence of both my father and my grandfather. They were, as usual, dressed in their funeral clothes, black overcoats with velvet collars, tile hats and stout boots. It was decided that I, small boy though I was, should also attend to represent the third generation. Bob Forrester and Aunt Helen, my mother's sister, had no children, but they kept a massive dog called Nipper, some kind of an irish terrier, and never particularly friendly. We three, my father, my grandfather and me walked to the funeral, rather, they walked and I ran along behind in my stout hobnailed boots.

Being a wealthy old boy, there was a wake, and the congregated relatives and friends participated generously in good food and the very best of whisky. Everybody patted my head and complimented Will on his youngest and brightest. Very quickly I was relegated to the kitchen to keep old Nipper company. I confess I was horrified to see him lift his leg by the door and let fly. He totally ignored my harsh objections, then growled hoarsely until I was subdued enough to withdraw. The road home was a real adventure. Shortcuts were taken through farms and estates despite the fact that it was already dark, and in the typical Scottish climate, raining. I had the greatest difficulty following the swaying top hats, and most of the time I had to run to keep up. Fortunately for me, every now and again they would stop to light a smelly old pipe, thus providing a beacon for me to follow. There were times when I was sure that they had forgotten me entirely. From then on I avoided funerals like the plague. I had nightmares for a while wherein I was constantly chasing two ghostly figures in tall hats and long black coats.

Thinking about nightmares reminds me of another ritual at the old farmhouse worthy of record. Just to the east of the farmhouse and the garden there was a large open field. Now it is totally built-up with houses and the whole area is called Millerfield. At that time it was always in grass, and any function in the village would be held in the field. One regular user was John Brown, an evangelist from Glasgow, and every now and again he would appear with his enormous tent and hold a revival. Whilst my mother never really approved of evangelists, she liked John Brown, and she described him as a very sincere preacher. He was an exceedingly jolly man, constantly surrounded by very nice people, who kept saying, 'Hallelujah' after everything he said.

So John Brown had free use of the field to pitch his great tent and hold his revival. To attract the greatest congregation, he was obliged to serve tea and goodies. For the mass production of tea, our wash-house was the ideal place. I had to set to work, well in advance of his arrival, to clean out an enormous copper boiler wherein all our dirty laundry was boiled each week. The boiler was set into a large brick foundation with a coal fire underneath. I had to climb inside and polish the copper till John Brown could see his face in it. Then it was filled with water from the pump and a huge fire built underneath. Being the big wheel in the tea-making business, I qualified for first pick of all the goodies, and I got to sit in the front row with my mother to listen to his lengthy sermons. My grandfather disapproved of the whole exercise but I was able to blame the entire affair on my mother. I had many nightmares about fire and brimstone.

By 1931 there were whispers about a depression and everything seemed to be really bad. It was difficult for me to understand, because we always had a table laden with good food, we had lots of warm clothes, and each year there were always whispers about the receipt of feu-duties to pay off all our debts. It seemed that the farm, whilst no longer a farm, still produced enough money for us. Elsewhere we read about people starving, coal mines closing, ships tied up, hunger marchers chaining themselves to the railings of Princes Street Gardens in Edinburgh. Emmanuel Shinwell was in the thick of it all and my mother lectured the locals on the worthless Labour Party. However Emmanuel must have done some things right because he lived to be a hundred, and he was well admired as a politician.

The Depression did have some effect upon us as a family. My older brother Bobby, about six years older than me, should have been working, according to my mother. But, Master Bobby was disinclined to chase after jobs, and he preferred to lie in the sun on the flat-topped stone dyke that separated our house from the road. He could take on the look of a very aggrieved and unjustly treated young man whenever my mother would take my grandfather's stick to him. However he was finally persuaded to go to work as a railway porter pending his recruitment into the Edinburgh police force, where it seemed that yet another of my father's cousins had influence.

No matter where we went, we would meet all kinds of people who would tip their hats to my grandfather with a 'Fine day, Donal. How's the Laird?' Most times my grandfather identified them as some other cousin or second cousin of the Millers. I found it very difficult to keep track of them all, the Braes, the Bowies, the Alexanders, the Stewarts and the Hendersons. All of them called me

'Wee Don', and it was quite impossible to persuade them that my name was Ian. Some of them reminded me that even when I was christened in St Michael's Kirk my mother had an argument with the Minister at the baptismal font. As always, Miss Belle prevailed, I was formally christened Ian Alexander Miller. Nevertheless, I had no alternative but accept both names, and 'Wee Don' it became, even when I went on to the Academy.

CHAPTER II

THE ACADEMY YEARS

The Academy lay at the east end of town, beyond the palace and the kirk, and it was slightly more than a mile from The Farmhouse. Most of the time I walked both ways, and in addition walked home for lunch. No doubt the four or five miles a day, coupled to wild bouts of rugby or soccer, helped me to grow up into a very muscular young man. Amateur boxing was my principal interest, and the skills developed from it stood me in good stead later on in life. The academic skills developed within us were important too and I was fortunate to have inherited my mother's brains. The learning process came easy to me, although I must confess I often wondered why the Headmaster kept pounding on my head with a heavy, round ruler. I think he believed that this would ensure the correct conjugation of Latin verbs.

We studied Virgil and Caesar's Gallic Wars, but I have yet to understand how I profited from it. Yet it was a splendid school and the friends I made were great. Most of the male teachers were veterans of the Great War of 1914-18 and some of them had lost limbs. The female teachers were young, handsome and stylish women, and as students we were always preoccupied with the possibilities of romance within the teachers' meeting room. Alas, we were totally wrong, the elegant ladies remained spinsters. We had forgotten that so many of our young menfolk had been killed in the war.

The Linlithgow Academy was instituted in 1894, in the Longcroft Hall at the West Port, directly across the road from the public school where my mother and her sisters had taught. Over the subsequent eight years the staff grew from two members to six, and it was recognised that there was a growing need for such an institution. About the year 1900 it was decided that a new building should be constructed at the eastern end of town and the chosen site bordered upon the grounds of the palace, and backed on to Linlithgow Loch. The new building was of solid stone, with a grey slate roof, an imposing tower at each end, and with spacious grounds.

It is recorded that the Rector, James Beveridge, led his fifty-two pupils along Linlithgow's High Street from the school's original premises at Longcroft Hall.

They were accompanied by the local pipe band and the streets were bedecked with flags for the big occasion. Pupils walked to the school from as far away as Bo'Ness, at least three miles away, and many of the school graduates went on to become prominent citizens, and some became Members of Parliament. With the population of Linlithgow at only 2,500 at that time, it is clear that very few youngsters enjoyed the privilege of a secondary education. Even when the school leaving age was raised only the very able ones went on to the Academy, all of the others were educated in supplementary classes at the public school.

By the time I first arrived at the Academy it was well staffed and by then the roll had reached about 200. I remember being particularly impressed by the massive stone gate on Blackness Road and the enormous expanse of glorious lawn which was separated from the carriageway by thick shrubbery. The single storey accommodation was arranged symmetrically around the central block, with a tall, circular tower at each entrance. At about this time Mr Beveridge retired and Mr Milne became Rector.

In addition to his duties as Headmaster Mr Milne personally conducted the classes in Latin. He carried a round ruler, about an inch in diameter and about fifteen inches long. I doubt if he had ever forgotten his days in the army. Most of the other teachers were gentle but strict; the very thought of being invited to visit the Rector's office was enough to sustain discipline.

There were special teachers for everything: Miss Brodie for Physical Training, Miss Meek for French, Mr Burt for English, Mr Dawson for Mathematics, Mr Johnston for Science, and they were supplemented by the elegant Miss Straiton and Miss Fisher. In addition, one of Mr Beveridge's daughters was on the staff. Each of the teachers had their own idiosyncrasies. Miss Brodie was a very muscular lady, always in a very brief gym dress, and forever blowing on a shrill whistle. She was a stickler for discipline and many times refused to allow students to leave the class for the bathroom. I remember clearly one little farm girl who insisted on raising her hands to be excused was ignored by Miss Brodie, and finally the little girl lost control and flooded the floor.

Miss Meek, a tiny little lady always in very high heels, just loved to pull my hair. Miss Straiton and Miss Fisher were always conscious of the boys ogling their legs. Mr Johnston, who had lost a leg in the war, had an automobile, an AC, a name I have never heard of since, but we surely envied him at the time. Mr Burt was constantly quoting Tennyson or Byron but never Robbie Burns. Mr Dawson cycled to school very sedately on a very expensive Raleigh. It had chain covers and a three-speed. He seemed to be very prim, and he would climb down and push the bicycle uphill. He was an Englishman and I assumed that they were all like that. To my surprise, later in life, I discovered that they were much like us.

We had cricket grounds, hard tennis courts, lawn tennis courts, a soccer field, and to avoid discipline, we could jump the wall into the palace grounds. These grounds, the Peel, were always beautifully tended, and all the summer social activities were conducted there, amidst massive trees and green, green grass that seemed to be almost indestructible, a tribute to the Scottish weather, no doubt. I do not ever remember a shortage of rain. A few sailboats, row boats and canoes on the loch added greatly to the enjoyment of the outdoors in summer. However, bearing in mind that Linlithgow is about fifty-six degrees north latitude, and therefore on a parallel with Churchill, Manitoba, it is not surprising that the winters were very severe.

As a very small boy, I can remember when the loch became frozen solid and hordes of people came out from Edinburgh to conduct great curling matches. In the depths of winter, if the sun shone at all, it would be up for only a short few hours, dark till nine-thirty in the morning, and getting dark again by three-thirty in the afternoon. The experts say that the climate is changing, and it most assuredly is at Linlithgow. Truly severe winters have become a thing of the past.

Sports were the joy of my youth. There were no sports stars being paid millions of dollars for batting a little ball around. We were all amateurs and nobody got paid. Even in the first-class soccer teams, where thousands of spectators paid to see the game, the players were paid only reasonable salaries and sponsorship was unheard of. There was keen competition between the many secondary schools throughout the region, bus trips to the games at the Bo'Ness and Bathgate Academies were hilarious and the spectators had as much fun as the players. In addition, within the region, we had several junior leagues for soccer, rugby and cricket teams. The players were adults, but the league was considered junior when compared to the big teams in the senior and premier leagues.

All of us boys aspired to become soccer players within the Linlithgow Rose Football Club, or to be cricketers in the West Lothian County Cricket Club, but only the really talented players could make the grade. However there were additional options. All of the paper mills had their own cricket clubs and belonged to a league. When the teams played at home or away the entire scoring record had to be maintained in a special book, well beyond the capabilities of the local fellows to understand. I therefore travelled as twelfth man with the Avon Mills club to keep score and to participate in the event of absence or accident.

This early association with grown men, mostly family men, broadened my horizons in a hurry, and whether they realized it or not, they shortened my period of adolescence. Their lives, both physical and emotional, were an open book. Their stories were often sad and told in the most vulgar language, but on some occasions the life stories were quite hilarious and really down to earth.

I still found time for exploration with my grandfather. These were great adventures, and in many ways very important to me as a student, particularly in history. There is scarcely a castle in Scotland that we failed to inspect. Stirling Castle, Edinburgh Castle, Glamis Castle and Balmoral Castle were my favourites, but even those that were little more than ruins came alive with my grandfather's tales. Battlefields were big with him. Many times we tramped over Bannockburn and paid homage to Robert the Bruce. On occasions, at a battlefield like Culloden, I would cry over the inscriptions on the boulders marking the mass graves. My grandfather was familiar with the history down to the last detail. I enjoyed visits to the Wallace Monument at the Bridge of Allan, as Wallace was one of my favourite heroes, and the Battle of Stirling Bridge was his greatest victory. Once, when he had escaped from the English, he slept in a cold stone bed on top of Cockleroy, a hill not far behind our house.

Churches, cathedrals, abbeys, they got our full attention too. Here again, my grandfather was an expert on the Reformation and he lectured me constantly on the merits of being a good presbyterian. We went to St Giles Cathedral and St Mary's Cathedral in Edinburgh, to Melrose Abbey, to St Andrews, and to almost every church in the kingdom. John Knox was one of his heroes and we spent days raking around in Knox's house in Edinburgh, located in the high street, the aptly-named Royal Mile. Palaces like Holyrood, Scone and Linlithgow were so familiar that I can see them now, and in my mind I can count the massive stones on the palace gates. Remembering my grandfather today convinces me that he was the best and kindest individual I ever had the privilege to meet and I truly treasure his memory.

School uniforms were in vogue in those days, and the Academy colours were in very good, conservative taste. Navy-blue blazer with school badge, white shirt, grey trousers, and a tie with diagonal stripes, alternating navy blue and royal blue. The girls wore gym dress, white blouse, navy-blue blazer, black stockings, and navy-blue bloomers. Most everyone took great pride in the school colours. The Rector, Mr Milne, always dashed about in a mortarboard and black gown. I am sure he was genuinely pleased with his appearance when he was in full regalia and he was rarely seen without the menace of the round ruler.

I had many close friends in school, one in particular, Charles McLean, a police superintendent's son. Our friendship lasted throughout the school years and on into wartime. Finally, in 1941, he was killed in an Air Force bomber over Brest, in western France. Some forty-five years later, I received a letter from him which had never been mailed. Instead, it was shipped to his mother as part of his personal effects. Mrs McLean never did summon the courage to open the package, and only after she died years later, his sister Effie forwarded the letter to me. Regrettably, nearly all of my school friends were killed in World War II, the war to end all wars, they were told. However, at school, in the fun years of our youth, not one of us ever dreamed of wars, and death, and devastation. The world was ours to conquer, each according to his own ambition.

In 1929, the education authority changed the rules, and shortly thereafter the Academy ceased to be a fee-paying school. It was now the secondary school and the school roll increased very quickly. Additional buildings were constructed in the school grounds and the teaching staff increased considerably. My two surviving sisters attended the Academy now and I had no option but to appear to be well-behaved. The school now had its share of handsome, older seniors who kept the young ladies spellbound. It became somewhat amusing, and at times downright obnoxious, to be a witness to the budding romances in the school grounds. Fortunately the young ladies were kept busy with domestic science in addition to normal studies and this helped to restrict the opportunities for romance.

Nevertheless, and remarkable though it may seem, even at the tender age of fourteen and fifteen true romance did flourish and in many cases was sustained to the point of matrimony. The girls and boys involved were given a rough time by their peers and their personal feelings, and their relationships, must have been sorely tested. I had no real interest in girls in those years, but I was always fortunate enough to be invited to special girl birthday parties and had therefore to tolerate the jeers and jibes of all my friends. Only the very well-to-do had parties, like Dr Garand's only daughter Doris, or Dorothy Stein, whose father managed the local omnibus company. Receipt of such invitations was never allowed to go to my head, my sisters saw to that.

By 1931 I had begun to generate a keen interest in geography, in particular, economic geography, and this in turn created a desire to see the world. Even then, without specific ambition, I remember feeling a tremendous admiration for one of our local dignitaries, a man who had lived in my grandfather's time. His family home was Bonside, a mansion house not far from a farm I used to visit. It was the birthplace, and at one time the home, of Sir Charles Wyville Thomson (1830 to 1882), who was chief of the scientific staff on the world-famous Challenger Oceanographic Expedition during the years 1872 to 1876. In St Michael's Church, in the centre window of the apse, there is a beautiful stained-glass window dedicated to his memory. It features a fleet of ships, such as that which accompanied the explorer on his charting of the world's oceans. Each Sunday, as I sat in the church, with Dr Coupar scowling down at me from his pulpit, I was staring at that window, sailing an imaginary vessel on the oceans of the world, braving the worst of hurricanes, and all to expand the British Empire.

How dull school would have been without holidays. Each break-up for vacation, whether Easter, summer or Christmas, was quite a ceremony. Easter and Christmas were relatively quiet, because religious holidays with the good christian folks in the village were generally restrained and very much for children. Summer was different, the feeling was heavenly, the days seemed to last forever and even when we went to bed it was still daylight.

We had a fabulous time with sports of all kinds from morning till night during the week and on weekends we had scout outings. We took off, pushing a two-wheeled gun carriage loaded up with tents and stores for overnight adventures in Carriber Glen. Each year in the month of July we went to the Highlands to Comrie, on the banks of the River Ruchle, for at least two weeks. On one memorable occasion there I felt desperately hungry in the middle of the night, so I sneaked off to the mess tent to partake of some bread and jam. Unfortunately for me someone had omitted to replace the top on a pot of raspberry jam and by now it was full of wasps. Being dark and being hungry, I spread the jam, wasps and all, and dug into what I thought would be a delicious sandwich. I spent a few days in hospital recovering from innumerable wasp stings in my mouth. It was a most unpleasant experience and one I was never allowed to forget.

The highlight of the summer holidays saw most of the family, brothers, sisters, Mother and Father, off to England, to the Crawford farm at Lexsden, near Colchester. Aunt Annie Crawford, my father's older sister, was a very austere lady, always with a black choker around her neck. Uncle John Crawford was a large, heavy-set, gruff man. They had four sons and four daughters. The old farm had great Clydesdale horses, enormous binders and hay carts galore. I liked the great change from home. Even the railroad trip on the London and North Eastern Railway was exciting. The main part of the trip was done on the 'Flying Scotsman' route, and back then; Edinburgh and London were the boundaries of my world.

As time passed by the older brothers developed different tastes in holidays and the holiday gang reduced year by year. Even my sisters ceased to be tomboys and generated an interest in young men. Brother Willie's 'Blue Dominoes' dance band was a thing of the past, and the young people were now riding in Alexander's Bluebird buses to Falkirk, to the modern dance halls. By now Willie had married his ladyfriend, Letitia. They lived somewhere off in Falkirk, about seven miles away, and they already had a son. This boy was the new William Miller, born in 1931, the third generation from the Auld Laird. Brother Donald had disappeared for a spell, but reappeared without explanation. Bobby still had not made it to the Edinburgh police – he was still a railroad man at Falkirk High Station.

Technology was in process of development, transportation by rail and by bus was improving rapidly and telephones were spreading their tentacles throughout the land. We did have a hard surface tarmacadam road but that was the upper limit until 1932. The electric overhead wires were extended throughout the village and in no time at all we were literally floodlit. Running water came next, and my versatile brother Donald wired the entire house and completed the internal plumbing. It is really difficult today to remember just how enormously different it was to have running hot and cold water and on/off electric lights instead of Aladdin oil lamps. My mother could scarcely conceal her excitement and she would invite total strangers into the house just to see the bathroom.

I would be remiss if I failed to mention the Riding of the Marches. Linlithgow, being a Royal Burgh, on a special day each year, organized a procession to ride round the borders of the Burgh, thus retaining all the rights and privileges appropriate thereto. In the early life of the town the magistrates were protective of the boundaries and the annual riding thereof was begun. From as early as 1389, when the Royal Charter was first awarded, it is likely that an annual inspection of the boundaries was made on foot. The first actual riding is reported to have taken place in the reign of James V in 1541. Bearing in mind the likelihood of inclement weather, the selected date kept changing, until in 1767 it was fixed on the Tuesday after the second Thursday in the month of June, and has remained so.

In the 1920s and the early 1930s, the Riding of the Marches was a great day for all of us. A huge procession, headed by the Lord Provost, the deacons, the guilds and their visitors followed by decorated vehicles loaded with schoolchildren and decorated horses ridden by farmhands. The entire procession was headed and tailed by pipe bands and they stopped at various strategic watering holes, for both horses and men. As children, we thought the whole affair was fabulous. In addition, a circus and charabancs loaded with special rides were set up just outside of town. Grown-ups and children alike enjoyed the entire day regardless of the weather.

Special meals were arranged in the homes, huge steak pies were ordered from the butcher and served with great mounds of potatoes and vegetables from the garden. The table groaned under the weight of fruit pies and cakes. Relatives appeared from far and wide and The Farmhouse was considered the place to be in view of the parade being compelled to pass through the village twice, the stopping point being the big pub over the brig, a watering hole truly capable of serving the needs of both man and beast. Commencing at about five in the morning, the festivities were opened by the happy sound of 'Drum and Fyfe'. The parade took until breakfast time to assemble and be properly marshalled. It then negotiated its way through town and arrived in the village in time for an early lunch. At the watering hole there were judges appointed and awards made to winners of different categories of vehicle and horse.

Meanwhile the gathering at The Farmhouse took place and my mother's sisters, with husbands, a few cousins and the Crawfords from England would all arrive at different times. The Marches were a big draw, a never-to-be-forgotten day. I recall too, how each year seemed to re-emphasize the fragile nature of our lives as each year some other relative had passed on. The death was mentioned, briefly discussed, then promptly forgotten, at least for the remainder of the day. Yet there was always a sour note on that day too, as the Marches were one day when Uncle James and his brothers could not stay away. They never dared to come to The Farmhouse but they always made a point of entertaining their cronies at the pub. My mother, with all her friends and relatives, wandered over there too to join the crowd. I often saw her pointing out Uncle James to all and sundry as a real blackguard. I do not believe that he ever recognized me at all.

None the less he smiled and waved to all his boozy friends and he raised his tile hat to the local dignitaries. Usually, during the main meal, my mother would let loose a diatribe about Will's brothers. My father would smile or nod sagely in support. Aunt Annie was always there with her husband Robert Crichton and she always struck me as a bit of a snob, always playing at being the great lady. Aunt Jeannie and her husband Harry Candler came out from Joppa, an eastern suburb of Edinburgh. My grandfather took me there on occasions and I always enjoyed the food, the electric tram ride and the train journey. Aunt Nellie with her husband Bob Forrester, the lawyer from Broxburn, never seemed to be very happy about anything. She was the first to be widowed and spent her declining years on the island of Madeira. The youngest, Margaret, or Meg, had committed the almost unforgivable sin, she had married an Englishman.

Actually, Tom Trowsdale was really a very nice man, but his brothers-in-law never did approve of him. His family were from Darlington in the county of Durham in the north of England, where they ran some big wholesale grocery business under the name of Trowsdale & Stevenson. His wife, Aunt Meg, the youngest, always made sure that everyone knew that she was the youngest. She had become more English than the English, and her accent irritated my mother, who quite often told her so. However, they were a jolly crowd on the Marches day and during the passage of the parade they were all in the front garden in their finery, being admired by all the boozy men in the charabancs. All the windows in the house were taken over by my sister's girlfriends, where they were hanging out yelling and screaming to make sure everyone saw them.

But there were some dark clouds drifting over the land in those days. Nothing much was said about the state of the economy and it seemed that we lived day to day, oblivious to the rest of the world. Gradually, however, the news trickled down to us adolescents, particularly when the paper mills started to cut production. My cricketer friends were worried and preoccupied with trying to hold on to their jobs.

At fifteen years old, at the Academy, we were being reminded constantly by our teachers of the importance of qualifying in order that we might go on to college for a lifetime career. Quite suddenly the fun and games era had ended. We were now conscious of what was going on in the real world. The United States stock market crash had not affected us much at all, but the townsfolk who had emigrated to America in the twenties were now returning. Apparently the seventeen shillings they got from the dole at home was better than selling apples on the street corners of Chicago. By the time the hunger-marchers started to chain themselves to the railings of Princes Street Gardens, the message came through loud and clear. Life was no longer a bed of roses. We grew up.

For the next year I concentrated upon the need for a career. Recognizing the state of the economy, and my own special desires to travel throughout the world, I had no alternative but to find a way to travel at someone else's expense. That year my older sister was keeping company, as the townsfolk would say, with Jock Braithwaite, the son of prominent publicans in the town. He was chief engineer on a British merchant ship sailing all over the world. I was quickly persuaded to apply to Bank Line Limited to join the British Merchant Navy as a cadet. In due course I was accepted, having passed all the examinations and tests, and I found myself indentured to the Master of the SS *Tymeric* to sail from Liverpool, England for foreign parts in April 1934. Meanwhile, we received news that Jock Braithwaite had died at sea, his body being consigned to the deep in the Great Bight off South Australia.

As a consequence of acceptance, and whilst still at the Academy, some of the bigger fellows wanted to take me out to celebrate. After all, I was sixteen and big for my age. In those days there were strict rules and the publicans observed them. We were all rather bitter about it, but later on it became the fun thing to find out all there was to know about pubs. St Michael's Hotel, or McCombie's, as we called it, was close to the school and the bars therein were first class. During market days the farmers patronized the place. At all other times it appeared to be the haunt of the élite and the intellectuals. All the doctors, dentists, veterinaries, bankers, lawyers and schoolmasters patronized McCombie's, and in many cases, too well. Fortunately for most of the patrons, bicycles were still in vogue and there were few automobiles on the road. Only the rich could afford them.

Robert Crichton, my uncle, Managing Director of Scottish Oils, did have a splendid limousine complete with chauffeur. It arrived every Monday morning at The Farmhouse to pick up my grandfather McDiarmid to take him to Philpstoun to spend the day with daughter Annie. He didn't care all that much for those Mondays and he would much sooner have stayed home. He preferred the charabanc, as he called the bus, and he and I continued our explorations right up to my last weekend at home.

The bar and the car come to mind because of an incident some years later and there was a lesson in it. Our good Rector had over-indulged in McCombie's and in his additional capacity of session clerk of the church he had squandered some of the funds in high living. In a fit of remorse, and in true military style, he blew his brains out in the Rector's office in the Academy. Everyone felt very badly about the affair because his wife and family were very popular. I was told that the car and Mr Crichton arrived at the scene, the affair was quickly disposed of and the church funds replaced. In those days the élite took care of one another.

My departure from the Academy to join the good ship *Tymeric* was uneventful. I remember that Miss Meek cried, grabbed me by the hair, pulled my head down and kissed me on the cheek. My friends were casual about the whole affair and seemed to believe I might be back in a couple of weeks. Their world, at that time, was small indeed. My mother cried a good deal too. My sister Jean handled most of the preparations, and by then, she seemed to be taking charge of everything. I really had no idea what lay in store for me but I do remember thinking very fondly of the old farmhouse, the Academy and about Linlithgow. All of a sudden, all of the quiet discussions I had had with my grandfather became meaningful to me. The history of Scotland, Linlithgow, a great place to be born, all of it began to make sense. Before I even joined the ship I had suddenly developed a great pride in my heritage. I was Ian Alexander Miller, bred from the McFarlanes, the Stewarts, the Alexanders and the McDiarmids.

Linlithgow, with its thousand years of history, retains its powerful attraction and always leaves me with the feeling that I should never have left it. There are Scottish people all over the world with the same sentiments. Our culture, our history, our music, our individual celebrations, all relate back to 'Our ain folk', perhaps a throwback to the old clan days, when everyone had a sense of belonging, a sense of community and a tremendous sense of pride. It will not be easy to compress a thousand years of turbulent history into a few thousand words. Nevertheless, it is worth a try in order that one might realize that sense of excitement generated at the moment of departure was tempered by a great sense of sadness that remained forever, etched deep within my memory.

CHAPTER III

LINLITHGOW, SCOTLAND

The royal and ancient burgh of Linlithgow is located along the south shore of Linlithgow Loch, in an attractive valley lying between the Bathgate Hills to the south and the River Forth, about three miles to the north. It lies about midway between the cities of Edinburgh and Stirling, on the old road to the Highlands. The town reached its peak in the fifteenth and sixteenth centuries, at this time enjoying charter rights to a lucrative monopoly of trade along the River Forth shore, between the Rivers Almond and the Avon. From time to time it hosted the royal court, and the town therefore contained the houses of courtiers and diplomats, thus providing a legacy of exceptional architecture.

For as far back as the retreat of the Ice Age, when the loch was formed from melting ice left behind by the shrinking glacier, it is believed that the town's earliest dwellings were within the loch itself. The likely group of homes is referred to as a 'crannog'. The waters of the loch provided protection for those early inhabitants during Scotland's dangerous prehistoric times. Evidence of these has long since been destroyed but there is plenty of evidence of occupation by Celtic tribes in the local hills. Almost two thousand years ago the Romans' outermost line of defence, Antonine's Wall, started close by. A well on a local farm, the Walton, was originally sunk by Roman soldiers. A farmer at Boroughmuir turned up a pottery urn full of Roman coins whilst ploughing his land. This find, in 1781, is documented by the Minister of St Michael's in 1843.

History records that King David I, who reigned from 1124 to 1153, erected a hunting lodge at Linlithgow. The site selected was on a high promontory jutting into the loch. The hilltop location offered splendid views in all directions and at the same time the waters of the loch on three sides provided protection from attack. In those days there was constant danger from rival nobles and extreme caution was necessary. Presumably such a lodge was a large wooden structure, with a big hole in the roof to permit smoke from a large central fire to escape. Skins and furs on the walls and floor were the likely furnishings.

On this same promontory there existed, even at that time, a Kirk of St Michael's. It was a time-honoured custom that churches dedicated to St Michael should be built on high ground. The first mention of the great church of Linlithgow is in a charter of 1138, in which King David I gifted it, 'With all its chapels, lands, and other rights, to the Cathedral of St Andrews'. One of the earliest written mentions of Linlithgow thus comes in the records of the church at St Andrews, where it is stated in the register for the years 1162-72 that, 'The Chapel of the Knights of St John at Torphichen, is bound to pay one silver mark annually to St Michael's, as a substitute for burial dues.'

The twelfth and thirteenth centuries were a time of comparative stability in the region. King David was followed upon the throne by King Malcolm IV, and thereafter by King Alexander II. Unfortunately his son and successor King Alexander III perished when thrown from his horse. He and his young French bride left no children. His heir, an infant granddaughter, the 'Little Maid of Norway', died without completing the voyage from Scandinavia. This created a problem of succession to the Scottish crown, and by now King Edward I of England had subdued the Welsh and saw his opportunity to turn his belligerent attention to Scotland.

Heroic resistance was organized by Sir William Wallace who defeated Edward at the Battle of Stirling Bridge, but later, in 1298, the Scots were routed and Wallace was forced to flee. As boys we used to lie in his cold stone bed on top of Cockleroy, and we often played in Wallace's cave on the banks of the River Avon where he successfully sought refuge from the English. The conquering King Edward I returned to Linlithgow on several occasions and is credited with building the first real fort, described as the Peel, in place of the hunting lodge. The stone walls of St Michael's Church were incorporated within his defences. The church itself served as his military storehouse and granary, while supplies were brought from England by ship to Blackness.

However, only a very few years later the so-called English Settlement feared for their safety and petitioned the King to be admitted to the Peel. Soon afterwards their position became even more uncertain by the King's death and the succession of his son Edward II. He, in turn, occupied Linlithgow in 1310 as he tried to counter the ever-increasing resistance by Wallace's successor, Robert the Bruce. In the year 1313, a Linlithgow farmer, required to deliver hay to the English garrison, delivered instead eight well-armed Scottish soldiers under the hay who slew the English sentries. Farmer Binnie manoeuvred the heavy cart so that the drawbridge could not rise and the portcullis could not fall. The garrison wisely surrendered to the irate townsfolk.

Shortly thereafter Edinburgh Castle was retaken by the Scots and in 1314, at the Battle of Bannockburn, near Stirling, Bruce routed Edward II's army and left them no choice but to flee. This was one of the most famous battles in Scottish history and the field, preserved to this day, is dominated by a massive monument to King Robert the Bruce. In greater than life-size, he is in full armour astride a beautiful horse. Many times I have wandered throughout the battlefield with my grandfather extolling the virtues of good King Robert, one of our greatest heroes. Bruce's heir, David II, succeeded to the throne when but a child. Edward III of England seized this opportunity to annexe Linlithgow once again and put his puppet, Edward Balliol, on the throne. However, as an adult, David II recovered the throne. He visited Linlithgow several times and in 1350 arranged for the repairs to the castle within the Peel. Additional records show that in 1365 King David II paid for the good and plentiful supply of wine for the banquet given during his royal residence.

The death of King David II marked the coming of the Stewarts to the Scottish throne. The Scottish nobles gathered at Linlithgow upon the death of their king and after due deliberation determined that the first of the Stewarts, Robert II, grandson of the Bruce, was the legal heir to the throne. Robert's father was the Lord High Steward of Bathgate Castle and it was from that title that the Scottish Royal Family derived the famous name of Stewart. During his reign King Robert II stayed at Linlithgow several times. On one such visit, on 23 October 1389, he conferred upon the town the status of a Royal Burgh. This royal charter was written in Latin, the language employed on all things legal.

During this period Linlithgow saw itself established as a member of the Scottish Court of the Four Burghs. Thus Linlithgow was rated along with Edinburgh, Stirling and Lanark as one of the most important places in the whole of Scotland. Roxburgh and Berwick-on-Tweed were considered too close to the English for comfort.

This charter was very important to the town because it meant that the people could choose their own magistrates, or baillies, as they were called, without interference from the King. King Robert died in 1390 and his successor, Robert III, continued the royal interest in the town and supported repairs to the royal manor. Except for the occasional expeditionary forces from England setting the town ablaze, Linlithgow prospered. Bearing in mind that much of the town was of wood with thatched roofs, the entire place could be recovered quite quickly. The final invasion took place in 1424 and this time the Royal Manor and the kirk were engulfed in the blaze.

Rebuilding began promptly thereafter and the new buildings are what we see today, on their shared promontory above the loch. This time the building of the King's manor was to be of stone and reconstruction took much longer. Nevertheless, when King Robert was succeeded by the first of the James's, his Queen Joanne was able to worship in St Michael's in 1429. The building of the palace proceeded incrementally, and certainly by 1437, the year James was murdered, much of it had been completed.

Records of purchases of cloth, paint and tapestries serve to indicate how the palace construction advanced year by year. James II succeeded to the throne, but he was too young to rule and little progress was made on the palace. In 1449 he married and brought his bride to the town, but during his turbulent reign he favoured Edinburgh and Stirling as his residences as they were easier to defend from his noble rivals. The Douglas family were constantly threatening trouble and the Livingstons were plotting against him. James dabbled with cannon and he was proud of his prowess with these new weapons of war. Unhappily it was the explosion of one of these big guns that killed him.

His widow, Queen Mary, and her six children remained at Linlithgow Palace. The heir to the throne was nine-year-old James III. At the age of eighteen he married Princess Margaret of Denmark and Linlithgow Palace was part of her dowry. In turn, she gave to Scotland the islands of Orkney and Shetland. An outbreak of pestilence in Edinburgh compelled them to complete at least one long stay at Linlithgow. However, like others before him, he failed to exercise control over his nobles and he too was defeated in a battle with the rebels. Subsequent to this loss, he was murdered in a nearby cottage at Sauchieburn in the year 1488.

He was succeeded by his son James IV who was but fifteen years of age but assumed the reigns of government almost at once. His period is considered to have heralded a golden age for Scotland in which Linlithgow played a prominent role. The palace at Linlithgow became his favourite residence and he obviously devoted time and money to its improvement. He married Margaret Tudor, the daughter of King Henry VII of England in 1503 and this was described as the marriage of the Thistle and the Rose. Rather foolishly, though, he decided to turn against his in-laws in England in an endeavour to support the French in 1513. Despite the warning by a so-called supernatural apparition, James IV paid the supreme penalty at the Battle of Flodden and many young Scottish nobles died with him.

His successor James V, a son born to Queen Margaret just one year before the death of her king, completed the final touches to the massive palace. As a child he was under the control of the powerful Douglas family and as always other jealous and ambitious noblemen were willing to risk their all to usurp that control. When he was fourteen a major battle was fought at Linlithgow Bridge where the Earl of Lennox endeavoured to seize power. Instead he died on the field of battle. However, at the age of sixteen, in 1530 James was able to assume control in his own right.

James V's queen, Mary of Guise, whom he married in 1537, is reported to have compared Linlithgow Palace to the noblest chateau of France. James's behaviour towards his nobles and to members of his court left something to be desired. As a consequence of the routing of his army by the English at the Battle of Solway Moss in 1542, James withdrew to Falkland Palace and died there only six days after the birth of his daughter, Mary, at Linlithgow. Mary, Queen of Scots, was born in the Royal Palace of Linlithgow and she was probably christened at the baptismal font in St Michael's. It is she who provided Linlithgow with worldwide historic fame.

It was in the reign of James V that the Riding of the Marches seriously began in Linlithgow. It is always deemed likely that the boundaries were inspected annually and on foot prior to this date. The procession involved tells much about the town as it existed during those middle ages. Led by the Provost and his baillies followed by the deacons, the bulk of the participants were members of the Linlithgow Trade Guilds and Incorporated Crafts. The original eight were the hammermen, the wrights, the baxters, the coopers, the weavers, the tailors, the cloth fullers and cordiners. Reading about these guilds always convinces me that therein lay the foundation of all of the early labour movements with their individual unions. For instance, the Guild of Hammermen included all of the craftsmen in Linlithgow who worked in any form of metal including the goldsmiths and the silversmiths. Each guild had its headquarters in a special public house wherein they held all of their meetings in comfort and with the added luxury of their favourite beverage. The population of the town at that time was about 2,500.

The leaders of these guilds were proud craftsmen and exercised a great deal of control over their trades. The cordiners, who worked in leather, including tanners, glovers, harness-makers, saddlers and shoemakers, became very important to the town in the seventeenth and eighteenth centuries. The plentiful supplies of pure fresh water encouraged growth in the industry. The same water supplies were used later on in the explosive growth of the paper industry. Yet both the tanneries and the paper mills subsequently disappeared. In their stead today there are electronics, communications and a wide assortment of modern high-technology industries.

Nevertheless, it is worthwhile to remember that in the days of James V in the middle of the sixteenth century, those incorporated trades maintained a strict monopoly, regulating the admission of apprentices, their promotions to craftsmen after at least five years of supervised service, the fixing of wages, payment of dues, quality control and methods of manufacture. At times they even dictated the price of goods. In addition, and by their own choice, they supported various expansions to the Church. During these same days the reformers were at work and the threat to the dominant Roman Catholic Church became real. John Knox preached reformation in Edinburgh and a fever seized Scotland in 1559. On 24 June of that year the Lords of the Reformation descended upon Linlithgow to cleanse the Church. They systematically destroyed all evidence of the Roman Catholic faith.

Meanwhile, Mary, with the agreement of Parliament, stayed either at Linlithgow or Stirling, as the Queen Mother preferred. Alas, it was well known that King Henry VIII of England desired Mary as his Queen despite her tender years. The English fleet visited the River Forth as if to threaten union by force. However, the nobles recognized the need for safety, so they removed her to France where she was married off to the Dauphin of France at the tender age of sixteen. The country she left behind was in turmoil and prominent citizens of Linlithgow died at the stake to become martyrs of the Reformation.

Mary returned to Linlithgow in 1561, a widow, after a marriage that was never consummated, according to report. St Michael's had been saved from the worst excesses of the Reformation mostly because the town magistrates had acted wisely and refrained from drastic action. The Queen, with her French courtiers and servants, enjoyed French picnics in the countryside and golf in the grounds of the Peel. Several place names throughout the county are distinctly French as a consequence of the influence they exerted. Along the length of the high street the substantial, stone-built, slate-roofed houses of the Spanish and the French ambassadors, and the elegant townhouses of the nobles, are still much in evidence.

Along that same street, running east and west through the town, there were ten wells. Each well gave its name to the street feeding into the high street. Linlithgow was quite famous for its wells and the general good health of the town was always ascribed to the 'excellent springs and the east-west air flow'. The names of the wells are unusual insofar as they were a mix of say, St Michael's, St Magdalene's, Friars Well, the Dog Well and the Lion Well. By far the most famous of the wells, of course, is the Cross Well. This is the focal point of the town, the centre of the weekly market, and the place of execution. My grandfather McDiarmid claimed that as a small boy he attended the last public execution at Linlithgow Cross.

At that time too the town was protected by a wall of which there are few traces left today. The names remain, nevertheless, so we have the West Port or gate, and the High Port, the east gate, and the Low Port on what is still the road to Blackness.

Without doubt, the lords and ladies and their families led very comfortable lives in Mary's day. In fact, apart from a small middle class of merchants and tradesmen, things had not changed much from the days of the barons and serfs. With tournaments, fishing, hunting, golfing, archery, tennis, bowling, curling and frequent banquets with the fountains flowing with wine, the gentry did live well. Doubtless the merchants and the men of the guilds had decent homes and adequate entertainment. But for the poor there was the roughest of lives. Those who became servants were at least warm and well-fed, but all others were compelled to scrape a livelihood out of the leftovers. The highland clansmen, poor though they may have been, lived in a less stratified society where all men were essentially equal. Even so, for all our technological progress, society remains stratified with the rich getting richer and the poor getting poorer.

Queen Mary, by now married to Lord Darnley, no doubt at the insistence of her councillors, paid several visits to Linlithgow. On one occasion she spent time at the palace while her husband marched on to Glasgow to put down a revolt led by the Earl of Moray. By 1567 Darnley was already a sick man and he was murdered rather clumsily in Edinburgh. His death was linked to Lord Bothwell who abducted an obviously willing Mary and the story goes that they were lovers. Mary was subsequently imprisoned in Loch Leven Castle, followed by her escape and flight to England. It is recorded somewhere that Bothwell died in a dungeon in Denmark. Poor Mary spent years under house arrest in England and was subsequently executed by order of Queen Elizabeth of England. Mary's baby son remained in Scotland.

Mary's only son James VI paid his first visit to Linlithgow at the age of twelve. In 1591 he travelled to Denmark to marry Princess Anna. Several of the Scottish parliaments were held in Linlithgow Palace because of an outbreak of plague. The highlight of James's reign was the offer of the English crown in 1603 on the death of Queen Elizabeth, the virgin queen. His departure for London must have been a grand celebration, but it was fourteen years before he was ever able to return. No doubt he had his difficulties with the English Parliament and there was considerable danger in travel in those days, even as a king. By 1617 he had returned and he was given a rousing welcome. His money problems had been resolved to some degree by the discovery of silver in the Bathgate Hills, near Linlithgow.

It may be that King James VI of Scotland, and at the same time James I of England, is best known because of his order that the Holy Bible be translated from Latin into English. It is interesting to note that, even in the recent printing of the Bible, the opening page has inscribed thereon, 'To the most high and mighty Prince James, by the grace of God, King of Great Britain, France, and Ireland, Defender of the Faith . . .'

King Charles I succeeded his father James VI in 1625 and he made a royal tour of Scotland in 1633. He was the last monarch ever to reside at Linlithgow Palace. Great change was about to come to the entire country with the coming of the Commonwealth, headed by Oliver Cromwell and his Roundheads. King Charles was executed in 1649. Cromwell used the church as a storehouse for his army and a stable for their horses. The Roundheads used both the inside and the outside of the church for musketry practice and they sharpened their swords on any suitably projecting stone. The Provost and the magistrates had scampered across the River Forth to Fife when they heard that Cromwell was about to visit.

As it turned out, the hated English soldiers were not as bad as they were reputed to be, the magistrates returned and made their peace with Cromwell. They had no alternative but follow the Cromwell law of the land. During the Cromwell rule the moral code was strictly enforced and the residents adjusted accordingly. For instance, the Linlithgow markets were always held on Saturdays but because of all the drinking and sometimes rioting that took place on Saturday night, it was not considered a suitable prelude to the sabbath. Market days were switched to Fridays to resolve the problem. The records of St Michael's contain details of how, after Sunday service, the elders patrolled the streets to see that no children were out playing and that the families were at home reading their bibles. The Christmas celebration, so popular in Linlithgow, was forbidden.

Oliver Cromwell died and to everyone's relief his son failed to succeed him. The monarchy was restored and Charles II assumed the throne in 1660. There was still unrest in the land because of the conflict in the Church between those who supported the restoration of episcopacy, as the King desired, and those who wished to remain faithful to the covenant. The Duke of York, brother of Charles II resided at Linlithgow Palace and during his stay he was made a Freeman of the Burgh. He succeeded his brother Charles on the throne, and became James VII. He admitted his Catholic faith and produced a Catholic heir. Unhappily he was dethroned by the so-called Glorious Revolution of 1688 and was the last of the Stewart kings. He and his family left for France.

The Protestant William and Mary of Orange came to the British throne, and this completely altered the political and religious outlook in the entirety of Scotland. In fact, a great number of Scotsmen have never recognized the so-called Royal Family since. They are mostly condemned as 'furriners' and considered to be a quite unnecessary expense. Despite the English, Linlithgow appears to have prospered in the eighteenth century. Water was piped directly into the wells from the local springs and this no doubt contributed to the health of the town. Trade flourished through the port of Blackness, dues levied in the markets provided funds to lay cobbled streets and the textile industry prospered and grew. The main exports through the port of Blackness were cargoes of coal, salt, woollen cloth, skins and hides, and on occasions corn, oats and wheat. The imports were exciting to the townsfolk, such as velvet, tapestries, fine linens, fruit and spices of all kinds.

Unfortunately, in the midst of their prosperity, the threat of another rebellion disturbed their hopes and dreams. In 1715, James Edward Stewart, dubbed the Old Pretender, and son of James VII, appeared from France. Meanwhile, King

William and Mary were succeeded by Queen Anne and in 1714 by George I. James's rebellion was short-lived and he returned in haste to the comparative safety of France. But in 1745, Prince Charles Edward Stewart, the Young Pretender, put in an appearance from France and was well received in the Highlands. He was far less enthusiastically received in the south, although his campaign was successful up to a point. He is reported to have marched into England and on as far as Derby, but resistance stiffened and he was forced to retreat. Various skirmishes were fought until the two armies finally faced each other at Culloden.

The English general, the Duke of Cumberland, defeated the Prince who had no alternative but flee. He escaped back to France through the Island of Skye with the help of Flora McDonald. Cumberland ordered that the wounded, and the women and children, were all to be slaughtered, and according to the record books he earned his title, the Butcher. Records show that the slaughter was totally unnecessary and it remains a blot on English military history.

To add to Cumberland's dreadful reputation it is recorded that when he and his troops left Linlithgow, on their way to final victory at Culloden, they left huge fires burning and unattended at the palace. Having left heaps of straw and old bedding around in the palace, the blaze spread rapidly and became uncontrollable. It was never thereafter repaired. It stands today, a glorious ruin, a monument to the violent history of the town.

By now, George II was on the British throne, giving way to George III who reigned till 1820. He died when the Auld Laird was eight years old. The years of the Napoleonic Wars were over as a consequence of the Duke of Wellington's victory at Waterloo where Napoleon was captured and subsequently exiled to St Helena. The authorities were by then more concerned with travel and communications. The biggest project underway at that time was the digging of the Union Canal. This was one of the last canals to be constructed in Britain and it stretched for thirty-one and a half miles from Edinburgh to Falkirk, on exactly the same level for its entire length. It finally connected with the Forth and Clyde Canal near Falkirk and offered what was then a comfortable and relatively rapid means of transport for both people and goods. The canal was opened to traffic in 1822.

However, the slow travel time, when compared to the railway, allowed the proponents of speed to convince the Government to finance a railway from Edinburgh to Glasgow, which opened in 1842. The nature of the countryside is such that great aqueducts were necessary for the canal, and equally large stone-arched viaducts for the railway. Armies of Irish navvies laboured for decades on their construction and maintenance. The results were widely acclaimed on both occasions, canal completion and railway completion. They were built to last, the canal survives to this day as a tourist playground and the express trains from Edinburgh to Glasgow speed along those tracks and over the same massive viaduct.

The principal use for the canal was the transportation of barges laden with coal, hauled by large Clydesdale horses on the towpath, with fresh horses supplied at various way stations. The passenger barges were well-equipped for passenger comfort and included bars and dining halls, and some offered entertainment. An overnight express service was employed for businessmen and merchants. It is interesting to compare the travel time, say, by coach over rough, unsurfaced roads of five hours, with the comfort of the 'Fly-Boat' for seven and a half hours. The new railway offered the same service at about the same price in a time of two and a half hours. Understandably, the railway thrived and the stage coaches disappeared.

The canal stopped taking commercial traffic in 1933, and was officially closed in 1965. However, as is customary in Great Britain, a Union Canal Society sprang up and is dedicated to its preservation. Much of the canal has been cleaned up and it is used for a variety of recreational purposes. A canal museum is now established at Linlithgow turning basin and electrically-powered barges carry tourists over the most attractive sections of the canal which includes the great aqueduct at Carriber Glen.

The improved transportation in the nineteenth century permitted Linlithgow to expand. The paper industry thrived and trade improved by leaps and bounds. Meanwhile the exodus to the United States and Canada had gathered momentum. This, in some ways, contributed to prosperity insofar as mostly the poor and the unemployed took advantage of the North American promise. The British Government devoted most of its time to expanding and sustaining the Empire, another good way of utilizing excess labour. King George IV reigned for only ten years, from 1820 to 1830, and he was succeeded by William IV who lasted only seven years. Then Queen Victoria ascended the throne in 1837 and she reigned until 1901. Her reign heralded a long period of progress both at home and abroad. The Auld Laird was a young man of twenty-five years when Victoria came to the throne and took us into the twentieth century.

By the time I was old enough to be interested, the population of Linlithgow was close to 3,000, and perhaps 3,500 by the time World War II commenced. Today there are more than 12,000 inhabitants, not because of industrial expansion, but because it has become a dormitory for Edinburgh and Glasgow. High-speed trains, excellent roads, good communications, proximity to Edinburgh Airport and its potential as a tourist centre, all have contributed to its growth. This can be bad or good, depending upon one's concern about traffic and general congestion, or in the case of the Kirk of St Michael, its expanding congregation.

As a boy, I can remember Sunday services at St Michael's, with fewer than thirty people in the congregation. Dr Coupar would stare down from his pulpit and lament upon the degradation of moral and christian values. By comparison, today there is standing room only in the kirk at times, and this with two morning services. None the less, on that last Sunday in April 1934, before I left for Liverpool and my career at sea, the church was almost deserted. I sat on in the Miller pew until I was alone, absorbing the history and the majesty of that ancient House of God. Walking through the emptiness of that great church never fails to impress, and when the sun is shining, the enormous, stained-glass windows almost come alive.

The high-backed wooden pews provided little seating comfort, no doubt designed to keep the congregation awake. The cold stone floors induced a numbness in the feet, and the massive stone pillars glowered down upon the body of the church, lending an air of antiquity, as if to encourage ghosts of the past. I stood by the baptismal font, remembering the reported argument the Minister had with my mother over my christening. In the vestry I looked up at the ministers' names carved in stone from the year 1200.

Standing in the centre aisle, and looking east towards the splendid window in the apse, reminded me once again of Charles Wyville Thomson, the great oceanic explorer, whose memory the window commemorates. The row upon row of black wooden pews, the great oaken doors, the floor of plain grey stone under which hundreds have been buried over the centuries, all bear mute testimony to the tens of generations who have worshipped here. My eyes were drawn to the aumbry, built in place of the old leper's squint, through which the diseased might watch the service. I mumbled a prayer of thanks for my own good health.

The lectern is in the form of a massive, bronze eagle settled upon an orb. The pulpit is of beautifully carved oak and features the figures of the three Queens: Margaret, Mary Stewart and Victoria. At the beginning of this century, the infant Samuel window was installed in memory of Esther Struthers Ferguson, daughter of John Ferguson, the Minister at that time. This Minister's other daughter drowned after falling through the ice on Linlithgow loch with her fiancé. I walked from St Katherine's aisle to sit in the elders' stalls beside the communion table in the apse. Finally I tiptoed across the lush red carpet laid between the choir stalls where my mother often sang and on down the centre aisle to the west door. Stepping into the sunshine from the sombre majesty of the church and facing the monumental ruins of the great palace reminded me of our turbulent history.

Recalling my grandfather's stories about the Reformation and the Covenantors reminded me of the kirk session records and their constant references to the need for restoration. So many efforts in this regard were brought to naught when

Oliver Cromwell decided to billet his troops and stable their horses in the church. To correct the consequent deterioration the town council levied a tax upon the entire burgh, collected under penalty of quartering. Not enough was collected and it was then decided to raise more by selling off the right to use a pew. This decision created great difficulties at a later date. Most seats soon belonged to someone and those who could not afford one had to rely on the generosity of others to allow them to sit in the church.

The eighteenth-century Church of Linlithgow followed general Scottish patterns, and I quote from St Michael's Church documents:

The Church was dominated by the Minister and his Kirk session who rigorously guarded the community's moral life and enforced fines for any breach of Church discipline. The money collected was used to help the poor of the Parish.

The Church was equipped with a repentance stool, on which any wrong-doer had to sit in full view of the congregation, and a set of Jougs at the Church door to chain up by the neck, anyone guilty of repeated transgressions.

The Kirk Session minutes are full of references to such moral lapses; drunkenness, adultery, whistling, working or washing clothes on the Lord's Day, or not keeping Elder's hours.

A typical Church service lasted up to four hours. A sand-glass was attached to the Minister's pulpit in order to ensure that he spoke (ex-tempore, for all notes were frowned upon) for at least two hours.

Singing was led by a precentor and was unaccompanied as music in the Church was frowned upon. An organ was referred to scathingly as a 'Kist o' Whistles'.

St Michael's was visited by the poet Robert Burns, in 1787, and he described it as 'a grim, comfortless Church'. Sir Walter Scott had much warmer comments to make during his visits. Yet these were grim times. In February 1819 a 'Linlithgow Mortsafe Society' was established to hire out a huge metal cage, which was placed over a grave to deter the grave-robbers from resurrecting the body and selling it to the anatomy lecturers in Edinburgh.

Wandering through the churchyard I came upon the same stone, erect upon the ground, where I stood each Sunday with my grandfather, remembering his forebears, and pointing out the inscription on the tombstone which referred to one night in the 1870s when he lost five siblings to scarlet fever. I would scrape moss from horizontal gravestones commemorating the Millers back to the sixteenth century. Others, lying flat upon the ground, are too weather-worn to divulge their secrets.

I walked down the Kirk Brae towards the town, remembering Sundays when as a small boy I was marched to church both morning and evening, just about three feet ahead of my grandfather's black, hawthorn walking stick. These were the memories I carried with me to the train that would take me to Liverpool to embark upon an endless journey around the world.

PART II

CHAPTER IV

THE MERCHANT NAVY – SS TYMERIC (VOYAGE 1)

The train journey to Liverpool was uneventful, although I must confess to a certain level of trepidation. This was a new adventure and one that I must undertake on my own. Liverpool's Lime Street Station and the trip to some outlandish suburb on an elevated railway did nothing to assuage my foreboding. My destination was Bootle, the end of the line I was told. Even the name worried me, I had a feeling that I was about to fall off the edge of the earth. The railroad tracks, the rickety staircase to the street and the appalling stench of the surrounding warehouses made the place even more uninviting. Across the street there was nothing but row upon row of dingy tenement houses. The docks, large and small, big ships, small ships, enormous cranes and men scrambling like ants amidst an ear-splitting noise were busy.

Suddenly I remembered an early day in April with my brother, by this time a policeman in Edinburgh, when he took me to Leith to see the docks there so that I might have some idea about my new world. I was not unduly impressed. Nevertheless my brother kept insisting that the *Tymeric* would be a much classier vessel than any of those we had inspected. One that we saw just after sunset had the name *Keelung* painted on her stern and the port of registry was Taipei, Formosa. She was obviously empty, awaiting cargo, and towered above the dock. Just as we passed the gangway a trio of Chinese men were stringing oil lanterns on the gangway rail and suddenly all the ship's lights went out. The ship was immediately shrouded in the shadows of dockside darkness. We could hear the crewmen babbling in Chinese. An officer, obviously European, stood amidst the shadows on the bridge deck, high above us, then we turned away. For some peculiar reason a shiver ran up and down my spine.

My brother hastened to explain that if no night work is planned on the dock the ship shuts down power completely, including generators, in the interest of economy. He suggested too that many of the ships trading there had Chinese or Malay or Indian crews, with British officers, again in the interest of economy. 'Things are tough all over,' he said with a laugh. Then as we passed the manilla headlines holding the ship against the dock he pointed out the galvanized steel discs fitted over the ropes, 'Tough on the rats, too, these are ratguards to keep them on board.' Indeed, I discovered later that he was right, everything was done to prevent rats escaping from the ships into the warehouses. I shuddered as I don't think I had ever seen a rat.

A stevedore I questioned responded in a peculiar Liverpudlian dialect and pointed across the dock. I followed his gesture and within minutes I was gazing up at the same clipper stern as the *Keelung*, but this one spelled *Tymeric*. The same enormous hull towered out of the water as if to emphasize its emptiness. The gangway leading to the amidship section looked uninviting. There was no red carpet here. But this was 'it'. The owners, the Bank Line Ltd, were headquartered at 21 Bury Street, London EC3. The Chairman was Lord Inverforth, in his youth Andrew Weir, a shipping clerk from Kirkcaldy, Scotland, who started the company and built the largest sailing fleet in the world. The very last of these, the *Olivebank*, a four-masted barque, was bought by a Norwegian shipmaster to run grain from Australia. By then she had been renamed the *Hercagon Cecilie* and she ended up on the rocks off the coast of Wales in the mid-1930s.

But this was April 1934 and uninviting though it might be I had no alternative but to climb the near vertical gangway. A Chinese quartermaster met me on the deck. He took my dufflebag and escorted me to the Captain's quarters, located on the boat deck, at the moment an island of peace and comparative quiet. I could see numerous crew members, all Chinese, peering up at me from the main deck where the hatches were being battened down.

I responded nervously to a voice saying, 'Come in'. I stepped into the Captain's quarters and it was though I had entered another world. This was his day room, in dark, polished oak panelling, with brass lamps slung in gimbals. A very pretty, middle-aged lady sat in a comfortable lounge chair, knitting. She smiled, obviously recognizing my discomfiture. Captain Bulman sat at a large mahogany desk with masses of papers spread in front of him. When he turned to face me I could have sworn he was the officer from the *Keelung*. However, he did introduce himself and his wife, then quickly escorted me down an oak-panelled staircase to the saloon. In a large cabin next door sat the greatest bear of a man I had ever seen. He was Thomas Fraser from the Shetland Islands, the Chief Officer. 'Aye,' he said to the captain, 'I'll take care of him.'

With very little ceremony I was advised to sign here, here and here. I simply did as I was instructed, scarcely knowing what the documents were all about. I learned later that I was now formally indentured to Captain Bulman for a period of four years, and was to be paid the princely sum of seventy pounds sterling for the entire period. I learned also, to my extreme disappointment, that the aforementioned seventy pounds merely covered my insurance dues to His

Majesty's Government. This, I was told, would provide me with unemployment benefits and an old age pension, which I have yet to receive, some sixty years later. I was also advised that on the following day I would have the privilege of signing the ship's articles at the shipping office.

'Now I'll show you where to park your body,' said Thomas Fraser. Across an alleyway, lined with steam pipes, there were cabins for the 2nd Officer, the 3rd Officer and a double-berth cabin for the cadets. A large bathroom was located at the end of the alleyway. Everything was truly antiquated but nevertheless spick and span. The cadets' cabin had two bunks, each with spotlessly clean linen, a double wardrobe, a fold-away wash-hand basin, a desk and a settee. A small bookcase was fastened to the bulkhead and this contained all the necessary text books on navigation, seamanship, meteorology and ship's business in general. 'Make yourself at home, son,' the Chief Officer said. 'You'll be here a long time. Your shipmate arrives tomorrow.' With a sweep of his arm he indicated the saloon, 'Dinner's at six. You're second sitting,' and with that I was alone.

Unpacking my few belongings took very little time and when it was done I sat on the settee feeling absolutely lost. I could not summon the necessary courage to go out on deck. I heard a bell ring but paid no attention, then suddenly the cabin door opened and in the alleyway stood the 3rd Officer. 'John Noble,' he said, and stepped inside. 'That's the first sitting for dinner. We go in in half an hour.' He shook hands warmly and within ten minutes I felt as if I had known him all my life. He had 'finished his time', as he said, had acquired his papers at college and this was now his first berth as third mate. In the next twenty minutes, and then over dinner, only two of us, I learned all the positive things about ships and seagoing. His optimism was infectious. He looked great, all six muscular feet of him, in a brand new uniform complete with the single band and diamond in gold braid.

I remember being impressed by the dinner. Damask tablecloths, linen napkins with silver rings, silver water jugs, silver utensils and crested dishes complimented the polished panelling on the bulkheads. Special pedestal-type mahogany chairs were screwed to the deck. The Chinese stewards said absolutely nothing but they brought plates of delicious, steaming hot soup followed by fish with a special sauce, then pork chops with all the trimmings. All this was followed by caramel custard, biscuits and cheese and coffee. I left the table stuffed to the gills. I promptly went to bed and slept like a log despite the unaccustomed throbbing from the engine room. The main engines were silent but generators vibrated and whined. In the morning I felt and behaved like an old hand.

Signing on was a dull experience and the shipping office, a typical dusty, humourless place. I was glad to get back on board. To my surprise my shipmate had arrived complete with mother and sister to see him off. I felt superior as a consequence and I gathered that his sister thought I was an old-timer which did much for my ego. We were sailing the following day for Baltimore, Maryland in ballast. That meant empty. The Chief Officer brought the Bo'sun to talk to us, to tour the ship and to allocate duties. He was Chinese, from Hong Kong, and spoke good English. The 2nd Officer, Mr Betts, who had just arrived back from leave, took us to the bridge and the charthouse, and advised us in firm tones that he personally was in charge of our education. We both decided that he was a bit of a windbag but deserving of cooperation.

Sailing day dawned bright and clear. We watched as tugboats manoeuvred the ship around the various docks to the lock gates. We departed and dropped the pilot about an hour later. We were soon into the choppy Irish Sea and poor Charlesworth, my shipmate, had to retire to his bunk. I was fortunate as I never ever suffered from seasickness even in the worst of weather. Soon we were heading south-west and then around the south coast of Ireland. My first voyage had begun and we were heading across the North Atlantic.

Days turned into weeks and the learning process was extremely rapid. Whilst at sea, we were on what was called watch and watch. In other words, four hours on deck and four hours below. The duty hours changed each day during the dogwatch, that is four to eight in the evening, when each group switched to two on and two off. That way we hit the 'death watch', midnight till four in the morning, only every second night. Despite the appalling pounding when we ran into rough seas, that is when the bow rises with the head sea then comes crashing down into the trough, we could all sleep like logs. The trouble was it was hard to wake up.

By the time we sighted the east coast of the United States, we cadets were old salts. Arrival in Baltimore was an experience in itself and Chesapeake Bay was glorious that May morning. However the glory disappeared at the dock. We berthed at the east end of East Baltimore Street, amidst mile-high wreckage because this was the scrap steel yard and we were destined to load for Japan. Huge electric cranes with magnets hovered over the piles of scrap metal, then swung their ungainly loads over the ship's holds and turned off the juice. The heavy metal tumbled into the hold making the most ungodly clatter. I had the impression that the stevedores actually enjoyed what they were doing but fortunately they only worked in daylight. By night the ship was in an eerie darkness and silent as the grave. In the shadows cast by the giant piles of scrap, the ship, the dock and the greasy water merged and became one huge blot on a bleak landscape.

By now Charlesworth and I had become friends with the engineers. They ate separately from us in a cosy mess room because they were always dressed in messy dungarees. The Chief Engineer, Mr Henderson, always dined in the saloon. Meal hours in the saloon were staid and boring but somehow more exciting in the engineers' mess as they were always telling dirty jokes, describing their various amorous adventures or boasting about how great their last ship was. They were determined to take us ashore to show us the ropes, or so they said. It was later that we realized that East Baltimore Street was an area where it was extremely desirable to travel in groups in the interest of self-protection.

East Baltimore Street in those years was world-famous amongst seafarers. It was known as the reddest red light district that anyone could imagine. One dingy bar after another lined the street and street-walkers galore lounged on every corner. The most brilliantly lit of these dens of iniquity was the 'Oasis', a few blocks east of the Lord Baltimore Hotel. The bars in the 'Oasis', the music, the half-naked dancers and the brilliant lights attracted the sailors of all nationalities. By late evening they were no longer sober and most were bent upon starting a war. When real trouble started the barman simply turned off all the lights, the ladies dissolved into the woodwork and it was difficult to tell friend from foe. I doubt if any of us ever knew how we were thrown out or how we managed to stick together, but most of us carried the marks of the brawl for quite a while. However it was all part of the learning process according to our shipmates.

Mr Fraser looked us over in the morning with a critical eye, shrugged his massive shoulders, and mumbled a warning of some kind. The loading resumed and the hellish noise precluded further conversation. We were soon over the bow on a bos'un's chair, dangling on the end of a rope, repainting the name 'Tymeric' on the bow, and the filthy dock water splashing below us erased any last remnant of any appetite we may have had. It was a great relief to head out to sea. We were only half-loaded, about 5,000 tons of scrap metal heaped indiscriminately in the bottom of the ship's cargo holds and bound for the Japanese munitions factories. The concentrated weight acted like a pendulum in the half-laden ship and she rolled and wallowed round like a deflated blimp. To avoid the north-flowing Gulf Stream we hugged the shore southbound for the Panama Canal.

Days passed quickly and each new day brought new dimensions to our little world. We had to shadow the bos'un or the ship's carpenter or the lamp-trimmer storekeeper and learn about every nook and cranny in the ship. There was an important daily need for soundings. Every compartment in the ship from forepeak to double-bottom fuel tanks, deep tanks, bilges, fresh water tanks, every single one of them was carefully sounded, morning and night, and the readings carefully recorded in a log book. Every valve, chain or moving part on deck or between decks was carefully oiled daily. The ship could alternate between coal-fired or oil-fired boilers, depending upon what part of the world we were in. On our way to Colon on the Atlantic side of the Panama Canal she burned coal.

Stokers and trimmers worked watch and watch as the deck crew did but with added duties. At the end of each watch the men surfaced from the over-heated stokehold drenched in sweat. After a shower and a meal they still had to dump the ashes before retiring. Each watch in the stokehold were compelled to draw the fires and discard the red-hot ashes into a corner of the stokehold at the end of their watch. They were then hoisted by drum and winch up the massive ventilator shafts to the main deck, then dumped into the sea through an ash-shute conveniently placed in the rail on the lee side of the ship.

In addition to the hard work, we had a taste of the more interesting aspects of seafaring, by special permission of the 2nd Mate. In those days the Captain was considered to be the monarch of all he surveyed and seemed to do little else but pace up and down on his spotless, oregon-pine boat deck. The Chief Officer, the big man from the Shetlands, ran the ship including cargo loading and unloading, assisted of course by his junior officers. The 2nd Mate was the Navigator, in charge of the wheelhouse, the chartroom and all matters pertaining to the whereabouts of the ship. The lowly 3rd Mate was in charge of the lifeboats, all life-saving, fire and safety equipment, and sustained his watch on the bridge.

The Chief always stood the 4 to 8 watches, the 2nd Mate the noon to 4 and midnight to 4, and the 3rd Mate the 8 to 12's. The Captain usually appeared on the bridge about noon to check the navigation and to make the final decisions on the ship's position in terms of latitude and longitude. The Radio Officer used these to report by low-frequency radio and on occasions he received messages from Rugby, England where a massive radio signal station was maintained.

As always, each had additional duties. The Chief with bills of lading and cargo plans and records, the 2nd Mate was also the Doctor and handled sick parade, and the 3rd Mate handled the money and maintained great ledgers and financial statements. The Radio Officer usually acted as Purser, and lent a great deal of mysterious assistance to the Captain.

The sick parade was always something of a joke bearing in mind that in the thirties medicine had not advanced all that much from the middle ages, except for the discovery of chloroform. This was found and developed by a humble chemist in my own home town, Linlithgow. Being big, as opposed to Charlesworth being of slight build, I was selected to be the assistant in the medical business and I rather enjoyed the whole process. We had little medicine in the so-called medicine chest, other than black draught, cascara sagrada, calomine lotion, friars balsam, permanganate of potash, and a big container of iodine. There was no such thing as antibiotics. Each candidate with a complaint was compelled to take a healthy swig of black draught before being permitted to describe his symptoms. This tended to keep the line pretty thin.

Most of the complaints were minor accidents, burns, black eyes, the odd broken limb and venereal disease. However we did have an occasional death due to accident or sickness, like heart attacks, and as the assistant medic I fell heir to the additional duties of undertaker. I had the job of sewing up the body in canvas, then lashing a heavy firebar thereto and at a time specified by his majesty the Captain, the corpse was placed on a hatch-board resting upon the gunwale and draped with the Red Ensign.

On a given signal, the officer of the watch rang the telegraph to stop the engines, then Captain Bulman, in full uniform, read the burial service from the Bible, raised his hand and the hatch was tipped. The body slid into the ocean, the ensign was retrieved, the engines rung full ahead again and the service was over. The 2nd Mate acting as ship's doctor made an appropriately solemn entry into the ship's official log. There was usually a great clinking of crystal glasses at the first sitting in the saloon on such a day. Charlesworth and I assumed that the Captain had cracked open a bottle of the good stuff to toast the departed spirit as well as good King Neptune. Alas, we were not invited. Mr Fraser could be seen smacking his chops as he paced the bridge on the second dogwatch.

Brief glimpses of the coastline emerged as we rounded Yucatan, Honduras, Nicaragua, then on to Colon. There was some excitement amongst the married officers who received mail from home. The London office received mail and forwarded it to an anticipated port of call by fast passenger liner leaving directly from England. My concern was the canal and the locks and the mechanical donkeys on rails that hauled us through the locks. I was fascinated and tremendously impressed by this great feat of engineering. Karun Lake and the tropical forest added wonder to the entire transit. I was still raving about it to my shipmates as we loaded fresh water and stores in Panama City prior to departure into the Gulf of Panama and on into the Pacific. This was the other half of the world to me. We studied the charts, made estimates of our progress and dreamed our individual dreams of adventure.

The *Tymeric* progressed majestically, at the colossal speed of ten knots. On average we made about 240 miles per day. We burned coal and created buckets of ash like crazy in so doing. The trimmers, pushing coal towards the slips into the stokehold, were working harder than ever to move the ever-diminishing supply of coal. It was then that we learned from Sparks, as we called the Radio Officer, that we were to take on fuel oil and convert in San Pedro, near Los Angeles. Thereafter we were to proceed to Vancouver, British Columbia to top off with dressed lumber, all for Japan. We all agreed that lumber was vastly better than scrap.

There was little to see at San Pedro and plenty to do. Engineers were busy changing fire brick and fire doors and connecting pipes and valves to the fuel tanks. Meanwhile, about 2,000 tons of black oil that looked like molasses were pumped from shore into the fuel tanks. These tanks were carefully watched throughout the process, continuous soundings were taken and real panic gripped the deckhands responsible for making sure there was no overflow. Awaiting steam pressure for the main engines provided some respite. We were able to go offshore with John Noble in one of the lifeboats. This provided him with a valuable report on lifeboat drill, safety and sailing. It provided us with great blisters on our hands from having to row all the way back to the ship when the wind died on us. Next day we put to sea once more heading northwards along the west coast of the United States.

The voyage was uneventful, the weather in mid-summer almost perfect. Watch on deck, watch below, followed one upon the other somewhat monotonously, despite the fact that we were kept busy washing down, cleaning decks, cleaning fresh-water tanks, painting, varnishing and polishing in every part of the ship. Interest increased significantly as we approached the straits of Juan de Fuca, bound for the Port of Vancouver. The scenery was incredible and this contributed much to our excitement at reaching port. We took a pilot on board, and some hours later we were berthed and ready to load. Timber was a great departure from scrap but according to our Chief Officer it represented a highly complimentary-type cargo, and the freight rates were satisfactory.

The heavy scrap lowered the *Tymeric* to only about half her permissable loaded draft but left ample space in the holds for the dressed lumber to be loaded. We crossed the harbour to north Vancouver and when the holds were completely filled the hatches were battened down and we were ready to sail. At this time we were advised to proceed to Port Alberni on the west side of Vancouver Island to load deck cargo, till she reached her allowable plimsoll mark for the North Pacific. We sailed under blue skies.

Leaving one port and arriving at another provides a sensation that is very difficult to describe. Perhaps it is the sea voyage itself that creates the effect. Sailing on the high seas utterly alone, at the mercy of nature, lends an impression of peace and tranquillity on the one hand and a wild excited feeling of being absolutely alone in the world on the other. Alone at midnight in a swaying crow's nest in utter darkness except for an occasional flash of phosphorescence can play havoc with a man's mind. Stability is recovered somewhat at the sight of land and a new excitement is generated. The actual adventure of being in port in a strange land may turn out to be very dull indeed. However such an experience has absolutely no detrimental effect on the renewed excitement upon reaching the next port of call.

The Pilot for Port Alberni was hard to find in a lashing rainstorm, but patience and forbearance displayed by the imperturbable Captain Bulman paid off. A brief break in the weather and the pilot cutter was alongside. The harbour was like something out of National Geographic magazine. I had the feeling that we were in the midst of a tropical rain forest except for the bite in the westerly breeze. Port Alberni was a real frontier town in our estimation. The stevedores were big men built like professional wrestlers. Most of the time they stank of stale beer and they seemed to take great delight in creating sparks from the steel decks with their heavy lumberjack books; they seemed to be ready to fight at the drop of a hat.

During the final stages of loading, when the deck cargo was piled no less than twenty feet high on the main decks, great chains were bolted to the gunwales and stretched tight across the top layers of timber. Being the final day and therefore a cause for celebration the smell of beer became almost overpowering. On the main deck aft a great hulking brute of a man started to swing a huge hammer over his head. This was the hammer to be used to slip the chains and the deck cargo in the event of violent weather conditions. 'I am the crazy Finn,' he kept shouting in a peculiar accent, then he let go with a string of obscenities at the foreman stevedore. 'I'm da crazy Finn,' he yelled again. Work promptly ceased and an instant audience was created, all well out of range of the swinging hammer.

I was careful to stay within the shadow of the big man from the Shetlands. 'Get the Mountie,' he said to someone and I felt a thrill of excitement. I had read all about the redcoats and I could hardly wait to see one arrive. I was sure it would need an army of them to subdue the crazy Finn. The audience fell silent and the crazy one yelled obscenities at everyone of us. I never did find out why. His accent was too difficult to interpret.

The Chief Officer moved towards the gangway and I followed him. A Model T Ford trundled down the wooden wharf towards us. A slim young man in a dark suit and trilby hat got out and mounted the gangplank. I could not believe that the mountie had arrived. He looked over the situation, walked across the timber piled high on the deck and by this time the 'Crazy Finn' stood nonchalantly leaning on the hammer, saying nothing. The mountie walked directly up to him, a full head shorter. He reached up with both hands, firmly grabbed his hair, jerked the head down, and at the same time he brought his knee up sharply to meet the crazy Finn's chin. It was curtains. The mountie pointed to two men and waved his hand. They picked up the limp Finn, dumped him unceremoniously on the dock, then bundled him into the car. The mountie drove off without a word.

The boss stevedore treated us to beers at the local hostelry before we sailed. Port Alberni has always remained in my mind as a unique place, just tottering on the edge of the world. I have never been back in sixty years. I have no doubt that great progress has been made and by now it could be a west coast paradise.

We departed on a very dull day but calm and with a glassy sea. Seals and sea otters lounged about upon the surface of a flat Pacific Ocean, taking full advantage of their kind of weather. Before nightfall the coastline had disappeared astern and we were once more alone on the high seas. As inexperienced as Charlesworth and I were, we were aware that the North Pacific could be a mighty unfriendly place when nature so decided.

We were headed west and maintained a course designed to keep us well south of the Aleutian Islands. Rough seas slowed the heavily-laden *Tymeric* and tons of seawater washed over the decks. The Bos'un and the ship's carpenter devoted full time to nursing the chains that held the deck load. On several occasions Charlesworth and I had to trot behind Mr Fraser, who would stand with his feet widespread upon the timber, whilst the ship heaved and rolled and creaked, almost as if in her death throes. He instructed us to climb down to inspect the shackles holding the chains to the gunwales and test the slip rings to make sure that one blow from the hammer would spring the chains loose. I can clearly remember hoping that such a decision would never have to be made.

Meanwhile we were learning navigation and we were even allowed to practice the art. In addition we had long periods of study dealing with knowledge of principles, mathematics, navigation, meteorology, ship's business, ship construction, etc. under the tutelage of Mr Betts. Navigation in the 1930s was indeed an art. We had the appropriate charts, the nautical ephemeris providing data relevant to sun, moon and stars, a chronometer, sextants, a crude radio direction-finder, a magnetic compass and a deep-sea, hand leadline. The bottom of the lead weight used with the leadline was stuffed with tallow to acquire a sample of the ocean bottom. Surprisingly, the old-fashioned way worked really well. A sand bottom, or shell, or mud, was easily identifiable and could be compared to the chart.

The key to successful navigation was the chronometer and this instrument was the prime responsibility of the Navigating Officer. The chronometer was wound at precisely the same time each day with a special key. The clock itself, a delicate instrument, was set permanently in gimbals to sustain it in a level position and was housed in its own mahogany, brass-bound box. As often as possible, and from different low-frequency radio stations time signals were received and the error of the chronometer was carefully recorded, so that when celestial observations were taken by sextant accurate time to the nearest half second could be obtained. One second error in time can create an error of a quarter of a mile in position.

We, the cadets, always enjoyed the opportunity to observe the ship's position, through time and sextant observation, followed by fairly lengthy and complex calculation. This is something that can be done today by pushing a button on a satellite navigation system and in addition the depth of water under the vessel is constantly displayed and recorded, and an auto-pilot, based upon a gyro compass, is in constant use. Very efficient one might conclude but no fun when compared to bracing oneself on the wing of the bridge when dawn breaks and shows a clear horizon. The sextant observations were always taken by two individuals, the results compared and how close we came to one another was a thrill in itself.

Despite the rough weather we finally found a calm sea under the lee of the northernmost island of Japan. Within hours we were berthed in a tiny port called Miiki, a small town perched upon a hillside overlooking enormous stacks of coal. Again we went through the ritual of conversion from oil to coal. The process of reducing steam pressure, changing the furnaces then raising steam again, allowed the crew time to obtain shore leave. John Noble, the 3rd Mate, had the job of issuing the requested allowances to the crew members. Upon signing the ship's articles, each man allocated the major portion of his wages to his family through the appropriate shipping office and the funds remaining accumulated to his account. He could draw upon this in the relevant currency at his discretion through Mr Noble. A very complex set of disbursement records had to be kept and it was very necessary that we learned how to do it.

Shore leave in Miiki was not an entirely successful venture. Before we arrived at our discharge ports, Osaka and Nagoya, the sick parade had expanded to include a few cases of gonorrhoea. The 2nd Mate was obliged to report those cases to the Health Officer in Osaka. The Japanese medical officer refused to believe that venereal disease had been contracted in the brothels of Miiki, and declared that the Chinese crew members were carriers of the disease. He did nevertheless sign the international health cards issued to each infected man and then recorded the recommended method of treatment.

The treatment of gonorrhoea was always a source of great amusement to all concerned with the exception of the victim of course. A hot-water bottle was filled with a solution of permanganate of potash and then hung upside down from a hook high on a cabin door. Instead of a stopper this bottle had a tube four or five feet long with an insertion stem and a clamp at the end. The victim himself was obliged to insert the stem into his penis and then release the clamp to allow the fluid to completely fill his bladder. He would hold the fluid for as long as possible before relieving himself with squeals and groans of relief. It is said that this procedure feels just like pissing razor blades. This performance was repeated several times each day and for about two weeks. Despite the obvious agony of the cure it did not appear to act as any great deterrent to the victim's sexual activity.

Syphylis, a more serious complaint, was treated with more respect and the victim was quarantined. In those days injections of bismouth were jabbed into the buttocks, but no one was quite sure of any benefit they provided. Such cases were put ashore in hospital and their health cards duly signed off. The British Consul in the relevant port accepted the responsibility of returning the man to his home port after appropriate treatment. As far as we were concerned it was only slightly less severe than a sentence of death. Small wonder then that our experience with the sick parade rendered us impervious to the wiles of the harlots who haunt every port in the world.

Osaka was a bustling port and a city of lights and lanterns. The Japanese food was strange to us and very cheap, as we were given about seventeen yen to the pound. Even one yen went a long way. Off-loading the cargo was an interesting experience in itself and caused us to rub shoulders with the Japanese stevedores. They were a peculiar lot; they wore socks that fitted around their big toe so they could wear the wooden sandals with toe straps. To me they were all tough little guys and peculiarly arrogant. At every opportunity they tried to make fun of us and they would laugh uproariously at their own jokes. So long as they were in the majority in the cargo hold they chose to be insultingly arrogant, but the moment they were in the minority, or alone with us, they quickly became subservient. Obviously they found it difficult to understand our disdain.

Nagoya was a carbon copy of Osaka. The few days it took us to off-load the scrap became very boring indeed. I was very relieved to learn that we were headed for Yokohama, to anchor in the outer harbour and to wait for orders. The rush and bustle of cargo handling gave way to absolute peace and quiet. Very quickly thereafter the officers produced a detailed plan for the refurbishment of the entire vessel. The engineers shut down every single machine on board and proceeded with extensive maintenance. No one knew how long we might wait for orders. Freight rates were low and ships were laid up all over the world. However, as Mr Fraser often reminded us all in the saloon, 'Thank your bloody stars you're all getting paid. Your families are living the life of Reilly.'

It was not all hard work. At weekends a workboat made the rounds of the ships to provide an opportunity for liberty. There was a Flying Angel Mission to Seamen in operation in Yokohama and the Padre was a very popular guy who loved sports. He organized soccer games, cricket games, swimming competitions and all kinds of indoor sports including boxing. The sports became highly competitive with different ships fielding teams. Chinese crew members played soccer in their bare feet and they could lay on quite a performance. Some of us provided training in boxing in exchange for training in ju-jitsu, an earlier version of karate. Any awards in the various competitions were simply bottles of Kirin beer.

Charlesworth and I, approaching our seventeenth birthdays, had begun to grow upwards and outwards as a result of the hard work and the exhilarating exercise. After only six months at sea I felt sure our parents would fail to recognize us. Fortunately clothes were cheap in Japan as we had already grown out of everything. On odd occasions a boat would call with stores and mail. The only mail I received was a cable from the owners instructing Captain Bulman to inform me that my father had died suddenly in the Edinburgh Royal Infirmary. There were no details. I remember being terribly sad but a conversation with the Padre the following Saturday convinced me that sadness should be brief. 'Life is meant to be given away,' he said. 'Everything and every one of us belongs to God. The Lord giveth and the Lord taketh away.' A long letter from my sister arrived at the ship weeks later with the details and by then, in my mind, my father had gone to a well-earned rest amongst his ancestors.

Finally we were advised from Rugby that we were to proceed with all speed to Nauru to load phosphates for Australia. John Noble explained to us that Nauru was a tiny island in the Pacific, near the equator, that had been built up on a coral reef through the millenia, by birdshit, as he put it. Through time this pile of phosphate had grown to several square miles in extent and it was now considered to be a very valuable fertilizer, widely used in Australia. A sister island, Ocean Island, a few dozen miles away, offered the same bounty.

There were a few Europeans, administrators and engineers on the island, some with families. They resided in very attractive bungalows amongst the palm trees, close to the coral beach and the blue Pacific Ocean. All the labour on the island were men recruited from China and under contract. They resided in barracks, played soccer against us in bare feet and we lost. The phosphates looked like dirty greyish-white rock but to my surprise there was no offensive odour. Loading of the ships was accomplished through giant cantilevers with moving belts.

As we were loading there a beautiful white-painted schooner sailed close in to shore and moored to a buoy. John Noble, Charlesworth and I spent an evening on board. It belonged to the British High Commissioner who was not on board. There was one British officer and a crew of Kanakas. The officer, an Englishman, was an expert on the Hawaiian guitar. We lay on the spotless, white, oregon-pine deck of the schooner, on a flat calm sea, counting the stars in the heavens and listening to his incredible music. For the first time in almost a year I felt truly civilized. The following day the schooner cast off and disappeared over the horizon.

Shortly after we battened down, fully-laden and headed south for Australia. The Bank Line sustained an office and a marine superintendent in Sydney, New South Wales who advised us by radio to off-load in Port Kembla and Geraldton and thereafter to proceed to Suva for a cargo of sugar for Liverpool, England. This news made the married men very happy indeed. The Australian Ports were much more exciting to us than those in the Far East. Everywhere we went we were treated like old friends. Even the hard-nosed stevedores who always referred to us as 'Pommy Bastards', asked us to carry messages home for them. The Flying Angel missions in each port, whilst run by a dedicated padre, were whole-heartedly supported by ageing, expatriate British women, many of whom I am sure were seeking potential husbands for their daughters.

Indeed some of the daughters were extremely attractive and were happy to attend dances and picnics but they were all very well chaperoned. From time to time we heard of officers who fell by the wayside and were escorted down the aisle. About a year later John Noble joined the happy throng and became an expatriate in Wanganui, New Zealand, having wed the well-endowed daughter of the local baker.

Being in the southern hemisphere we were basking in the splendour of an early summer in New South Wales. This was shortly after the new Sydney Harbour Bridge, but well before the Grand Opera House. However we were sent on to Port Kembla, a grubby little port just south of Sydney. The people, both young and old, were constantly swilling beer despite the appalling depression existing at that time. In those days before air-conditioning, the drinkers would spill out of the bars and taverns onto the sidewalk, if only for a breath of air. Melbourne seemed to be more conservative and sedate than Sydney. Most of the men wore blue serge suits and bowler hats despite the early summer heat. Flinders Street Station was the very hub of the city and the buildings, though squat by today's standards, were imposing and like Edinburgh gave the impression that they were there to stay. We off-loaded at Geelong on the west side of the bay and it was a change for us to ride a train to and from Flinders Street.

Departure for Suva was a mixed blessing. Whilst we were happy to put out to sea once more we had to face up to some very hard work. In readiness for a cargo of sugar the holds had to be washed down several times to remove all traces of the phosphates. We stopped at Newcastle, just north of Sydney, to top up with coal bunkers for the long voyage ahead, little else but water being available in Suva. All the bilges were cleaned, cement-washed and dunnage wood laid on the steel 'tween decks to allow air circulation within the cargo. Arrival at Suva some ten days later was something of a relief. We were at anchor in Lausaka and loaded out of barges.

The stevedores, Fijian Kanakas, were a happy bunch always singing and dancing. They were big, handsome, brown men with fine features and intelligent, happy faces. They liked to work but they insisted on lots of breaks too. During rest periods the island girls, with flowers in their hair, appeared with buckets full of some concoction made out of coconut milk. We were always invited to share it and we found it quite intoxicating. However it seemed to energize the good Kanakas and they were able to throw the 200-pound bags of sugar around at will. The bags were stacked in piles of twenty to a rope sling. The ship's derricks and winches raised these slings from the barges and deposited them within each cargo hold. The stevedores then stacked the bags tightly together until the hold was filled to capacity. Then they moved into the 'tween decks.

As the bags were hoisted into the ship, tally clerks were stationed to provide an accurate count for each hold. We, the cadets, were supposed to ensure that the tally was correct and formally signed off for each shift. There was always utter confusion about the whole affair because the tallymen could scarcely read or write. But there was always Mr Fraser, and the fore-and-aft draft marks, the plimsoll line and his hydrometer to ensure that we lay in salt water. Given all his numbers he could calculate the entire load quite accurately, provided he could measure how much coal and fresh water etc. remained on board.

In any case care was exercised to ensure that the ship was never over-loaded, and woe to anyone prepared to steal a 200-pound bag of brown sugar. The sugar was to be delivered to Messrs Tate and Lyle and the freight paid in accordance with the Chief Officer's calculations. At the discharging end there was always another bunch of tallymen and the situation was always chaotic. However on the basis of hundreds of years of experience these great maritime problems were amicably resolved by bearded men in business suits and glasses clinked in an appropriate celebration.

With the hatches battened down and Mr Fraser happy we put to sea, with the Kanakas on the barges shouting and singing their farewells whilst imbibing generous gulps of their favourite brew. We headed for Panama, glad to be underway and too disinterested to worry about the thousands of miles ahead of us. Fully-laden, the old *Tymeric* had to struggle to make good her ten knots. When we asked John Noble, 'How far to go?' he would say, 'Ask me again in a couple of weeks.' I remember vaguely that Christmas came and went without Santa Claus, although I do remember the plum pudding. After about three weeks of steaming we sighted Panama and we were glad to see the loads of fresh stores come aboard. The meals on the eastbound transit of the canal were of more interest than the scenery. We gorged ourselves on fresh fruit and vegetables.

Good weather and a couple of days of full speed ahead brought us close to Cuba, we replenished our bunkers in Guantanamo and then took advantage of the Gulf Stream to head northwards and on into the Atlantic. The weather grew colder, the skies heavier and the wind threatening. The vessel, fully-laden to her winter North Atlantic marks, appeared to struggle a bit. The ever-faithful main engines, triple expansion steam, churned the propeller around at sixty-odd revolutions per minute. Heavy seas began to roll over the main deck. Mr Fraser ordered the lifelines laid out and all hatch covers to be lashed down. Brand new manilla ropes were hauled out of the forepeak and stretched along the fore and aft well decks to provide a measure of protection against getting washed overboard. The lashings on the hatches were stretched taut with the bottle screws and all the main ventilators were removed and plugged.

'Prepare for the worst,' I heard Captain Bulman say to the Chief Officer. 'We are in for a mighty bad crossing.' His prophecy could not have been more accurate, however, as a result, we were prepared. The sea and swell grew worse by the hour. East of Bermuda the wind rose to gale force and the horizon completely disappeared. Navigation from then on was by dead reckoning, as Mr Betts described it, as he instructed me to read the log. This was a very simple instrument but reasonably effective most of the time. A brass device, shaped like a tiny torpedo with vanes, was towed astern and the special towline was attached to a clock display. When properly calibrated the log could measure distance travelled, so long as you were willing to ignore currents or the terrible drag of a heavy swell. The distance as registered by the log and modified by the mariner's experience, coupled to the adjusted magnetic compass course, provided the data necessary for Mr Betts's 'dead reckoning'.

The very name sounded ominous. By the following morning the wind was screaming around the bridge and green water was breaking heavily over the bow. Captain Bulman reduced to 'half speed' and the old ship ceased to creak and groan temporarily. By nightfall, just when everyone thought the worst was over, the wind, the weather and the state of the sea worsened to a frightening degree. The Captain slowed the vessel even more and altered course to starboard, enough to keep the swell just off the starboard bow. During that night the first of the SOS messages came in from a British cargo ship, the SS *Millpool*, which later foundered with all hands. A second SOS from a Japanese ship brought assurance of assistance from a Norwegian tanker. By morning there was a third distress call but at least a hundred miles from us.

Sparks kept a grim watch on his radio equipment, recording all the calls for assistance and the offers of help. A second ship foundered but many of the crew were saved. How on earth they were rescued under the prevailing conditions was a mystery to me. By now the seas were as high as six- or seven-storey buildings and solid, green, menacing water lashed over the decks. A hurried conference between the Captain and the Chief Engineer divulged that the stokers and trimmers were too terrified to go below and many were hiding in the 'tween decks prepared to die. The junior engineers were in the stokehold firing the boilers. Mr Fraser, the Bos'un and the ship's carpenter were streaming oil bags from the fo'castle head to smooth the breaking seas.

There was no more watch below. Soon those of us on the bridge, gasping at the ferocity of the seas, heard the Captain give the order to 'heave too'. By that he meant to sustain only sufficient speed to keep steerage way, thereby keeping her head to wind and sea, thus avoiding the devastating breakers rolling aboard. The Captain feared the smashing of the forward hatches, the Chief Engineer feared for his boilers. Those of us who were mobile were sent into the stokehold to assist. We stood, legs wide apart, almost up to our knees in oily water sloshing about as the stricken vessel was tossed about in the storm. It is difficult to remember how long the violent weather lasted. Sparks maintained that there were seven separate distress calls. John Noble swore that we survived only because the old ship had been built in Glasgow.

I didn't really care. We had gone without food for two days, we were constantly soaked to the skin and I could not remember when last we had slept. As the wind and sea abated our stokers and trimmers reappeared, their faces as inscrutable as ever. It was at least two more days before we could pick up speed and proceed. When the overcast sky finally dissolved into sunshine, I was happily amused by the antics of our Navigation Officer who had observed and calculated a position at least 150 miles behind his dead reckoning. He stood in awe of the North Atlantic weather. He took several more sights to confirm to himself what was unimaginable. Instead of making progress eastward we had been blown backwards.

Captain Bulman received messages of congratulation from the owners upon arrival in Liverpool. Our cargo, despite the appalling weather, was in good shape and the old ship, whilst sadly rusted and sorely in need of paint, had weathered the storm of the century with only minimal damage. As a result we all knew that Mr Fraser had padded his replacement orders for stores like rope, hawsers, paint and stuff, and got away with it. 'The Scots are a canny lot,' said Noble. 'But these guys from the Shetlands can show us a thing or two.'

The sugar was off-loaded in a remarkably short space of time. Those officers unable to get leave had their wives come aboard. We, the lowly cadets, were either forgotten or ignored. However the ladies made a nice uplifting change in the saloon and the stewards and crew were all on their best behaviour. With the cargo safely delivered we had a brief spell in dry dock, then we departed for Swansea and the wives sailed with us. There, we loaded a cargo of anthracite to about 70 per cent of the ship's capacity then topped off with coal bunkers, in order that we could make the long voyage to Tasmania round the Cape of Good Hope without stopping anywhere. In addition to the voyage being non-stop for reasons of economy it was also to be undertaken at reduced speed to conserve fuel. This involved a voyage of some fifty-five days and we were to store all the necessary rations.

In 1935 merchantmen like the *Tymeric* did not have the luxury of freezers or refrigerators. We had a massive storeroom into which was packed ten tons of ice with the fresh stores packed around it, and these lasted no more than ten days in the tropics. To ease this burden and to satisfy the demands of the crew we were obliged to carry live chickens, sheep and several fat pigs. Fortunately the farmyard was sustained on the poop deck as far aft as you can possibly get and an appropriate place for pigs.

In due course we were ready for this horrendous voyage at the stately speed of seven knots. We wined and dined like royalty on the last night in port, to impress the ladies, no doubt. There were tearful farewells in the morning when the Pilot boarded to take us out to sea.

CHAPTER V

SS TYMERIC – *(VOYAGE 2)*

In early 1935 the *Tymeric* proceeded on her latest voyage at the reduced speed of seven knots. As a consequence of our spell in the dry dock she looked brand, spanking new except for the tell-tale ancient profile. 'Built by the mile and cut off by the yard,' they had said during the 1914-18 war when she was built in Glasgow. Next morning we were awakened at daybreak by the crowing of an aged rooster. It was difficult to figure out how he had managed to escape the keen eye of the Chief Steward. The ship's chandlers were notorious rascals in those days and the rooster was probably their idea of a joke.

To save Suez Canal dues the selected route took us down the west coast of Africa and round the Cape of Good Hope. During that part of the voyage, with the weather still reasonably good, much of the coal taken aboard and stowed in the 'tween decks had to be transferred into the amidships bunkers. This was a messy exercise but it felt good when it was completed as by then we were in sight of the Cape and about to undertake the last, long leg of the voyage. By now fresh fruit and vegetables were long gone, so we were served lots of lime juice to avoid the spread of scurvy. The meat was turning green and smelled, the flour was crawling with weavils and even the potatoes had become unrecognizable. From here on it was rice cakes and beans with everything. However the chickens, including the rooster, provided an occasional light change in the diet. On those days when one of the pigs was slaughtered it would be a regular squealing circus. The Chinese had their own peculiar way of doing things and we stayed out of the way, but it was difficult to stay out of earshot.

Somehow the reduced speed, coupled with the length of the voyage and the awful food, began to wear on the officers' nerves. The Chinese crew members seemed to be serenely unconscious of the strain and happily demolished great mounds of greasy rice and pork, prepared by their own cooks. Charlesworth and I could hear the irritation in the voices in the saloon. Places at the meal table were vacated earlier than usual and sometimes not occupied at all. Mr Henderson, the Chief Engineer, invited us to his cabin on odd occasions for coffee and we could tell by his gruff response to our queries that relationships were becoming strained.

'It's only a temporary lapse in the good humour,' he said in response to a direction question. 'Once we get to Hobart, everything will be normal again.' He was a kindly Scot, Mr Henderson, but he took some strange delight in starting arguments that he would always win at mealtimes in the saloon. He was a great student of the *Reader's Digest* and from this great source he studied the facts relevant to some peculiar technology. Thereafter he introduced the subject in idle conversation in the saloon, nurtured the resulting discussion and argument, then destroyed his adversaries with the detailed knowledge he had only recently absorbed. When we complained of the slow speed he responded with a smile, 'My engines never had it so good.'

Finally, after treating the sick parade for rashes, boils and all kinds of stomach problems, we crossed the Great Australian Bight. Despite the winter season in the southern hemisphere the weather was calm and hordes of sealions barked at us as we proceeded slowly eastwards. I remembered that it was here that Jock Braithwaite, from my old home town in Scotland, had been consigned to the deep. A brief shiver rippled up my spine. I was glad when Tasmania finally appeared on the horizon. We rounded the south shore anticipating orders for Hobart, but the powers that be routed us to St Margaret's Bay, a tiny hole in the wall with scarcely a communication link to anywhere. There was a carbide factory nestled in the high end of the bay and it was here that the anthracite was needed. For the first time in my life I learned that carbide could be the basis for a profitable enterprise.

The local Tasmanian people were somewhat overwhelmed by us and I could sympathize with them. Seeing groups of Chinese men marching along behind their serang did nothing to inspire confidence in the locals. The growing pile of anthracite at their factory was a source of great relief, no doubt, as this assured them of continued employment. As there was absolutely nothing for us to do in the entire area we were all very glad to depart, although we were more than thankful for the excellent stores of food we were able to get. Orders arrived advising of our charter for cargoes of phosphates out of Nauru and Ocean Island, for Australian ports.

The voyages up to the equator and back to Australia were a kind of holiday for us. The weather was not unpleasant, the voyages short so the food was fresh and plentiful and good. The phosphates charter took us to places like Port Kembla, Adelaide, Geraldton and often to Newcastle for bunkers, which allowed us to make friends. Weekends were always pleasant in the smaller Australian ports as no one could induce the Aussie stevedores to work during weekends in those days. As a result the entire population donned their Sunday best and wandered down to the wharf to visit the ship. So many of them seemed to be desperate to speak to someone from their old home town. Scottish people by the dozen came looking for us. They were most hospitable and invited us to their homes. Most of them admitted to an insatiable desire to return to the Old Country but few had the necessary funds.

Just as we were about to become accustomed to the luxuries of the tropical climes our orders were changed. We proceeded to Bunbury and Fremantle on the west coast to load grain for Calcutta. The trip up the Hoogli River in the Ganges estuary was a unique experience. There were dhows, bellums and boats of all kinds, tugs, barges and sailboats, and on land nothing but wall-to-wall people. Because of the oftentimes five-foot tidal bore, a wall of water that raced up the river at the turn of the spring tides, we tied up to enormous moored buoys, using anchor chain both fore and aft. On a wet morning, watching the native river traffic, listening to the incessant yelling and screaming, made me think of the underworld. In Kidderpore Docks, where we loaded coal for Aden, it was like Dante's Inferno. Yet at the Marine Club, where we were obliged to attend in clean white shirts and tropical uniform, the world ceased to spin wildly and all of a sudden we were engulfed in a quietly luxurious outpost of the Empire, complete with turbanned servants, cold Allsops beer and hot curry.

Many of the local memsahibs, complete with families, attended the functions at the Marine Club. Garden parties and outdoor dances were held regularly. At weekends the club was swamped with exceedingly handsome Anglo-Indian girls, many of whom found husbands among the ship's officers. However romance bypassed the *Tymeric*, perhaps because we were a very tough-looking lot and a far cry from the very nice young men who were officers from the British India Steamship Line passenger ships. When we left Kidderpore the ship had to be scrubbed down from truck to keel and it was a real pleasure to play around with the high-pressure hoses. Just putting out to sea from the mouth of the river lowered the temperature considerably.

The trip to Aden was hot and uneventful and the discharge of the cargo in Aden harbour was an indescribable hell. There was no air-conditioning of any kind but we went off on shore leave to get away from the dirt and grime. There was absolutely nothing to do on shore and the natives obviously resented us. We were glad to leave and head for the Red Sea and the Suez Canal, then on to Naples for dry dock. From Italy we steamed along the north shore of Africa to another hot oven called Melilla to pick up iron ore for Alicante in Spain. By this time General Franco had commenced his agonizing conquest of Spain and we were obliged to paint huge British flags on the hull and also on the deck of the flying bridge to ensure neutral recognition by aircraft. Union Jacks are not easy to lay out, particularly from a swinging bos'un's chair.

Alicante was subdued and relatively quiet but had as yet seen very little of the civil war. On our approach we were checked out by several ageing destroyers and a rusty cruiser, all flying the Spanish flag. Upon formal recognition, they assured us of eternal friendship and brotherhood, and a share in the eventual victory by the revered Generalissimo Franco. We were not impressed but nevertheless we were obliged to obey the flag signals displayed for us.

It is interesting to note that by international agreement the letters of the alphabet are each represented by a unique flag. Each ship is identified by a four-flag signal. In the case of British ships, the signal letters all start with the letter G. Each single flag signal has a specific meaning, like a B for, 'I am carrying explosives.' P stands for 'I require a pilot.' Two-flag signals are for emergencies and three-flag signals can be used to string messages together. Each signaller interprets the signal from an international code book printed in his own language.

We obeyed, we discharged our cargo and we departed unscathed for Gibraltar harbour where we lay at anchor awaiting orders. One night we had a very interesting experience. The night was very dark, calm and with no moon, and I was on anchor watch. There were really no restrictions on where one might be on anchor watch, provided you were wide awake. There was always a quartermaster on duty in the wheelhouse and an officer-of-the-watch, probably dozing in the saloon. It was cold so I chose to be in the galley smelling the bread baking for the following day. It was about midnight when I heard the cry, 'Hombre, hombre.' From the deck I could just see a head bobbing in the water. In the quickest time I have ever seen it happen, we launched a boat and picked up the bag of bones in the water. He was naked and spoke only Spanish, but already he was obviously delirious. We wrapped him in blankets and hoisted him gently on board.

It was hours before he stopped shivering. Anything we gave him to eat or drink he would promptly vomit. By dawn he had settled down and fallen asleep, except that every now and again he would awake screaming. The Captain decided that he must have escaped from the military-political prison on the other side of the bay. To avoid complications that very morning we rowed ashore and delivered him to the British authorities. I never heard of him again. That same afternoon the Spanish military visited the ship with questions for which they received very little response. Mr Fraser bore the brunt of the questioning. He merely grunted in response and shrugged his massive shoulders. I doubt if the Spaniards understood the Gaelic he used. He smiled broadly and saluted smartly when they were leaving.

We sailed the following day for Black Sea ports, via Naples, for bunkers. The ship's officers were glum, the trips undertaken in ballast were becoming all too frequent and the *Tymeric*'s freight record was much in doubt. They feared we might be sailing for the scrapyards in Greece. However we entered the

Bosporous and pressed on. Orders came for Odessa, Batoum and Novorossiysk, to load general cargo for Vladivostok in eastern Russia. Everyone sighed with relief but wondered if the freight rate might ever be paid. Just at that time Britain and Russia were involved in some serious court disputes and the rhetoric was getting tougher by the day.

To my eternal surprise we ran into thick ice in the northern section of the Black Sea, ice so thick that the vessel was brought to a standstill. Ice-breakers came out from Odessa to break us free, then they escorted us into port. It had never occurred to me that it might get that cold in these low latitudes. Loading the cargo in this very cold weather created all kinds of problems. Many of the stevedores were females and mostly dressed in rags against the cold. Many of them had no shoes and simply wrapped old sacks around their feet. The loading process was slow and no one seemed at all interested in speeding things up. It seemed that they were paid on a time basis, so the longer they made the job last the more they got paid, which was a truly self-defeating process.

Shore leave was an exercise in frustration. Instead of money we were given a sheet of paper with roubles marked on one side and kopeks on the other. The government store was the only place to buy anything, even if you could find it, and there the cashier dug out an enormous pair of scissors to clip off the appropriate amount. I could never understand how anyone could exercise control over such a monetary system.

However in their defence let me say that they maintained an 'Entouriste', a club for sailors, international in scope, and there one could get haircuts, play pool, eat fine food and on occasions become involved in Russian-style parties. The females who were allowed to attend the club were able to get some sort of allowance for clothes. Everything like soap, cosmetics or jewelry was considered currency. It was freely said that anything and everything was available for a bar of soap or a pair of stockings. Conditions in Batoum and Novorossiysk, where we loaded machinery, were similar. Our Chinese crew members had a ball but they paid dearly for it.

By the time we had reached Port Said, headed for the canal and the Red Sea, the sick bay was overcrowded. At least one third of the crew members were infected with venereal disease of one kind or another and we were due to call at Hong Kong to change crew. These men were going home. We were compelled to acquire a large number of rubber bottles and a large quantity of permanganate of potash. Sadly there were a couple of cases of syphilis. We, the medics, worked overtime. Every now and again there were bouts of hysteria, aggravated by the serang berating them. As a consequence I learned more Chinese 'oaths' that month than at any other time in my life.

On arrival in Hong Kong the Medical Officer gave them all a clean bill of health and sent them on their way. New faces, but with the same Cantonese tongue, took over and our medical problems were written off, something I found to be disturbing, but no one seemed to care. With stores and water we headed north-eastwards for the Taiwan Strait and on into the China Sea. The weather was kind to us, the winds no more than light airs and the sea calm and smooth as glass. The journey from the Black Sea to eastern Russia was many thousands of miles but Mr Henderson's engines behaved faultlessly. 'There's nothing to go wrong with an up and down steam job,' the Chief stated forcefully. 'It's those new-fangled diesel jobs you better watch out for.'

During one of our frequent discussions with him we passed very close to a Jardine-Matheson liner, bound from Shanghai to Hong Kong. We exchanged identification signals as we passed within a few hundred feet of each other, close enough for us to see the scores of fashionably-dressed European passengers on the promenade deck, and at the same time the orientals travelling steerage in the lower main deck aft. I noticed a massive steel fence that covered the entire set of passenger decks and prevented any possible exchange between those passenger decks and the steerage compartments. I questioned the Chief about it and of course he was happy to spend the next hour regaling us with his experiences in Butterfield-Swire liners sailing the China Seas in the 1920s.

As he explained it there had been a considerable amount of piracy on the high seas in his earlier days. Chinese pirates boarded those passenger liners as humble steerage ticket-holders, and slept on the main deck just like the peasants. At some predetermined point in the voyage they appeared on the bridge, well disciplined and well armed. At the same time they occupied the Captain's quarters, the radio room, and the engine room. They took over control of the vessel briefly, robbed the passengers, raided the strongroom and the cargo if desirable. Later, they would rendezvous with several large junks, disembark and simply disappear.

On several occasions, when ship's officers carried firearms, the pirates did not hesitate to shoot and many fatalities were recorded. Precautions like steel fences, armed security and navy patrols, kept the piracy from spreading but it never did entirely eradicate it. The Chinese are an inventive lot and while some of the schemes described by the Chief did sound a bit far-fetched many were verified by other officers with similar experience. For years thereafter it was my declared intention to head for the China Sea to join Jardine's liners. They were a well-established Scottish firm with more than a hundred years of experience on the China coast trade from Shanghai to Macao. They are still a financial power throughout Asia today.

We progressed from the China Sea through the Korean Strait, then into the Sea of Japan and on into eastern Russia. Vladivostok harbour was even more desolate than Odessa had been and there was very little activity of any kind. We did berth alongside an extensive wharf but the discharge of cargo, all supervised by armed soldiers, was really a transfer of cargo into several smaller Russian ships berthed alongside us. We were given the impression that we were involved in an exceedingly important operation. We visited the other ships and were quite impressed by the calibre of people on board. The ships were ancient rust buckets but were nevertheless reasonably comfortable. A high percentage of the officers were females, particularly the radio officers and several spoke very good English. From bits and pieces of conversation we gathered that the crates of machinery we carried were vital to the construction of a submarine base on the Kamchatka Peninsula. No foreign ships or personnel were allowed to visit there.

Indeed, some thirty years later, during an exercise with the United States Navy in the Bering Sea, we were briefly within binocular range of Petropovlovsk, the massive, modern submarine base, right there on the Kamchatka Peninsula. I remember wondering if the precious machinery shipped there in 1936 had contributed much to the growth of the naval base. The submarines that the US Navy planned to track throughout that region were based there in Petropovlovsk. The peninsula was a forbidding place, about as bleak as could be found anywhere. It reminded me of Cape Wrath on the west coast of Scotland on a stormy winter night. Yet as I shivered and wondered why anyone would want to stay there in these conditions, I suddenly realized that Petropovlovsk was about the same latitude as my home town in Scotland, only a few degrees below the Arctic Circle.

Becoming friendly with the Russian officers made shore leave much more pleasant. We roamed the town with them on rickety buses and visited the strangest places. One young man insisted on taking me to visit the grave of his family just outside the town. The graveyard was almost like a disaster area. A large construction crew were cutting a highway through it without much concern for the wreckage of the graves. It appeared that grieving relatives liked to leave pictures around, with evidence pointing to the reason for sudden death. Lots of graves were marked by the banged-up steering wheels from automobiles, with a picture of the victim attached. Surprisingly, many of the graves bore the remnants of fresh flowers. The young man wept openly and without embarrassment. Later, we went to the Entouriste centre and stuffed ourselves with food and beer.

On one special day, we were invited to an afternoon tea party at the centre, for local naval dignitaries. Several of us attended decked out in clean shirts and pressed uniforms. Sparks was with us and as he prided himself on his linguistic abilities we left the ordering to him. When we selected a table and sat down a very attractive waitress hovered nearby. Sparks started babbling in his textbook Russian and the young lady's face was a study in astonishment. She took off shaking her head. When she returned with pots of steaming tea and lemon, she said, in perfect English, 'Would you like to come to the counter and choose your own cakes.' Fortunately all of us refrained from laughter as we learned later that the lady was a volunteer and the wife of a young submarine commander.

We departed from Vladivostok leaving good friends behind and headed south for Nauru and the highly profitable bird droppings for the Australian farmers. After only two round trips we were ordered to the west coast, Fremantle and Bunbury, to discharge our phosphates and then load grain for Land's End for orders. I saw very little of either port due to a minor accident that put me in hospital in Bunbury for most of that period. The hospital was run by nuns and I shared a room with an old Scotsman, seventy-five years old, who cursed and swore all day long from behind drawn curtains. The nuns were horrified but forgave him because he had lost a leg in some accident with a binder on his up-country farm. I never did learn the whole story as the old boy always launched into unintelligible oaths out of sheer self-pity.

He did cheer up though on the arrival of a plump little woman of about forty who I mistook for his daughter. She turned out to be his wife and behind her trotted four little kids, the youngest of which was only three, a little boy with golden curls, obviously his old father's pride and joy. They were a happy family and I had to promise that one day I would come to visit them. 'Ships that pass in the night,' Mr Fraser said when I told him about it. 'You're a hard-case sailor now. What the hell would you want with a farm?'

Loading was completed shortly after my return. We headed for Aden for bunkers, then into the Red Sea past the hot, barren island of Perim, then northwards to Suez. The canal transit was a bit boring for us although the pilots used to get a bit upset about how the old *Tymeric* would suddenly yaw without reason. They were accustomed to passenger liners that respond well to the rudder and the *Tymeric* was not like that. She needed to be understood and any sudden lurch to port or starboard had to be instantly counteracted. A southbound ship, tied up to allow us to pass, would be in grave danger, according to the Pilot. He got so nervous the imperturbable Captain Bulman brought him a double Scotch. However we reached Port Said and moved onwards without incident.

Land's End for orders translated into a Liverpool destination. The docklands at Bootle seemed to be our destiny but this time with a difference. We were advised that the Chinese crew were to be shipped back to Hong Kong, the crew accommodation overhauled and a white crew signed on. Presumably activity by the Seafarers' union and the high rate of unemployment in the UK convinced the owners to make the change. To us, Charlesworth and I particularly, it made little difference, and mistakenly as it turned out we looked forward to it. By now we had more than two and a half years of sea time behind us, 1937 was close at hand and we felt as hard as nails. To us the future looked bright.

Meanwhile the weather was anything but bright in Liverpool and this delayed the discharge of cargo. Allowing heavy rain to pour down the holds onto the grain would be disastrous. Nevertheless, progress was made, the cargo discharged and the fo'castle refurbishment finally completed. Christmas was celebrated quietly on board but several boisterous nights were spent amidst the bright lights of Lime Street in downtown Liverpool. A new cadet, John Clarke, from Elgin in Scotland, joined us.

Our Chinese crew departed, homeward-bound for Hong Kong and Canton. After an endless shuffling around at the shipping office, a truly motley crew of sailors and stokers, led by a muscular bos'un, finally appeared and took over the fo'castle. Initially it was difficult for us to determine who was a donkeyman, and who was an oiler, or a stoker, or an able seaman, or an ordinary seaman. It was equally difficult to identify who was the Storekeeper and who was the Lamp-trimmer. The Bos'un, the Carpenter and the quartermasters, were easier to recognize. These designations had been used for hundreds of years and although inappropriate for these modern times they were still used. The Chief Steward, the cooks, the stewards, the cabin boys, were something to behold. They were a real bunch of comedians and functioned as members of a team going from one vessel to the next, voyage after voyage.

The ship's Carpenter, also the self-elected barber, was a very important member of the crew. He was the Chief Officer's good right arm. He was a grand fellow, already in his forties, an exercise nut and a body-builder. He elected himself to be our coach and trained us in boxing, ju-jitsu, soccer, swimming etc. He was a very happy fellow, with a happy family he left behind each voyage, always cheerful and thoroughly dependable. He and the Bos'un were the undisputed headmen amongst the crew and both reported directly to the Chief Officer. The Bos'un was a big, muscular fellow, tough as nails but not particularly bright.

At the very last moment we learned that Captain Bulman was leaving us for extended leave. Mr Fraser, the Chief Officer, assumed command and a new chief took over. Once again we were ready to undertake a new voyage.

CHAPTER VI

SS TYMERIC – (VOYAGE 3)

Sailing day finally came around a couple of days before my nineteenth birthday on 10 January 1937. Again we proceeded to Swansea to load bunkers, with additional bunkers in the 'tween decks for an extended voyage. Our orders were to proceed to Antwerp to load a cargo of slag for New Zealand. This implied another long, non-stop, round the Cape of Good Hope voyage, this time all the way to Auckland, New Plymouth and Wanganui. The news was greeted with dismay and the officers wondered how the newly acquired white crew might react to the hardships. They had good reason to feel nervous.

Our stay in Antwerp was eventful insofar as our valiant crew managed to get themselves involved in serious brawls in the bars in the red light district. The local paddy wagon made nightly visits to our gangway to deposit drunks. I am sure the local constabulary were delighted to see us cast off from the dock. These docks in Antwerp were truly memorable. Most were surfaced with slippery cobblestones and the drenching rain made them glisten like diamonds. Mid-January, amidst the fog and the rain, and I was never so cold in my life.

We made good time even at reduced speed as we progressed down through the English Channel and on into the rough Bay of Biscay. The cold and the damp weather kept us off the decks till beyond the Canary Islands. Then we faced the customary hard work of shifting bunkers from the 'tween docks, and we had the same appalling rations after ten days or so at sea. We carried the same farmyard and lived through the same monotonous days of watch on deck and watch below. This voyage, at reduced speed, took us seventy-six agonizing days of threats and squabbles and fist fights. Fortunately the weather was kind to us and the trip across the Great Australian Bight was tolerable but depressing. Discussions we might have with shipmates were usually morbid and the stories exchanged were sad.

One of my shipmates, a junior engineer from Glasgow, named Wildridge, persisted in telling me all about his personal ambitions. Apparently he had always been keen to get a shore job on the Island of Nauru, and even more so after he had seen the beautiful white schooner there. He had applied and been accepted but grumbled about not being permitted to leave the ship. I can remember thinking how crazy he was, but very soon afterwards he made it. The Chief Engineer, old Henderson, finally let him go when he found a relief engineer, an American. Wildridge took off laughing and singing. I saw him again months later in residence in a neat bungalow and very happy in Nauru. He was still there a few years later when the Japanese took over. I have never heard of him since. His chances of survival were exceedingly slim.

On board he had a wind-up gramophone, a portable, which he had bought in Liverpool before we departed. He purchased a few records too but there was one he kept playing over and over again. It was a dance tune called 'Who made little boy blue?' When I saw him again in Nauru he was still playing it. He also carried a framed picture of his sister, a very beautiful girl. He told me a very sad story about her.

In the early thirties, whilst he was serving his time in the Glasgow shipyards, his sister, a trained nurse, had a burning desire to travel and see the world. She had come to him one day full of excitement about a job she had found in Antwerp as a nanny to a wealthy South American family in their country's foreign service. Very shortly afterwards his folks received a letter telling them that the family were homeward bound for South America and she was very excited to be going with them. She was never heard from again, ever. In those days there were occasional reports of the dreaded white slave traffic and he was sure she had become a victim. Her picture haunts my memory to this day.

When we finally arrived in Auckland, darkness had just fallen. We dropped anchor in the harbour to await daylight. During the first anchor watch at least half the crew dived overboard and disappeared. Dawn came and in the early morning light we berthed. With the sunrise, and the early morning sunlight streaming over the city, the entire harbour looked almost fairy-like. Only then was I fully convinced that the agonizing voyage was finally over and normal life might begin again. The first order of business was to treat our stomachs with tender loving care. Daily trips to the oyster bars that lined the main Auckland streets helped us to get back into shape.

Each day the Bos'un was obliged to update a list of missing crewmen, and Captain Fraser and Mr Henderson had to sustain contact with the local police. Quite a number of the missing men were recovered from the drunk tank in the Auckland jail, nevertheless a few never did reappear. They were replaced by locals or Kiwis as we called them and they had no problem settling in.

At the next stop, New Plymouth, we acquired another cadet, Boyd O'Reilly, son of the local Customs Chief. Boyd was a great lanky guy with an irrepressible sense of humour and a constant urge to chase girls. His family were good to Charlesworth and I, and we enjoyed their company and the good home-cooked dinners they provided. Both of us fell madly in love with Boyd's sister, Terriora, a cheerful, gangly girl in her late teens. Wisely, she elected to string both of us along, but the romance never had a chance to flourish as we departed from New Plymouth and never returned.

Wanganui was a delightful spot, a small town with one main street but absolutely full of young people like ourselves. They had a smashing bakery shop in the centre of town where they sold the most remarkable stuff I have ever tasted. It was a regular stop for us each trip ashore. An additional attraction was the baker's daughter, a beautiful, plump girl with whom we all fell madly in love. She had eyes for no one but John Noble, the 3rd Mate, and he was truly smitten. Some time later when the Captain obtained a relief for him he was off to marry his true love in Wanganui. Later he joined the Union Steamship Company, and the last we heard of him he was on regular runs from Auckland to Vancouver, Canada sailing on the SS *Aorangi*, a large passenger liner.

The *Tymeric* departed from New Zealand for Nauru and Ocean Island again, and thence to Australia. First we went to Port Kembla, then to Newcastle where Charlesworth was transferred to another Bank Line vessel. On our return trip for more phosphates we picked up three or four nuns who were bound for one of the Pacific Island leper colonies. They were a strange lot, very gentle and devout ladies of the Catholic Church. They appeared to be a bit uncomfortable with us although the officers did everything they could to make them feel welcome. We were obliged to launch a lifeboat in order to land them. We could see from a distance the pitiful creatures there to greet them. They were landed with all their worldly goods, a cardboard suitcase each. They bade us a cheerful 'bon voyage' as they stepped ashore.

Our tropical runs did not last long however. Much to O'Reilly's dismay we were off to Hong Kong for a long-delayed twenty-four year survey in dry-dock before he had a chance to say farewell to his accumulation of lady friends. I remember someone's gramophone playing 'I saw the harbour lights', with O'Reilly close to tears. A few days at sea headed north and he had fully recovered and was ready to take on Hong Kong. For all of us it turned out to be one of our greatest and most dangerous adventures.

Some hours before we arrived at Hong Kong the first indications of typhoon weather could be observed. The old salts like Captain Fraser and Mr Henderson were heard voicing some truly dreary predictions, feelings in their bones, presumably. However we did make the anchorage off Taikoo dockyard in Wanchai, and there we were to remain until further orders. No shore leave was permitted. Typhoon warnings were flying at the weather station up on the Peak, above the city. The Harbour Master advised all ships to maintain emergency stations as in his opinion the typhoon was heading dangerously close to Hong

Kong.

O'Reilly and I spent a whole afternoon on watch on the bridge, admiring all the passenger liners tied up to buoys in mid-harbour. We were fascinated by the ferries darting madly about between Hong Kong and Kowloon on the mainland. How on earth they manoeuvred unscathed through the scores of dhows, junks, sampans and barges I will never understand. O'Reilly spent most of his time admiring the ladies on the pier through a high-powered telescope. John Clarke expressed some concern about the peculiar greyness within the afternoon sunlight. The weather was hot and muggy but he was actually shivering, a premonition perhaps. Shortly afterwards a port launch passed alongside with a loud hailer, advising us that the storm was headed directly towards us.

Captain Fraser ordered steam to be raised and a second anchor to be dropped to secure our mooring. The Bos'un and crew stretched lifelines on the main decks and lashed down every item on deck that might move. Storm doors were closed and the forepeak entries were plugged with locking bars attached. Hatchboards with their tarpaulin covers were lashed down with manilla ropes. Darkness fell and an eerie silence settled over the harbour. By now absolutely nothing moved. The thousands of sampans with their Chinese families aboard were huddled close to shore without fires or lights of any kind. There was still only a fresh breeze blowing in from seaward and there was no sign at all of seabirds. The Captain and the officers gathered on the bridge and held huddled conversations. For the first time in all of our voyagings I could detect a note of real concern in the Captain's voice. Even the watch below preferred to remain on deck.

Heavy cloud rolled across the sky, the wind rose a little and a few waves lapped against the steel hull. The wind made an eerie sound in the rigging, but by now most of us had breathed a sigh of relief. Quite a few of us really believed that the typhoon had veered away out to sea and by morning all would be normal again. At four bells of the second dogwatch, those of us going off watch headed for our bunks. Our optimism was ill-timed.

Just then, real darkness fell like a shroud over the island and the rains came. Lights could no longer be seen anywhere. Visibility was reduced almost to zero. The wind rose quite suddenly up to a screaming force eight and a low swell rolled into the harbour, just enough to set the vessels into an uneasy motion. The wind tore the tops from the waves then lashed them against the bulwarks with a vicious crackling sound. I could hear the clank of the engine room telegraph and I felt a terrible desire to get back on the bridge if only for the company of my shipmates. It wasn't easy negotiating the companionways as the wind tore at everything in its path. I reached shelter on the lee side of the bridge and breathed a sigh of relief. It was short-lived. The anchor chains were leading straight ahead and tight, and the ship's engines were running at half speed to ease the strain. To the eastward of the harbour, the rain had ceased and visibility rose to about a mile. An awesome light spread across the harbour entrance, then all hell broke loose.

Very few of the details were ever remembered. Everyone had a different tale to tell. Fortunately we were all alive to tell our stories in the morning. I remember Captain Fraser ringing full ahead on the engine room telegraph as the anchor chains creaked defiance at the strain. Suddenly the entire flying bridge, the charthouse deck head, took off in the wind and smashed into the funnel. Two lifeboats on the weather side were reduced to matchsticks. The storm centre passed over us with the wind screaming at nearly 200 miles per hour. I can remember a sudden, brief period of near calm when I took off for the main deck and huddled behind the steel stanchions supporting the gunwale. Then there was a wind shift and an ear-splitting roar followed by a peculiar screeching noise. The old *Tymeric* heeled steeply to starboard, then she grounded astern and the engines came to a grinding halt.

It was dawn before anyone could move. As daylight flickered in the wind and the rain the typhoon reduced its ferocity slightly, and in one's and two's crew members drenched to the skin, gathered in the galley and huddled around a miserable fire, banked by the chief cook the night before. By noon the rain had cleared, the wind reduced and it was actually possible to go on deck, still clinging to the lifelines. The stern of the *Tymeric* and her massive propeller were lodged within a group of swimming pools. The anchor chains had held, but the anchors dragged with the force of the wind despite the assistance by the engines. We were fast aground with a heavy starboard list.

Odd as it may seem we all felt happy and safe, lodged firmly against the shore. It was later that we learned that it would take three months to fix. Waiting for tugs and available space in Taikoo Dock was like a holiday. The starboard list was a bit awkward but not insurmountable. Meals were uncomfortable in the saloon but there was plenty of humour around.

News spread like wildfire of course and much of it was treated with scepticism. However, much of it was easy to verify as we were in the very midst of it. No fewer than twenty-three ocean-going ships were run aground with differing degrees of damage. Several of these were declared 'Constructive Total Loss'. Some of the passenger liners were Japanese. One in particular, the *Asama Maru*, was lifted into nine feet of water by the tidal wave in Repulse Bay. The Japanese arrived in force from Tokyo, cut down her superstructure, removed her engines, then used nine powerful tugs to drag her back into deep water. She was rebuilt and back at sea in less than six months. One large Jardine's vessel finished up with her stern astride the tram lines on the main Hong Kong waterfront.

Unhappily the poor, as always, suffered the most. It was estimated that 10,000 Chinese lost their lives from the sampans where whole families lived out their lives on board. It was difficult to check such estimates but I do remember the harbour awash with dead bodies. The port craft spent days and nights collecting the corpses for some mysterious ritual burial. The damage to the cities of Hong Kong and Kowloon was enormous, but in typical Chinese fashion hordes of coolies tackled the clean-up and the construction men worked around the clock. By the time we were ready to head to sea the scars were no longer visible.

Our stay in the Taikoo dockyard required that all of us live ashore in Wanchai as the ship was uninhabitable. We ate in local Chinese restaurants and there were times when I thought that the food was more dangerous than the typhoon. However there were lots of sports facilities available through Taikoo dockyard. Nevertheless Mr Betts still insisted upon our study periods and we derived some benefit from the review necessary to bring O'Reilly up to scratch.

On those occasions when money was available we usually got into trouble. Most of the crew were constantly in trouble and apparently accustomed to it. At all times someone was blamed. In one particular case it was the Seaforth Highlanders, a regiment on duty in Hong Kong, and large gangs of Yanks from visiting cruisers in the harbour. The dance halls were ablaze with sound and light and laughter, and hordes of elegant female partners for whom one had to purchase tickets lined the walls. Late in the evening tempers flared and brawls broke out. A protective steel mesh was unfurled in front of the orchestra while they continued to play at an ever-increasing tempo. The ladies gathered their elegant, slit skirts and departed in haste. The main lights went out and almost immediately the sirens could be heard. Meanwhile the dance floor resembled a giant boxing ring.

Having grown accustomed to these gang wars, Clarke, O'Reilly and I were smart enough to ease our way out in time to escape the US navy shore patrol or the local gendarmes. On occasions we might be more circumspect, when invited out by a member of the shipyard staff, most of whom were British men with Chinese wives. Many very pretty eligible daughters were paraded before us but Captain Fraser warned us with a threat of dire consequences to avoid romance at all costs.

O'Reilly was in his element on those occasions and offered us all kinds of sage advice on how to sample the temptations without getting caught on the hook. But he too was glad when sailing day finally came around. The *Tymeric* looked brand, spanking new despite her out-dated contours. New flags fluttered from her masts and being Hong Kong the officers had all invested in new wardrobes. By that time ships were arriving from Shanghai with large numbers of white Russians, all anxious to avoid the war zone. The Japanese had already launched their brutal attack on the Chinese mainland. We were bound for Kobe, Japan with general cargo. A minor accident to my foot landed me in hospital there, a hospital run by nuns from Holland, something that took me completely by surprise. However I was assured by the good sisters that Holland had a long history of trade association with the Japanese.

The same day that I arrived back on board the crew had managed to break into some precious cases of expensive liquor in the cargo, and many of them became so roaring drunk and threatening that the 'Mutiny on Board' flag signal had been hoisted. The Chief Steward had already been thrown overboard, followed by every available lifebuoy, and some of the firemen were beating up the cooks and the stewards. The arrival of the Japanese police quietened things down in a hurry but they insisted on taking the ringleaders ashore. On their return about forty-eight hours later they were chastened individuals. By their account the police had practiced ju-jitsu with them as victims and literally bounced them off the walls.

Again we headed out to sea and south to Nauru for Australian ports in the Spencer Gulf, then on to Adelaide and back to Nauru again for Australian ports. However after completion we were dispatched to Fremantle and Bunbury to load for Calcutta. By now it was March 1938 and I was counting the days to the end of my four years. Sure enough it had clicked at head office. Orders came, I was to be dropped off in Colombo and there to await the arrival of the MV *Myrtlebank*. To my delight I was installed for a few days in the fashionable Galleface Hotel in Colombo. I lived like a king for a brief period, signed chits for everything and enjoyed the thrill of it all immensely.

For a very short while I missed all my shipmates on the good ship *Tymeric* and as it turned out I never ever saw any of them again.

CHAPTER VII

MV MYRTLEBANK

The MV *Myrtlebank*, a much more modern cargo liner than the *Tymeric*, finally arrived from Calcutta to top off her cargo of tea, jute and gunnies for South America. The officers and crew were a happy lot. There were three cadets, all junior to me, so that when the 3rd Mate was discharged sick, I was elected to take his place. This was a happy circumstance for me as it meant that I suddenly fell heir to a handsome salary and a first-class cabin to myself. After four years of near slavery this development was really something to be savoured.

Before leaving Colombo, bound for South American ports, the cargo derricks were lowered and a giant crane placed large cages thereon, and these were lashed down securely. A little later, about 800 lively and incredibly noisy monkeys were transferred into these cages. On the main deck aft several other cages were loaded to accommodate more glamorous animals like black panthers. Our menagerie on the foredeck was exceedingly noisy but highly entertaining, whilst on the main deck aft the caged beasts paced up and down in menacing silence. At least they were well fed.

We called at Cape Town for mail, fresh water and stores, and then on to Tristan da Cunha to drop off some official stuff, using one of the lifeboats. West of the island the weather took a turn for the worse and quite quickly the laden vessel was rolling and pitching, and shipping heavy seas over the decks. The monkeys screeched their objections and some of them were quite ill. As we were approaching Cape Horn, during the darkness of the middle watch, one of the cages was partially smashed. Monkeys poured out, all anxious to take advantage of their new-found freedom.

By daylight they were all over the ship swinging about in the shrouds. Crew members hustled to make the repairs and some effort was made to catch the escapees. Most of the larger ones found their way to the fo'castle head and as the bow slipped through the water they stared down in fascination at the bubbling phosphorescence, and then they jumped, one by one. Many of the smaller ones followed them but finally order was restored. The research centres in Chile and Argentina, to which they were bound, were a number short of the bill of lading.

Cargo was discharged into barges in the various ports, then we returned to the east coast to Buenos Aires, Montevideo and Sao Paolo to load general cargo for London, England.

One minor adventure in Buenos Aires soured me on shore leave for a while. As 3rd Mate on the *Myrtlebank* I was a man of means and I located some Scottish friends in the port who had wealthy relatives in the city and were members of the Jockey Club. As a result we wined and dined and made out like bandits in the fashionable clubs along the Avenida de Florida. As luck would have it we ventured into the Boca area, a very rowdy and dangerous place, and we were involved in a brawl. This led to our arrest and we were hauled off to jail.

The punishment there was swift and effective. We were locked behind bars, but promptly at five in the morning we were provided with a large bowl of lumpy porridge and milk. Then we were herded onto a truck, dropped off at the top end of Avenida de Florida and each presented with a large broom. We were compelled to sweep the entire avenue to the dock area, arriving there about eight o'clock, where we were promptly discharged and the brooms collected. The punishment was effective and I did not venture ashore again during the remainder of our stay. Montevideo was something of a rest stop and Sao Paolo kept us so busy that shore leave was out of the question.

We arrived in London at the end of July and my indenture period was now completed. I was eagerly looking forward to the Nautical College in Edinburgh. Arriving home after more than four years was a real thrill and I was treated like the prodigal son. I felt that I was a somebody now, as opposed to having been the dogsbody on the *Tymeric*. I had money in the bank, I was husky and weatherbeaten, and I believed I was the most experienced, mature guy around. In addition to going to college I had the mistaken notion that I might give the girls a treat.

To my everlasting disappointment the girls had all grown up, they had matured and they were now very selective in their choice of male companions. I guess I must have carried the 'Mark of Cain'; I was supposed to be that wild merchantman, a sailor, and was not the ideal escort for the ladies of the day. But I had a dog, the most beautiful, pure-bred Alsatian, a male called Nipper. He had already been at The Farmhouse for a couple of years but he and I became instant friends. When I was not at school he and I went everywhere together. He used to sit at my feet in the Star and Garter Hotel in Linlithgow and he would swig the occasional beer. He especially liked it out of a crystal ashtray.

I lived at The Farmhouse with my mother, now a widow. My father had died whilst I was in Japan some years earlier. My grandfather McDiarmid had died the previous year at the age of ninety-seven. He was accustomed to his daily walk and took off with the dogs as usual that day. Nipper came home alone and my sister followed him to where the old man lay dead by the River Avon. By then my older sister Nancy had married Earnest Schofield and moved to Rochdale in Lancashire. My sister Jean married the son of a farmer from Balfroan, about thirty miles west of us. Her husband, Jock Morrison, moved into The Farmhouse and they stayed on there for about thirty years and raised a family of three. At that time they already had a little boy, Ian Morrison, and I do believe the second child was on the way.

The village had changed although The Farmhouse and the garden remained. The surrounding land was covered with council houses. One of the earliest and largest groups, right alongside the old farm, had been named Lennox Avenue, but my mother, ever the indefatigable Miss Belle, marched into the county buildings and refused to move until the name was officially changed to Millerfield. It remains so to this day.

I rode the bus to the college in Edinburgh but occasionally I stayed over at my brother Bobby's digs in London Road. He and about four other policemen lived there so my mother was confident that I could stay out of trouble. He had a terrific car, a Lanchester, made by the Daimler Company, and it had fluid drive. To my surprise he was always willing to loan me the car. Jock Morrison taught me how to drive in his Morris Oxford in which he took enormous pride. He parked it in the most inaccessible space in the old stable where I remembered the old horse had died. Nevertheless one could always see one's face in this jet-black limousine with leather seats. My mother, now in her sixties, derived most of her real enjoyment from being chauffeured around in that car. 'Makes me feel like a duchess,' she would say.

We took off at weekends, Mother, Jean, Jock, Wee Ian and I for picnics in the highlands. My sister had a special Coleman stove and all the necessary equipment. She prepared all kinds of meals ready to heat, with potatoes and veggies to boil. These were pleasant, happy, carefree days, despite the undercurrent of menace from Nazi Germany and Mr Neville Chamberlain's futile negotiations.

Everything was so cheap in those days. Fellow students and I sneaked time off in the afternoon to go to a film in the Edinburgh Playhouse, a splendid theatre. If we were there before two p.m. it cost only sixpence, equivalent to about two pennies today. We saw some classic epics like *Viva Zapata* and *I was a Fugitive from a Chain Gang*. Then we would go to one of Crawford's delightful bake shops and stuff ourselves with Scotch pies and rhubarb tarts. It was a thrill to have money in the bank; with good food, good beer and my splendid dog I was perfectly happy and the world was nothing but sunshine. I remember my mother and sister being terribly proud of me. They wanted so badly to see me as

Captain of an ocean liner and because of that I really did work hard at college.

I also made several new friends in Linlithgow – men who were older and had been friends with my older brothers. One in particular, James Edgar, was with Sanderson's Vat 69 Whisky in Edinburgh and we often rode on the bus together. Another, James Brock, one of Brock the Builders family, did lots of work for my mother. Our friendship lasted throughout their lifetimes. At different times they exerted considerable influence on my life. In addition there was always my special buddy, Charles McLean, now a banker, and a spare-time RAF pilot. There was a distinct bond between us. Unhappily, he died in a bombing raid over Brest in western France in late 1941.

On 28 October 1938, having qualified at the Nautical College, I was appointed Third Officer on a brand new vessel, the MV *Inverlane*, lying at moorings in the River Fal at Falmouth in England. I was obliged to say my farewells once more but this time the parting was much more mature. Mine was an honourable profession and they were proud to see me go with a cheerful 'Bon Voyage'.

STREAMBANK, a typical BANK LINE cargo liner, about 11,000 tons gross.

Today, these ships are fast disappearing as much general cargo is now transported by air-cargo planes. The modern fleets of cargo liners are comprised mainly of Container Ships, massive Oil Tankers, and Bulk Carriers.

CHAPTER VIII

THE WAR AT SEA – MV INVERLANE

Reporting on board a new vessel is always something of a mixture of dread and expectation, but sailors are such a breed that all kinds of characters are readily accepted, provided they fit the general mould. Quite quickly new shipmates are accepted as old friends and with everyone knowing precisely where he fits within the different responsibilities there was rarely an excuse for internal conflict. Of course there are always certain preferences in all of us, for instance, I was vastly relieved to find that the Captain, John Robertson, was a Scotsman from Grangemouth, very close to my own home. While he did not welcome me with open arms, I did detect a certain warmth in his greeting. He was a surly old bachelor, aged about forty-five, old to me then, but he was a born shipmaster and respected by everyone.

The Motor Vessel *Inverlane*, a brand new tanker, was a delight to see – truly modern, with graceful lines, black hull, white superstructure and a buff funnel with a black top. She had luxury accommodation by comparison with my earlier experience, loads of deck space, lounges, smoke-rooms and very good food. To my surprise she was flying a green, white and gold ensign, the flag of the Irish Republic. She was registered in Dublin, owned by the Crusader Petroleum Company which was merely another branch of the Bank Line. She was one of seven sisters, named after Irish rivers like the *Invershannon*, the *Inverliffey* etc., and all built in Bremen, Germany. It was said to be some peculiar way of getting company money out of Germany. It is interesting to note that all seven of these ships were sunk by German submarines in the first year of the war. The *Inverlane* was the first to go.

She had been laid up in the River Fal for a couple of months prior to undertaking her maiden voyage. Her powerful engines were German MAN diesels, which looked as shiny as silver plate. However, according to the engineers, the castings were all lousy and they were constantly plagued by pump rods collapsing and a lack of appropriate spare parts. Nevertheless, from a deck officer's point of view, the ship was a dream, with the entire bridge, the charthouse and the control room all very much up to date. She had the first echo sounder I

81

had ever seen; it provided a continuous record of the depth of water under the keel. Whilst we had the very latest in radio direction-finding equipment, it was still very necessary to practice the art of celestial navigation and the heart thereof was the 2nd Mate's precious chronometer.

Within days we were prepared for sea with stores, fresh water, fuel and a full complement of white crew. These men were entirely different to those of my earlier experience, a much more technically-oriented group. The ship's hull was divided into forty separate tanks, all with inter-connecting pipelines, so that various types of oil might be carried. One tank load could be transferred to another and all were controlled from a massive pump room wherein the main controls were housed. However each separate tank was gated from the main deck by a master valve operated by hand. Also special piping for use in carrying steam for cleaning, or safety against fire, was run in parallel to the main lines. Cargo loading and discharging control was complex and had to be learned from scratch. Mistakes could be costly and at times life-threatening.

The maiden voyage of the *Inverlane* took us to Port Arthur, Texas where we loaded petrol for Santa Cruz de Tenerife. The stay in Port Arthur was brief but at least I had time to visit Beaumont and Orange, just to find out if they were all just wild Texas towns. Everybody was in the oil business and most people seemed to be in transit. The single claim to fame in Port Arthur was Proctor Street where every second house was a cathouse and the rest were bars. We survived the visit there without casualties on the sick parade. The Chief Engineer was extremely pleased with the crew performance and claimed that for the first time in his experience he had acquired a highly competent crew.

Fully-laden with petrol, the voyage to Tenerife was uneventful. Considering that it was winter the weather was quite reasonable. There were rough enough periods when it was a pleasure to observe the sleek vessel ploughing through rough seas and throwing off green water with ease. The steel decks, the heavy tank lids and the special catwalks made everything seem to be almost invulnerable to the worst of storms. She sliced through the water like a yacht, leaving a bubbling wake of phosphorescence behind her stretching almost to the horizon. Despite the gloomy skies we managed to get the important sights and position determinations. Constant practice whets one's interest in acquiring an intimate knowledge of the stars and the planets. My interest in celestial navigation never flagged.

It was on my morning watch when we first caught sight of Tenerife, a giant 12,000-feet high mountain on an island. The peak could be seen on a clear day for more than fifty miles. We anchored off Santa Cruz with instructions to wait until the freight was paid. We had reached that stage in business where everyone was so nervous that they wanted to see the colour of the money before delivering the goods. General Franco's credit was not all that good and cash on the barrel-head was the order of the day. Orders finally came and the cargo was duly discharged. Santa Cruz has changed for the better no doubt but back then it was a total disaster. We were happy to cast off, bound for Texas again, this time to the port of Galveston.

By now, officers and crew were proficient in the loading and discharging of cargo and the whole process could be accomplished in less than a day unless a mix of different gravity oils was specified in the manifest. We did have a couple of nights in Galveston and at that time in early 1939 it was a buzzing town. We were told that the whole place was run by the mafia and whilst this was something of an exaggeration there is no doubt that the entertainment business was run by the boys from Chicago. There were dance halls on a long pier that stretched out to sea, with music, and dancing, and gambling, and dancing girls, and lots of very dubious entertainment. The seafront was lined with cocktail bars where every barman had a hair-raising story to tell. It did not take long to treat the tall tales with the proverbial dose of salt. After all, this was Texas.

Our orders were for Spain, to Alicante and to Malaga. Off-loading was difficult due to war damage to the port facilities. The Spanish civil war had dragged on and on and only now, with General Franco in more or less full control, things were settling down. But they were far from being properly organized. Everywhere we went there was desolation, starvation, begging, homeless, shortages and as a consequence crime was rampant. The army was in control, but without noticeable discipline, and in most cases it was every man for himself. Each day on the docks a line would form consisting of people begging for the excess food from the galley. They brought their own containers to carry away anything that was edible. We were welcomed everywhere until our money gave out and then we were just men who made good targets. Desperate people could cut a man's throat for the clothes on his back.

Saddened by the desolation, we were nevertheless relieved to depart. We were ordered to Venice, Italy to dry dock. I remember being surprised as it had never occurred to me that Venice was an active sea port. I was also horrified to discover how cold it was, something I did not expect in sunny Italy. We were up-river in dry dock with everything shut down, no heat, no lights and even with the bar closed. The mornings were misty and damp just like Scotland. The delays in the dockyard were an engineering problem so we, the deck officers, had lots of time to visit the sights of Venice proper and I must admit to being enthralled by the entire city. The beautiful buildings, the variety of museums, the art galleries, even the pigeons held us spellbound.

Back on board one gathered the impression of urgency in the orders from headquarters, so obviously the demand for tonnage, for oil shipments was heating up. We were advised to proceed with all speed to Tripoli in Syria. There, no one is ever closer to shore than about five miles. In those days we edged our way in to shore until we spotted a buoy to which the pipeline was attached. We anchored, recovered the buoy with a hawser attached and winched up the pipeline. This had to be attached to the main gate valve, we then hoisted a flag signal and the crude oil began to flow. Several hours later, by flashing light, we advised the shore staff to ease the flow then shut off when we were fully laden. The pipeline was capped and dumped. A little man in a boat arrived with the bills of lading and we were off to Marseille in the south of France.

Our visit to Marseille was brief but exciting. On our night out in the Place de la Bourse, in a bar called, of all things, 'Snow White and the Seven Dwarfs', we were involved in a heated discussion about the impending war with Germany. There were seamen there from Norway, Sweden, Germany, Holland and France, of course. Later on in the evening the discussion became so heated that they decided to start the war there and then. Very soon the tell-tale whine of the French police sirens could be heard and we were lucky to escape through a basement window into a back alley and thence to the safety of the docks.

We departed that morning bound for Corpus Christi, Texas. The saloon conversations were dominated by discussions about war, about Mr Chamberlain and peace in our time, and about how the Nazis could never hope to conquer the Maginot Line. We argued constantly about how the war would last only a few short weeks, how the French would triumph on the ground, and through the Entente Cordiale, the great British Navy would turn the screws on Adolf Hitler. We were all supremely confident of a quick victory. We had already forgotten the carnage and desolation in Spain. Somehow or other that could never happen to us.

Corpus Christi was a delightful place but a bit of a disaster for me. I had often heard of the term, 'a Mickey Finn', but here, for the first time in my life I experienced one. In the warmth of a Texas evening, the cocktail bars, mere roofs with lattice-work walls and clinging vines, looked cool and inviting, and the entertainment was boisterous. Having visited a few I remember entering a large, glamorous place, then nothing. I finally regained consciousness when the vessel was already twenty-four hours at sea. Captain Robertson had taken my watch on the bridge. He had me on the carpet but to my surprise and relief seemed more concerned than upset. I did have to suffer a lecture but the subject was never mentioned again. I had not lost much: a watch, some money, a good pair of hand-made shoes and absolutely all of my dignity. As the Captain said, I was a very lucky young man. The Bos'un and his shore crew had found me and lugged me aboard.

Again to Spanish ports, but this time to the Bay of Biscay, to Santander and

Bilbao, with the usual wait in the Bay pending payment of freight. I was soured on shore leave and happy to head out to sea again bound for Abadan in the Persian Gulf. This took us through the Mediterranean to Port Said, then canal transit and down the Red Sea, then round into the Persian Gulf. We departed from Abadan in August 1939 with the usual Land's End for orders, but this time with dispatch. Fully-laden and at full speed was something of a thrill in the Persian Gulf where the water was crystal clear but just deep enough in places for loaded ships. Looking ahead from the bridge one always gathered the impression that we were just about to run aground. Being summer the water was as smooth as glass and the temperature of the atmosphere somewhere around 120 degrees Fahrenheit. We were glad to arrive at the Mediterranean end of the Suez Canal again, even if only to cool off.

By now all hands would gather around the radio receivers anxious for news, but still supremely confident of a very brief war and a brilliant victory. Discussions at meals in the saloon were constantly based around Hitler and his Nazi forces. Great argument took place regarding the relative strengths of the various navies, with all concerned supremely confident of the superiority of the British. Some of the younger set, myself included, were more interested in discussing Hitler's great 'strength through joy' movements and I believe that some of us secretly envied the young storm troopers their fancy uniforms and most certainly their gorgeous, blond, Aryan girlfriends. Most of us had several outdated American magazines extolling the virtues of the youth movements and I must confess that much of what we saw and read made everything sound great, provided you were a Nazi.

As we approached Land's End we were ordered to German ports. However on 3 September, just as war was declared, we were in the narrows of the English Channel. Captain Robertson wisely put in to Zeebrugge to await developments. On the night of 5 September we slipped across the strait shrouded in darkness and headed for anchorage at Southend at the mouth of the River Thames.

We lay in the anchorage there for many long weeks. The entire crew and some of the officers, including Captain Robertson, left the vessel for well-earned leave while a new crew was signed on. No doubt much of the delay was due to deliberations prior to the Royal Navy impounding the German cargo, changing the port of registry and the ensign and the need for the vessel to be painted battleship grey from stem to stern. Finally, in early December, we were ordered to proceed to Invergordon Naval Base in the north of Scotland, and when a convoy of about fourteen ships was assembled off Southend we were ready to set sail. The Captain was ferried ashore to participate in some great, secret conference and on his return we weighed anchor and got underway.

The convoy was assembled and after much hair-raising manoeuvring established itself in the desired formation and we proceeded at a reduced speed of about twelve knots. Meanwhile an escort of naval vessels appeared and darted about at great speed just like broody hens. There was some excitement on the bridge when the destroyer HMS *Kelly* was recognized and the Captain advised us that she was under the command of Lieutenant Commander Lord Louis Mountbatten. The pronouncement fell a little flat as most of us were Scotsmen and not unduly impressed with the aristocracy.

Our overall progress northwards through the North Sea towards Scotland was relatively slow, because of the Royal Navy's faith in zig-zagging and manoeuvring around, supposedly to fool the submarines. Unfortunately they were not fooled for long. It was about high noon on 14 December 1939 and those of us on duty were on the bridge taking sunshots for latitude when the first torpedo hit. To my surprise it was not the explosion that shook us, it was the roaring wall of flame that shot up from the pump room. The torpedo had hit the diesel fuel tanks and exploded, then ignited the highly flammable crude in the cargo tanks. The flames were instantly about 400 feet high. Either the sudden heat or a second torpedo blew the heads off the tanks and flame spewed out like giant fountains. The engines shuddered to a halt but the hull still forged ahead leaving a trail of black oil blazing on the sea surface. A southerly wind on the starboard beam sustained one lifeboat in the clear. On our port side a second tanker full of aviation spirit blew up in flames then disappeared from view.

Those of us on the bridge were able to launch the starboard lifeboat but it was a miracle the boat stayed upright. Within minutes the *Inverlane*, carried forward by her own momentum, was far ahead of us. We had to row like hell into the wind to avoid the flames whilst some of the crew members were dragged out of the icy, oil-slicked water. By now several square miles of sea were ablaze with a great column of oily, black smoke rising into the heavens. Finally the destroyer *Kelly* hove alongside the lifeboat and we clambered up the rope nets slung over her side dragging the half-drowned crew members behind us. Shortly afterwards, before we had time to thank the Gods for our good fortunes, the *Kelly* hit a mine which blew most of her stern off, with massive loss of life.

Within minutes the naval escort vessel *Wallace* came to the rescue and the survivors from the *Inverlane* and the injured from the *Kelly* were transferred. Thereafter she proceeded at full speed for Rosyth, a naval yard in the River Forth. The *Kelly* remained afloat and was towed into Newcastle-on-Tyne, and Lord Louis was decorated with the Distinguished Service Cross. The burned out hulk of the *Inverlane* drifted ashore on the English coast some days later. It was already dark when we docked in Rosyth. Most of us were soaked in a mixture of oil and seawater but sitting on the steam-pipe casings on the *Wallace* dried us out to some degree.

There was much confusion at Rosyth. Thus far the organization of the Sea Transport section of the Royal Navy had not caught up with the needs of Merchant Navy survivors. None of us had any British money and there was no way the Royal Navy could advance us a few shillings. We did finally get travel vouchers and a Navy vehicle dropped us off at the railway station. We found a train for Edinburgh at some ungodly hour in the morning. I remember the group, about nine of us, having a heated discussion with some Sea Transport officer at Waverley Station in Edinburgh. It was cold and we were hungry and there was still no available money. I took off up the steps to Princes Street and on up to St Andrew's Square. There was a bus leaving for Stirling which would pass the old farmhouse door. I climbed aboard and promptly fell asleep, probably stinking of oil. The bus conductress had recognized me; she stopped the bus at The Farmhouse door and yelled for my sister Jean.

Jock Morrison, my sister's husband, was home and together they assisted me off the bus and straight into the bathroom. With a bath, breakfast and much good Scotch whisky and a warm bed I was a brand new man by the following day. I woke up with Nipper licking my face. Telephone calls to the shipping office assured me of three weeks survivor's leave. Welcome home!

That day, when I woke up at the old farmhouse, 16 December and just nine days before Christmas 1939, was a remarkable one for me. My mother, my sister, her husband, their babies and Nipper the dog made so much fuss I wondered how I ever survived. Even the folks in the village would look at me in awe. Up until that time I don't believe anyone paid much attention to the war. It was all happening elsewhere. No one really cared until Dunkirk, and then of course the bombers came. However it was all very strange to me to be totally devoid of personal possessions. I had absolutely nothing but the clothes I stood up in and those stank horribly of oil. Nevertheless life had to go on and in short order the wardrobe was replenished, but with an eye on economy. After all, the chances for continued survival were not all that good. All my expensive camera equipment, good binoculars, sextant and navigation instruments were reduced to cinders and at the bottom of the sea somewhere. I had no plans for their replacement and from that moment on I decided to travel light.

Linlithgow, certainly those who knew me there, made much of my adventure and my old friends organized many rowdy parties. There were times before Christmas when Nipper, the ever-faithful dog, looking sorely neglected, would abandon me and leave for home by himself thus alarming the folks at the brig. Much of the clowning and celebrating came to a head on old year's night in 1939. Charlie McLean threw a part at his family home up on the canal banks. We were celebrating his call-up to the Royal Air Force out of the auxiliary training section. There was quite a group of us, including his sisters, Margaret Wotherspoon and Jimmy Brock, and it was one of the coldest nights on record. The canal was frozen solid.

Someone, somehow, started some crazy game of climbing the walls of an old hump-backed bridge that crossed the canal close by. In bright moonlight, reflected from dazzling white snow, amidst howls, catcalls and general encouragement, I managed to get halfway across when my feet slipped on the polished stone and I went crashing down onto the solid ice. Unfortunately I fell face first, I was a sight to behold. Patched up with 'new skin', one side of my face totally black and blue, I looked like the wreck of the Hesperus. The heavy navy uniform cushioned my fall and I was able to walk without a problem. When I arrived home near breakfast time my mother almost had a fit. It took hours of explaining to finally calm her down. To everyone else it was a badge of honour, a sort of war wound to be much admired. To my relief I was advised from London to join a ship in Birkenhead at the end of January. It was a reminder to take life more seriously.

By then James Brock and another friend, James Edgar, had decided that Edinburgh might be more our style and plans were discussed for weekends in the city. James Edgar, a few years older than I, had started work in St Magdalene's Distillery in Linlithgow in the late twenties, and by this time had a senior post in Sanderson's Vat 69 whisky distillery in Leith. He spent his entire life in the whisky business, finishing up as a Director of the Distillers Company Ltd., a very prestigious post indeed. However, James had a secretary who had a female cousin and a female friend, and with the changing wartime attitudes it was not considered too improper to organize a blind date. I was always quite certain that all these arrangements were eagerly made by the secretary because she was keen on him. The big day of the blind date was Saturday 13 January.

James Brock and I made a special effort on that day, he in his best civvies and me in a brand new uniform. We felt as though we were the best-dressed men in the entire city. We joined James Edgar in the sample room of the Vat 69 office for a couple of quick ones to upgrade our self-confidence as blind dates were a new experience for us. The weather was kind on that day, a winter sun shone from a cloudless sky and at three in the afternoon on Lothian Road the air was glorious. The meeting place was outside the Regal Cinema, the girls were already there and I recognized Jean Samuel. She was tiny and so was the other who turned out to be the cousin. I can vaguely remember saying to the lads, 'I'll take the big plump one.' By then we were close and the girls smiled up at us. Quite quickly I realized that the big one was not all that big at all, it was just that the other two were so small. I cannot say that I remember the introductions or the arrangements. I do remember going to the sweet counter to pick up a box of Black Magic chocolates and somehow or other we found our seats in the cinema.

It has been pointed out to me on many occasions since that I ruined the whole film by insisting on trying to make conversation. In retrospect I can only conclude that I was smitten almost from the first moment I saw her and I was anxious to make a good impression. After the film all six of us went to the Empire and danced to the music of two different orchestras. I hadn't danced all that much till then so it wasn't my dancing that convinced her we should have a second date. The evening ended in quite a walk. Jean Samuel, Jane Malcolm – the 'sweater girl', Jim Brock called her – and I finished up on a tram, and because Jean lived beyond the end of the line we walked her home. Then I walked Miss Jane home, holding her hand. Finally I had to walk another mile back to my brother's flat to spend the night.

However I walked with a light step. The sweater girl had agreed to another date the following Saturday. I don't believe I really knew why I felt so light-hearted nor why the future looked so bright all of a sudden. I do remember the moon shining almost as clear as day and I felt good. It was when I saw her coming towards me the following Saturday that I knew. There was no shred of doubt in my mind – for the first and only time in my life I was in love. Thereafter we met every day until the end of the month. Being presented with a large framed picture seemed to confirm that the romance was consolidated. We parted, she cried and I remember wondering if I would ever see her again.

CHAPTER IX

MV CEDARBANK

I reported to Birkenhead, near Liverpool for duty as Third Officer of the Motor Vessel *Cedarbank*, a twin-screw cargo vessel recently arrived from Sierra Leone with a massive salvage patch on her port side. She had been involved in a collision there with another ship but allowed to proceed to the UK with a crude salvage patch because of the war. It was decided while the vessel was still in Birkenhead that she should be redesigned internally for rapid loading and off-loading of vehicles like tanks, Bren gun carriers and trucks. Such vessels were urgently needed to ferry the British Expeditionary Force's equipment to France.

Unfortunately, upon leaving Birkenhead, we had a serious collision with another vessel and we sank her in the ship channel while both ships were under pilotage. It seems odd to say she sank for she really only sank about three feet and stayed absolutely level, sitting on the muddy bottom. We returned to port for bow repairs. The need for haste precluded the possibility of a general repair so to save time they welded light steel patches externally to the bow then filled up the forepeak with cement. When we finally put to sea in ballast, bound for south of England ports, the *Cedarbank* sailed only very slightly down by the head, as a sailor would say. Before we reached our destination special messages were received advising us to proceed with all speed to the port of Leith, in Scotland. In other words, almost back home in Edinburgh.

Special cargo awaited us there but no more special than what we had been specially redesigned to carry. Great loaded trucks, Bren gun carriers, tanks etc. could be loaded by crane, and thereafter under their own power in the cargo holds driven to specially located ring bolts to hold them in position. Guns, bombs and ammunition in the 'tween decks, and on the main deck, crated aircraft, drums of fuel and other motley stores. Shore leave was discouraged supposedly to avoid information leaks but somehow or other my policeman brother found out that the *Cedarbank* was in port and he came looking for me. Captain Calderwood gave me special permission for leave in view of the fact that Mrs Calderwood had shown up in Edinburgh.

My fiancée, as I had described her to the Captain, and I had a dreamy couple of days in the city. I do believe we were both walking on air. Much of our time was spent at my brother's flat in Merchiston Grove so that in the event of an emergency he could find me in a hurry. By this time most people knew that there were expeditionary forces bound for Norway to defend the northern reaches against the Nazi advance. The *Cedarbank* had the dubious honour of carrying the necessary armour for such a force. By this time April Fool's Day had come and gone.

After a tearful farewell from wives and sweethearts we left port shrouded in fog and headed north-eastwards at full speed towards a rendezvous with the troop-carriers. We assumed that we were bound for the Narvik region of Norway, as after all we needed shore-based facilities to off-load. However when the two Blue Funnel passenger liners with escorts hove into view we knew that the troops were ready and waiting. We carried everything but their rifles. A flurry of flag signals and flashing Aldis lamps advised us to join the happy throng and participate in the usual zig-zag manoeuvres. We had scarcely settled down when a message arrived ordering the *Cedarbank* to proceed independently and with all speed to Kirkwall in the Orkney Islands. To our dismay, we learned later that the military had omitted to put anti-freeze into the radiators of the various vehicles despite the fact that we were heading for the Arctic Circle.

To give the Navy due credit Kirkwall was ready for us. At anchor in Scapa Flow, an army of men and equipment descended upon us and in less that twenty-four hours we were underway, bound for northern Norway again and a new rendezvous. I can vaguely remember plotting the position on the Captain's instructions and calculating the time of arrival running independently at full speed. We should have been there at 8.30 a.m. on 21 April 1940 but at about 8.20 a.m., just as we sighted the Royal Navy destroyer *Jaguar* approaching us, we were hit by two torpedoes within seconds of one another and both on the starboard quarter.

The *Cedarbank* immediately began sinking by the stern and within thirty seconds or so the bow began to rise out of the water. Just as she became totally vertical, she started to slide away slowly and then with a violent upheaval she disappeared under the water. I learned later from the Navy that the entire process of destruction took only ninety seconds. Being Third Officer I had reported to the bridge, fully-dressed, at 7.45 a.m. to take over the watch at 8.00 a.m. I checked our position by dead reckoning, took an azimuth of the sun to check the compass error and adjusted the course to be steered accordingly. I had taken my first sip of tea brought by the steward when the *Jaguar* hove into view, her flashing Aldis lamp signals advising us to close ranks with the troop-carriers. The sea state was calm but icy cold. We were already well within the Arctic Circle. We were at full speed and fast approaching our predetermined rendezvous.

At about 8.20 a.m. I was about to take a shot of the sun to check our longitude when our whole world turned upside down. James Soutar, the Chief Officer, and Captain Calderwood were arriving back on the bridge to check out the *Jaguar* messages just as we were hit. As the vessel heeled slightly to starboard the helmsman joined us as we stepped over the rail to the boat deck to release the lifeboat. We did not quite make it.

I found myself in the icy water staring skyward at this enormous ship now vertical in the water. I could clearly see the port anchor, something that weighed about five tons, suddenly clear the hawse-pipe and come hurtling down towards me, missing my head by inches. As the giant hull slipped into the icy sea there was the most horrendous roaring sound then a terrible drag downwards. I was sure I was going with her till all the air in my heavy uniform and bridge coat acted like an air bubble and threw me back up to the surface, gasping for breath. A raft, automatically ejected from the shrouds, floated nearby. I dragged myself aboard with six or seven others.

Within minutes the *Jaguar* steamed slowly alongside the raft and we grasped the rope nets thrown over us. She picked up about a dozen of us but several never regained unconsciousness. Later, they were buried whilst still at sea. Those of us who survived were frozen stiff, unable to move, but grateful to be alive. The icy dip must have drained us as I am sure we all slept for hours on board the *Jaguar* in any old bunk we could find. The Captain of the *Jaguar* was Philip Vian, later to become Admiral Sir Philip Vian, one of the Lords of the Admiralty. He must have been a very senior officer to have earned command of the *Jaguar*, one of the very latest of the Royal Navy's destroyers. He had become quite famous as a consequence of a very daring capture of the German supply vessel *Altmark*. She was endeavouring to slink back to Germany carrying many British Merchant Navy shipmasters and chief engineers as prisoners in her cargo holds, thus precluding the possibility of British submarine attack.

However the destroyer *Cossack*, under Vian's command, slipped alongside of her one moonlight night off the coast of Norway. She was boarded in the old-fashioned Navy fashion with swords and pistols. She was considered to be a major prize. This adventure did much to revive British morale in the midst of so much other doom and gloom at that time. At a later date, by then a squadron commander, he played a very important role in the sinking of the German battleship *Bismarck*, again acquiring naval recognition and public acclaim.

When sufficiently recovered and with our clothes dried out we learned in the wardroom that as a consequence of the loss of the *Cedarbank* the expedition had been called off. The *Jaguar*, now alone on a lonely grey sea, was proceeding at high speed towards some new destination. We soon learned that we, the survivors, would be landing somewhere in Norway. Destroyers simply do not have accommodation for passengers and usually fewer than four berths in the ship's hospital. In any case the *Jaguar* already had new orders, new commitments and the best solution for everyone was to put us ashore. Very soon we were proceeding into a Norwegian fjord not far south of Trondheim. It was very cold and wet with traces of late winter snows still clinging to the sheer cliffs on either side of us.

The *Jaguar* put a line ashore on a wooden wharf and about nine of us, the *Cedarbank* survivors, limped off. By the time we had our bearings the ship was gone. We trudged up the long jetty to the town of Andalsnes, a town I judged to be of about 1,400 souls, and as I remember it there was not a single soul in sight. I remember thinking to myself how nice it was to have absolutely no baggage to worry about. We did try what appeared to be the local hospital, hoping for some first aid, but there was no one available. We finally met up with some Norwegians and Swedes who were scouring the coast in the hope of picking up a ship bound for Britain. According to them there were Germans everywhere in Norway and Andalsnes was likely to be occupied soon.

Somehow, out of nowhere, word came that we should head for Alesund. Suddenly everyone seemed to be convinced that there was a ship there, the last one, leaving for Scapa Flow. It was amazing how quickly the mood of depression and fear for the future dissolved in favour of this slim hope at Alesund. Indeed, it turned out to be true. From a high knoll we could look down on this small fishing village and there in all her grey colour was a ship flying the Red Ensign. It turned out to be the *St Magnus*, a small cargo-passenger vessel, more at home in the Orkney Islands. It amused us later to discover that such a small vessel belonged to a company with such a large name, which was the North of Scotland, Orkney and Shetland Island Shipping Company. But on that day the *St Magnus* rivalled the *Queen Mary* in my mind.

There was no question of, 'Who are you?' or 'Where are you going?' just 'Welcome aboard'. She was crowded but we were all singing when she left the dock. Outside the harbour the wind was whipping the white tops off the heavy seas. We knew it was going to be a cold crossing and we searched around for a dry space on deck to crawl into. A Norwegian sailor-shipowner and I crawled under a four-inch gun turret on the after deck. We were sheltered from the wind and spray and we had one blanket between us. I did not know what the gun crew were firing at, but I did almost jump out of my skin when the gun went off. My head had been against one of the steel supports to the gun base. Finally, when I got rid of the ringing in my ears I realized that we were being shelled by a German surfaced submarine whilst at the same time Stuka dive-bombers were whining overhead.

Providence was on our side that day. In less than an hour and still unscathed despite the enemy fire we were shrouded in dense fog. It hung over us like a protective blanket until we reached the Pentland Firth. We berthed at Kirkwall and as we clambered ashore we were greeted by harried officials who had no shelter to give us. They were already overcrowded with refugees. Some of us were invited to lodge in the county home, but my Norwegian friend and I decided to fend for ourselves. We managed to acquire a bottle of Scotch and we retired to the lee side of a drystone dyke.

That night, as we lay there, the moon rose into a cloudless sky. The stars were as bright as searchlights. We were reasonably warm, sheltered from the wind and aglow with the warm whisky in our stomachs. We were at peace with the world, but alas, the world had something else in store for us. It was the night of the biggest air raid ever over Scapa Flow. It was not a successful one for the Germans as more than a score of planes were shot down. We lay quite still, our eyes skyward, counting the anti-aircraft shell bursts and feeling rather sorry for the German fliers. When the guns fell silent we fell asleep. We awoke at dawn aching in every joint.

In the morning we were led like sheep to Scapa Flow and there we boarded an anchored passenger liner which turned out to be the naval headquarters. After being processed, and later that same day, some of us were taken out to board a small ferry, the *St Ola*, to take us across the Pentland Firth to Scrabster, a small port on the northernmost shores of Scotland. There we climbed aboard a ramshackle bus to Thurso where we waited for hours for a train. Finally we got to Wick and lots of the local ladies there fed us on tea and sandwiches. We began to feel like human beings again.

In those days I believe it was a one-track railway over the mountains to Inverness. It seemed to take forever, with occasional shunting about on sidings, whilst trains passed going in the opposite direction. Here again though, out of nowhere, the highland women appeared with their tea and snacks; I do not know what we would have down without them. From Inverness we progressed more quickly and finally reached Edinburgh. My favourite bus conductress dropped me off again at the brig. I was dirty, unshaven, in a tattered uniform with no cap, but she smiled at me and said, 'We'll have to stop meeting like this.'

The welcome home at The Farmhouse was overwhelming. The womenfolk cried a lot at first but soon afterwards, when I cleaned up a bit, we were laughing and joking excitedly. Nipper, to his delight, was allowed into the kitchen, a rare treat for him, so he lay at the hearth with his head on my feet and his behind almost in the fire. I must have told my story a dozen times as the neighbours came and went. My homecoming was quite an event at Linlithgow Bridge. After all, as far as they were concerned, the war had not really started yet. The radio blared out songs like, 'We're gonna hang out the washing on the Siegfried Line'. Everyone still believed in our invincibility and there were no real shortages yet. However the telephone lines had not yet reached The Farmhouse, so my sister got the police to call my brother in Edinburgh and he, in turn, informed the Malcolms of my arrival home.

I must have been a seedy looking character when I arrived at Hutchison Road, the Malcolm home. I had cleaned up a bit and my sister had done the best she could with my clothes. I badly needed a haircut and I had no hat. Nevertheless the greeting was nervously warm whilst I met her parents and her sixteen-year-old brother, Edwin. Later, when we were alone, we were strangely silent and aloof for quite a while. Finally Jane broke down and cried and I had great difficulty consoling her. I believe that we both felt as though we were living on the edge of a precipice. However once I was assured again from London of my survivor's leave we started to enjoy life again and make plans for the future.

By now it was the beginning of May 1940. Spring had already blossomed into summer, the nights were growing shorter and together we walked for miles in the gloaming over Arthur's Seat and Holyrood Palace. It was on such a night, whilst strolling over the hills, that she agreed to marry me, but adding, 'You will have to ask my Dad.'

Fortunately her dad's bark was infinitely worse than his bite. While he objected vehemently to any thought of matrimony during the war, he saw no reason why we should not get engaged. Jane was overjoyed because in those days an engagement was a solid commitment and she would have a ring to show off to all her friends. She did not enjoy meeting my mother for the first time, though, as she was queried about her religion and her background, and then told in no uncertain terms that Master Ian could have found a wife much closer to Linlithgow. Nevertheless after a few visits they became firm friends and Jane quite enjoyed being shown off to all the locals.

She really enjoyed the ring selection process in Ritchie's Jewellers in Leith Street. She finally chose a ring with thirteen small diamonds on it because we were engaged on 13 May 1940. Indeed we first met on 13 January 1940. This date was to be inscribed in the ring and she could scarcely wait to get it. As it happened the number thirteen was lucky for us. I signed on to my next ship, again in Liverpool, on 13 June 1940 and the good luck stayed with me. There was a sadness when we parted but having learned to face up to the tragedies of war we tried to make the best of things and we pretended to be happy.

CHAPTER X

MV MYRTLEBANK

These were anything but happy times for the British. The entire Norwegian Campaign was being abandoned and the troops withdrawn. Hanging out the washing on the Siegfried Line had become a ghastly joke. The much-vaunted Maginot Line, an expensive farce, was simply by-passed by the Germans and their blitzkreig methods swept all before them. On 26 May of that year, 1940, the horrendous withdrawal from Dunkirk began. Nine days later, nearly three hundred and fifty thousand men had been ferried back to England. On 14 June the Germans marched into Paris. The threat of invasion of our own homeland became horrifyingly real.

As we sailed out of Liverpool on the *Myrtlebank* on that day in June our spirits were at an all-time low. As we headed out north and then west through the Irish Sea and the north channel, and into the broad western ocean, I am sure that each one of us aboard seriously wondered if we would ever make it home again. Officers and crew were strangely silent on the bridge and in the saloon the radio provided us with a sad romantic message from Vera Lynn. Each one of us was constantly alone with his thoughts of home and a gnawing fear for what invasion might bring. We were all already well aware of Danes, Norwegians, Poles, Dutchmen and Frenchmen, now refugees, and already serving in the Merchant Navy.

When we broke from convoy and headed south at full speed into the mid-Atlantic where hundreds of Allied ships had already been sunk we were reminded of the deadly battle of the Atlantic by our Captain Evans. He would lecture us daily on the need to stay alert and to be on constant lookout for the tell-tale wake of a submarine periscope or the smoke stacks on the horizon that could turn out to be an armed merchant cruiser. They, with their supply ships, had already taken a heavy toll in the South Atlantic.

To raise our spirits we recounted to one another the saga of the pocket battleship *Graf Spee*, where Commander Harwood of the British cruiser *Exeter*, with the *Ajax* and the *Achilles*, had finally crippled the *Graf Spee* and sent her creeping into Montevideo for on-board repair. Three days later, as the British waited for them outside the mouth of the River Plate, the German crew scuttled their ship and then blew her up.

The pocket battleship *Scheer* sank thirty-seven ships in one Atlantic convoy and did extensive damage to our worldwide shipping lanes. The battleship *Hipper* was a constant threat whilst sheltering in Brest and on her occasional forays into the Atlantic spelled death for a score or so of merchant ships. The supply ships for the German raiders were hard to track down. They had an advantage over us insofar as every ship they sighted was an obvious enemy, while for us, we never knew which ship on the horizon might turn out to be an enemy. Radio silence was a strict naval order. However the Radio Officer was constantly on watch, listening carefully in order to intercept messages. Unhappily, most of the messages were distress calls from ships we were not permitted to assist. Our precious munitions cargoes were of much more value than a few human lives.

Whilst we sailed under sealed orders with specific routing instructions, to be opened only when appropriate, we all knew that we were bound for India via the Cape of Good Hope. At the last moment, just before we left Liverpool, we were in receipt of two large crates, each weighing about two tons for storage in the strong room. It was obvious that both crates were packed solid with silver rupees. I learned then for the first time that these silver rupees were minted in England for the Indian Government. A veritable treasure one might think but a treasure that would be difficult to steal without the benefit of a crane. With Italy now a German ally the transit through the Mediterranean was essentially cut. We had no alternative but to go around the Cape.

The *Myrtlebank* was a twin-screw motor vessel powered by diesel fuel. This meant that we had a very long range and a clean smokestack. On a clear day we could sight the masts of another vessel more than ten miles away, but the heavy smoke from a steamship might reveal her presence from twenty or even thirty miles. We proceeded at full speed by what seemed to us a circuitous route, but 'Father knows best,' Captain Evans would say. 'We follow orders.' By now it was July and the weather in the southern hemisphere was wintry, visibility was limited and we liked it that way. The seas were rough and therefore really tough on an old diesel-powered submarine.

We rounded the Cape without ever seeing it and put into Port Elizabeth for stores, water and fuel. In those days the sun shone, the air was brisk and the countryside was breathtakingly beautiful. We, in company with other ships in the port, were entertained at a concert and later on at private homes. We were treated like long-lost brothers and there was much celebration until word came through that a lifeboat full of seamen had been lost in the mountainous surf off the coast. It turned out that a British ship had been sunk off Réunion Island and survivors had made it all the way to the South African coast only to fall victim to the vicious surf. None survived.

We headed for Bombay, more alert to the dangers on the high seas than ever, but we reached the Indian coast without incident. Off-loading was a slow process because of the direct discharge into trains for shipment across the continent and on into Burma. By the end of August we were on our way to Calcutta, Madras and Colombo to load a full cargo for South American ports. October was gone before we cleared Colombo heading for Cape Town. Again we were directed by a circuitous route, apparently to avoid the last known areas where ships had been destroyed by German raiders. Fate smiled upon us as we headed west across the South Atlantic after a brief stop in Cape Town. We sailed for only a couple of days before being directed southwards to escape some unspecified foe and we were mighty close to Antarctica before heading directly for Cape Horn.

We off-loaded in the west coast ports, mostly small parcels of cargo, a few hundred tons here and there into barges, and this was mostly tea, jute and gunnies. The return trip around the Horn was violent despite the summer season. We had orders for Sao Paolo in Brazil. The English community there had organized what they called the 'Liberty Inn', where the ship's officers were entertained to parties and dances. Several major British shipping lines, like Blue Star, were regular traders there. The kindness and the concern expressed by these people was enough to convince us that the entire world had not gone insane.

I remember being sorry to leave Sao Paolo but our orders called for a return south to Rio Grande dol Sul to load a full cargo of bully beef, wet hides and great barrels and puncheons full of intestines used in the making of sausages. It amused me to think of the miles and miles of sausages, good old English bangers, that might be made from each barrel. The ship was loaded to the summer plimsoll lines and as we departed for Sierra Leone in rough seas I had the feeling that we could be mistaken for a submarine. Both the weather and the enemy were good to us as we arrived without serious incident but not without the customary emergencies. Every day at sea carried with it the constant threat of torpedoes, a sudden violent explosion without warning, and we were just like sitting ducks.

It was really hot in Freetown, Sierra Leone and we had to wait quite a while for the arrival of enough ships from diverse sources to form a convoy with some minimal protection from a couple of ancient naval escorts. Even at this time, early March 1941, the escort ships were all too few. Nevertheless there was some sense of comfort in a convoy as it surely made us feel a lot less lonely. It is hard to remember just how desolate it could be in the middle watch, from midnight till four in the morning, on a blacked-out ship, steaming at full speed through the black darkness. Shadows played tricks with our eyes. On occasions another vessel might slide past close by with just the swish of her bow wave and leaving only the bubbling phosphorescence of her wake behind her. Heartbeats quickened, followed by a deep sigh of relief.

Twice the convoy was scattered and regrouped as a result of submarine attack. Three or four ships were lost on each occasion. We wondered about survivors but we had our orders. There was no way we were permitted to stop. We used to wonder if it might be better to be blown to bits on an exploding tanker or munitions ship rather than be a survivor from a grain carrier and be left to swim forever in the icy-cold Atlantic. I was in constant demand when the guys were depressed. 'What was it like to be blown up in a tanker?' and 'What do you think about on a sinking ship in the high Arctic?'

However when we finally reached shelter in Loch Ewe, on the west coast of Scotland, on a golden spring morning, most of us felt that all was right with the world. For the first time in eleven long months we all received great mounds of mail from home and most were love letters. Homecoming was truly sweet, despite the fact that Britain was an island fortress, standing alone against her power-crazed enemies. We could see the rhododendrons blooming on the hillsides. Radios blared with dear Vera and her songs of love and romance. But again we had to wait until there were enough ships in the loch bound for English ports. We were warned of a hectic run down through the North Sea.

At last we headed out into the Minch, about fourteen ships with a destroyer escort. We were promised air cover when necessary. Cape Wrath glowered down upon us in all its majesty, on one of the all too few clear days of the year. We laboured through the Pentland Firth with the tide running heavily against us. The skies were a brilliant blue and cloudless, perfect weather for the dive-bombers, but we were totally ignored until we got to the mouth of the River Forth. During an air attack we had no option but to continue on our course as big merchantmen are really too cumbersome to manoeuvre with any hope of dodging bomber runs. Given sharp eyes and an alert helmsman we might avoid a floating mine or dodge the odd torpedo. Like us, the torpedoes were comparatively slow in those days. We did get the promised air cover and it did much for our morale when the occasional German bomber was shot down.

We were hustled up the River Thames with tugboats standing by for it was essential that we were safely berthed before darkness fell as nights in the London docks, except for an occasional moonlit night, were black as pitch. Not a light to be seen anywhere, yet before sunrise the stevedores streamed aboard like ants to off-load their precious cargoes. Despite the appalling bombing raids they were remarkably cheerful guys with cockney accents we could scarcely understand. But we all spoke the same language in the great public houses whilst quaffing their watery beer. Our favourite pub was the 'George' where we spent several hilarious nights.

On 15 May 1941 I was signed off and headed for home with three full months college leave to upgrade my papers at Leith Nautical College. I boarded the train at King's Cross with a light heart. The train pulled out of the station during a bombing raid but within half an hour we were speeding through the countryside in complete darkness. I nodded off to sleep while counting the sparks flying from the old steam locomotive.

I now had two homes, each offering the warmest of welcomes. From a celebration at the old farmhouse to a warm and loving reception in Edinburgh. It was more than a man had a right to expect. Within days of my arrival Jane was arguing with her father about the merits of matrimony. He and I had many amusing moments in pubs before he lightened up sufficiently to agree. The night he did agree it was already close to midnight when he got home and he was anxious to hear the radio news; I do believe that he agreed just to keep us quiet. Later on, after a generous toast, he entertained us to a raucous rendering of 'We'll gather lilacs in the spring again'.

Next day there was the beginning of feverish activity. A wedding was arranged at North Merchiston Church for 14 June, with a reception to follow at the Troquair Rooms. Invitations were churned out in haste and thereafter there was much discussion about the bridal wardrobe. There was a serious matter of clothing coupons to worry about. Meanwhile I scampered between Linlithgow, Edinburgh and the Nautical College in Leith, and I left the entire affair to the women.

Nevertheless I was compelled to take some interest in clothes. The easiest thing for me to do was to buy a new uniform as I did not need coupons for that. On the other hand Jane could do very little without coupons but she was an absolute genius with a sewing machine. She spent the coupons on a jazzy outfit for the wedding, then because she needed a winter coat for later in the year she bought a very nice lime-green, woollen blanket, without coupons, and from it she made a very elegant winter coat.

The wedding day was sunny and warm and everything went off like clockwork. The Reverend John Penman, a bachelor, was a very solemn, conservative minister. He took great care to remind me of the grave responsibility I was about to undertake and then I got a long lecture on the need for true love and unending loyalty. 'Till death do you part,' he intoned with a peculiar firmness. When we signed the register I believe I knew that it was forever.

The wedding reception was terrific, about seventy guests, mothers, brothers, sisters, in-laws, nephews, nieces, aunts, uncles; it was a huge success. There was only one in a kilt, my five-year-old nephew, Ian Morrison. The guests must have enjoyed themselves as we learned later that two of my brothers became hopelessly inebriated and late at night made themselves objectionable at the ticket office in the railway station. One, the policeman, escaped on a moving train leaving for Glasgow but the other did not and he was arrested. The following day he had no choice but to call my new father-in-law to come and bail him out. We, the young ones, saw the humour of the situation, but my mother never allowed either of them to forget it. 'I was absolutely black affronted,' she kept saying for years afterwards.

Just as Adolf Hitler committed his gravest error by invading Russia in June 1941, Jane and I spent a blissful four days honeymooning at Earlston, a quiet town on the Scottish borders, with Jane's favourite aunt and uncle and her grandmother. Four days was all the time permitted because Jane, like everyone else, was subject to wartime discipline and told to return to work at an aircraft plant. We had rented a furnished bungalow in Craigentinney, a suburb of Edinburgh, for a period of three months and therein we preserved our very own love nest till duty called once again.

CHAPTER XI

MV ETTRICKBANK

In September 1941 I was ordered to report to the Motor Vessel *Ettrickbank*, berthed in Swansea, Wales and loading munitions for the North African campaign. At the same time she was being provided with her own armament, a four-inch gun on the stern, Bofors anti-aircraft guns fore and aft and water-cooled machine-guns on the bridge. In addition there were handy little rockets on the flying bridge, easily fired and trailing a few hundred feet of piano wire. These wires were capable of slicing the wings off any dive-bomber and they were very effective. The German fliers were very soon dropping their bombs from much higher altitudes and as a result many of their bombs landed in the water with a disappointingly dull thud.

Together with a naval gun crew, the leader of which was an Australian, a very funny bloke, we were hastily pushed through a gunnery course. Fortunately most of our gunnery exercises were simply fun times, those shots we were obliged to fire in anger were usually far off the mark. It is not easy controlling a four-inch gun on a ship that is rolling and pitching about in a heavy sea. Luckily for us the enemy fought on the same playing field and firing from the watery deck of a surfaced submarine was no picnic either. In those days diesel submarines were relatively slow even on the surface and we could easily outrun them. Being Second Officer, and when necessary the Medical Officer, I now had the added responsibility of Gunnery Officer. Being busy was probably the best medicine under the circumstances.

In October 1941 we sailed into the Irish Sea and headed north to join a convoy which took us out to mid-Atlantic before we swung south and took off independently. During the month of October, much to our relief, the Royal Navy had sunk two German raiders, the *Kota* and the *Pinney*, both of which were supply ships for long-range submarines. We amused ourselves by thinking about the subs running out of fuel and stores in the South Atlantic, then patiently waiting at some outlandish rendezvous for a supply ship that would never appear. In November we were further cheered by the news of the sinking of the *Atlantis*, a dangerous German raider, by the cruiser *Devonshire*.

Captain Watkins, Master of the *Ettrickbank*, was a jolly sort and a bachelor who liked his liquor. Nevertheless he ran a tight ship and insisted on doubled-up deck watches, no straying from the pre-determined courses and strict adherence to Admiralty orders. We were sorely in need of a rest when we finally made it to Cape Town. A brief stop there then out into the Indian Ocean before heading northwards towards the Horn of Africa and on into the Red Sea. During the month of December some several hundred miles off the coast of western Australia, HMAS *Sydney* had run up close to a suspicious merchantman called *Kormoran*. To their surprise the German ship threw off her camouflage and opened fire. Both ships finally sank without survivors. Our leading gunner had served on the *Sydney* only a few months earlier. He mourned the loss of his shipmates for months thereafter.

We off-loaded deck cargo at Suez, mostly aircraft parts, then on into the Suez Canal. From Port Said we proceeded to Alexandria to off-load the badly-needed ordnance for the North African campaign. We were loading for Malta when other orders took priority and we returned to Port Said in the early days of January 1942. A brief refit there and we were ready to transport several hundred Australian troops with their armour to bolster the forces in Malaya. Then down the Red Sea and out into the Indian Ocean once again.

The weather was not unpleasant, and the shipboard deck space was more than adequate to permit freedom of movement to the entire force of wild Australians. They spent most of their time gambling on the spin of two copper coins onto a blanket spread on the deck. Meanwhile someone had won an accordion belonging to a real musician in a card game and he insisted on taking lessons just outside the saloon portholes. Some of the officers were strange men who had spent most of their lives in the isolation of sheep stations. The war to them spelled a certain freedom and much excitement.

As we approached the west coast of India, where we might acquire some air cover, we had a very strange experience. We were still a couple of hundred nautical miles off the coast when an old biplane appeared on the horizon, then approached us head-on. As the plane passed overhead just a few hundred feet above us we could see the aviators waving their arms. Moments later they banked steeply then dropped into the sea. Captain Watkins abandoned his normally conservative rules in this strange situation and decided to pick them up. Both pilots were Sikhs and had flown out of Cochin when engine problems compelled them to seek our assistance.

We proceeded into Cochin harbour to anchor for the night and to confer with the authorities. Captain Watkins and I were invited to a dinner at the Royal Indian Air Force base at Cochin. It was a unique experience for me and a glorious celebration for all concerned. We had a great deal of difficulty hoisting the good

Captain aboard at the end of the evening. We were greeted by cheers from the Aussie soldiers lining the decks. They were more than a little envious of the royal treatment we had received, and the glorious send-off provided.

By dawn, it was anchors aweigh, and we were off heading for the southern tip of Ceylon, and on to Singapore. We were within a day's run when new orders came. On that day, 15 February 1942, Singapore had fallen to the Japanese. We were ordered to Western Australia, and we berthed at Fremantle some days later. Whilst the news of the Japanese advance was anything but cheerful, nothing could dampen the enthusiasm of the Aussies when we tied up to the dock. They were given leave and we were ordered to Sydney with their equipment. In the saloon, we discussed our good luck. Without the break in the voyage at Cochin, we might all have been Japanese prisoners of war. A couple of weeks later our Aussie soldiers rejoined us and they were transported to Port Moresby in New Guinea. We never heard of them again.

We were ordered to New Zealand to load general cargo for the United Kingdom. We were loaded in record time, and we proceeded from Auckland and Dunedin to Port Napier on the southern tip of South Island where we received our sailing orders. Once again around Cape Horn, but first, a long lonely haul across the South Pacific, with our route taking us way south into the Antarctic zone presumably to avoid submarines. The days and nights were utterly boring as we sailed along with a typical Antarctic swell on the starboard beam. The *Ettrickbank* rolled excessively, but Captain Watkins often emerged from his suite at the oddest hours, just to ensure our adherence to the specified headings.

About three days short of the Horn, a howling gale descended upon us without warning, and within hours green seas were washing over the decks. In the black darkness of the middle watch the vessel rolled very heavily to port, then on the reverse roll to starboard a wild wave hit us with unbelievable force. Lifeboats were ripped out of the davits, the bridge was damaged and the decks were swept clean. We had no alternative but to alter course and reduce speed.

Captain Watkins appeared on the bridge cursing a blue streak. However, he was venting his wrath against the 'Great white fathers at the Admiralty', as he called them, with innumerable obscene embellishments. 'We'll head directly for Cape Horn,' he said. 'To hell with the Admiralty. Submarines couldn't survive in this kind of weather.'

We rounded the Horn without ever seeing land and pressed on northwards through the South Atlantic, making what repairs the ship's crew could accomplish. We made good speed and at the slightest sign of smoke on the horizon we altered course and pulled away. That year, 1942, the months of January to April were particularly bad off the coast of North America and we were well aware of the raiders in the South Atlantic. No one was taking any bets on our making it all the way to the UK. Nevertheless, we reached the safety of New York harbour on 25 May 1942. The authorities there simply ignored the damage and loaded the decks with crated aircraft; these were lashed down with chains fastened by ringbolts welded to the deck.

Three days later we were heading up the East River and out into Nantucket Sound. We spent a glorious morning heading through the Cape Cod canal, then on to Halifax, Nova Scotia. We joined a convoy in process of assembly and headed eastwards towards home. The convoy was comparatively small and made up of mostly modern ships, with the result that we made good time. We suffered fewer submarine attacks than predicted and lost only four ships, which was something of a record. By 14 June 1942 we were heading up the Manchester Ship Canal and all of us were in very good spirits.

On the following day we signed off and then immediately signed on again during the one visit to the shipping office. We were committed to another voyage to God knows where, but at the time we didn't care because we had been in contact with home and the wives were already on the way. I remember sitting for hours at the railway station waiting for Jane. It was the dreariest of nights, drizzling rain and scarcely a light to be seen anywhere. I am sure that hers was the last train to make it that night and she was the last to get off. She was totally bewildered when I caught her, she had never been to Manchester before, and come to think of it, she had never been to many places before at all. I had arranged a room at a so-called first-class Hotel, the Grosvenor, yet when we checked in I had the feeling that they thought we had just met, till they saw the baggage.

After ten long months of separation, I will not dare describe our feelings. Suffice it to say we were in a kind of seventh heaven. The two weeks she spent on board were great fun. Other officers' wives were there and almost every evening was a celebration of some kind. Every night bordered on the hilarious as the two of us were obliged to squeeze into one bunk. It was just as well we were both young and happily optimistic. We never spoke of the hazards of life at sea. We lived only for those days we were together and beyond that we lived on some indestructible hope for the future.

Our general cargo from New Zealand was discharged in less than three weeks, and we were to sail in ballast. The farewells were dry-eyed and haltingly cheerful. All of us accepted our fate and we were grateful for our time we had had to spend with our wives. For them, no doubt, the long dreary days of waiting began again. The chances of receiving a letter from abroad were remote and the chances of receiving a telegram of regret from the Admiralty were pretty high. It was the end of June 1942 when we sailed and the entire year was a very bad one for the Merchant Navy. History tells us that in the year 1942 alone 1,664 Merchant

Navy ships were sunk by enemy action, a total of 7,790,000 tons. The number of lives lost was never mentioned. In those days of war, the measure of success or failure was presented in statistics that included only materials like ships, tanks, guns and aeroplanes.

As was customary we proceeded out into the Atlantic in convoy for about ten days before breaking off and proceeding independently. An outward-bound convoy with many of the ships in ballast probably made a less attractive target for the U-boats. Undoubtedly their preference would be for a deep-laden munitions ship or a loaded tanker. We escaped with very few losses to this particular convoy. In mid-Atlantic we headed south to avoid the U-boats skulking off the coast of the United States and the eastern Caribbean.

Our route took us almost to the north coast of Brazil at the mouth of the River Amazon, before heading westwards for Port o' Spain. Within two days run from Trinidad, offshore from Paramaribo, we sighted a single lifeboat adrift on the blue tropical sea. There were no clouds in the sky and scarcely a breath of wind. Captain Watkins promptly doubled the lookout watches and had the guncrews standing by. The U-boats had the reputation of hanging about sub-surface near lifeboats, waiting for ships crazy enough to try a rescue, and the good Captain was well aware of their subterfuge. However, as we passed close by, through binoculars we could see about a dozen survivors in the boat, mostly too weak to move. The Captain ordered the helmsman to swing around to a reverse course and slowed speed. Meanwhile we dropped a lifeboat into its chocks, as they were normally kept swung out on the davits, and held fast to the hull by slip-ropes.

As we approached the drifting boat, the boat-falls were made ready to hoist, with the Bos'un dangling from the lower block. A long bowline was stretched from the foredeck, ready to hook the boat, and sailors dangled from lifelines ready to make the jump when the order was given. The *Ettrickbank* slid alongside at slow speed, the bowline was hooked on and the boat-falls clicked on to the appropriate lifeboat hooks. Being in ballast, and looking down from the ship's bridge, the boat looked small and fragile, and the poor creatures in it were a sorry sight.

We had gathered full speed again before the lifeboat was at main deck level. We gathered them in, about a dozen men, only one of whom had the strength to speak. He was badly swollen, burned almost black, and could scarcely keep his eyes open. They were the survivors of a British ship, the *Marylyn*, out of London. We had a small ship's hospital with four bunks and the gunners willingly vacated their quarters for the remainder. We made those that were still alive as comfortable as possible and headed directly for Port o' Spain. Officers and crew were strangely quiet thereafter, each with his own thoughts no doubt. I kept remembering the phrase, 'There, but for the grace of God, go I'.

The Medical Officer in Port o' Spain picked them up in a special launch and we headed round the coast to Pointe Fortune where we loaded eight thousand tons of asphalt in drums, for Australia. We wondered at the urgency for asphalt, but soon realized that Australia dreaded the possibility of invasion from the Japanese and airport extensions were needed everywhere for defence. In those days there was no source of oil in Australia and certainly no giant pitch lake like they have in Trinidad. Messy though the cargo happened to be, it was very quickly loaded and we were on our way.

The Panama Canal transit was a welcome relief from the constant threat of being blown to pieces, although we did manage a little humour in the new situation. We debated about how many torpedoes would be needed to sink us and how frustrated the U-boat commander would be to see his target speed on by with scarcely a tremor. We were all convinced that the drums of asphalt would act like a sponge on the explosion and would tend to keep the ship afloat more or less for ever. As it turned out our theories were never tested. There was never a shot fired in anger during the entire three-week run to Sydney, New South Wales.

After several days in Sydney we took the remaining cargo to Melbourne. In the west coast ports of Australia we loaded general cargo for Egypt. By now the war in the Pacific had reached its deadliest peak, but it did appear that the Japanese supply lines were stretched to the limit. Certainly the Australians breathed a little easier, and their troops in support of the Americans were achieving some small successes. The news for us did not change much. It was acknowledged that there were at least five U-boats operating off Cape Town and at least nine off the coast of Brazil. There were also vague reports of two Japanese armed merchant raiders operating in the Indian Ocean.

Whilst on our way back to the Suez Canal we listened to radio reports wherein one Japanese raider was sunk and another damaged in an engagement with the Royal Indian Navy, and this not too far behind us. Our worst scare was in the canal itself where we barely escaped a serious collision with a speeding warship. Christmas 1942 was approaching as we left Egypt again bound for the Far East. This time we were in good spirits. Montgomery had thoroughly defeated the Africa Corps at El Alamein, and Rommel's forces were in total retreat. The previously victorious German Armies on their eastern front were now bogged down at Stalingrad. In November the great North African landings had been successful at Casablanca, Oran and Algiers. Without doubt the tide of war had turned.

During these better times we were less inclined to be depressed about our own appalling losses at sea. Nothing much had change for us, but somehow we managed to be a lot more optimistic. Early February 1943 in Calcutta was not all that bad. Bearing in mind the fall of Burma to the Japanese, and their armies being close to the borders of India on our previous visit, by now the dangers appeared much less severe. The Battle of Midway, a decisive defeat of the Japanese Navy, had done much for everyone's morale.

They were playing cricket on the Maidan, the elegant green lawns of Calcutta where the big hotels were located. The ballroom at the Continental was crowded every evening. Excellent food and wine was served by turbanned waiters in long white coats and red sashes. There was a peculiar feeling amongst us: it was as though we had come upon an elegant oasis in the midst of a world gone mad. After a few days we felt more civilized again and certainly more sympathetic. We realized that the army officers we rubbed shoulders with in the hotels had come on leave from the disastrous Burma campaign, a leave they had earned the hard way.

Even so, peace or war, our world trade had to be supported. South America depended upon us for thousands of tons of exports from India. We stopped at Madras and Vizagapattam to top up, and headed out to sea again. As always the Indian Ocean was the happy hunting ground of several raiders and the usual pack of submarines kept their silent vigil in the waters off the Cape of Good Hope. Their supply ships were reported from time to time in African ports.

We were routed so far south of the Cape that we were getting close to the icebergs in Antarctica. April should have been reasonably good weather, even as far south as we were, but the Gods smiled upon us through heavy clouds and winter fog. We very rarely saw the horizon and we navigated mostly by dead reckoning. On some odd occasions, a peek at the stars at dawn was enough to provide us with an approximate position and a compass correction. By early May we had sighted the southern tip of South America and from here the real nightmare began. Our lookouts had developed the jitters from the news reports they had heard and to them every white-topped wave disclosed an enemy periscope. Fortunately the sightings, the alarms and the gunnery stations all fizzled out. What submarines may have been there must have been thoroughly confused by our zig-zag courses. It was extremely difficult to keep track of our position with so many alterations of course and with so few opportunities to determine our location. I remember seeing Bahia quite clearly one day through binoculars and we had absolutely no business being there. Finally we made it to the entrance to the River Plate, deep-laden with cargo, but down to the last ton of fuel.

Buenos Aires was a city of lights. There were no shortages of the good things in life there. Obviously many South Americans were becoming rich because of the war and many of them flaunted it. The English-speaking community there, and it was a large one, was extremely hospitable, and many of the families went out of their way to be kind to us. The railway and hospitals were run by Scottish people, as far as I could gather, many of them claimed to have been there for generations and they even claimed to have built the railway. Several of the big businesses were run by Britishers who wielded a great deal of influence on our behalf.

We caught up with all the war news, like General Montgomery's North African victories and his advance into Tripoli. We read about Rommel's return to Germany to make his peace with Hitler and finally, at the end of April 1943, the defeat of the German and Italian Armies in Tunisia and their wholesale surrender on 13 May. These victories, coupled to the breaking of the siege of Leningrad in January and the German disaster at Stalingrad in the early spring, made this a banner year for us. There was much to celebrate and plenty of places to celebrate in Buenos Aires. Our crew members were in constant trouble with the police, but I must admit, they were all returned in good shape and without great penalty.

Cargo discharge kept us fully occupied and immediately thereafter we had to prepare to load for the United Kingdom. We were advised that we should depart Buenos Aires about two thirds loaded and we were to top up in Montevideo, Uruguay. The prospect of being homeward-bound again enlivened all of us. There were great plans for gifts for the families, how best to acquire them and how best to store them. Nylons, underwear, chocolates, fruits, there was a long list of desirable items, but the trip across the equator in the stinking heat of the West African coast could ruin most of the items on the list. I bought inlaid nests of tables, sewing boxes, materials, nylons, chocolates, underwear etc. In those days, there was a 'Harrods' shop in Buenos Aires which could supply almost anything the heart could desire.

The junior engineers produced loads of empty four-gallon kerosine drums and these were carefully steam-cleaned. Thereafter the goodies were packed, the drums soldered airtight and were placed in the deep-freeze. The days in Montevideo were painfully slow in passing and when we departed we were ready to cheer. We anchored at the mouth of the River Plate in international waters, then took off in the dead of night. By daylight we were well over a hundred miles off-shore and in deep water. Our race against time and the ever-present enemy began again. We sighted several ships inward-bound but we altered course to give them a wide berth.

The voyage to Freetown should have taken less than ten days, but the route dictated to us kept us clear of Brazil and east of Ascension Island. Whether it was the route or the vigilance we maintained, we made it to Freetown, Sierra Leone, where we were roasted for about ten days waiting for a convoy. Our impatience to get home only aggravated the situation. Finally, almost at the end of out tether, the convoy was assembled and we were off on our circuitous route, ending up in mid-Atlantic before heading east for Loch Ewe on the west coast of Scotland. We were fortunate to lose only a couple of ships and doubly fortunate insofar as the ships on either side of us were the ones to go. One, a fully-laden tanker, went up in flames and drifted through the convoy like Dante's inferno. Only minutes later another loaded cargo vessel, immediately alongside us, took two torpedoes and dropped slowly astern.

Darkness fell, and we breathed a sigh of relief, but with mixed emotions. One could never quite forget seeing those ships in their death throes, wondering how long they would take to sink and were there any survivors? It was mid-summer, their chances were reasonably good, but we never did know their fate. There were no published statistics with ships' names and crew identification, only the number of ships and the accumulated tonnage. Homeward-bound, after how long? There would be wives and families waiting in vain. Who might be next? The next day, a lone Sunderland flying boat appeared on the horizon and provided a much-needed morale boast.

We were constantly on the alert for long-range enemy aircraft, but on this occasion we were much more fortunate. Two ships in the convoy were fitted with fighter aircraft on the foredeck, perched upon a steam catapult. With enemy aircraft sighted these planes were launched and on termination of the sortie the pilot ditched and hoped to be picked up by a trailing escort. I never envied them the job. However it was said that they did keep the German long-range planes at bay. Soon we were under the umbrella of Coastal Command and finally within sight of the Irish coast, then Scotland. Entering Loch Ewe in that month of July was like entering the Garden of Eden. The surrounding hills were alive with their summer colour and the sun shone out of a cloudless sky. Then some absolutely beautiful Wrens arrived with bags of mail, the first news in almost a year.

Again, days waiting for convoy assembly, then the slow majestic pace of the slowest ship. Cape Wrath was shrouded in fog and our passage through the Pentland Firth was made in drenching rain. Our progress down through the North Sea, zig-zagging to confuse the submarines and with doubled lookouts scanning the sea surface for floating mines was painfully slow. As action stations were frequent we slept in our clothes and mostly on station. Under the protection of the Coastal Command we made it to the Thames without losing a single ship.

We were hustled into the Port of London and the welcome mat was out for us at the 'George'. During every hour of daylight the stevedores laboured to off-load. We were home at last, the wives were arriving and all was well with the world. At night the bombers came, but we scarcely noticed, they were someone else's problem. We were not allowed to use the ship's armament in port but the noise of the big anti-aircraft guns was music to our ears. The saloon was a constant hub of excitement and good cheer. The women were happy and the married men were ecstatic. Captain Watkins, a bachelor, smiled benignly upon us all. He was never happier than when he could share his unending supply of liquor with visitors. Consequently there was a constant stream of people to his suite, after all the really good stuff was in very short supply.

Jane was bubbling with excitement as it was her first visit to London and the first time in years she had seen such mounds of gifts and goodies. Like the other girls she flaunted her nylons like they were some kind of uniform. She had saved her ration of clothing coupons, done her own dressmaking and looked extremely elegant in the midst of the rush and bustle of shipboard life. On our nights off she would skip down the gangway in high heels, as though she had been a seafarer all of her life. On one particular night in the 'George', amongst lots of friends, and slightly inebriated, she was boasting about all the nylons, the underwear and the stuff her devoted husband had brought her from Buenos Aires. She almost died with embarrassment when the friends identified themselves as customs officers. She got such a shock she burst into tears but the tears subsided when she was assured, in the midst of great hilarity, that they were off-duty.

When we got back aboard that night she had a confession to make. Whilst I was gone, she had invested in a fur coat, but had not had the courage to wear it. It became one of the ship's jokes the following day and she had to put up with a great deal of ribbing about it. By 22 August 1943 we were advised of the arrival of relief officers. Miss Jane departed for home in Edinburgh, but happy in the knowledge that I would follow in two or three days. We both knew that I had accumulated enough sea-time to qualify for three months' college leave to acquire my deep-sea master's papers. She was waiting for me on the platform at Waverley Station in Edinburgh and despite the warm summer evening she wore the fur coat. To me, she was the most beautiful sight in the entire city.

Jane had already arranged a furnished house for us in Plewlands Terrace, Morningside, a very desirable district in Edinburgh. It was a two-storey house and stood in its own grounds, surrounded by a high wall. Much too big for us but we did not have a care in the world. It certainly was a long tram ride to the Nautical College, but I didn't mind that a bit. It gave me time to catch up in Naval Architecture, Meteorology, Knowledge of Principles, or any one of the many subjects we were compelled to study. However, I was well prepared for I had spent hours on end during monotonous sea voyages preparing for this. I had no intention of failing.

We quickly forgot all about the war. Perhaps we were being selfish, but after all there was little we could do to influence either the conduct or the outcome of the war. It would be time enough to remember after Christmas. We were within walking distance of Slateford where Jane's family lived and we were able to do quite a bit of entertaining. The menus were a bit skimpy, and even when we went out we were limited to dried egg or beans on toast. Nevertheless, having connections in the countryside was of considerable help. From Linlithgow and the surrounding farms we could always get a few fresh eggs and the occasional chicken. With my good friend James Edgar, by now General Manager of Sanderson's Vat 69, we were never short of a bottle.

The autumn weather was good to us and we spent fabulous evenings on the Braids Hills. The snow was late that year and as the nights drew in, as they say in Scotland, we had comfortably warm bedrooms upstairs. It may have been hard work at college, but it was a never-ending honeymoon at Plewlands Terrace. Christmas and New Year came and went, we hosted several great parties with friends and relatives from out of town and our Hogmanay party had a few morning surprises. In one bedroom, four girls were sound asleep in a large bed with a young man, a cousin of Jane's from Duns, stretched across their feet and snoring like a walrus. He was never allowed to forget his little indiscretion. Every available bed was occupied and I am not really sure I even knew some of the occupants. I do know that the bar was totally dry and that we had assuredly toasted the coming of the New Year.

Nineteen forty-four was, for us, the beginning of victory. The German war machine was worn a bit thin and we all waited with bated breath for the invasion of Europe. On 10 January 1944 I was twenty-six years old, and on that day I had the feeling that Jane's mother was mightily concerned. With a war raging on it was not considered prudent for young wives to be left pregnant. As it turned out her concerns were justified. Before I left for sea again Jane was ready to admit that she was pregnant. We were both very happy at the prospect of a first-born, but somehow or other it raised the level of concern. In early February I was qualified for command, and it was decision time again.

CERTIFICATE OF COMPETENCY

MASTER

AS

OF A FOREIGN-GOING STEAMSHIP

No. 61556.

To *Ian Alexander Miller.*

WHEREAS you have been found duly qualified to fulfil the duties of Master of a Foreign-going Steamship in the Merchant Service, the Minister of Transport, in exercise of his powers under the Merchant Shipping Acts and of all other powers enabling him in that behalf, hereby grants you this Certificate of Competency.

SIGNED BY AUTHORITY OF THE MINISTER OF TRANSPORT and dated this ....2nd........ day

of ....September........ 19 42.

Countersigned

Registrar General

A Deputy Secretary
of the Ministry of
Transport.

REGISTERED AT THE OFFICE OF THE REGISTRAR GENERAL OF SHIPPING AND SEAMEN.

THIS MASTER'S CERTIFICATE IS IN THE FORM OF A BOOK FOR EASE OF CARE AND CARRIAGE. The Exams were passed in February 1944, but due to the restrictions of war only a yellow chit was issued. It took till 1949 for the Registrar to track us down.

CHAPTER XII

SS HORSA & *SS* MAJORCA

Instead of reporting back to the Bank Line in London, I decided to stay closer to home. I joined a shipping company in Leith. I was well aware of two of their ships, the *Horsa* and the *Henquist,* which were referred to locally as the bacon and egg boats. They carried refrigerated cargoes and passengers from Copenhagen, Denmark, to Leith before the war. Danish butter, eggs, cheese, bacon and other delicacies were delivered at high speed across the North Sea, however they were now engaged in supplying the American troops in Iceland. For some peculiar reason, best known to our fearless leaders, massive quantities of army stores were shipped out of New York to Scotland, then transhipped to Iceland. The ships were fast and they ran independently out of Leith, round the North of Scotland, then westwards into the North Atlantic past the Faeroe Islands and on to Reykjavik.

We discharged there great quantities of frozen beef, crates of Coke, hundreds of tons of potatoes and all kinds of good stuff that the folks at home could not get. It was treated like gold at both ends and with a high level of security. The return voyage was much more interesting to me. We headed around the north coast of Iceland in totally uncharted waters, to load frozen fish in Akureyri. We picked up several thousand tons of the stuff in the refrigerated cargo space. The fish was packed in fifty-six pound cartons and in each carton there were eight separate seven-pound slabs, each with a different kind of fish, all beautifully filleted, e.g. cod, sole, haddock, flounder, plaice etc. As officers, we were each presented with a case.

Back in Edinburgh, in Slateford where Jane lived with her parents again, the neighbours waited for my return with great anticipation. After all, no one had domestic fridges in those days. The fish had to be kept in the sink, all fifty-six pounds of it, so without question it was shared with the neighbours, every one had a feast for a couple of days and I was very popular. With Jane now visibly pregnant, I brought back canned fruit, chocolate and ovaltine, and she became quite chubby and the envy of the neighbourhood, still a working girl by order of His Majesty's Government.

MINISTRY OF WAR TRANSPORT.

LIBERATION OF EUROPE

PAY SHEET

ame .... MILLER
(BLOCK LETTERS)
tian Name) Ian Alexander
A No. R204920.   Rank or Rating 1st Mate
ficate of Competency: Grade .... Number 51439
ENDANT Full Name Jean Miller
Address 13 Atholian Rd. Edinburgh
Relationship Wife   Post Office Slateford, E'burgh

T OF KIN Name
(If different from above)

Address and Relationship

rs' Pension Fund Membership No. Bank Line Provident
(If in private fund, state company)

S. Membership No. 1

oved Society and No. 1
(including particulars of Court, Lodge, etc., where applicable)

o paid for but deferred ...7... days. Income Tax Code M

Local Office & Serial No. ...7...
:02] 49011/4211 800 pads 1/44 M&C Ltd. 51/1

Pay as below commences on 7. 5. 1944

		£	s.	d.
Basic wages per week	...	6	12	5
War Risk Money per week	...	2	6	8
Consolidated Rate per week	...	1	10	—
Total earnings per week		10	9	1

of which :—		£	s.	d.
Allocated to dependant per week	...	6	—	1
Income tax deduction per week	...	1	16	1
Officers' Pension Fund per week	...		4	10
N.U.S. contribution per week	...			
Health & Pensions Insurance per week	...		11	
Unemployment Insurance per week	...			
Total deduction per week	...	8	10	—
NET WAGES per week	...	2	8	3

equals £ : 6 s. 11 d. per day

Signature of Seaman Ian Miller
Signature of Superintendent Eleanor Cecil Taylor

DATE STAMP

LIBERATION OF EUROPE:- This Pay-Sheet was issued by the Department of Transport to those of us who volunteered for the invasion fleet. In 1945 the exchange rate was more than four dollars to the pound Sterling – the salary was therefore approximately $250 US per month.

115

The voyages were considered to be high risk, although at least they were of short duration, but like all good things the Iceland cruises came to rather an abrupt end. A few months earlier, like most other Merchant Navy officers, I had volunteered for the invasion force.

On 6 May 1944, I was transferred from the *Horsa* to the *Majorca* as Chief Officer. She was fully laden with munitions in Bristol, England. We knew immediately why, but of course nobody really knew when it would really happen. We were all well prepared and distributed around different ports in the south of England. We went out on a few exercises and obviously there were hundreds of ships laden with troops and military supplies. We finished up in Penarth, in south Wales, to await zero hour. I don't remember much about it as I was hospitalized with a health problem the good medical officers could not understand.

When I finally woke up I was surrounded by long faces, I was shipped home and the prognosis was poor. Apparently I had collapsed a couple of times whilst on duty and no one could figure out what was wrong. After grave discussions it was decided that I had some severe infection in the muscles of the heart, they provided an unpronounceable scientific name for it and it was hinted that it might be life-threatening.

When I reached Edinburgh, I made an appointment with Doctor Ian Farquharson, a renowned heart specialist. After a lengthy period of probing, testing and measuring, he finally called me in for a personal interview. In a very few terse sentences he voiced his opinion, 'Absolutely no sign of any organic problem of any kind. A very peculiar, but certainly not life-threatening, functional problem.' I breathed a long sigh of relief but was so overwhelmed I did not ask him a single question. As I was leaving he handed me a letter. In the event of any subsequent medical examiner appearing alarmed when he sounded my heart, I was to present this letter. I needed it eight years later.

I was released from further Merchant Navy service on 7 July 1944 and was therefore a free man. The fact that we were about to have a family and that we had a life ahead of us took a little time to sink in. We found, through friends, a very nice apartment at Sighthill, a new development on the west side of the city and meanwhile I had to find a job. One of the instructors at the Nautical College advised me to check with British Overseas Airways Corporation who were badly in need of navigators for a fleet of flying boats they hoped to put into service. I was invited to visit them at their headquarters in Bristol, England, and whilst I was there Jane gave birth to a daughter, Lynn Anne.

She was in a private nursing home in Chester Street in Edinburgh, where everything was spic and span and there were excellent doctors in attendance.

But according to Miss Jane she may as well have given birth in a tent. There were no drugs of any kind available and she had a prolonged and difficult labour. I was never forgiven for not being there. Nevertheless, Miss Lynn Anne was the most beautiful, brown-eyed baby I had ever seen. Within weeks she had the most gorgeous head of beautiful blond curls and she was the most admired child in all of Edinburgh.

However BOAC plans were temporarily on hold. My uncle, the Managing Director of Scottish Oils, used his influence to place me with the British Tanker Company in their London office. I reported thereto but discovered that they had moved out of their palatial headquarters in the City of London in favour of safer quarters near Shepperton-on-Thames. I found myself with the job of trying to straighten out the lighterage accounts for one of their vessels in Abadan. She was employed in the loading of oil cargoes in Abadan to top up the larger tankers leaving their berths to pass through dredged channels, not necessarily fully-laden. About twenty miles to seaward, beyond the outer bar, this vessel, the *British Soldier*, tied up alongside the larger tanker to bring her down to the allowable plimsoll marks. It was an absolutely boring mess. I lasted less than six months before I decided to go home.

Whilst there, it was not at all unpleasant. I lived in digs, as the English called it, with a little plump, matronly lady, a butcher's widow. It was a very large house with hordes of rooms. There were several spinster ladies of varying ages in residence and each weekend the ladies really let their hair down. Mrs Blackwell, the landlady, had lots of influence in the ration book business and she managed to get enormous roasts of beef that no one else could get. On Sunday mornings she put the roast into an enormous pan in a coal-fired oven. Meanwhile I peeled the potatoes and cleaned the vegetables. Then off we all went to the local pub for a couple of pints. On our return the roast was bubbling away like crazy and she made up some mixture she called Yorkshire pudding. The roast was removed and this concoction was poured into the boiling gravy. Within minutes it rose and took on a beautiful golden colour and later it browned on the top. We fed like fighting cocks on roast beef, Yorkshire pudding, roast potatoes etc., followed by apple pies, baked by the other ladies in competition one with the other. I was talked into being the judge. It was never easy.

One afternoon, just as we finished digesting the apple pie, we could hear the putt-putt of a flying bomb. I thought there might be something to see when the drone was silenced. I had just put my hand on the handle of the back door when the explosion shook the house. The back door was blown off its hinges and it smacked me squarely in the face. I walked around for days with two beautiful black eyes and was the butt of everybody's jokes. 'Fallen out with all the gorgeous girls, huh?' they would ask. I had no choice but grin and bear it.

Air raids, bombs and V2s were less frequent now; the Germans were running out of aeroplanes and concentrating only on rockets. We read about them each day and sometimes we heard the explosions, then the fire engines, but somehow we managed to ignore it all. Christmas and New Year was a miserable time and Jane was getting restless. I could not see a future for us there, and I simply decided to quit and go home. It was spring and I planted a garden full of vegetables. Miss Lynn, now about eight months old, was a picture in her fancy English perambulator. This was my first experience with baby-sitting and I pushed her around for miles, all the way over to Corstorphine and back. But there were bills to be paid and we badly needed a plan for the rest of our lives.

After considerable discussion I persuaded Jane that our best hope for a worthwhile future was to go abroad. The Crown Agents for the Colonies in London was the best opportunity for merchantmen and I paid them a visit. They accepted my application but they could not promise a posting pending the cessation of hostilities in Europe. At least I felt that I might begin a new career at the end of the war and all I needed now was a job to keep me going. I found such a job with Younger's Brewery. The salary was meagre but I got to drink their beer every day to wash down a very good free lunch.

To my great relief the Allies were progressing towards victory in Europe and morale was now high. The June 1944 landings in France had been successful and by August Paris was once again a free city. In January 1945 the Germans suffered another defeat in the Ardennes and by March the Allies were preparing to cross the Rhine. In April 1945 Italy was close to surrender and the Russians were closing in on Berlin. Full German surrender came on 27 May 1945 and both Hitler and Mussolini were dead. It was estimated that more than thirty million people died as a consequence of their desire to rule the world.

There is no such thing as a happy ending to a war. There were millions of people in Europe, displaced and living amongst the ruins, and hundreds of thousands of others were wandering from place to place seeking food and shelter. But the politicians kept talking about this war to end all wars and pointed to the dawn of a new beginning. Without doubt it behove each of us to seek out his own fortune. Waiting for the politicians to provide it could take till the end of time. By mid-May 1945 I was back in London, awaiting processing for an appointment in Iraq.

PART III

CHAPTER XIII

THE CROWN AGENTS FOR THE COLONIES

The Crown Agents for the Colonies had, and still have, a long history of service to the British Government, to the Governments of the Colonies, and to a variety of protectorates in odd corners of the globe. From the golden days of the British Empire, they had been the purchasing agents and suppliers of British goods and services to the colonies. In most cases, many civilian, professional personnel were recruited and posted to those Governments in support of the various facilities supplied. In the case of protectorates, and some foreign governments, the Crown Agents performed the same services, supplying ships, tugboats, dredgers, hydrographic ships, light-tenders and all things mechanical like cranes, barges etc., with the people to operate and maintain them, under direct contract to the Crown Agents.

The colonies, e.g. Canada, Australia, New Zealand, South, West and East Africa, India, Ceylon etc., and the protectorates like Trinidad and Tobago, Falkland Islands, the Fiji Islands and several Arab states like Palestine, Transjordan, Iraq, Bahrain, Kuwait, Oman, Trucial Oman, and Abu Dubai etc., were all clients of the Crown Agents at 4 Millbank, London, England. Professional personnel were under direct contract with the Crown Agents and seconded to the colonial or foreign government as necessary.

All personnel under such contracts were, by Order in Council of the British Government in 1939, compelled to remain at their posts until such order was rescinded. This order was not rescinded until October 1946. This was pointed out to me in London when I was accepted and seconded to the Government of Iraq. Indeed, this was very significant insofar as it would create a general exodus of personnel due for retirement during those years 1939 to 1946, during which they had no option but to stay on. It was obvious that such an exodus in 1946 would create good opportunities for quick promotion.

With the war in Europe over, I was on my way. In early July, appropriately documented, I joined the *Bardistan* in Glasgow, bound for Port Said and then to the Near East. In peace we sailed through the Mediterranean under sunshine and blue skies. Jane and I were parted once more but there was a firm promise that she would be permitted to join me as soon as accommodation became available. The *Bardistan* was a freighter of some 7,000 tons employed in the trade to the Persian Gulf. She carried only six passengers, but with the off-duty officers we were able to organize games of bridge and some sports on deck. Two of the passengers were ladies, travelling to the Middle East, to join husbands in Crown Agent postings.

During the ten-day voyage I spent time in the ship's library, studying the entire middle eastern area. Within a very short time, I found myself engrossed in the geography, the biblical history and of course the turbulent history of the last hundred years. The increasing importance of the Middle East stemmed from the voracious appetite of the British to establish and sustain an Empire that stretched around the world. As it turned out I was privileged to witness the decline of the this great Empire, but with a certain amount of pride and gratitude to providence, I believe that the British withdrew with dignity.

The seventeenth and eighteenth centuries were the years when Britain established her far-flung Empire, supported by great sailing ships following in the wake of the great navigators like Captain Cook. However, in 1869, the completion of the Suez Canal by Ferdinand de Lesseps, coupled with the introduction of the steamship, created an entirely new situation that required massive investment and some truly entrepreneurial effort. Expanded trade meant an urgent need for fuel and fuelling stations and in those days this meant coal, of which Britain had a plentiful supply. Very quickly, and taking advantage of existing strategic possessions, the British rose to the occasion thus opening steamship routes to the Persian Gulf and to India.

The shift from wind power to coal power was accomplished quickly and coaling stations were established at Gibraltar, Cyprus, Port Said and at Aden, a protectorate in South Yemen. With this accomplished the British were then able to dominate all trade to middle and far eastern countries. The massive four-masted barques and the great tea-clippers continued to compete for many years, but the Industrial Revolution doomed them to failure. The last major four-masted barque, the old *Olivebank*, renamed the *Hercagon Cecilie*, and loaded with grain from Australia, was wrecked on the coast of Wales in the early 1930s just as I went off to sea.

However oil was rapidly becoming a more useful fuel and vessels were being built both faster and larger. The need for modern navigational aids, like lighthouses and radio beacons, gave rise to the need for international agreements, under British leadership. It was then that truly large numbers of professionals were recruited by the Crown Agents for service in the growth and maintenance of foreign ports and facilities, to permit the shipment of oil and encourage the expansion of trade.

In Scotland, back in the 1850s, oil was extracted from shale, which was mined in twenty-six different locations throughout the area where I lived as a child. There were eleven small refineries and together they made up Scottish Oils Limited. My uncle, Robert Crichton, was Managing Director there until well into the 1950s. Earlier, in 1901, an associated corporation, D'Arcy Exploration Company, was established and they made the first major discovery of oil in the Middle East, in southern Persia, now Iran, in the year 1908. This was developed into the largest oil port and the largest refinery in the world in 1914.

Prior to the First World War of 1914-18, at the time of the waning of the Ottoman Empire, the British, the French and the Russians increased their influence. In 1907 the British agreed to divide Persia, keeping the southern half and leaving the northern half to the Russians. By 1914 the British occupied Egypt, Aden, Cyprus, Gibraltar and Malta.

At war's end in 1918, the British and French divided the middle eastern spoils. The French seemed to be happy with Syria and Lebanon, while the British took Transjordan, Iraq, Kuwait, Bahrain and the Sheikdoms of Trucial Oman. They paid King Ibn Saud of Saudi Arabia, the sum of £25,000 a year not to side with the Turks. In 1938 the Americans found oil in Saudi Arabia, to their everlasting advantage. The old King Ibn Saud died in 1952.

However, development slowed in the post-First World War period and did not recover much until the early thirties. Nevertheless, oil was discovered by the British in Iraq in 1934 and the Persian fields expanded enormously. By 1936 the oil companies had discovered that Kuwait literally floated on oil and smaller fields were found in Bahrain. But there were problems throughout these areas, in particular in Persia. In 1921 an army officer, Reza Kahn, took control of Persia, and added Pavlevi to his name in order to show a connection to an ancient dynasty. In his own self-interest he cooperated with the British to a limited degree.

But in 1941 the British found it necessary to occupy Persia, Reza conveniently abdicated and left his son, Mohammed Reza, to reign in his stead. But the restlessness within Persia persisted. Like all occupied nations they nurtured an intense desire to overthrow their masters. It was in 1951 before they saw an opportunity to rebel, which of course I did not know whilst I browsed in the Bardistan library.

My special interest was Iraq, a country of some 170,000 square miles and 15 million people. In 1914 the British Army occupied Basrah, Baghdad, Mosul and Kirkuq, the major cities in Iraq. They crowned a twenty-nine year old Arabian prince, and he was called King Faisil I. The entire country was granted independence in 1932. The King died in 1933 and his son Ghazi succeeded him.

Voyages Into Eternity

Unfortunately young King Ghazi was killed in an automobile accident in 1939, and he left a beautiful, widowed Queen Alia and her infant son, King Faisil II, to reign in his stead. Crown Prince Abdul Ilah took over as Regent, pending young Faisil's coming of age. The seat of government was in Baghdad and it was clear from the written descriptions that Baghdad was a modern city.

Whilst studying the modern history of Mesopotamia and examining charts I felt compelled to look back and remember our old church bibles. The final pages always contained maps of Middle East areas as they were believed to be in biblical times. Even from those it was clear that the two major rivers in Iraq, the Tigris and the Euphrates, had their sources in the mountain ranges of eastern Turkey and flowed through Syria before entering Iraq.

In my grandfather's bible there is a map of the ancient world. This is a John Brown bible, published in Glasgow, Scotland, in the year 1837. The map is truly remarkable insofar as general perspective is concerned. In terms of distances there may be measurable discrepancies and many of the names, and certainly all of the boundaries, have been changed through the years. According to this map the city of Babel, or Babylon, was located at the junction of the Tigris and Euphrates rivers, a few miles inland from Basrah. Nasiriyah is on the banks of the Euphrates, a short distance further north. The Garden of Eden is also clearly marked at the point where the Euphrates reaches the Persian Gulf. Ninevah, located on the banks of the River Tigris near the modern city of Mosul, was in the far northern reaches of Iraq, in Kurdish territory.

By the time the good ship *Bardistan* arrived at Port Said I was looking forward to my posting. The need for haste dictated that I disembark at Port Said and travel overland to Baghdad, a unique experience for me. I travelled by car from Port Said to Al Quantara, a railway station where the railway from Cairo to Haifa crossed the Suez Canal on a massive swing-bridge, and the train I boarded in the early evening travelled eastward across the Sinai Desert by night to avoid the appalling heat. It was sometime in the early afternoon of the following day when we arrived in Haifa. There were serious troubles in Palestine at this time and trains certainly did not move at full speed. After an overnight stay I learned from the British Consul all about the proposed route to Baghdad.

It seems that a transportation company had been started by two New Zealanders who stayed on after the 1914-18 war. They called their company Nairn Transport, and for some twenty-five years or so they had been quite successful. I was taken by car from Haifa to Jerusalem and there I joined a bus with other passengers for Damascus, Syria. After an overnight stay in Damascus I took another bus to Al Rutba, where we boarded the big desert transport that would take us to Baghdad, an overnight run of some 300 miles. The desert transport was a most impressive vehicle, it was the largest I had ever seen and must have had about sixteen wheels supporting a heavy steel frame, with an air-conditioned chassis, in which there were aeroplane-type seats and a chemical toilet. The driver's cab was a separate unit and perched upon its top there was a powerful searchlight. It turned out that the route was well marked with white-painted stone cairns every few miles and these were easily picked out by the searchlight.

In addition to this great vehicle there was a regular caravan of ancient vehicles of all types hauling freight and carrying passengers, trailing behind us in no particular order. Apparently it was very necessary that the proper route be followed very carefully as failure to do so could result in the vehicles sinking to the hubs in the fine sand. During the night, and at high speed, a couple of tyres blew out with a real bang, but the driver kept on going. It was not considered advisable to stop. I did not envy the passengers on the decrepit vehicles behind us: presumably if they fell by the wayside they had to wait to be picked up by the next transport following along in a couple of days. I wondered how they could possibly survive the terrible desert heat. I was told that we were lucky, this was only July and the real searing heat did not start until August and September.

At dawn we arrived at Al Ramidah, not too far from the River Euphrates and from there there was a rough tarmac road to Baghdad. I was relieved to check in at the Semiramis Hotel overlooking the River Tigris in the centre of the city of Baghdad. I finally had an opportunity to wash the sand out of my hair. The trip from Baghdad to Basrah, in southern Iraq, was accomplished in the comparative luxury of an air-conditioned train, my first experience of such luxury. I was surprised to find out how well everything worked. Hotel elevators, cabs, trains, telephones, these things really did properly function. I learned later that all things technical were handled by Syrians. The Arabs seemed to be content to watch the dates grow, and at that point in time I had the impression that everyone was happy with his lot. The Syrians dreamed of vacations amongst the cedars of Lebanon and the Arabs were happy to dream of a pilgrimage to Mecca.

The city of Basrah, something of a disaster area even in those days, was located in the desert, quite a way from the river. A more pleasant town, Ashar, was located on the river. The headquarters of Basrah Port Directorate, of which I was now a member, was about five miles further upriver from Ashar, at Marqil. This was a truly pleasant spot, close to the broad river, with clean, efficient wharves and dominated by a massive headquarters building which was surrounded by great eucalyptus trees; tree-lined avenues led away from it to modern bungalows occupied by the senior port officials. In the centre of what might be called a European compound there was a very large and very imposing Marine Club.

The club, open to all Directorate employees, and to selected guests amongst the European community in Ashar, was a sight for sore eyes. Swimming pools, tennis courts, indoor cinema, outdoor cinema, restaurant, bars, billiard rooms etc. were maintained, and service was provided, by white-coated waiters, mostly from India. A short cab ride away there was an international airport and a very large, modern hotel. At that time, in the early days of the Super-Constellation aircraft, Basrah was rapidly becoming the hub of the Middle East. All the major airlines were represented there, Pan-Am, Trans-World, British Overseas Airways, Swissair, Air France, KLM etc., and all with support staff in residence.

CHAPTER XIV

THE PERSIAN GULF SERVICE

By the time I reported to headquarters, I must confess I was very impressed and absolutely convinced that Jane might enjoy life here. I was very happy with the terms of my contract, with my salary, the earned vacations and impressed by the potential for promotion. I thought everything in the garden was lovely until I learned the whole story, which was not entirely a disaster, but at least I was brought down to earth. It was clear that one had to start at the bottom and work back upriver to Marqil. The significance of the Order in Council, likely to come within a year, was finally brought home to me.

The broad river I could see flowing past the lush, green lawns at the Port Director's beautiful residence was referred to as the Shatt-al-Arab, the junction of the Rivers Tigris and Euphrates, and about twenty miles to seaward, additionally joined by the River Karun flowing from Persia. I was invited there to lunch and drinks and a jolly good old British sermon. The Port Director, Colonel Johnston OBE, was a political appointee and concerned himself primarily with public relations and all dealings with the Government and embassies in Baghdad. I was rather glad to get out from under, and get back to headquarters for a more down-to-earth briefing.

From Basrah to the outer bar, where the pilot vessel was stationed, was a distance of 126 miles. Despite the fact that a few miles downstream from Basrah the east bank of the river became Persian territory, the absolute control of the entire river rested with the Government of Iraq. Some historical agreement dictated that all the way up to the high water mark was Iraqi territory, much to the chagrin of the Persians. There were three ports on the Persian side, Khorammshar, Abadan, and Khosrowabad, and at this point in my indoctrination I was told that Persia was to be referred to henceforward by its new name, Iran. On the Iraqi side of the river there was Basrah, Ashar and near the mouth of the river, Fao, a large engineering depot, later to become another oil port. This combination of ports accounted for the handling of more than 600 ship movements in each calendar month, making it one of the busiest shipping areas in the entire world at that time.

There were 126 miles of pilotage involved, and more than 40 miles of dredged channels, thus creating the need for five of the largest drag-suction dredgers in the world, a complete hydrographic service and appropriate port facilities. In support of these operations, a pilot vessel was stationed outside the outer bar and a control vessel immediately inside the inner bar. The dredgers worked around the clock and the hydrographic vessels produced the necessary channel charts. These were supported by a fleet of tugboats and launches all of which were maintained by the engineering depot at Fao. In addition, the Port Directorate handled all of the harbour masters at the individual ports and supported an ocean-going light-tender to service the navigational aids throughout the Gulf. Finally, there was a beautiful 4,000-ton yacht tied up at the airport jetty, at the disposal of the Royal Family.

A period of learning was required for all new staff and this meant service in the dredgers operating out of Fao at the very mouth of the Shatt-al-Arab. At that time Fao was accessible only by boat; a road was planned for the near future. Meanwhile for those hardy souls who loved the desert, one could make the run at high speed over the fine sand. Too bad if you got stuck. Captain Ainsley, the Port Captain at Marqil, was very jolly about the whole affair and he and I spent an evening imbibing at the port club. When he escorted me to the launch heading for Fao the next day he reminded me again that I could look forward to being upriver in eighteen months.

The journey downriver was restricted to half speed on the launch due to the possibility that the wake created might damage the bunds which protected the date palms. All the way down, almost to the very mouth of the river, a supply of fresh water was maintained because of the massive outflow. The palms were fed from the river by a series of shallow channels dug by hand. It was fascinating to watch the ships, the various Arab villages and an occasional town go by. Abadan, by now a massive oil refinery, and a busy oil port, was a small city by itself. In the reach, a long stretch of water below the port, about a dozen large tankers lay at anchor awaiting a berth to help transport some 40 million tons of oil per annum worldwide.

The launch itself was a model of comfort. A barefoot crew of six, white pine decks scrubbed clean, an outside recliner on the bow and a spacious cabin in the rear allowed room to move about. Comfortable deckchairs, cold beer and excellent sandwiches helped pass the time away. My first glimpse of Fao was reassuring to some degree. There was an extensive compound essentially reserved for Europeans and senior Iraqi staff guarded by sleeping soldiers with nineteenth-century rifles. The need for guards was driven more by the need to create jobs rather than protection from marauding bands of Arab Bedouin.

Within the compound there was a large marine workshop, a boat repair yard and a plant for the production of acetelyne gas to fuel lighthouses and buoys. There were comfortable bungalows for the marine engineers running the depot, a large marine club complete with swimming pool and a very large house for the officer-in-charge. The entire area was surrounded by palm trees and within the compound there were attractive gardens full of fig trees, eucalyptus trees and hordes of shrubs like oleanda.

The obvious office to report to at this hour was the bar in the Marine Club. The Depot Superintendent, Stanley Gray, his assistant engineers, the Iraqi administrators, the Port Doctor, and others had already assembled there. To my surprise there was one elegant lady to whom everyone paid uncommon respect. She was Mrs Charman, the wife of the engineer-in-charge of the gas plant. Together they had occupied the supreme level of high society in Fao for many long years, and more recently without benefit of home leave. Ma Charman, as most of the officers called her behind her back, had dominated the entire area for years. When she rose to leave the bar, everyone respectfully stood till she disappeared out of the door. The wives of the Iraqi officials never showed up at the club at all.

The engineers who ran the place were Gray and McKnight, two dour Scotsmen. Whilst they were helpful enough in their own way I found them to be most uncommunicative. Instead of answering my queries they kept on ordering drinks from the bar. By the time I was ready to depart for the outer bar, and duties aboard the dredgers operating there, I was already two or three sheets to the wind. The send-off was nevertheless congenial. Being a fellow Scot I gathered that they paid more than the usual attention to my needs, and being the first of many more new arrivals yet to come, perhaps I had peaked their interest.

The launch stopped momentarily at the control vessel for introductions to one 'Ali' Broad, a Cornishman given the nickname Ali, presumably due to his long service on the control vessel. 'Only an Arab could stand it,' said Ali, as I departed. We paid our respects also to the pilot vessel, the *King Faisil*, a gorgeous yacht, at one time the property of the Duke of Beresford. The Pilot-Master, a Captain McKnight, lived in the splendour of the Duchess's suite. No one had ever complained so the vessel remained in her original gaudy decor. The pilots, transients all, could not care less. The next ship heading inwards and preferably bound for Basrah was their primary interest.

Finally I boarded a dredger, one of five, and most with peculiar names derived from Lion and Tiger. There was the *Liger*, the *Tigon*, and the *Onger*. Fortunately for the dignity of the marine fraternity, before delivery of numbers four and five, all from Simonds' yard in Glasgow, Scotland, a new superintendent had taken over and named them the *Basrah*, and the *Baghdad*. These were the largest drag-suction dredgers in the world at that time, each being capable of pumping sand at a rate of 2,000 tons per hour. This was very necessary as nearly forty miles of dredged channels had to be sustained at specific depth levels. During the flood season, in particular, the run-off could be intense and some 12 million tons of sand and silt had to be moved.

These vessels operated twenty-four hours per day, five or six days a week, and even seven days a week in the flood season. For this reason alone they were so constructed as to permit truly spacious accommodation, adequate deck space and a fully-automated bridge with all controls hydraulic. All were fitted with radio telephones to coordinate the necessary tasks, and in support of these vessels a small hydrographic fleet was maintained. At hydro-labs in Fao, and in Basrah, up-to-date channel charts were prepared on a daily basis for the dredging-masters. Full-scale Gulf navigation charts were constantly up-dated.

On those weekends when dredgers could be spared one might steam all the way to Basrah for two days of liberty whilst the remaining four berthed at Fao. I need hardly comment upon the celebration at the marine club during these liberty days. The party began as soon as the vessels docked and reached a fever pitch of jollification by the first night, then gradually tapered off until sailing time. Needless to say the bar staff doubled, the shore gang became the centre of attention and Ma Charman disappeared into purdha for the entire two days. Nevertheless the job was done, the objectives were met and few of the officers met with serious injury, although like everywhere else there were a few deaths recorded.

One dredging-master, Dai Griffiths, a Welshman and a teetotaller, died suddenly of a cerebral haemorrhage. On another occasion I had to enter the Chief Engineer's suite because he failed to appear for breakfast. He was dead in bed, already turned partially blue, and the situation was critical with the outside temperature hovering around 125 degrees Fahrenheit. The Chief had been a drinking man and had just returned from an extensive leave somewhere. The cause of death was never of any real concern except when filling in the death certificate. An early burial was by far the most important task of to be undertaken so we steamed directly to Basrah. The ship's carpenter assembled a simple wooden coffin and by five p.m. that same afternoon the coffin was placed upon a gun-carriage, draped with the British flag and marched to the cemetery where Ted Matchett, the Irish Padre from St Peter's Church in Ashar, read the burial service. Then we all adjourned to the bar for a rather solemn celebration.

Meanwhile another new shipmaster, Christian Rodskjaer, a Danish citizen married to an English girl during the war, joined me in a crusade to have wives join us in Fao. The excuse that accommodation was unavailable was wearing thin, building was proceeding apace and most of the executive agreed that wives at Fao might very well raise the standard of behaviour level of the entire staff.

130

Finally headquarters gave permission, based upon completion of a desert road from Fao to Basrah, thus ensuring adequate transportation and hospital services for the memsahibs and the children.

The road was something of a triumph for the Russian engineer, Lennotovski, who directed its construction. It was really only a broad bund, that is sand piled up, then flattened out by a bulldozer and thereafter lots of thick black oil spread on the surface. There was never any real road surface at all. However, trucks, buses and taxicabs buzzed along at tremendous speeds with only an occasional fatality. Lennotovski was inordinately proud of his historic feat of engineering.

My first year of service there was interesting enough as there was lots of marine engineering work and river conservancy methodology to be studied. We spent long hours of duty on the bridge and the time passed quickly. But weekend liberty grew boring and the boisterous parties, so amusing in the beginning, soon soured. When Rodskjaer and I received word that the two wives were to board the *Bardistan* for the voyage out, we had interests outside the club. We knew that we would have to share accommodation in the beginning, but because the Port Directorate supplied everything, including furnishings, linen and crockery, we were prepared well in advance.

Jane had Lynn, now nearly two years old, and Sheila Rodskjaer had Christian, an infant boy, with them. We had a typical sailors' joyful reunion and the gang threw a big party at the club to celebrate. Their uneventful voyage through the Mediterranean, the Suez Canal, the Red Sea and around into the Persian Gulf had taken three full weeks, but both girls and the children had enjoyed the voyage. Being sailors' wives they were treated like royalty during the trip.

It surely must have been a shock for the girls, straight from Britain, to land at Fao of all places. Even so they quickly made the house into a home and settled down to a reasonably well-regulated existence. The children thrived on it and Lynn, with her yellow curls, her brown eyes and a truly unique personality charmed her way into everyone's heart. Even Ma Charman really loved her.

For some reason Lynn was absolutely fascinated by the Iraqis and the older and uglier the Arab, the better she liked them. She very quickly learned enough of the local Arabic to cover all of the social niceties, so all of her scruffy Arab friends brought children from miles around just to look at her. Within weeks she was swimming like a fish in the swimming pool and really enjoying life.

Meanwhile the community grew quite a bit and we had one or two real characters join us at Fao at different times. For instance, one of our chief engineers, a Welshman, had returned to the United Kingdom on a six-month leave during the summer of 1946. Apparently he had quite a bank account and he stayed at the swank hotels in London, probably half-canned most of the time, and his evenings were spent at vaudeville theatres. Inevitably he fell madly in

131

love with an acrobatic dancer, a member of a team, just about ready to retire as the ladies were on the shady side of forty and I guess the high kicks and the splits no longer come so easily at that age. Not surprisingly they paid a visit to the local registrar and were married. The lady dancer's reaction to Fao was a real blast. She took to entertaining the entire company in the club and often when inebriated would do her act, at great risk, atop the grand piano. The ladies' fashions at that time were never designed for elegance whilst standing on their heads. The honeymoon was relatively brief but the lady did get an uproarious send-off from a most appreciative audience. I never heard of them again.

On a happier note Henry Hall, the hydrographic chief, and his wife, moved down to Fao from Basrah and became our next-door neighbours. This gave Miss Lynn access to additional attention and entertainment from Mr Hall and she could help herself to all kinds of fruit from the orchard surrounding the big house. Fresh figs became her special favourite. On occasions we would ride the transport to Marqil and the ride was an absolute nightmare due in part to Lennotovski's road but mainly because of the crazy drivers and their thirst for speed. Jane enjoyed the visits to the souk, the native bazaar, where everything was sold through barter. The entire performance could be both fascinating and hilarious. Negotiation for something as ordinary as a wristwatch might necessitate several visits before the deal was finally done.

Of much more interest to Jane were the several new bungalows under construction in Marqil. Each house had two large bedrooms, each with its own bathroom, a very spacious lounge, a separate dining room, a broad front porch and a wide verandah all around. The floors were completely tiled throughout and the cookhouse was separated from the main house by quite a few feet. Each house had at least a half-acre garden and was totally air-conditioned. There was also a bug-proof sleeping enclosure on the flat roof for those hardy souls who loved fresh air. Every house was completely furnished and staffed with an Indian cook, a houseboy, topass and an armed guard who slept at the gate around the clock.

Both Jane and Sheila could scarcely contain themselves until the houses were allocated. When their names showed up on the list we had a big celebration. The house for us was but a few minutes walk along a tree-lined avenue to the Marine Club. The girls were in seventh heaven with swimming, tennis, film shows and each with a Syrian female nanny for the children. The biggest advantage of all was the additional company of the headquarters wives, the lady club members from Ashar and the airline representatives from the airport.

In Ashar there were a variety of consulates as well as business representatives and this provided a real mix of expatriates, both young and old. By now there were several more shipmasters like Rodskjaer and myself, they too had wives arriving and some of them had children. The staff at the club were delighted to entertain the kids, and they scampered around everywhere except the bar and the hallowed halls of the billiard rooms.

Meanwhile, to keep the ships, the dredgers, the pilot vessel etc., in good shape, all of them, in rotation, had to be taken to Bombay, India for overhaul in the Gray McKenzie Engineering yards there. The facilities at Basrah and Fao were adequate for maintenance but not for dry dock and periodic overhaul. These brief voyages provided a break. Whilst in Bombay the Chief Engineer and I stayed in a hotel uptown and enjoyed life knowing that everything on board was in good hands. There was a fabulous racecourse in Bombay. Thoroughbreds were shipped in from Australia, as were the high-priced jockeys to ride them, and the sport was highly popular.

Meanwhile the work at Fao went on day after day and the ships, freighters, tankers and passenger liners passed safely through the channels with only a very occasional grounding. Even this emergency was well taken care of by powerful tugs. During flood season in the spring, the effort needed was sometimes back-breaking. The River Karun carried heavy sand which would deposit on the Karun bar and dredging there was a nightmare in the high-velocity current of the combined rivers. Within another year, 1947, there was a sufficiency of staff in Fao, so Rodskjaer and I were promoted upriver for training as harbour masters. There was an on-going requirement for two at Basrah, six at Abadan and one at Khosrowabad, and all responsible to a port officer at Basrah, and at Abadan. By now a few of the senior men were on their way to retirement.

The principal duties of a harbour master was the berthing of the ships. The pilots brought empty vessels upriver from the outer bar to the reach below Abadan and there they would anchor to await their berth. On the first of the ebb tide, all the fully-laden vessels at their berths were properly documented by the loading officials, then a harbour master, with two tugs in attendance, took each one off from the jetty and swung her around in the river with the assistance of the two tugs. Bearing in mind that at that stage of the tide there might be only one foot of water under the keel, and a 600-foot long vessel had to be swung around in the river less than 800 feet wide, it was a nerve-wracking process, especially if the main engines failed or if the river was in flood. With the vessel turned and heading downriver, and properly in the ship channel, the harbour master handed over to the pilot. Then a quick signature on the ship's documents, a large scotch to bid bon voyage and a scramble into a launch to board the next ship due off. Meanwhile other harbour masters brought the empty vessels from the reach to the appropriate berths without benefit of tugs.

It may all sound very simple but it had its moments. There have been occasions when a wrong move by a harbour master, or a misinterpreted order, resulted in several million pounds of damage within a matter of minutes. There were exciting times too. In the event of a fire at the refinery, and there were many, all vessels loading, including if possible the one on fire and the two above and two below, had to be removed from their berths and anchored in the reach. Some with 20 or 30 thousand tons of aviation spirit were just like floating bombs. Once or twice we had fires that engulfed the loading ship and the vessel ended up a burned-out hulk, and with several casualties. The vessels came from almost everywhere and were bound for South America, Europe, USA, Australia, Japan, India, etc. We made many friends amongst Norwegians, Swedes, Greeks, Frenchmen and Spaniards, seamen from all over the world.

Jane sometimes visited the ships with me for dinner parties and film shows, and many of the captains and chief engineers had their wives sail with them. In those days, and much to the amusement of the ship's crew lining the rail, Miss Jane could scramble up a Jacob's ladder like a real sailor.

The berthing process could have its moments too, especially if there was lots of wind across the river, and very little current. Those were times when the dock had to be approached at a faster speed to provide steerage way, and then an anchor dropped and dragged to slow her down. Those operations were exceedingly delicate and each harbour master took great pride in sustaining a damage-free record. I was fortunate as in my seven years of service I had not one single damage claim. It was not a matter of nerves of steel, but more of an intuitive sense that comes with experience.

As harbour masters we provided both medical and customs clearance to each vessel we handled. In many of the regular British ships, particularly those that were homeward-bound, the Captain might wish to clear out the ship's bar, leaving only a sufficient supply to last until they arrived at their home port. This way made the process of handing over to a new master much simpler, as the entire bar, run on a non-profit basis, was funded by the current master. Consequently we might load up our launch with cases of the finest liquor at bonded store prices, in those days about fifty pence a bottle. This was both a good thing and a bad as many of the officers ashore overindulged. However, for those of us capable of self-control, it meant that we could supply all of our friends with the very best. Some of the regular traders brought cases of frozen steaks, lamb chops and other delicacies from New Zealand or Australia for our personal larders.

At our quarters at Abadan we maintained accommodation on the Iraq side of the river and this was always referred to as Harmaq. Having residence permits for both Iraq and Iran, we were free to go wherever we pleased, and wearing an Iraqi naval uniform made it even easier for us. Abadan had many facilities, clubs, cinemas, etc., and all of us made friends there. There were approximately 3,000 Europeans in residence and these were backed up by thousands of Syrian technicians. Ours was a busy life, the first of every ebb tide dictated the commencement of our duties, and we were on duty for four days, then two full days off in Basrah. Each of us had a splendid suite of rooms, surrounding a central lounge-dining room, all air-conditioned. The drive to Basrah was little more than forty miles over the better section of the road.

Life in Marqil was becoming even more pleasant. New cars, both British and American, were appearing everywhere. The Airport, the hub of the entire Middle East and beyond, supported a large number of representatives and mechanics from a variety of countries, and all this lent a cosmopolitan air to the Marine Club at Marqil. There were now black tie dances complete with orchestra, all kinds of organized sports and sports competitions. Life was enjoyable and the future looked bright. By February 1948 it was time to think about home leave. We were allowed two and a half months leave for each year served and it was considered advisable to take leave whenever six months had been accumulated.

I made arrangements for Jane and Lynn to travel back to the UK on the SS *Afghanistan*, a brand new vessel commanded by a good friend of mine, Captain Stewart. Whilst I learned later that they had a hellish time in the Bay of Biscay, they made it to European ports without mishap. They called at Bremen, Germany and Jane was absolutely appalled at the misery there. The substitute currency was cigarettes, preferably American. She visited the war-shattered city with Captain Stewart, just to get an impression of what it must have been like for them in 1945. She brought back a silver key to the city which she treasures to this day.

By the time I arrived home in May by plane, Jane had already leased a furnished apartment in Warrender Park Terrace, in Edinburgh, overlooking some beautiful parkland and beyond to the Braid Hills. She enjoyed the unaccustomed housework and cooking so much that she literally polished me out of the door. I decided to take a course in shorthand and typing at a Business School in the mornings just to get out of the house. I never regretted learning to touch-type as I subsequently found it to be a most useful skill.

It was at this same time that I decided to try my hand at short-story writing and much to everyone's surprise, I achieved a measure of success. Blackwood's Journal and Chamber's Journal, two literary-type magazines published in Edinburgh, had always been favourites of mine. I was delighted to become a published author therein and I used the pen-name, Iain Alexander.

We really enjoyed Warrender Park Terrace as we could walk across the park to the city centre and we frequented the 'Golf Tavern', a very popular pub. Most of the theatres we liked were within walking distance, we had all the afternoons and evenings to enjoy ourselves and money was of no concern. My full salary and allowances from the Crown Agents was worth about four times the normal professional salary in Edinburgh. There was but one nagging worry to bother us and that was Miss Lynn's schooling. She was still only four years old but neither Jane nor I wanted her to miss a good education.

There were schools in Abadan and a school run by nuns in Basrah, but we felt that she would be better off in Edinburgh. We chose St Hilary's, an excellent school for girls with both boarders and day girls. We agreed that she should be a boarder there before she reached the age of six. Once our minds were made up we enjoyed our leave more and visited relatives far and wide. We took trips to the Highlands with Jane's folks, and Lynn kept busy organizing our entire daily life. She loved the old farmhouse where her Grannie Miller always had special treats for her.

Like most folks home on leave, we spent a good deal of time taking pictures of our ancestor's tombstones. At one point when we were concentrating on Jane's maternal grandmother's resting-place in Coldingham, we agreed we should take over temporarily the nursing duties for her paternal grandmother, bedridden in Earlston, in Berwickshire. She was being cared for in the home of her daughter and son-in-law, Jane's favourite aunt and uncle, who had not had a vacation in years.

It was sometime in August 1948 when we took over their comfortable bungalow in the valley of the River Leader, as it flowed through the town of Earlston. In a rear bedroom this bedridden lady was a very charming, jolly old soul and she was attended each day by a visiting nurse. She was not supposed to wear her false teeth in case she might choke, but she was constantly confiding in Lynn that she really must have them for appearances' sake. Miss Lynn, either through pity or sheer devilment, fetched the teeth and later on Jane was greeted with a broad toothy smile. There was also a large, fluffy cat and a beautiful garden full of fruit, vegetables and flowers. We were all very happy there for just a few sunshiney days. Aunt Ena and Uncle Sam had taken off for a horse-racing week at Ayr, on the west coast. We slept in spacious comfort in a large front bedroom, and with Lynn only four, we brought in a little camp bed so we might be together.

Because we had run out of shillings to feed the gas meter one rainy night, the lights fizzled and then failed entirely, so we retired to bed in the gloaming, figuring that we would fix it in the morning. By midnight, in pitch blackness, I awoke and heard the rain battering at the windows. Fearing that one might be open I swung my legs over the bed and found myself up to my knees in water. I became fully awake with a jolt and found Miss Lynn sound asleep, but floating around the room in her little bed. Jane awoke in momentary hysterics. There was no choice but to get out in a hurry. I was familiar with the location of the house and the river; without doubt there had been a cloudburst in the hills behind us.

Lynn, still sleeping, lay in my arms, and with Jane clinging to my belt we made it to the back door. As we stepped down the two steps to the garden path the water was up close to my waist. Just then the cat leaped onto my shoulders, dug his claws into my back and I had no option but tolerate it. Another step from the garden path to the road, with the water lapping at my chest, and I could feel Jane behind me with the water up to her armpits. The rain was lashing down and I must confess I was terrified in case a log came tumbling down on top of us. Then lights and voices, the town was aroused and there were men racing down the hill towards us.

Jane and Lynn were taken over by total strangers and the cat had taken an immense leap onto dry land whilst I and other men raced back to get the old lady. By the time we got into the house she was afloat on her mattress and we had to take her out through the top half of the window, then with about six of us carrying her shoulder-high, we got her out of the gate and up the slope to the town. She kept chortling away to herself, apparently enjoying the whole adventure, despite the fact that the rain was absolutely freezing. We were greeted by hordes of concerned country ladies, all directing us to the lobby of the 'Red Lion' pub. Jane, in a borrowed dressing gown over her nightdress, was busily cuddling Miss Lynn is warm blankets whilst humming a Highland song.

When the old lady was stretched out on a cushioned bed at the inn, with several old friends in attendance, she kept asking where she was. When they finally told her she was at the 'Red Lion', she demanded a large brandy and stated that she had always wanted to pay a visit there.

Men with lanterns were still bringing in waterlogged survivors from the flood and there was grave concern for the animals at the farm across the road from the bungalow. Fortunately the animals have some sort of built-in sensor that we don't have and most of them were already on high ground. Only the stabled horses and the milk cows had to be led to safety. When daylight came the flood was gone, leaving inches of fine sand and mud all over the house, with a dirty silt mark all around level with the mantelshelf. Jane and Lynn were left at the inn while I took off for Edinburgh to acquire more clothes for all of us. By the time I got back the damage was visible everywhere and further downstream a great lake had formed behind a high railway embankment. The coastal town of Eyemouth was in real danger if the embankment gave way. Army engineers drilled the necessary drainage relief and the crisis was over.

I was busy hosing out the house when Sam and Ena arrived home and was vastly relieved at how calm they were when they surveyed the damage. They were both so relieved to find their mother safe and well, and Sam, a really cool customer, took the whole affair in his stride. It took a while before everything was shipshape again, and Jane and I and Lynn were already back in Iraq before they were able to move back into the house.

Back in Iraq at that time life was really good to us. We had a beautiful air-conditioned home, a good salary, a job that I really liked, great friends and the future never looked brighter. There was a regular plane service now from Glasgow to Amsterdam, then on to Basrah with a stopover at Rome, Italy. The flying boats with their relatively short hops were already obsolete. We had settled down again in Marqil to a degree whereby we had more time to spend on the places and the culture around us. I was now one of the very senior Captains as so many of the older men had retired. As different vacancies cropped up they were offered to us first, such as Pilot Master, Master of the light-tender *Nearchus* or Harbour Master at Khosrowabad with accommodation on the Iranian side, or operations at headquarters. I decided to stay at Harmaq, Abadan with Jane at Marqil in her comfortable house. We had an excellent social life, with a great mix of people and a mix of cultures. By now, the end of 1948, there were many important social activities to which we were invited. These were Iraqi Government functions, Air Force and Navy celebrations etc., in addition to all of the regular club functions and social events in Ashar.

During those years in Basrah the British maintained an Air Force presence at Sheyba, not far from us, and an additional wing at an air base just outside Baghdad. The Royal Navy also sustained a dock just below Ashar and made periodic visits thereto, the ships being based at Bahrain. Their presence was never at any time overpowering and seemed to be either acceptable or totally ignored by the Iraqis. The officers joined us at the club and on occasions groups of us were entertained at their mess. Their presence was a constant reminder of the subtlety of British diplomacy.

Their role was always justified on the basis of some totally obscure need for the protection of Iraq from unspecified enemies, and the need for the training and development of an Iraqi defence capability that somehow or other never seemed to materialize. In the southern Gulf, in the sheikdoms of Trucial Oman, and in Oman, the defence forces there were headed by an officer corps, all of whom were British. The Sheik and some members of his Government always ensured that their sons served a few terms at the British Military Academy. It appeared to me at times that the elite amongst the Arabs were more British than the British.

Most of us there were well aware that we were living in the cradle of civilization and many among us were interested enough to visit the places of historical and religious interest. Ninivah, in the far north, in what the locals claim to be Kurdistan, is often referred to in the Bible. The ruins are clearly visible, and more recently, there have been several archaeological digs undertaken there. Closer to us, at Nasiriyah, it was possible to have discussions with the archaeologists. Clearly there is ample evidence to demonstrate the existence and indeed the location of the city of Babel or Babylon, and there, in what is now a desert, was a peculiar aura of peace and tranquillity. One can almost feel the history of the place and instinctively I found myself going back in time, certainly to my childhood years in church when we spent time in Sunday school studying the old maps at the back of the Bible.

There was a place where the taxi-drivers liked to take tourists, claiming it to be the site of the original Garden of Eden, complete with the tree of knowledge. I took Jane and Lynn out there several times and they were allowed to take a little twig from the tree to press within the covers of their bible. The site was so isolated and so free from exploitation that the local tale was almost believable. The tree was an ancient eucalyptus, probably old for a tree of that type, but not old enough to have survived from the days of Adam and Eve. However it was not unpleasant just to stand there and quietly believe. Even today the memory of it provides a quiet peace in these more stressful times.

It was there, seeing the natives living in their reed huts, that I was compelled to think about the weather. While the winter period in Iraq was most pleasant, and the gardens ablaze with flowers, the summer heat was unbelievable. During the dry season the temperature could rise to 125 degrees Fahrenheit in the shade. In the afternoons in the worst of it, we as harbour masters, boarding vessels in the reach, found ourselves climbing up Jacob's ladders forty to fifty feet high to scramble on deck, then having to walk along steaming, steel decks till we finally reached the shade of the 'midships section and thence to the bridge. Quite often too the wind blew very strongly, carrying sand and dust, just like a dense fog. This was the shimal, the wind from the north, from the desert. In mid-summer, as it has done for centuries, the wind regularly blew in from the south to ripen the dates. It blew in from the Gulf, just laden with moisture. This was the churgee.

During the south wind the temperature might drop to 97 degrees, but the humidity rose to almost 90 per cent and it was necessary to change clothes several times a day. Perspiration would run from every pore and condensation within the house would be such that water would drip from the ceiling beams. Hence the reason for the tiled floors and the Persian carpets. In such weather the duty days at Abadan were sheer murder and off-duty days at Basrah were spent in the swimming pool.

Regardless of the weather, there were highlights too in our schedules. The cargo ships and in particular the passenger liners were always a welcome relief from the tanker drudgery. There were four passenger liners in particular that contributed much to our social life. They were not large, just about 20,000 tons each, from the British India Steamship Lines. These were the *Dumra*, the *Dara*, the *Dwarka*, and the *Daressa*. They were referred to as the Bombay mail and ran constantly between Basrah and Bombay. The officers and engineers were British and the crew were Indian. Two or three of the captains were Scotsmen and good friends of mine. During their stay in port, parties and dances were organized on the promenade deck and the local ladies just loved the change of scene.

There were other vessels from England, Holland, Denmark, Sweden etc., some were a mix of cargo and passenger, and traded as far east as Japan. One Swedish liner with a beautiful spiral staircase sticks in my mind. She was tied up at buoys in the river at Ashar and was off-loading into barges. The Captain liked to live really well and he organized one of the best parties I can ever remember aboard ship. I had agreed to transport about ten young ladies in my launch and as it was my off-duty period, I spent much of the time with the canapés, the cocktails and especially the aquavite, whilst the ladies preferred to dance. There were several boatloads of the younger set and it was a cool, delightful evening with a full moon. There was dancing on the promenade deck.

When I finally climbed the spiral staircase to the upper deck I could hear the strains of 'Happy days'; I was feeling no pain. The elegant young lady, one of my charges, to whom I offered my arm for a dance, looked me up and down, then turned me down cold and with a haughty shrug of her shoulders she took off. It isn't often one gets such a brush-off, so I suppose it registered pretty firmly in my mind but I thought no more of it. The party proceeded apace and by the wee hours of the morning we were ready to break up. Bearing in mind the height of the ship's accommodation ladder, the instability of the launches and the groups of slightly inebriated ladies for whom we were responsible, we dusted off the cobwebs from our minds and provided appropriate escort. Getting them all aboard was finally accomplished, the headcount completed and the secunney cast off and headed for shore.

No doubt the moonlight, the cocktails and perhaps youthful exuberance induced one of my elegant female charges to move up to the bow of the launch while doing a neat little dance. As we were approaching the boat dock I recognized her: it was she of the brush-off. I was about to call out to her to sit down when the secunney put the engine into full reverse as he was approaching the dock too fast. The young lady took a nosedive into the murky water. When she rose to the surface we could do no more than advise her to stand up. The water by the boat dock was less than three feet deep at low tide and unhappily the river bottom was just stinking mud. As she stood up and we hauled her aboard I must confess I felt desperately sorry for her. She was black with river mud and stank like the devil. She was inconsolable. The cars were crowded and I think out of sheer spite she insisted on sitting on my knee as she wept on my shoulder on the drive back to Marqil. I was never allowed to forget it.

About that time the young King Faisil was home in Iraq from Eton, the school in England he attended. He was just eleven years old. There were several major celebrations laid on for him and the embassy people were there looking after the Prince Regent, Crown Prince Abdul Ilah. The British Ambassador, Sir Reginald Stonehewer-Bird, and Lady Bird, were amongst the guests and whilst they were temporarily in Basrah, they also threw a party. Jane and I have a great collection of invitation cards with gold lettering inviting us to these fancy affairs. She loved every minute of it, particularly the dressing up part, and insisted I wear white sharkskin dinner jackets. Miss Lynn always managed to push her way into the forefront of everything. Having taken command of the royal yacht *Queen Alia*, when the royal family were aboard, Jane and I qualified for all kinds of guest lists.

In general life was pretty gay and by 1949 we were dreading the day when Jane and Lynn would have to take off for Edinburgh, for Lynn's school. She was approaching five years old. She could converse freely in Arabic with the Syrian nanny and she carried on long conversations with the night watchman who slept at our gate each night. She had a great time with the servants, with the boat crew and she was always on good terms with Shahab, the cook. What on earth they talked about was hard to tell but the cook maintained he understood every word she said. Having yellow curls, a pale skin and brown eyes, the Arab children stopped to gaze at her. When she spoke they would run away. There was only one incident when we had a problem with Lynn and that was around her fifth birthday.

There was a desert storm warning with the likelihood of damaging winds and this happened to be the day when Lynn was nowhere to be found. Her nanny had lost track of her and no one could find her. I was just leaving the docks, having warned the ships of the impending storm, when the wind really started to scream. I was walking up Tanoomah Avenue past the Marine Club when I saw Jane who was almost frantic by this time. At the very last moment Lynn had been located in the club kitchen, being fed some special goodies brought in by aeroplane. We still had a couple of hundred yards to go to get home and the two of us were clinging on to Lynn's hands while I used the garden railings to help us along. Just then the wind ripped up the avenue with a screech like a banshee, and as we got to our garden gate the sleeping enclosure on the roof took off and disappeared skyward. For the first time ever the sleeping watchman was missing from his post at the gate.

Like most tropical storms it disappeared almost as quickly as it came. Even so it left a fair trail of damage behind it. Unfortunately Jane, with all her superstitions, took this as a warning from providence that it was time to take Lynn home to Scotland. We stretched it out for two or three more months but then she really had to go. Lynn was bursting with excitement and she scarcely noticed that I would not be around. She had lengthy conversations with all her Arab friends, explaining that she was going off to school, but she would return with a great fanfare when she became a big girl. For quite a while after they had gone I felt as though my life had ended. I stayed away from Basrah and spent my off-duty at Abadan.

Fortunately I met a very nice family there, the Kitsons. The father, about my age, was a consultant with Ewbank and Partners, and stationed at Abadan only temporarily. His wife Betty just loved the river, the boats and the launches, and her little daughter Hilary, about seven years old, was a real little doll. We became firm friends and took lots of river trips together. Later, when Jane returned, we saw a great deal of each other. Finally, when we parted, they were off to a new posting in the Caribbean, and they presented me with a very fine silver cigarette box with a hand-painted miniature embedded on the lid. However, like ships that pass in the night, we never saw them again. Many years later we heard from someone who claimed to have met them in Barbados, saying that Hilary had married a surgeon there.

It was 1950 when Jane returned alone from Edinburgh, by now Miss Lynn was decked out in the St Hilary's school uniform and from her pictures she looked to be quite the young lady. Unhappily her mother was deeply depressed as she didn't like the idea of being separated from Lynn at all. Some days when we might be with Hilary Kitson the tears would be streaming down her cheeks. However, and thankfully, our new neighbours, Jules and Pinky Gindreaux, helped to cheer her up. Jules was station manager for Trans-World Airlines, and he convinced Jane that he was in dire need of an efficient secretary, so she took the job. She enjoyed the work, the busy airport, the hordes of people coming and going. She got to know everybody in the airline business and there were real characters among them. She cheered up considerably.

She also developed a firm friendship with some of the people from Ashar. One was Liz Perry whose husband represented Caterpillar Tractors, and the other was Opal Lindsay whose husband Al ran a geophysical exploration company in Ashar. Both couples divorced a few years later, but when we knew them they were truly a hoot, as Opal would say. She was from Shreveport, Lousianna, had an almost unintelligible southern accent and was an incorrigible flirt. She and Liz threw some lively parties to which Jane and I, a couple of squares no doubt, would always be invited for the air of respectability we lent to the affair. There was an occasional visit from a US Navy warship, more of a survey ship than a warship, and on these occasions the parties were really big stuff.

There were some very odd characters in the Port Directorate, some in the airlines and indeed some in the consulates. Only the dedicated business people lived conservative lives. On one occasion in Fao, for instance, the Port Doctor, and one of the hydrographers got permission to go off somewhere into the desert for drinks before dinner with the Collector of Customs for southern Iraq. They arrived back three days later, looking very much the worse for wear. I can remember assisting the Minister up the steps to the pulpit for the Christmas Eve service and he leaned over the pulpit and preached the sermon of his very life. We caught him on his way back down the stairs. A couple of very nice young males from the American consulate were hustled on to an aeroplane before a scandal broke.

We had our little adventurers too. An English girl, the wife of one of our officers, loved to go off on camel caravans with the Bedouin for weeks at a time. One of the favourite sports of the Arab sheiks was to hunt gazelle in the desert. Unhappily for the fleet and beautiful gazelle, the hunters used jeeps and high-powered rifles. One could hardly call it sport. However they liked it and they often practiced their falconry whilst out in the wild. A couple of Americans took off in a jeep into the desert on a joint hunt and preliminary survey exploration. They never did make it back. Some time later they were found dead from thirst and heatstroke with the radiator still full of water.

Enough of tragedy; on a more exciting note the Crown Prince, recently married, decided that the family needed a cruise on the *Queen Alia*, the royal yacht tied up at the airport jetty. She had a permanent skeleton crew, for on the rare occasions when young King Faisil returned from England, sometimes with schoolboy friends, a cruise was in order. With advance warning the crew were brought up to sea-going strength, and the Chef, the Hotel Manager and several stewards were brought from the Airport Hotel. I took command and checked out all the preparations.

On such occasions it was customary for the Royal Family to throw several parties, the biggest always at the Marine Club and the embassy staffs joined us from Baghdad. Sir Reginald Stonehewer-Bird and his Lady always accompanied the Port Director on the podium, and together they attended to all of the appropriate niceties. The ladies always loved all the pomp and ceremony and to add to the interest this was a ceremony the senior Iraqi women loved to attend. The parties, the dancing and the celebration were truly remarkable to those of us accustomed to believing that muslims do not imbibe.

Being in command of the yacht, and fairly well-known to the Baghdad crowd, Jane and I were given ringside seats at all of these circuses, and I must say that there were many aspects of the entire affair that were most enjoyable. On the humorous side it was always rather intriguing to see all the Arab ladies from the royal court, including Queen Alia, now little more than thirty years old, arrive on board. Everyone, even the servants, and particularly the crew, were subdued and with eyes downcast. The ladies tripped up the companionway, encased in their keffiyehs, covered from head to toe, and complete with veils. The last mooring had scarcely been cast off when the gorgeous girls appeared on deck in sundress or swimsuit.

The menfolk usually arrived separately and most often by launch after we were underway. The Prince Regent, the young King Faisil, Nuri Sayed, the Prime Minister, and Jawad Ali, the Foreign Minister, and his beautiful, red-haired American wife, and many lesser dignitaries came aboard at the last moment. I gained the impression that most of the men were anxious to ingratiate themselves with the young Queen. To avoid any offence to the dignity of these male suitors it was customary for the Commander to sit at the head of the table. This way everyone felt that they were amongst equals.

The ship was really something to behold. Some 4,000 tons of luxury with four high-speed chriscraft in the davits. The dining saloon was spacious, with dark oak panelling and chandeliers. The carpets on the deck were priceless. There was a fully-furnished throne room and all the telephones were gold-plated. The various suites were spacious and luxuriously appointed. The voyage was conducted in leisurely fashion with various stops for fishing expeditions, clay-pigeon shooting and fun and games on deck etc. Courtesy calls were made to a few sheikdoms and a very special visit paid to the Sultan of Muscat. If heading for Bombay, and the weather was a little rough, I was asked to turn back. The return to Basrah was at high speed and within minutes of docking at the airport jetty the entire royal party was driven directly to the aircraft to return them to Baghdad. Noticeably, the aircraft crews were always British.

I was happy to be home and be able to transfer the royal responsibilities elsewhere. I never felt quite at ease with the guests on board and it was always difficult to gauge who was jealous of whom. Arabs have a remarkable inclination to conceal hatred for imaginary enemies and at the same time tend to nurture long-standing family feuds. There were times when I felt as though there was a bomb ticking in the room next door. Nevertheless it appeared that the young Queen was totally unaware of the atmosphere of threat that surrounded her. However, understanding her own Arab culture, and being aware of their history of violence, she must have suffered certain qualms when surrounded by her supposedly devoted subjects.

It was some years later when the political pot boiled over with a vengeance, and the young King, his Prime Minister and his Foreign Minister were slaughtered like pigs by the mobs in the Baghdad bazaar. Their heads were paraded around on poles in the markets for days afterward. I never did find out what happened to Queen Alia. Even then, in the winter months of 1950, the winds of change were starting to blow. One could sense the atmosphere of political excitement in the Iranian bazaars and there was a definite, but indescribable, feeling of menace in the air. International politics and business interests were working at cross purposes too, and each nation with interests in the oil business was busy making deals with upstart dictators, and generally contributing to the turmoil.

Meanwhile life in the Port Directorate, entirely divorced from politics, carried on with customary efficiency. There was always work to be done, schedules to be met, new responsibilities to be undertaken and many emergencies to be overcome. Jane was happy at her job, and with her friends in Marqil, so she rarely questioned my peculiar schedule of activities, like trips to Bombay for ship maintenance or so-called glamorous voyages on the *Queen Alia* in the midst of my regular duties at Abadan.

One additional emergency of interest did arise in the early spring of 1951. The Captain of the *Nearchus*, the Persian Gulf light-tender, decided it was time to retire. A substitute was needed in a hurry until a full-time successor could be found. I was asked to undertake the spring cruise. The *Nearchus* was a splendid old vessel, complete with bowsprit and clipper stern. Built in the earlier days of oil-fired steamships, she had spacious deckspace, teakwood accommodation, white pine decks and a splendid open deckspace on the stern. Her working gear was comprised mainly of the equipment necessary to the handling, maintenance, and recovery and launching of buoys, and the general supply of lighthouses. She had a very efficient crew, truly dependable engines and extra accommodation on the promenade deck for special passengers.

Her duties were simple enough. The light-tender was responsible for the maintenance of all of the navigational aids, such as lighthouses, buoys and beacons etc., throughout the entire Gulf region, as far as Jask on the eastern border of Iran, and as far south as Ras al Hadd on the Oman side. On taking off on a cruise, all she needed was a great load of cylinders of acetylene gas, maintenance gear, stores and one or possibly two buoys. In readiness for placement, each buoy was painted in the relevant colours and the characteristic of the flashing light adjusted to fit the particular location. A buoy in need of maintenance was retrieved and a refitted one launched in its place. On the way to the next one due for refit that buoy was chipped, painted and coloured according to its next location, gas cylinders replenished and light characteristic adjusted.

These buoys were anchored by a two-ton steel, cylindrical, inverted saucer on the seabed, and an appropriate length of heavy steel chain, sufficient to cover the depth and any rise of tide. It was necessary to wait for smooth seas at each operation so there was never any great haste involved. The maintenance of lighthouses, such as that on the Quoins, a small island dominating the entrance to the Gulf, was a different kettle of fish. Replenished equipment had to be landed on the island then hauled to the lighthouse, usually on the highest point, and all the necessary stores for the personnel manning the lighthouse were hand-carried. Contracts called for a lighthouse keeper and usually two assistants, but it was comical to see the large number of their extended families scurrying for any available hiding place as soon as they caught sight of the *Nearchus*.

In addition, the vessel performed some very special duties for the British Government. The Political Resident for the region, at that time Sir Rupert Hay, had his official residence at Jufair, in Bahrain. On certain occasions he used the *Nearchus* to conduct his political tour of his region of interest. Such duties had emerged and became established over the years from about 1903. Bahrain was a British protectorate and in those earlier days before oil, Bahrain was one of the centres of Persian Gulf trade in fishing, pearl diving, slave trading etc. Manama, the main city on the island, was a thriving port and with oil being discovered in 1934 it became very prosperous. The *Nearchus* had work to accomplish in Manama and I was summoned to Jufair, to go over Sir Rupert's itinerary for his proposed cruise.

To get to Jufair and to his most impressive residence there it was necessary to travel by taxicab across the island. The Chief Engineer, the Public Relations Assistant and I travelled in a cab procured directly from a dealer headquarters. It was a brand new Cadillac with less than one hundred miles on the clock. The driver selected asked permission to carry his very good friend with him in the front seat and to this we agreed. The driver, who spoke very good English, advised us that he knew exactly how to get there, that he was an excellent and thoroughly well-trained driver and a very responsible individual. He seemed to be very proud of the fact that he had been selected by the dealer to drive such an automobile.

We took off into the desert along a hard surface road and the speed kept on increasing despite our admonitions. 'Don't worry Sahib, I am a very well-trained driver,' he kept saying. A little later on we were racing through an ancient Arab burial ground, and by this time I am convinced that the speedometer was touching 120 miles per hour. He was still babbling, 'Do not worry, Sahib,' when we rounded a bend in the road and hit a rock no bigger than a football. We left the road on a level keel and landed in the sand with the Cadillac travelling at incredible speed. It took about a quarter to half a mile before we finally came to rest. Fortunately, with three grown men in the rear seat, we were locked together more or less. When the dust cleared and we clambered out I could scarcely believe my eyes. The driver and his very good friend were running as fast as their legs could carry them towards the distant horizon.

The Cadillac was an absolute shambles. The engine cover and all four doors were gone. The tyres had been ripped from the wheel rims and a dreadful hissing sound was all that was left of the engine. Presumably the well-trained driver had no intention of facing up to his boss in Manama. He and his friend were headed for distant parts. We shook the stiffness out of our limbs and shuffled back to the road. About half an hour later we were picked up by a truck bound for Jufair. Sir Rupert's daughter Mary thought the whole adventure was a huge joke. Miss Mary was something of a tomboy. She loved to ride Arabian horses at the racecourse in Manama, and was well liked locally.

Sir Rupert was a jolly, stout fellow, and very good humoured. His itinerary was detailed to us and we agreed to pick him up at Jufair on the following day with his staff. I was very impressed when he boarded. We, the officers on the *Nearchus* were dressed in naval tropical uniform but Sir Rupert put us to shame. He was resplendent in an all-white uniform, complete with brass buttons, medals and spiked helmet. He was indeed a sight to be seen, a worthy representative of the British crown.

We proceeded from Jufair to the sheikdoms of Abu Dhabi, Dubai and Trucial Oman. At various contact points, usually far from any apparent civilization, we anchored off-shore and awaited the arrival of an Arab dhow. The Sheik himself came aboard, with great ceremony tea was served on the after deck and there, after lengthy conversations, a yellow chamois leather bag full of golden sovereigns changed hands. Later the Sheik departed, and then his number one son came aboard for a lesser ceremony, and a much smaller bag. We understood this to be the traditional British method of buying their continued allegiance to the Crown. In general, it seemed to be a very successful manoeuvre as it smoothed the way for the entry of many British corporations involved in the search for oil.

I find it odd today to look back on how Abu Dhabi was once only a cluster of mud huts in a greasy old creek. Today there are high-rise buildings, six-lane highways going nowhere and an inexhaustible supply of Cadillacs. The once poverty-stricken Sheiks are now billionaires, all practising President Reagan's theory of trickle-down economics. Without doubt only a trickle of the oil revenues finds its way down to the desert Arab. However, a fairly large and reasonably successful middle class has emerged and they, quite naturally, are dedicated to the Sheik.

Our political cruise culminated in a splendid courtesy call upon the Sultan of Muscat. Ridiculous as it may sound, we had a small cannon set up on the fo'castle head and we fired the royal salute upon entry into the harbour. The Sultan himself had been educated in England and had developed a taste for all things British, plus all of those luxuries to which he had become accustomed within his own culture. This was truly a case of enjoyment of the best of two worlds. During our mission there the subject of a manned lighthouse on Ras al Hadd was discussed. This was without doubt the longest stretch of unlighted coastline in the entire shipping world. However the Sultan, in his wisdom, advised that the lives of the lighthouse keepers could not be guaranteed for but a few days. They would be slaughtered for the clothes on their back by marauding Bedouin, he said, and this was 1951. Earlier, a Greek ship that ran aground in that area was beseiged by pirates. Some very few years later the Sultan was forced to abdicate in favour of his son and spent his declining years in residence at Claridges Hotel in London.

Our return trip was less eventful, we dropped Sir Rupert off at Jufair with the usual fanfare and proceeded back to Basrah with the cruise completed. The good ship *Nearchus* was handed over to the safe keeping of a new Shipmaster and continued her duties under the direction of the Persian Gulf Lighting Authority, another one of the organizations sustained by the British. She was relieved in later years by an ultra-modern light-tender built in England, and with the incredibly stupid name of *Relume*, more evidence of the utter lack of imagination employed in the naming of these very important vessels, which were in themselves outposts of the British Empire.

I was glad to be home again and I spent a few days in Marqil before returning to Abadan. Very quickly we reverted to routine and the Harmaq drudgery, as we called it, started all over again. Jane had reached the stage where she too needed a change of scenery. As it happened, the port of Khosrowabad, or Kabda as we called it, was in process of expansion. The oil company insisted on having a Harbour Master in residence there and supplied all the accommodation and transportation. There were quite a number of very comfortable bungalows at Kabda and it was only a fifteen-minute drive to Abadan. Jane liked the idea so we volunteered to go there for the summer of 1951.

We were very comfortable there with a fully-furnished house and servants supplied by the oil company. I maintained the usual comfortable launch with a secunney and a crew of six on constant standby. The boat crews were all exceedingly happy fellows, with very good jobs by their standards and all kinds of opportunities for smuggling or thieving or whatever took their fancy. They arranged their own relief crews. I suspect that several of them maintained wives in Fao, and in Basrah, but these matters were always considered very private and totally ignored until an accident or death, when several different families would appear, each claiming rights to the few scraps of property left by the deceased.

While social activities in general in Abadan were as jolly as ever on the surface, it was very evident to us that all was not well in Tehran, the capital city. It seemed that the Shah was in constant conflict with his ministers and there were several instances of blood-spilling uprisings in the bazaar of Abadan, and more seriously at Khorramshar, with a much larger native community demanding a greater share of the spoils. Yet on the Iraqi side of the river, in Basrah, and in Baghdad, all was apparently well. Nevertheless, being close to thirty-four years of age, I was obliged to look into the crystal ball and determine what kind of future lay ahead of us. I could not see enough years remaining to provide me with a comfortable retirement. On odd occasions Jane and I talked about it.

With Lynn at school in Edinburgh we had arranged for her to spend her vacations at Earlston with Jane's aunt and uncle. They were both happy with her and Lynn's grandfather acted as chauffeur. We got an occasional letter from them, usually in Lynn's holidays, and some from Lynn's school with brief notes in them from Lynn herself. When we received such letters it was easy for me to see that Jane would gladly give up the fancy boats and cars, and the bank account, just so we could be a family again. Therein lay food for thought.

To keep up with all the changing rules and regulations it was necessary for me to visit Basrah and on those occasions Jane would accompany me there. There were times too when we were invited to special functions going on at Fao, by now developing into an evermore important base of operations. One such occasion in the late summer of 1951 is worthy of record. We had an invitation to some very special celebration at Fao wherein the entire community was involved in the affair with partying starting early in the day, sports activities, and sports competitions taking place throughout the afternoon, and all this culminating in an outdoor ball in the late evening. Our secunney decorated the launch in anticipation and no doubt they too had a party planned.

It was a splendid affair and we were both amazed at the changes, at the number of families there and the level of sports activities they managed to generate. It was quite a cosmopolitan crowd, with several Polish engineers, several Dutch engineers with wives and daughters, and a few Russians here and there, in addition to the British contingent. One Dutch engineer, a good friend, was married to an Australian girl Alice who was caught in Holland for the entire war whilst husband Jerry had no choice but to serve in the British Merchant Navy. They were separated for four long years. Meanwhile their little daughter Judy grew up and Alice had some horror stories to tell of the German occupation of Holland. The daughter, by then about sixteen, was the belle of the ball.

In the early hours of the following morning we had to head upriver to Kabda where there were loaded ships waiting to depart on the next ebb tide. Jane was absolutely exhausted, perhaps still mildly inebriated and decided to have a nap in the stern of the launch. She still wore her evening dress, in those days a divided affair with a long skirt and a halter, leaving a bare midriff. As she slept the sleep of the just, the launch rounded a bend in the river into Kabda Reach and we ran into a school of flying fish. Many of the little devils flopped aboard and several onto Madame's midriff. Her screams could have been heard all the way back to Fao. She had scarcely recovered when we reached the dock in Kabda in the black darkness just before the dawn.

Our bungalow was about a quarter of a mile from the jetty, just a very pleasant walk along a raised bund, but badly illuminated and there was no moon. We could hear the pye-dogs baying in the faint desert breeze. We meandered along, arm in arm, when suddenly there was shouting and scuffling and I could feel the sharp point of a bayonet in the small of my back. I could sense Jane's total collapse against my arm. However the excitement was short-lived when the Iranian army officer recognized my Iraqi naval uniform. He barked some instructions and the troops backed off. He apologized profusely but offered no explanation. Wisely I did not press for a translation and we hurried home.

Jane was reluctant to be left alone thereafter, so I arranged for her to be transferred to Basrah and the boat crew assisted her with all her personal things and her precious Persian carpets. I remained at Kabda, knowing full well that there was serious trouble brewing. Within a couple of days minor riots had taken place both at Khorramshar and at Abadan. We heard of major political upheavals in Tehran. Some weeks dragged by whilst the shipping carried on. Tankers, cargo vessels and passenger vessels came and went and everything on the river was normal.

By the autumn the real riots had started, several men were killed in the bazaar at Khorramshar and there were some fairly serious incidents on the wharves there. One black weekend a few people were killed in the bazaar at Abadan and the mobs ran amok with flags dipped in their blood. It was then that HMS *Essex*, a British cruiser, appeared at the outer bar, was piloted up the river and moored to the buoys directly across from the bazaar. Her six-inch guns were swung around to point directly at the souk. Fortunately for all of us, these were still the days of gunboat diplomacy, the riots ceased, the Iranian Army regained control and all was mysteriously quiet.

Not so at Kabda where the memsahibs were packing and departing for the airport and the husbands had already established bachelors' quarters close to the docks. The dogs were rounded up, herded into a garage and a cylinder of butane gas released. It was kinder that way. Given their freedom they would have ended up in the desert amongst the packs of pye-dogs skirting the civilized area. Such dogs were a mix of domestic animal and the desert jackal which could be dangerous in a pack if you were alone and showed the slightest sign of fear. I was ordered to move to Harmaq on the Iraqi side, just opposite Abadan, and to await orders. As always in situations like these there were rumours and counter-rumours, but very little of the real truth trickled down to us.

It was evident that the political uproar was confined to Iran. The Iraqis did expose a few more uniforms to the public, but had no obvious intention of interfering in Iranian affairs. All was quiet at Abadan, but movements of ships were slowing down, and quickly. It appeared that the Iranian military still exercised control, but the Shah himself had been removed from power in a bloodless coup, the Prime Minister Mossadeq took over and promptly nationalized the oil company. The British elected to exercise further restraint and ordered the cruiser to return to base in the Persian Gulf.

I remember very clearly the unusual fuss with the cruiser when it was decided she should depart. I was called to the Port Officer's office to discuss her movements. There were several political representatives there and it was apparent that few of them were well acquainted with the river. It was pointed out to them that the cruiser was well over 600 feet long and it might be very difficult to turn her around. Facing upriver and staying in the defined channels under pilotage was one thing, swinging her around to head back out to sea was something entirely different. Were she to run aground the political wallahs would be desperately embarrassed before hordes of unruly natives. It was reluctantly agreed that I should take her upriver beyond Abadan to the place we called Hell's Gates, the reach below Khorramshar.

There was both a Captain and a Commodore on board and I found it exceedingly difficult to explain to them the quandary we were in. Proceeding upriver to Hell's Gates, whilst a bit nerve-wracking with a cruiser, was considered acceptable, but sticking her bow into the river bank, and with helm hard over using the engines to swing her around, was agreed to only very reluctantly. To make matters worse I had no choice but to wait for a maximum rise of the tide level resulting from a high spring tide at Fao.

Finally, on the bridge, flanked by the good commanders, I gave the appropriate orders and the cruiser glided into mid-river and gracefully proceeded at slow speed upriver to the wilderness of Hell's Gates. At the point in the river where I elected to turn, with the bow deeply embedded in the mud against the river bank, I could sense the nervousness of the officers behind me. To be honest I had butterflies in my stomach as I watched her swing. What a difference from the average merchantman, here there was real power in her several screws. She balked a bit whilst at right angles to the bank and mud swirled around her stern. I could hear sighs of relief as she gathered momentum. When almost completely around and with all engines astern she withdrew slowly from the river bank. An engine switch to full ahead and she straightened out like the racehorse she really was.

There was a distinct hubbub of excitement and relief on the part of the officers and crew. As we headed downriver at reduced speed past Abadan there was much saluting and flag-waving, and then one final blast on the ship's siren. It can be said that all parties breathed sighs of relief at her departure but I felt sure that the Europeans remaining felt a little less secure. Very soon it became evident that the oil cartel had a good deal more to say to Mr Mossadeq. They decided to boycott the refinery in its entirety, then they simply shut it down. There was considerable sadness when the last tanker left the dock in Abadan. We shook hands firmly with all the government dignitaries and left. I was ordered to Basrah where I took over as Harbour Master, and the shipping business there was busier than ever.

Jane and I were together again and by then, close to Christmas 1951, I had already accumulated lots of home leave. We had many discussions about our plans for the future and decided that the best thing to do was for Jane to fly home in the spring and I would follow in the early summer. My current contract with the Crown Agents was due to expire in September 1952. I am sure that when Jane left Basrah by Super-Constellation for London she knew she would never be back. She simply could not wait to get home and be a mother again to Miss Lynn.

I was a grass widower again in Basrah for a few months of spring and early summer of 1952; this was by far the best time of the year in Iraq. Business and shipping both continued to prosper there and the airport was busier than ever. Whilst the facilities at Abadan remained closed and the embargo tightened its grip the only loser was the Iranian Government. The average Iranian who derived no benefit whatsoever from the oil revenues really cared little about the outcome. However to anyone familiar with the overall situation it was obvious that things would never be the same again. Without doubt the situation might be resolved but only temporarily. There could be no real possibility of long-term stability under the existing regime and no one knew who might be its successor.

By the month of May 1952 I had made up my mind that it was time to go elsewhere, despite the excellent accommodation, the fat salary and the senior appointments. I convinced myself that there were more important things in life. I paid my final visits to the contacts in Baghdad and in Basrah, and even visited Fao for the last time. At the end of the month I advised the Directorate that I would take leave in the UK and that I would contact the Crown Agents in London for final settlement as I would not be returning. I should record the fact that the Directorate were most generous. I was given full salary and allowance to the end of my contact, and with accumulated local leave, home leave and provident fund contributions I qualified for a very handsome lump sum settlement. I left with absolutely no regrets.

The first-class flight home by KLM to Amsterdam and on to Glasgow was an event in itself. I knew then that an era of my life had ended and I had all these hours flying to mull over in my mind all the possibilities for a new life somewhere, anywhere, but no longer in the Middle East. When I saw Jane and Lynn at the airport I knew I had made the right decision. I had visions of a rousing, riotous reception but instead it was restrained and a little chilling. Jane was obviously nervous with Lynn, not knowing how she would react. Lynn, now a day-girl at St Hilary's, and dressed up in her school uniform complete with hat, looked quite grown up to me. She looked me up and down before making up her mind that I was acceptable. After all she was nearly eight years old and a very self-confident little lady after a couple of years of boarding school.

We had arrived home in Edinburgh before the ice really melted and Miss Lynn decided that she might call me Daddy. It was indeed a relief and only then did I truly believe that I was back home. I did get a big hug before she went off to bed and Jane kept me entertained for the rest of the evening telling me stories about Lynn and her school holidays. Jane's dad, Lynn's grandfather, having spent his life in the motor trade always drove a large modern car. He picked Lynn up at school to take her to Earlston. Miss Lynn would not ride in the front with him at all, instead she insisted on sitting in regal splendour at the back. She insisted that she got nothing to eat at the school but tapioca pudding. Her grandmother, who loved her dearly, would describe her as an impudent little besom, independent, demanding and always getting her own way. She never did change very much.

That very night Jane and I made the final, irrevocable decision. We would seek a new family life together elsewhere in the world after a suitable holiday. With this happy thought in our minds we slept like tops and in the morning we woke to find that Lynn had crawled into the middle of the bed between us. It was a good omen for the start of a new adventure, another voyage so to speak, for the three of us.

PART IV

CHAPTER XV

CANADIAN LANDED IMMIGRANT

Our four-month holiday in Edinburgh was the holiday of a lifetime. Lynn was a day-girl at St Hilary's, but soon her end of term came along and the three of us were inseparable. Lynn clung to her mother as though she was scared she might leave again. She told us wild stories about boarding school just to convince us that she should never be sent back. She kept saying that she got nothing to eat but tapioca pudding, which was truly an exaggeration, because she was by far the healthiest looking child around.

She enjoyed our visits to the old farmhouse at Linlithgow Bridge and her grannie Miller doted upon her despite the fact that she already had lots of grandchildren. Another attraction of course had to be the three Morrison children, now quite grown up. My sister Jean and brother-in-law Jock Morrison were still there, complete with a talkative budgie and a handsome alsatian called Laddie, one of Nipper's off-spring. There was Ian Morrison, a big lad like his father, about fifteen years old, then Miss Belle, a demure thirteen, and finally little Miss Katie, pretending to be ten.

We had our picnics in the country and our tours of the glorious highlands, and I had lots of opportunities to revisit the old haunts my old grandfather and I had visited so often. For the first time that I can remember I really missed my father and my old grandfather. They had been so much a part of the old house that nothing seemed to be the same without them. I managed time alone with my mother and she and I went to the theatres in Edinburgh, something she truly enjoyed. In those days, at the theatre interval, the men rose to go to the bar, but meanwhile most had arranged for a coffee tray to be served to the ladies at their seats. That was always the highlight of my mother's evening.

Our time in Edinburgh was divided mostly between Jane's parents and her younger brother Edwin, now married to Chrissie and already the parents of two daughters, Diane and Christine. Quite separately though I had a very good and lasting relationship with Jane's father John Malcolm. He was in the motor trade, as he called it, and spent most of his time selling fleets of trucks and buses. He was a very popular man with hordes of friends, and he loved life, music and song, but most of all he loved the pubs. He and I were good friends and together we had many a truly Scottish adventure. He was always trying to convince Jane and I that we should buy a pub, his choice being the 'Castle Bar', in Castle Street. Happily we never did. Oddly enough he had spent most of the 1914-18 war in Mesopotamia as it was called then. He shared many unpleasant memories of his terrible experiences there.

Being a man of considerable means, and bent upon making a good impression in my new endeavours, I had a brand new wardrobe hand-tailored by Simpson's of Hanover Street. We used to joke about it quite a bit but now out of uniform, and in temperate climates, it was very necessary to spruce up. It was fortunate that we had a busy social life with all our old friends during our vacation because beyond that happy period, and I did not know it yet, I had many a long, lonely day to spend before I could afford it again.

We had tossed a coin to determine whether to consider Australia or Canada, and fate determined Canada to be our next goal. I had read great stories about the tremendous development about to begin in the St Lawrence Seaway, and the opportunities there were reported to be fantastic. Once the decision was made there was no time wasted. I visited the immigration offices in Glasgow and fortunately I had the good sense to take with me the letter from Doctor Ian Farquharson. The young doctors at the immigration office giving medical examinations were joking with one another that they could dance to the peculiar beat of my heart. However the letter convinced them that I was okay and within days I was documented and ticketed first class on the SS *Atlantic*, out of Southampton for Quebec city, with an arrival date of 1 October 1952.

Once again Jane and I parted, but at least she had Lynn with her, they lived in a nice apartment in Edinburgh and would await the good word to follow me to Canada. Lynn was quite sad at my departure, it was difficult to assure her that there were good schools in Canada and she would not have to become a boarder again at St Hilary's. Nevertheless I was so optimistic about the entire adventure that I was able to convince them that we would be together again soon and they were dry-eyed at our final parting.

I joined the SS *Atlantic*, the Home Lines flagship, to find that she was really a reconditioned Matson liner that once ran from San Francisco to Hawaii. She was berthed at Southampton and she made a call at Cherbourg to pick up additional passengers. During the stay in both ports I met and made friends with the Danish Marine Superintendent of the company and he had a most unusual name: it was Axel Bitch. He recognized me as a seafarer, introduced me to the Captain and his wife, made the staff aware of my presence and ensured their attention and service throughout the voyage. He asked me as a friend to seriously look around the vessel and write to him about any deficiencies I might observe.

Voyages Into Eternity

At the end of September the North Atlantic was already a little rough and many of the passengers were seasick. In first class the bars were literally empty and the entertainment was very low key. I did meet one young lady who was very pretty but her name was something of a mismatch. Her surname was Hogg and they had christened her Alexandrina. Her father was some bigshot on the railway somewhere. As it happened she was fascinated by the daily sweepstake based upon the number of nautical miles the vessel travelled and this was published on the noticeboard shortly after noon. She insisted that I explain the day's run process to her and advise her of the likely winning number.

Each day her number was very close and I always took the number one above or one below hers. As it turned out it was my number that came up and I won about four hundred and fifty dollars. I mention it only because that was a lot of money in those days and as fate would have it it helped me get through the winter in Montreal. In those post-war years, because of the weakness of British currency due to a disastrous war, those of us who departed were permitted to take only a maximum of six hundred dollars per year, and not one cent more. To put these numbers in perspective, the average professional at that time earned about three hundred dollars per month. I stepped ashore in Quebec city with a total of one thousand dollars in my pocket.

The immigration process was brief, courteous and final. I was an instant landed immigrant with the freedom to settle anywhere in the entire country and with authorization to work. Another application, at a later date, was all that was required if I desired to become a citizen. I must admit I suffered a momentary lapse of determination and endured a few pangs of sadness as I felt that I was abandoning my native land. However such lapses are understandable, and purely momentary. Life must go on, one step at a time.

I took the first train out for Montreal and on the advice of a friendly railway man I headed for what he called a tourist home at the west end of St Catherine Street, where rooms were three dollars per night. I was pleasantly surprised, the bedroom was comfortable and there was a decent bathroom down the hall. Within walking distance, straight down St Catherine Street, there was an abundance of restaurants, the majority of which were spaghetti houses, all boasting of the number of tons of the stuff they had dished up in the current year. I spent the first week finding my way around and seeking information. I quickly tired of spaghetti and became one of the regulars at Ben's delicatessen.

Before the week was out I had recognized my first grave mistake. The cold, bitter, Canadian winter was moving in and within weeks everything that was marine would be shut down. The so-called mega project, the St Lawrence Seaway, was as far as I was concerned a ghastly farce. The equipment and the methods

159

they were using were so antiquated it was beyond belief. A brief discussion with one of the executives of Morrison-Knudsen convinced me that I would be better off on a farm in Saskatchewan. I had blundered badly as I should have arrived in the spring. The port of Montreal was about to shut down and the line-up at the unemployment office was something to behold.

Nevertheless I had no choice but to make the best of it so I sat down and wrote a long letter to Jane, telling her all about the beautiful city of Montreal. Then I decided to winterize and economize. I moved from the tourist home into digs in Notre Dame de Grace. I had a warm, comfortable room in a nice Jewish home and I unpacked my typewriter and went to work. First it was resumés seeking employment in the spring, then fiction, short stories for the popular magazines.

I had my share of rejection slips before I hit the jackpot in February 1953. My response to an original fiction competition advertised by Fawcett Publications, a US firm, was a winner. A short story, 'No flies on Brannigan', won second prize for me and much to my surprise they sent me more money when they published it. It must have earned me more than 1,200 dollars. Meanwhile I did find the odd temporary job to keep the wolf from the door and some of them were rather amusing.

In one case there were truckloads of telephone directories about to be delivered to the railway station for loading on to goods waggons. The previous year the shipment had been very badly damaged because so many packages containing ten directories had been stored on end instead of flat. I was considered to be the very person they needed to supervise the gang of hoodlums who were hired to load the cars. It was my responsibility to see that every package was stowed flat. I was far from flattered by the compliment, but I took the job. I sincerely hope I am never again obliged to supervise such a bunch of idiots but I can never quite forget the raucous entertainment they provided.

I spent some weeks working in a basement in Champs de Mars, in the very heart of the red-light district, for an outfit called Levitt Safety. They were always organizing the stupidest training programs for salesmen peddling work safety equipment. During these sessions, run by a stout fellow from Cairo, Egypt, who was constantly humming 'Glow little Glowworm', the owner himself would appear. Without saying a word to anyone he would walk into the classroom, pick up the chalk and write on the blackboard, 'X number of calls equals Y number of sales'. Then, having dropped these pearls of wisdom, he would simply depart.

About that time in late March I received a very welcome letter in response to one of my many applications. I had an interview, a beginning, I thought. This was at Robert Reford Company Ltd., local shipping agents for Flota Mercante

Gran-Columbiana and several other enterprises. They needed a Marine Superintendent to supervise the off-loading of vessels in the port of Montreal. The old boy who interviewed me was from Dundee, in Scotland, but as it turned out he was an accountant and not my cup of tea. However I was glad to take the job and promptly found myself back in the Champs de Mars area amongst all the pimps, whores and dockworkers, and of course, Levitt Safety.

By 1 April 1953 I was on the docks supervising the unloading of the MV *Cuidad de Caracas*, just in from South America. Much of the cargo for Montreal was coffee in 100 lb bags, each bag worth at least a hundred dollars, and every stevedore on the entire dock was just dying to steal one. The duty hours were frantic. At times I was on the dock by 4.45 a.m., and dragging myself back to Notre Dame de Grace on a tram at ten or eleven at night. Meanwhile my accountant boss from Dundee was weeping and wailing about the number of bags of coffee going missing. I could scarcely wait for the day when I might be able to advise him where to shove his coffee.

It was because of my activities on the docks that I met Captain McIntyre, very much my senior and very sympathetic to my cause. He convinced me that the shipping business and the seaway were not for me. He had a friend in Ottawa, a Mr F.C.G. Smith, the Dominion Hydrographer, and he recommended a personal visit. It wasn't easy to find the time but because of a delay in arrival of one of our vessels I was able to sneak away. In less than ten minutes Mr F.C.G. Smith convinced me to fill in the necessary forms of application, and he assured me that within weeks I would be accepted and that I should promptly bring my wife to Ottawa. Meanwhile he put me in touch with D'Arcy Charles, one of his senior officials.

I spent a number of hours in Ottawa looking around and found it to be a most attractive city. I celebrated in the club car on the way back to Montreal whilst I mentally composed my letter of regret to the man from Dundee. I wrote to Jane that very night and in a very short time she had her passage booked to Montreal on the *Empress of Australia*. On my recommendation she and Lynn travelled first class in view of the likely hardships they might face in settling in Ottawa. By early June she was on her way and by some good fortune Captain McIntyre had located another young Scottish sailor willing to take my place at Reford Co. Ltd. Later on I learned that my substitute and old man Dodd, from Dundee, got along famously.

I was on the dock to meet the beautiful *Empress*, and although nervous about the new job I was delighted to see my womenfolk again. Miss Jane was in the height of fashion and Lynn, now almost nine, was quite the young lady. She wasn't too happy about having left all her friends behind but she was reassured when I promised that she would be going to a really good school. Their baggage

161

included Persian carpets, carved Chinese chests and all kinds of stuff. How we ever got it all through the customs then on to Ottawa is still a mystery.

In preparation for their arrival I had signed a lease for a new apartment on Tilbury Avenue, close to the Carling and Cole intersection. Beyond that intersection, Carling Avenue was a gravel road leading directly out to the sticks. The apartments were six to a block and were just in the final stages of completion. Ours was indeed complete but still in something of a mess. The bath was full of cartons and sawdust and the kitchen had obviously been used as everybody's storehouse. I could see Madame's nose crinkle dangerously and braced myself for an onslaught.

It was not so much the state of the apartment that horrified her because we cleaned it up in a hurry. It was when I told her that I was obliged to head for the Arctic for the hydrographic survey season which carried on until the end of October that she rebelled. I had to admit that, henceforward, I would be gone for six months of the year. We argued quite a bit and there was the occasional flood of tears with Lynn joining in. We had no furniture that first night so we had to sleep on the Persian carpets. However, before I took off, the basic furniture was delivered and they were at least comfortable, but very much alone. The real estate people assured us that the building would be fully occupied within a week.

The day I left for Seven Islands to begin my new career Jane was consoled to some degree, knowing that I had a permanent job. The salary was dismal: 300 dollars a month, plus a 300-dollar field bonus for each summer. In addition, come 1 October, she would get another 600 from our Bank in Scotland. I kept saying, 'Before you know it, we'll have a car,' but she was not impressed. However she did assure me that she would not take off back to Scotland. She promised me a comfortable home to return to for the winter.

Getting to Seven Islands was not easy and I was relieved to finally catch sight of the survey vessel at anchor offshore. The *Kapuskasing* was an algerine class ex-naval vessel, now manned by a civilian crew, mostly Newfoundlanders. The hydrographers – there were seven of us plus a couple of student assistants – were headed by Ralph Hansen, the party chief. The primary purpose of hydrography is the production of nautical charts, and it is a very serious business involving hydrographers, cartographers and draughtsmen, producing charts back in Ottawa from the wealth of data and information accumulated in the field. The survey work must be done to a very high level of accuracy and can be very interesting as well as being a very rugged way of life.

At that particular time the objective was to produce an accurate chart of the recently constructed port of Seven Islands, the terminal for the export of iron ore from Ungava. Very shortly that objective had been met and we moved on to

162

the east coast of Cape Breton Island. I have to confess that, after my palmy days in the Middle East with the Crown Agents, and the ego-building experience of being a senior burra-sahib, I felt like very small potatoes as the new man on the *Kapuskasing*. Operating out of launches, climbing mountains to build triangulation stations, lugging theodolites around to measure horizontal angles, was a far cry from being the monarch of all you survey. Nevertheless it was a lesson in humility and I managed to swallow my pride.

On 31 October we were on our way back to Ottawa and a clear six months at home. It was an exhilarating thought and we all had quite a celebration on the train journey to Ottawa, some 1,100 miles. We travelled in some sort of second-class comfort, described as a roomette, wherein we could sit during daylight hours, and come nightfall, if you were something of an acrobat, a bed could be disentangled from the wall. Fortunately we had access to a little Nova Scotia rum which helped to ease the pain.

Arrival in Ottawa at Union Station was the highpoint of the entire operation. There were loads of folks there to greet the train and Jane and Lynn were among them. By now their apartment building was full and they had made friends with other tenants. One of their friends had a car so we were delivered home in the lap of luxury. I was most surprised, Jane had really created a home for us, complete with washing machine with its own power wringer. In those days there were no dryers available other than long stretches of wire rope slung between sheaves attached to stout poles on the roofs of the garages. Jane took great pride in lugging baskets of wet laundry out there, climbing onto the garage roof, then dangling all her smalls from the wire provided. It was already wintry and the so-called washing was frozen stiff.

We had a high old time for a few days, running to the bank to get her allowance from the Bank of Scotland, getting our hands on the 300-dollar field bonus, then visiting stores like Freemans, and Robinson, Pringle and Tilley, all long gone by now. Our pride and joy was a brand new black and white television. We were the first in the entire building so the neighbours practically lived with us for a while. We used to watch the Ed Sullivan Show on a Sunday night with a house full of guests. Soon, RPT was doing a roaring trade and everybody had one. However, a car was still out of the question and I rode the buses and the trams.

The hydrographic headquarters was located in a crumbling, temporary building at the Carling and Preston intersection. It was a section within the Department of Mines and Technical Surveys. Our neighbours were topographic surveys, geological surveys, etc., all in all, a very interesting group. The entire department was headed up by a peculiar old boy by the name of Willett Miller, no relation, who constantly lounged in his office chair with his feet up on the desk and rolled his own cigarettes. Strange though it may seem, anytime I had occasion to visit his office I would be fascinated by his feet. The sole of one of his shoes was totally worn out and he had stuffed paper into the shoe to provide a measure of protection from the scuffed wooden floors of his office.

The hydrographic party chiefs, Ralph Hansen being ours, devoted many a long day to reminiscing, and most of Friday afternoons to the 'Last Chance Tavern' on Preston Street. But there was some sort of order within the various offices where the field data was carefully analyzed, reviewed, then transferred from field sheets to appropriate chart projections at greatly expanded scale, and described upon aluminium-backed sheets for stability. The scale was reduced later by photographic reduction methods. Some training was organized in the art of cartography and later on classes were started dealing with triangulation, with adjustments, and with the approved methodology for the calculation of latitude and longitude to a very high degree of accuracy. In the spring, when the weather permitted, we spent a good deal of time on celestial observations. These classes were conducted by Paul Brunavs, a nautical geodesist from the University of Riga, in Latvia.

It was obvious that the entire department was in process of expansion and awaiting approval of funding to permit construction of new vessels. They were short of qualified personnel and in dire need of the application of newer technologies. Sub-departments like Tidal, Levelling, and Sailing Directions, were equally short-handed considering the thousands of miles of Canadian coastline and the country's dependence upon world shipping. It was no real surprise when Mr Smith, the Dominion Hydrographer, informed us of his negotiation with Decca Navigator Company of London, England, for a special, electronic survey system to provide continuous horizontal control of the survey vessel, thereby speeding up the process of chart production.

Mr Smith had selected the *Kapuskasing* for the relevant trials and in view of my Deep-Sea Master's qualifications he had selected me as the initial guinea pig. Ralph Hansen remained as party chief but he was happy to leave the technology application to me. Training manuals, technical papers and methodology recommendations were supplied and it was determined that the initial operation was to be conducted off the north shore of Prince Edward Island, and as far north as the Magdalen Islands. The systems planning lent considerable excitement to our spring period, and by April's end we were ready to go.

By now Jane had learned to live with the idea of my annual excursions and she was good friends with many of the other hydrographic wives. D'Arcy Charles, with whom my early indoctrination had been conducted, became a firm friend and the friendship lasted until his death at the age of seventy-eight. However there was one big surprise before my departure. With Miss Lynn already over nine years old, Jane was pregnant. While she was not exactly jumping for joy at the prospect, it was only because of the terrifying labour she had endured in 1944. She was a very nervous prospective mother when I departed and I kept wondering about my own age, thirty-five, a little old to be a new father, I thought.

Despite my reservations and my concern about Jane and the baby, later that year, in the heat of July and six months pregnant, she and Lynn took off to visit her aunt and uncle in New Jersey. They rode the train from Ottawa to Montreal, then on to New York city. Her uncle Bill, her mother's brother, met her at Grand Central Station. They lived in Midland Park, New Jersey and considering that they had never met before they all had a jolly good time. I still have pictures of Lynn running around in a cowgirl suit complete with six-guns. The heat that summer was grim and I can remember feeling vastly relieved when I learned that they had arrived home safely.

However, schedules determined that we join the vessel in Halifax, Nova Scotia and there the Decca technical people joined us for the trip around the coast to Prince Edward Island. We had to erect a low-frequency radio transmitting-receiving station at a surveyed point in PEI, which was powered by portable generators and attended by two technicians who kept in touch with us by radio-telephone. A second station, exactly similar, was erected on the Magdalen Islands. A radio station on board triggered the entire system by transmitting on a harmonically related frequency. The receivers on board, when the transmitters were running constantly and phase-locked one to the other, converted the related signals to a common frequency for comparison and decometers provided read-out in a number of lanes distant from each of the slave stations on shore. Using the comparison frequency and the known speed of propagation over seawater, the width of a lane could be calculated in metres, down to thousandths of a metre.

Each station had a 150-foot transmitting tower and it was a really fun exercise erecting it. It was also advisable to locate the station close to the sea and on good soil to provide a base from which a strong signal might be emitted. Locally these stations created quite a stir, the country folks were absolutely fascinated by the whole process and I think some of them seriously believed that we were trying to track flying saucers. The visit to the Magdalens was an education in itself. We were guests of the Mayor and fêted locally. It was spring and the farmers were ploughing and spreading dead herring on their fields. The English boys at that station were wearing face masks when we left.

In preparation for the survey vessel to run lines of continuous electronic sounding, the field sheets were overlaid with concentric circles in colour code to provide ease of position plotting by range-range. We were constantly aware of our precise distance from each of the two slave stations, identified on the field sheets in accurate coordinates, and the plotting of our position was rendered simple. In addition, a track-plotter automatically portrayed our progress along any pre-determined line. Apart from the usual gaffes, periods of bad weather and occasional technical breakdowns, the system performed as planned. At the end of the season it was concluded that the *Kapuskasing* had increased her production immensely and that the experiment had been a great success.

Promptly on 31 October 1954 I arrived home to be greeted by the very pregnant Miss Jane, with Lynn not at all pleased by this turn of events and pretending some measure of embarrassment. It is difficult to recall the sensation I felt at seeing Jane about thirty pounds overweight and practically waddling. It was good though to feel the baby kicking like crazy every now and again. Thankfully Dr Barnes, her gynaecologist, decided that she was ripe for birth and ordered her into the civic hospital on the morning of 3 November. Right on time, Miss Janice Elaine appeared, and suddenly we were a family again. Even Lynn was dashing about full of unusual concern. She was delighted all of a sudden to have a sister, and to see her mother looking normal again.

About this time several persons from the Basrah Port Directorate showed up in Ottawa. John Ough, who had been a hydrographer with us in Basrah, joined the Department, Cyril Connally and Cyril Osborne, both surveyors in Basrah, decided that Ottawa offered more scope. John Ough moved on into the National Film Board, Cyril Osborne moved to the Army surveys, but Connally stayed on. At a later date another shipmaster with similar experience to mine, Harry Wood, also showed up from Basrah. He and his wife and daughter stayed with us briefly till he settled into the Department of Transport and was shunted off to Quebec city. They didn't like it and they returned to England shortly afterwards.

Back at the office, FCG as everybody called him, was delighted with the entire field performance of the *Kapuskasing* and he asked me to write a technical article describing the entire operation for publication in the *International Hydrographic Review*. This was the organ of a world body, headquartered in the principality of Monaco, and usually headed up by a retired admiral from some navy, usually British. Indeed the article was duly published, much to the satisfaction of FCG, but also to the delight of Decca Navigator Company who were in the business of selling these very expensive devices.

During the entire winter of 1954-55 I worked closely with Paul Brunavs in the creation of suitable training courses for the hydrographic office. He and I became good friends and I learned more from Paul Brunavs in the mathematics of geodesy, the intricacies of triangulation chain adjustments, the calculation of long lines, than from any college I had ever attended. He had some considerable difficulty with his English but was pleased to train me in order that I might thereafter train the others.

By the spring of 1955, with Janice bundled into a perambulator, Jane used to march off down Roosevelt Avenue in constant search for a nicer place to live. I thought the apartment was just fine but my views carried little weight against the combined opinions of Jane and Lynn. Her perseverance paid off. She found a wonderful new duplex, the top half of a lovely old home on Edison Avenue. The lady there, Mrs Tobin, just fell in love with Jane and her kids. She had never had any of her own and her husband Earl, who had a heating business, was a canny old soul with a large dog, a big cigar, and a constant smile. I believe that that was one of the happiest times of our lives when we moved into that brand, spanking new place. Jane was in seventh heaven.

Lynn and I often went off to the movies and picked up a bag of chocolate bars from a local confectioner called Joe's. It was always a great adventure together and something just between us. She was happy to leave her mother behind baby-sitting and on the walk to and fro she would confide all kinds of girlie stuff to which I would respond with elaborate seriousness. She and I were real friends while she was about ten and eleven. There were times, I think, when Jane thought that we were too close. It was then that she decided that we needed a car so we could all be out together. Shortly after that it became a crisis, we had to get a car, and she had to be able to drive it before I left for the following summer.

A brief search through the advertisements for used cars came up with a 1951 Rover, purported to be in excellent condition and for immediate sale. One phone call and the man was honking the horn at the door for a test drive. We loved it, it felt like a limousine. The deal was done, the man accepted cash and took off. We couldn't wait to get downstairs again to go off by ourselves. Unhappily, it failed to start. Jane had a bout of hysterics, but the man was long gone. When we recovered sufficiently to rationalize the situation it turned out to be a fairly simple problem with the starter motor. The less said about the driver-training provided to Miss Jane the better. However after a brief period including several serious fights, a few fits of hysterics and many anxious moments in the car, she could drive. From that moment on she used my winter sheepskin coat to cover the bonnet of the car every night in the garage. It was now her car.

Before my departure for the summer season of 1955 Miss Janice Elaine was christened by the Reverend Bruce McDonald in the Westboro United Church on Churchill Avenue. It was a very big moment in our lives. I suppose that we knew right then that that was it, our family, the four of us. Where Lynn had been a corn-coloured blond, Janice was a redhead, a beautiful copper colour. She was a very happy child, never ever a bother, and loved by all of us. I already enjoyed preparing all her bottles each evening, pushing her up and down in a pram and showing her off to everybody. We got to know the two boys next door, Peter and Andrew. Jane became good friends with the parents, Dr Ernie Weeks and his wife Gerda, during that summer.

In the hydrographic office there was an air of positive thinking and many of the staff were showing up with new cars. In fact some staff members took their cars with them to the maritimes for the summer in order to have transportation during weekend outings. On the *Kapuskasing* we had Gordon Arnold, who was a sort of bagman, as we called him, as he handled all the cash, ordered all the stores and retained all the relevant voyage expense records. He showed up in Halifax with a bright red Studebaker which everyone greatly envied. It turned out to be extremely useful at weekends in summertime, PEI and in Cheticamp on Cape Breton Island. It made everyone feel more prosperous and injected a feeling of optimism into the entire field crew.

That year we were back at our automated systems approach to surveying and with the aid of the Decca technicians from London everything went off exceedingly well. As a result of the initial success a second system had been ordered for another similar hydrographic ship, the *Fort Francis*, and she operated out of Ingonish on the Atlantic side of Cape Breton. As is customary on any initial venture many things went wrong and towards the end of the season I was transferred to the *Fort Francis* to assist in their correction.

By the time October came around the weather was unusually unsettled and by the end of the month we were all pretty well exhausted. An algerine in bad weather is not the most comfortable of vessels and with the restricted space the accommodation was spartan. However the food, whilst plain, was plentiful and without social distractions to bother us we worked very long hours. It was a great relief to return to Halifax to pack up for the summer. Gordie Arnold took off in his red limousine with all his financial records but we, the hydrographers, had to wait for the train.

Jane, Lynn and Janice were all bubbling with excitement when I got home. Not that Janice had much to say at only one year old but she did get quite excited when she saw me. It was difficult to follow the stories from Jane and Lynn, they were so excited about their big adventure. That summer they had decided to drive through Toronto and on to Hamilton to visit a friend, Jean Horseman. Earl Tobin had provided the necessary routing instructions and one of Jane's close friends, Pamela Flaherty, decided to join the trio. The entire trip had been a bit frightening apparently because no one had the slightest idea where they were going. Earl Tobin's map was all Greek to them. Nevertheless they had persevered, driven right through Toronto and on into Hamilton, and all this long before the existence of Route 401.

They finally made their objective, had a hilarious time and on the return journey brought Jean Horseman and her kids back with them. How they all squeezed into the old Rover I will never know. Providence must have smiled upon them because the tyres on the car had only a minimum of tread remaining.

Mrs Tobin was mightily relieved to see them back safely and just to celebrate their return the children were left in her care whilst the girls took off to the outdoor cinema drive-in. Alas, when all the ice cream and popcorn had been demolished and the film completed, the dependable Rover refused to start. It was the middle of the night before they made it home.

But we were saving money now and we had the Rover completely overhauled so that Jane could career around to wherever she wanted to go. It was just as well because FCG had been in touch with Decca who suggested that I be sent there to study their systems. At the same time he offered to arrange for me to undergo special training at the British Naval Hydrographic Office, in London, England. I was delighted to have the opportunity to go and to my surprise he also suggested a trip to Edinburgh, to recruit newly-qualified shipmasters from the Nautical College there. There were new hydrographic survey vessels under construction and he had big plans for expansion.

Jane was not entirely happy with the idea but she did recognize the worthwhile benefits for me and she was a good sport about it. It was the spring of 1956 and by then there was a regular North Atlantic air service out of Montreal, via Goose Bay, Labrador to London, England. The aircraft were souped up DC6s, with four gasoline-powered engines, terribly noisy, but considered to be relatively safe. We landed at Goose Bay with three engines remaining, number four having been on fire. We had to stay in a Nissen hut at Goose Bay for at least two days whilst an engine was flown in from Montreal. The trans-Atlantic crossing was accomplished without further mishap, but with everyone's ears ringing like Big Ben.

Decca elected to be the host and had arranged an elaborate itinerary. Whilst there I was wined and dined in some of the most fabulous restaurants I have ever seen. The company was run by an American, Harvey Schwarz, a small, insignificant man but a real dynamo at marketing. The Navigator Company was a subsidiary of the massive Decca complex controlled by Sir Edward Lewis. Schwarz's big success had been the primary utilization of the system in the D-Day landings. It was his dedicated purpose in life to expand the system throughout the civilized world and in particular into the country of his birth, the United States.

Roy Mitchell, an ex-squadron leader from the Royal Air Force and an associate of Sir Robert Watson-Watt, the British scientist credited with the development of radar, had been selected to lead the effort into the North American market. He had already convinced the Bendix Corporation to consider a North American licence. Like Schwarz he was a workaholic but he was also a very polished individual and exceedingly clever. By the end of the first week he had made up his mind that his North American organization had to include me. Fortunately I acquired a rest from all these high-priced entrepreneurs when I moved to the British Naval Hydrographic Office. I met Admiral St Bernard Stevens and his staff and I must say I enjoyed every day of my stay with them. I spent weeks at Cricklewood, the headquarters, then spent more time at their production facilities at Taunton, Somerset.

In particular, I enjoyed my time with Commander Ian Farquharson, Head of their Tidal Surveys division. I spent several evenings at his home in High Wycombe. He had two daughters, both British Airlines air stewardesses, a young son, Ian, and a charming wife, Kate. Their neighbours through the garden fence were Wendy Hiller and her handicapped husband. She was always my favourite film actress. Ian loved to serve large pink gins to all and sundry in his beautiful garden. The following year, upon their retirement from the Royal Navy, both Admiral Stevens and Captain Farquharson were brought to Canada by FCG. The Admiral came under contract as a consultant, and Ian Farquharson came to head up the Tidal Division.

On a more personal level I had sustained correspondence with a young student hydrographer who had sailed with me on the *Kapuskasing*. At the time, Douglas Kelly was very young, just out of college and had blown every cent he had on a brand new Hillman Minx. We became good friends and when he became aware of my background he leaned on me for advice about his future. I remember telling him very bluntly to go back to Ottawa, sell his car, quit hydrographics and buy a one-way plane ticket to London, England so that he might learn what life was really all about. To my surprise, he did precisely that. After sowing his wild oats he settled down, went to college and became a radio officer, flying with Eagle Airlines all over North Africa.

Now I had occasion to look him up, but finding him was an adventure in itself. The address I had for him was in Earls Court and the particular street where he parked his duffel bags was a long row of what had once been elegant town houses. The years of neglect after the war had wrought havoc with the interior and I found to my dismay that one could progress from one elegant town house to the next through holes created in the walls. At one time somebody had obviously tried to develop flats in the building but with little success. I remember staggering through the corridors, through holes in the walls, dodging ladies underwear strung on ropes in the alleyways, past open doors to apartments bulging with remnants and leftovers from the previous night's binge. Great empty fireplaces with lingerie dangling from the marble mantelpiece bore mute testimony to their past grandeur.

Finally young Doug's smiling face was easy to recognize as he had the most glorious set of glistening white teeth I had ever seen on any man. He must have been a real heartbreaker with the girls. We had a boisterous reunion, then he was gone. Years later he returned to Ottawa and became a successful businessman. From time to time we met, more by accident than design, but often enough so that we stayed in touch. Such is the way of life of sailors and adventurers.

One of the highlights of my trip was a visit to Herstmonceux Castle, as a guest of the Astronomer Royal. It had always been an ambition of mine to meet the people who prepared and published the 'Nautical Ephemeris', without which the mariner could not possibly calculate his position. Within this manual, published annually, were all of the data and information relevant to the celestial sphere, including the sun, moon and stars, with their hour angles and declination etc. The staff at the castle had preserved all of the old equipment, such as hollerith punchcard machines, and mechanical and electric calculators. Greenwich Time was their primary responsibility and within the castle, deep in the dungeon depths, were the original clocks as well as newer atomic devices.

I spent the last few days of my stay in the UK in Edinburgh and this provided time for a quick hello around the family at Linlithgow and in Edinburgh. I set up meetings, mostly in hotel bars, with some of the students from the Nautical College, who were studying for their master's papers. The level of interest was quite surprising, and I arranged for the relevant application forms and provided instructions in regard to documentation at the immigration office. As a consequence, within a very few months, we had seven or eight successful applicants and they were promptly posted to the various vessels.

I was glad to get home in mid-April with my overall mission accomplished. I had begun to feel that there might be some sort of future for me in Canada after all, although the thought of spending all of the summer months off in the field was no longer appealing. However the 1956 summer season was upon us and I had no choice but to join the happy group. Jane, Lynn and little Janice saw me off once again and I believe that they too were wondering when I might ever have a summer at home. However, by the time I reached Halifax and stepped aboard the *Kapuskasing* I was back to normal, prepared for one day at a time.

The summer of 1956 was like all the others, sixteen-hour days broken up by dreary liberty in port for water and stores. This season we operated out of Cheticamp, on the west side of Cape Breton Island, and as usual churned through the survey lines in very short order. One of the highlights of the summer was a venture into the Gut of Canso where a causeway linking Nova Scotia to Cape Breton was under construction. We were the last vessel to pass through the remaining gap before the causeway was finally closed off. Meanwhile back in Ottawa, F.C.G. Smith had retired due to age and Norman Gray took over as Dominion Hydrographer. A brand new vessel, the *Baffin*, was nearing completion and a second sister vessel was planned.

On my arrival home the first thing Jane said to me was, 'No more trips to

England without me. If you go, we all go.' However the entire winter was devoted to the development of training manuals and teaching the new arrivals the hydrographic gospel. During this same winter of 1956, Roy Mitchell moved from London to Toronto and established a Canadian office. He spent much of his time in Ottawa, negotiating with the various Government departments, and kept a suite at the Chateau Laurier. He had Jane and I out to dinner several times and obviously he had set his mind upon convincing Jane that I should move into his organization.

When April 1957 came around, and the survey departments were preparing for their summer expeditions, my own estimate of my future with them was pretty low. The brand new vessel, the *Baffin*, fitted with the latest Decca equipment, was to be manned by a slate of hydrographers which did not include me. I was posted back to the *Kapuskasing* once again and I found it difficult to understand why. I hesitated to question my fearless leaders in view of my rather close association with Decca. Instead I paid more attention to Roy Mitchell and his plans for conquering North America. A brief discussion with Jane and the decision was made. I was now Manager of Systems for Decca, Toronto.

By this time Ian Farquharson was already settled in and I well remember my discussion with him in regard to the possibilities as he might see them. He was a very cheerful, humorous guy, and we had many a joke about the whole Canadian operation. I was most impressed one day when he handed me a handwritten note. It was a profound quotation from Shakespeare: 'There is a tide in the affairs of men, which when taken on the flood . . .' From that moment on my mind was at ease.

The move from Ottawa to Toronto was abrupt, with little time for serious planning. To avoid another six months of plodding in the field I had no option but resign immediately. Jane was upset about leaving Mrs Tobin, but excited at the thought that we might have more time together. We withdrew the Government pension contributions and tallied up our meagre savings, then optimistically decided that we could afford to buy a house. The 50 per cent raise in salary I got had a great deal to do with our future ambitions. The old Rover trundled its way to Toronto and beyond to a little town called Oakville where we decided to stay.

We found a brand new house, ready for occupancy, on the fourth line, just west of Oakville. The overall price was 16,000 dollars and we could just manage the down payment. A few days in a motel where the heater didn't work, then our belongings arrived and we moved in. The neighbours were great, the schools were great, and out of sheer necessity I had to buy a decent car; so we were then properly settled in. Like most folks in Oakville, I commuted to the west side of Toronto, but not for long. After a couple of weeks I was on my way to the Gulf of Mexico.

The trip was something of an adventure because in those days everywhere in Texas, with the possible exception of Dallas, was still in a growth phase. Houston was still a hick town and the William Pitt Hotel and the bus station were the most exciting places in town. In Austin, the State capital, I swear I bumped into cowboys on the main streets. The London office of Decca had established a survey system in the Gulf of Mexico for Shell Oil who were running a geophysical survey needing accuracy of continuous position fix. Things were not going too well technically and I had the problem of getting the show on the road. With the technical deficiencies corrected it turned out that the real problem was one of communication and indoctrination. I had no option but to go to sea on their high-speed, ex-Navy, coastal patrol boat.

The entire venture had its amusing side as well as the down-to-earth business of indoctrinating the personnel with the proper methodology, the recognition and correction of momentary system failures and the constant need for vigilance. Quite quickly real production commenced and it was then rather difficult to convince them to head back into port to drop me off. Instead, I had to swing along with the production gang and fend for myself. The ship was too small to boast of cooks and stewards, or any other luxury for that matter. They merely kept a large pot of fat bubbling on the stove, one bucket full of raw chip potatoes and another full of shrimp, standing alongside. If you were hungry you chucked a handful of chips and shrimp into a wire basket and plunged it into the hot fat. *Voilà*, there was lunch. For dessert there was a large ice-chest on the stern, absolutely full of every kind of chocolate bar available.

I hastened back to civilization the moment the ship docked, but I did quite enjoy the entire adventure. Things were beginning to hum in Toronto under Roy Mitchell's prodding. Visiting engineers from London and mathematicians from the labs to train us in the more elegant mathematics involved in hyperbolic systems came and went their way. Meanwhile we were recruiting more staff. The really big promotion at that time was the 'Delrac System', whereby a massive transmitter in the Highlands of Scotland was to be phase-locked to a similar transmitter in Newfoundland, radiating on a different but harmonically related frequency, thus producing trans-Atlantic coverage for the growing aircraft traffic and the critical need for their adequate separation laterally, as well as in altitude.

Our end of the system required a 600-foot tower to be erected in Newfoundland, near Gander. To satisfy the mathematical equations in the calculation of the hyperbolic patterns of equal phase, it was necessary to make innumerable measurements of soil conductivity throughout Newfoundland. By now I had a competent staff and this kept us hopping on and off aeroplanes, and on one occasion involved driving over 4,000 miles over Newfoundland with a van loaded with equipment. Here again the life was rugged. A dearth of hotels compelled us to camp out and cook for ourselves in the backwoods of the entire island. Occasionally we ground to a halt on some country road, held up by two large bears sleeping in the sunshine on the warm tarmac. They would be angry at being disturbed and when they stretched their great forepaws skyward they looked eight feet tall to me. Fortunately they would merely grunt a bit, give out a roar or two then amble off into the woods.

At least I was home quite regularly and we were able to have some summer fun together as a family. Jane loved her house and garden, and kept me slaving at building fences and rockeries as well as completing the basement. She made lots of friends and made a good life for herself. Lynn was happy at school and Janice was running about, now almost three years old. When the top brass visited from London, Roy Mitchell organized elegant dinner parties at the Lord Simcoe Hotel where they served pheasant under glass, and flaming pancakes, and Jane positively glowed. It was always an amusing business, too, as we suffered constant telephone interruptions from London, from Spain, from Australia, etc. It lent an air of excitement to the whole business.

However such endeavours are not without setbacks. Just when Mitchell announced our success with a multi-million dollar proposal to the Canadian Government for a series of general navigation systems in the Maritimes and Quebec, the brand new CGS *Baffin* was run aground on Black Rock, in St Margaret's Bay, Nova Scotia in dense fog at full speed. There were two deep-sea master mariners on duty in the control room at the time and they blamed errors in the Decca system.

I was asked by the Dominion Hydrographer to provide an analysis of the entire disaster and this was done in confidence. However a higher authority deemed it necessary to conduct a public enquiry. This took up much of my time the following summer when the enquiry was held in Halifax under Chief Justice Poitier, flanked by two nautical assessors. The outcome was satisfactory as far as we were concerned and the officers involved were censured. Our attorneys made sure we stayed in our seats throughout the entire enquiry. It did some good for the hydrographic office as the court emphasized the need for an established line of authority on board and the need for the precise definition of command. The hydrographer in charge claimed that it was nothing to do with him as he was washing his hands at the time. As a consequence of subsequent rational measures adopted by the Dominion Hydrographer, such an incident did not reoccur.

Meanwhile our staff were busy building stations throughout Newfoundland, Nova Scotia and Quebec and the office work back in Toronto was building up. We recruited more experts from England and whilst we were still run off our feet, it was a truly exciting and rewarding business. The travel, the hotel living, the entertainment and the fat expense account made up for all the hard work. Around Christmas 1958 we were so excited with all our success and had several staff parties to celebrate. As always, just when everything is going great, look out! Roy Mitchell made an announcement that left us all momentarily stunned.

Decca was about to withdraw from North America and the Bendix Corporation had taken over the licence. This meant that the Surveys Division, my operation, must move to Ottawa under the wing of Computing Devices of Canada, a Bendix subsidiary. Roy Mitchell was off to New York City to take over Decca Radar Corporation there and whilst he invited me to go with him, I felt that I could not desert the nine or ten key people I had assembled in Toronto. The transfer of the numerous technicians involved was handled quite well but the proposed transfer of key personnel was badly bungled and it took several rather forceful arguments with the CDC President, Charles Hemberry, to convince him that either we came together or we did not come at all. His selected executives, who knew absolutely nothing about marine sciences, were unacceptable to us.

Christmas time was never a happy period for critical negotiation, but by 1 January 1959 we were all on the CDC payroll and we were all being moved to Ottawa at Bendix expense. It was not an ideal start to any operation, but the corporate executive apparently got the message that we did not plan on being pushed around and that without us they had little hope of success. I gathered the impression, through dealings with other major corporations, that they were run by marketing people who had little or no appreciation for the eventual need to produce; and in our kind of operations, we produced or we died.

Once again Jane was uprooted and we were somewhat nervous of our chances of selling the house in Oakville quickly. Lynn wanted to stay behind, she was fourteen and very self-assured. As luck would have it we had an offer on the house the same day it went on the market. Jane couldn't wait for moving day as she had already seen the house she wanted in Ottawa, on Adirondack Drive. To us it was expensive, 21,000 dollars, and close to completion. To Jane it was beautiful, it backed on to NCC parkland and had an extensive garden. Next door Janice found a friend her own age, a McDonald. Lynn was difficult for a while but like any other fourteen-year-old she settled down as soon as she made friends at school. Toronto and Oakville were very soon forgotten and Jane picked up all her old friendships very quickly. I took great delight in the 30 per cent salary raise that went with the transfer.

As always there was one sad exception. Jane's friend Gerda Weeks had died whilst we were in Oakville and Ernie was now a widower with two young sons to worry about. On a happier note it was extremely pleasant to recover our relationship with Admiral Stevens and his wife and of course with Ian Farquaharson and Kate. D'Arcy Charles was quite senior now in the hydrographic service and he and I used to see a great deal of each other. All in all it was just like coming back home.

Our start with Computing Devices, whilst inauspicious from the point of view of internal politics, was a howling success from a business point of view. We actually brought our business with us from Toronto and the major contract with the Canadian Department of Transport was bound to last for several years, so we had a feeling of confidence in the future despite the likelihood of competition. We continued our work with Shell Oil and developed further business with Spartan Air Surveys, in addition to all of the support we provided to the Hydrographic Office. We also became involved in some real pioneering work with the Polar Continental Shelf Project, run by Dr Roots, out of the Department of Mines and Technical Surveys.

This project was unique insofar as it involved the conduct of scientific studies of the high Arctic, with chains of electronic survey stations to be established on Ellef-Rignes Island, close to latitude eighty north. It was a first of its kind and due to the initial success in support of the scientists this project continued on for years. The rigours of the locale and the sheer loneliness were overcome exceedingly well by our technical personnel involved, many of whom had never even seen snow before. The rugged beauty and the stark landscape of the Arctic tends to bring the best out in a man. We had few accidents to record other than one technician being badly mauled by a polar bear and having to be flown out to hospital in Thule, Greenland.

All of these operations meant constant travel and supervision, supported by cartographic and computer capabilities back at headquarters. It was a highly profitable service operation mainly because all of the senior personnel, including myself, were paid consulting fees and travel expenses so that we cost the company nothing. By this time too we were conducting operations for the Canadian Navy and for the United States Navy. Indeed we were truly busy beavers with operations going on throughout the American continent.

The family settled into Adirondack Drive and loved it. Janice was now five and went happily off to school with her friend from next door, while her big sister, Lynn, was in high school and surrounded by friends. Business took me to London several times and I managed to get together with the families in Edinburgh at weekends. Jane's Dad and I remained firm friends and I often enjoyed his company. He retired in 1960 at 65 years of age, and from that moment on he went rapidly downhill. He died quite suddenly a year later and Jane returned to Scotland for the funeral. Miss Lynn, at seventeen, was housekeeper and did remarkably well in her mother's absence.

I maintained a close relationship with D'Arcy Charles who was involved in the planning and construction of new vessels. Jane and Colleen, his wife, had

176

become close friends and during some special cooking course they attended they met Mary Cook from Carlton Place, an author and broadcaster with CBC. From time to time other females joined the group, and they had regular outings and shared interests. The association and friendship goes on as intensely as ever to this very day. It is worth mentioning that all of these girls attended our twenty-fifth wedding anniversary, and twenty-five years later they were at our fiftieth.

By now, too, Ernie Weeks had tired of his bachelor status, with all the attendant problems of supervising two young sons, and was now prepared to start a new life. We were delighted to be amongst the first of his friends to meet the chosen bride, a McDonald from Prince Edward Island. Annalea and he were married in Kitchener, Ontario and Jane and I were guests at the wedding. Annalea was a teacher there and had been left a young widow with one daughter when her husband was killed at Dieppe. Ernie, a renowned economist and Rhodes scholar, devoted his life to public service and he and Annalea, and Jane and I, have always been good friends.

As a consequence of brief tasks undertaken on behalf of the United States Navy during 1958 our services were greatly extended thereto through Western Electric Field Engineering, the technical arm of American Telephone and Telegraph. The US Bureau of Ships had an increasing interest in offshore projects in the North Atlantic. Because of the highly classified nature of these projects it was necessary for me personally to supervise those segments of the operations that were dependent upon horizontal control. This involved much travel to Winston-Salem, North Carolina, and to Bell Labs in Whippany, New Jersey. All of these were major operations involving several service ships, and as was customary, such operations were carefully pre-planned, which involved numerous high-level meetings in Washington DC, at the Bureau of Ships, with Commander Joe Kelly.

I was given to understand from Navy sources that Kelly was the only officer in the US Navy who progressed all the way from commander to admiral without moving out of his office in Buships. He was a remarkable man and exercised more authority than any other officer in any military service that I ever dealt with. His Washington meetings were an exercise in military bureaucracy with admirals in attendance, but as soon as general approval was reached the bureaucrats disappeared into the woodwork and a highly efficient field team emerged. We assisted in major operations with Navy service vessels, and with helicopters, operating out of Argentia, Newfoundland; San Juan, Puerto Rico; Bermuda; Treasure Island, San Francisco; and Adak, in the Aleutian Islands.

This was the highly-successful US Navy 'Project Caesar', an anti-submarine warfare program acknowledged to be one of the most successful of the major Navy programs. It involved the emplantment of large arrays of hydrophones, up to 300 miles offshore, and interconnected to computer facilities onshore by heavy copper communications cables. These systems were emplanted in pre-planned positions, appropriately oriented in the prescribed directions, then calibrated and certified operational through the acoustic data flow to the facilities onshore. In this way, using a combination of systems all processing the acoustic data, it was possible to track ships and submarines of all types. Different vessels have different acoustic signatures and as the technology progressed it was possible to identify specific signatures, thus enhancing the use of the arrays.

In view of the operations out of Argentia, Newfoundland and with the tracking stations within Canadian territory, there was necessary liaison with the Canadian Navy. To simplify the procedures I undertook to copy the Royal Canadian Navy on the relevant reports, and provide liaison through the Joint Chiefs of Staff at the Canadian headquarters at 2450 Massachusetts Avenue, in DC. On many of my trips to Washington Jane would tag along and had a great time shopping in 'G' Street. She just loved the cocktail hour at 'Paul Young's', on Connecticut Avenue, and the stuffed cabbage rolls at 'Duke Seibert's'.

In the early years of these operations I spent a good deal of time at Argentia Naval Base and saw considerable sea service on US Navy survey vessels, and on the cable-layers, *Thor* and *Aeolus*. At the time there was an impressive US presence in Newfoundland. An air base, Pepperill, was maintained just outside St Johns and out of an airstrip in Argentia a fleet of Super-Constellations sustained a round-the-clock radar screen in the North Atlantic. The installation at Argentia was quite immense, with multi-storey, high-rise bachelors' quarters. All in all it was a little bit of America. However the road from Argentia to St Johns was anything but American-style. It was the roughest road in the world, as far as I am concerned, yet at times one of the most beautiful with acre upon acre of bright blue and purple iris growing wild by the roadside.

The early adventures with the cable-layers were at times hilarious. Massive copper cable, twenty-one quad, about six inches in diameter, was necessary, and every few miles an amplifier package was needed. About a hundred miles of cable represented a shipload and this we picked up in New England. The laying of the cable was not easy and because of its weight, and the danger of stretching the amplifier packages, the cable-layers paid out gently over the bow-sheave whilst being towed astern by a powerful tug. The inside end of the cable was attached to terminals within the ship's test room and constant checks were run to ensure the quality and the accuracy of the acoustic reception at any time.

However operations could become quite involved due to changing weather conditions. The entire hydrophone array had to be carefully laid on previously selected sites, oriented in a specific direction and thereafter the cable laid precisely along a pre-determined route. This was the true test of the horizontal control we provided, using specially located radio stations. The check on orientation, and the calibration of the various hydrophones in the array, close to a mile in length, was accomplished by having survey vessels at unique locations drop charges to be recorded through the hydrophones along the cable and into the test room. Having laid the first leg of cable, the cable-layer had to procure another load, and the splicing process on her return was a work of art in itself, taking up to thirty-six hours. This task was done by specialists flown in for the purpose. Just holding the vessel in position in a heaving Atlantic swell was a major task in itself.

Finally the near-shore end of the cable was laid, then Navy divers would perform their peculiar brand of underwater expertise and blast a trench for a quick burial of the cable. Each operation had its own special problems and many of the arrays differed in configuration. It took teamwork to achieve a successful emplantment and thereafter a final certification. Several position-controlled survey ships performed sonar exercises and dropped charges to ensure that the hydrophones were recording and relaying acoustic data. These exercises finally determined success or failure, fortunately for us, mostly success. As the projects progressed, improvements emerged like co-axial cable, much lighter and thinner, and much more effective. Test exercises were conducted at a special sonar range on the island of Bermuda and these took place several times each year.

Operations such as these, involving naval vessels, Western Electric engineers and Decca field engineers were expensive. No chances were taken as failure could have spelled disaster. Whilst engineering almost dominated the entire project, it cannot be forgotten that there was a considerable team of mathematicians involved. While the research and the operational instructions emerged from Bell labs, the practical processes that could only be done on board were in themselves complicated. We used a combination of range-range, and hyperbolic systems to provide the horizontal control for the entire set of operations. Every vessel, independently receiving coordinates, whilst dropping a circular pattern of charges, established the position of the various hydrophones to better than twenty metres, using reasonably well-established speeds of propagation of sound in seawater.

There were times when the mathematical resolution of these acoustic exercises really tested a man's patience. One individual, a scientist from Western Electric, Cherokee Johnston, was a full-blooded Cherokee Indian. He had degrees from Massachusetts Institute of Technology and a Ph.D. from London University, England. He was an absolute whiz-kid and was the numbers man with whom I had to work. He had survived the jungles of Bataan where so many others had died. Jane and I met his family, his wife was a Canadian Iroquois and they had two little daughters. The older one was called Seneca and at seven years old she was a regular little Indian princess.

These anti-submarine warfare projects were conducted in a variety of locations, in both the Atlantic and the Pacific. On the west coast the staging base was Treasure Island, San Francisco and the operational base was Adak in the Aleutian Islands. Sad to say, there was very little survey control from which to establish precise coordinates for our shore stations, and a good deal of reconnaissance and survey work was needed in advance of any major operation. This generally meant flying around in Navy helicopters in arctic conditions, where survival suits were supposedly a necessity. Unhappily I could never find such a suit to fit and had no choice but to travel light. Being accustomed to arctic conditions, I did not mind, but the Navy kept making me sign waivers of responsibility.

Getting to Adak was sometimes quite a hazardous adventure. The normal route from home was Ottawa to Chicago, to Seattle, to Anchorage, Alaska. That part of the trip was okay, but from there on one had to travel by Reeves Aleutian Airlines. They were using old DC6s, with souped-up engines, and took cargo, passengers or whatever happened to be profitable. Remarkably, each of their aeroplanes carried two of the most beautiful stewardesses one could wish to meet. I think the idea was to divert passengers' attention from the hazards of the trip. Getting down on some of those islands was a hair-raising business and most of the time the entire area was shrouded in fog.

The Aleutian Islands were something to behold. The US Air Force maintained a large base on Shemya, the westernmost island of the main chain. The US Navy, on the other hand, maintained their large naval base at Adak, on a separate island about 300 miles eastward. We had to visit many of the islands there and the wildlife was quite astounding. At one stage we had to investigate the islands in proximity to Shemya, the principal ones being Attu and Agattu. It was difficult to move on the beaches because of the large number of seals, massive walrus and seabirds by the thousands. The scavengers were alive and well too: arctic foxes, a bit small and scraggy, hung around on the fringe of the herds.

On Agattu, due to weather conditions, a group of us had to stagger across the island to be picked up on the lee side. On the way across this uninhabited chunk of hills and bogs we came across the wreckage of a Japanese Zero fighter with the skeleton of the pilot still at the controls. The wreckage was totally overgrown with weeds and sea grasses. With the arctic wind whistling through the high grass, it was enough to give a man the shivers. On many of the other islands we came across Nissen huts that had once served as shelter for the Japanese conquerors. Whilst in the region I read a most interesting book by a US Army brigadier about the Aleutian campaign. According to the book it was an absolute farce, with troops attacking islands already occupied by their own forces. Such is the nature of war.

A few of our missions came dangerously close to disaster. On one voyage on the *San Pablo*, a survey vessel, we were caught in a raging storm and before we were properly back in operation we were in sight of the Kamchatka Peninsula, with a Russian plane nosing around. Nevertheless, with the odd mission to Hawaii, or Bermuda, as solace we had little to grumble about. I had acquired a very competent staff, mostly stolen from the London base of operations, and these were men willing to go off to distant parts. We were busy to a degree whereby the Systems Division was run by telephone, and Jane was wondering when I might spend a little more time at home.

Lynn was over eighteen by now and had completed high school. Despite our offer of a university education she elected to take a job in a bank. We assumed that a year of work would do her no harm and hoped that she might settle down, then go off somewhere to a good university. We were sadly wrong: she continued to live with us but insisted on staying at work, and was equally insistent about her choice of a boyfriend, her high-school sweetheart. We did our utmost to dissuade her, but the romance culminated in a hasty wedding and an early pregnancy. I took her to Scotland with me for a few months' stay while the young husband found his feet as a technician training with Decca.

I brought her back home in February 1964, very much overweight, but absolutely glowing with good health. We were grandparents in April, and much to my embarrassment she kept shouting for her daddy during labour. There was no choice, they had to move in with us for a while, yet everyone appeared to assume that this was just great and envied us as youthful grandparents. After all this was the sixties: the younger generation was taking over and about to turn the world upside down.

Sometime earlier my brother Donald moved from Scotland to Toronto, with his wife, daughter and one son. Another son had already taken off for Australia and hadn't been heard from in years. Maureen, the daughter, was an airline stewardess and used to visit us regularly. Young Donald, her brother, a great swimmer, went to university in Toronto and supported himself through coaching at Etobekoe. He had made it to the British Empire Games as a swimmer, but more importantly he came out of school a pretty sharp operator and finished up in his own business. My brother never did fit in all that well in North America. He took off for a couple of years as Chief Engineer at the Castle Harbour Hotel in Bermuda and I was able to see him there quite often. Unfortunately he was involved in an accident in New Jersey and from a blood transfusion he contracted a peculiarly virulent bout of hepatitis which killed him.

Meanwhile I was caught up in other special operations for the US Navy, quite divorced from the regular ventures in anti-submarine warfare. One in particular was a rather delicate operation in Spain which involved reconnaissance and the establishment of special systems on the Spanish coast to provide control in the Mediterranean for the establishment of sub-surface Polaris missile sites. In those years, through the good offices of General Franco, the United States maintained a Naval Base near Cadiz on the west coast of Spain. In addition, in Madrid, they supported a Joint US Military Aid Group (JUSMAG), headed by Colonel Manley, and they could draw on resources available in London, England at Grosvenor Square.

On arrival in Madrid I was met by Colonel Manley, and Captain Smith, a Navy legal expert from London, joined us. They had already acquired an interpreter/liaison officer from the Spanish Navy, a young man by the name of Lt Cdr Huerta-Gray. We set off in Manley's Buick with the young man in the driver's seat. He just loved the car and he made sure all the pretty girls saw him driving it. He was the son of a Spanish admiral and his mother was a Gray, of the Gray-Dunns biscuit empire in England. We drove through Seville and on to Cadiz, then south to the Mediterranean coast at a leisurely pace and with all the appropriate diplomatic stops. Our objective was the area between Malaga and Barcelona and the critical need to acquire local approval for the selected sites. All the young commander's brothers and sisters worked for Iberia, the National Airline, and all of the officers' clubs were accessible to both military and airline personnel.

The Spanish Navy clubs were combined with Iberia and as a consequence much of our negotiation took place in the chummy atmosphere of the club. It was all a splendid lesson in European-style military diplomacy. However, the mission was accomplished and the real work began. Once again the field technicians arrived with the important equipment, and in good time operations got under way. A large US Merchant Navy vessel, the *Dutton*, had been converted into an oceanographic ship, complete with laboratory and production facilities. I had people all over the place, at Marbella, Almeria, Torremolinos and Malaga. During our operations there President John Kennedy was assassinated in Dallas, Texas and it seemed that the entire population of Spain genuinely mourned his passing.

The mourning period was brief and the need for project completion was urgent. Everyone was aware of the need for rapid deployment and none more so than the young lieutenant in charge of the shore stations. He felt compelled to make some hasty, last-minute inspections which involved a great deal of driving but his precious jeep broke down. Not to be outdone he thumbed a ride on the pillion of a motorcycle in drenching rain, then completed his journey in the back of a cement truck. By the time he dried out he had to be cut out of his clothes.

With the project successfully launched I hurried back to Canada to find that

I had obligations elsewhere. Nevertheless I found time to return to Spain when necessary and it was during these trips that I escorted Lynn to Scotland and later on back to Canada. About that time too, to make matters more complicated, a nuclear device had sprung loose from its cradle under the wing of a US aircraft. It had landed offshore and was spotted by fishermen in waters that were not particularly deep. The frantic rush to retrieve it was a product of military anxiety to protect its secrets. We were there in support of Westinghouse who were the experts at that sort of thing.

Rushing around the world involved in projects such as these tend to provide one with a reputation, often greatly exaggerated. But in dealing with one's peers at national seminars, it is possible to meet the right people in particular areas of interest. From my earliest years in the hydrographic office I had had a good relationship with my counterparts in Washington DC. Several of the senior officers from the US Coastguard and the Oceanographic Office visited us regularly. This resulted in some very close relationships with key experts in emerging areas of complex technology.

Several of my associates in Washington DC involved in geodesy, ocean engineering and the proposed field of space exploration decided to form a consulting corporation. This was 'Geonautics', the President was Floyd Hough and the Vice-President Bob Salin. I too was a consultant and shareholder, until the corporation was taken over by Computer Sciences Corporation years later. Hough's claim to fame was the development of the 'Hough Spheroid', the parameters of which were more relevant to space calculations. Together with several other experts, we were under contract to Project Mercury, the original space program. Bob Salin was the ocean engineer who moved to Computer Sciences Corporation with the takeover.

This kind of contract led to invitations to major seminar sessions at Woods Hole Oceanographic Institute where I met several of the operational submarine commanders who had seen duty out of the sub base in Scotland. During one tragic occasion, when the submarine *Thresher* went down with all hands, I was asked to join Admiral Stevens's investigative team operating out of Woods Hole. The concern was devoted to a determination of the cause of the disaster in view of the fact that she had gone down in about 800 metres of water just off the Continental Shelf. There was absolutely no hope of recovery. Sailors throughout the entire community felt an intense sense of grief at the loss.

Whilst there was much scientific effort expended in the investigation and many reports written, each with its own conclusions, it must be said that the consensus amongst our group was that due to certain likely failures in pipe connections, she failed to recover her surfacing capability and dropped to a depth at which she must have imploded. With the aid of lights and underwater cameras, operating at great depths, certain images were produced whereby wreckage was recognized as being from the *Thresher*. It was a very sad moment for all of us but life had to go on.

In the midst of all these projects and the emerging technologies, and with my airline credit card providing instant first-class travel to Europe, to the Caribbean, to Anchorage, Alaska, to San Francisco, or to Hawaii, I was suddenly face to face with a major crisis. In the autumn of 1964 Jane felt a lump in her breast and Doctor Gordon Renwick, our family physician, confirmed the need for a hospital test. With very little warning she was on the operating table and whilst Doctor Devitt, the surgeon, assured me it was caught in the earliest stages, he advised a mastectomy on the basis of the evidence in the biopsy. To be absolutely sure of full recovery he recommended radiation-induced menopause, and full radiation, post-operative treatment on the lymph glands. Jane was absolutely devastated but she suffered her way through it all.

After she was released from hospital Dr Renwick took great care of her as her nerves were shattered. There were occasions when she came to Washington with me for a change of scene and the whole of her shoulder and under her arm was covered in blisters from the radiation. It was truly a tragedy but from somewhere, somehow, she gathered the strength to overcome it and eventually came out of it looking remarkably well and as smart as ever. She served in the 'Reach to Recovery' program for years thereafter. Lynn and her baby, David, were a great comfort to her during that very trying ordeal.

I had to prepare to stay home a little more and I was fortunate to have a well-trained, dependable staff behind me, but there was always some new venture arising that required my undivided attention. Suddenly there was a need for the extension of the acoustic ranges at Cape Canaveral. The need extended into the Atlantic for hundreds of miles. To complicate matters the US Oceanographic Office decided that it was necessary to first improve the geodetic survey network throughout the Caribbean island chain. The original surveys were no longer considered to be sufficiently accurate to permit their extension seaward. Operating with Navy service vessels out of San Juan, Puerto Rico we set to work in earnest to upgrade. Our people with the electronic systems network did a great deal of island hopping to acquire the necessary observations.

For a brief period I was practically commuting to San Juan. For the acoustic extensions seaward, the Western Electric Group needed a series of self-setting, taut-wire buoy systems that could be launched quickly and set automatically. We located such devices at EMI – Cossor, in Dartmouth, Nova Scotia and they were quite successful. Like all ocean engineering operations the news got around and a Bendix division as far away as Los Angeles developed an intense interest in the technology. They were vitally concerned with hydro-dynamic positioning devices for other projects.

In parallel with our operation, another group of scientists had dreamed up 'Project Mohole', whereby they intended to use a floating drill-ship to drill completely through the earth's mantle and down into the hot core. The quickest way of doing this was to start the drilling in the deepest hole one could find in the ocean, like the Puerto Rican Trench, in almost 12,000 metres. A trial operation had already been undertaken and through Bendix I was soon in contact with Robert Taggert, of Falls Church, Virginia who was the Consultant Naval Architect on the experiment. The entire operation on 'CUSS 1', as he called it, had been a hair-raising business, but had demonstrated to the sponsors that the methodology was feasible and more trials were planned. With these in mind I visited Scripps Oceanographic Institute in California and spent time in North Hollywood with the Bendix Electro-Dynamics division located there.

At this time also, through Norman Gray, the Dominion Hydrographer, we had undertaken a large consulting contract. The intent was to study the various hydrographic services well-known in the world, observe their adopted methodologies and study new technology applications with a view to providing detailed system recommendations for the new Canadian hydrographic fleet. The important offices were the British, in London, England, the Swedish Hydrographic Office in Stockholm and the Finnish Hydrographic Office in Helsinki. It was a great pleasure to work with my old associates again and the end product helped establish the Computing Devices Company as a technical force in the area of ocean engineering.

By now we were well into the autumn of 1965 and it was made clear to me that I should spend more time in Ottawa. Whilst the Decca division had prospered the main business operations were something less than profitable. Bendix, who owned 60 per cent of the company, decided to go public. Whilst it was a good deal for the brokers, it did absolutely nothing for the bottom line. But there was always supreme optimism and major developments were always just months away from production – digital computers for classified aircraft, head-up displays for fighter aircraft and moving map displays for everybody. It was all very exciting but there were no contracts as yet. Finally, the executive had wakened up to that fact.

There were rumblings in Mahogany Row, massive changes were needed, rumours were rife, but nobody got fired, they just got moved around. Expenditures stayed the same and the income grew ever smaller. Bendix moved an executive into the Vice-President's office, further changes were made, but these were equally ineffectual. The marketing staff who had survived for so long on unjustifiable optimism were all from the Royal Canadian Air Force and all imbued with the notion that Computing Devices could conquer the world of avionics.

Much against my will I was moved into Mahogany Row as Marketing Director and within weeks I knew we were flogging a dead horse. Great teams of marketing engineers and project engineers flew off to Dayton, Ohio to the US air base there, to demonstrate their wares. At our invitation US Air Force generals flew up in their 'Thunderbirds' to visit our facility. Yet clearly from day one it was obvious that the corporate objective was to try to sell essentially foreign-built systems for installation in US classified aircraft. The 'not invented here' factor was decidedly against us and we were in direct competition with some of the largest defence contractors in the world. Quite apart from that our equipment never seemed to get beyond the demonstration phase.

It is indeed surprising how long it takes to convince a dedicated group that their dedication is totally misguided. We had offices in Los Angeles, in Washington DC, and in Rome, Italy, and a small engineering operation in London, England. They survived on the maintenance and support of outdated technologies, and the eternal hope for a huge installation order on some, as yet undeveloped, fleet of aircraft or helicopters. However, hope springs eternal, and the corporate image had to be sustained at all costs. By the spring of 1966 the President had planned a grand board meeting to be held in the Chateau Frontenac in Quebec city.

We all worked very hard that spring preparing massive proposals in response to US Air Force bid-sets, and making final presentations to Dayton, Ohio air base and to the prime contractors in Los Angeles. Meanwhile the bread and butter business of the company had to be nursed along, like airborne infra-red sensors for forest fire detection, airborne photo-reconnaissance systems, communication systems, Decca Operations and the Computer Sales Division. However, in all of these major marketing efforts in the defence business there comes a period of rest and ominous silence. A period of time is allocated to analysis and adjudication which terminates in a decision and finally a contract award. During this quiet period marketing activity was directed at more mundane programs and in places further afield like Dallas, Texas where many less glamorous aircraft were in production and might support some cockpit modification.

The plans for the big board bash in Quebec city were in the process of consolidation and I remember falling victim to Jane's persuasion and ordering a very expensive dinner jacket from Dovers in Bank Street. It fitted me like a glove and Jane was proud of her good taste. Unfortunately I never did get the chance to wear it in Quebec city as the big bash was cancelled. The President had developed cold feet. By mid-summer things were even more ominously quiet so I decided to take my first real holiday since coming to Canada. Jane, Janice, now eleven and a half, and I packed our things and took off for Scotland. Miss Lynn, her husband and the baby, in an apartment nearby, were left behind as caretakers.

We had the time of our lives with both families, in Linlithgow, and in Edinburgh. We hired the biggest car we could find and spent wonderful days touring and partying in the Highlands of Scotland. My mother, God bless her, had a glorious time and simply doted on her red-headed granddaughter. Jane's brother and his family, now two girls and a boy, and her mother were all well and together with them we spent many happy days on the Scottish borders at Earlston, Coldingham and Duns. All three of us were reluctant to leave when the time came for us to go home. On our last day, during a luncheon party in the 'Four Marys' at Linlithgow Cross, I was called to the telephone. They had tracked me down to pass on the bad news. As I had anticipated, we were not the winners on the glamorous aircraft contracts.

The flight home was something of an anti-climax. Our little world had been rocked quite a bit and I suppose we wondered how much longer we might maintain the lavish lifestyle. Jane had visions of my return to the Decca empire but I had reservations which I kept to myself. I was well aware of the increasing competition from US navigation systems, like Loran, but more importantly, with my experience with Geonautics, I knew that satellite navigation systems would eventually take over. I had made up my mind, I was in the market for a new career. It was 1966 and I was forty-eight years old, but in those days that was not considered too old to start afresh.

By now Western Electric Field Engineering Corporation in Winston-Salem had purchased several chains of Decca survey systems on behalf of the US Navy, and with training courses they had a capability of their own. Several of the senior technicians from our Canadian organization, already experienced in 'WECO' projects, transferred directly to Winston-Salem. As a consequence I had no feeling of disloyalty to the US Navy, and in any case I could always stay in close touch with the responsible groups.

In an odd sort of way, I chose to celebrate my decision by discussing with Jane the possibility of a twenty-fifth wedding anniversary party. Our twenty-fifth was on 14 June 1966, and she agreed that we ought to make a splash. She handled the whole affair with her usual enthusiasm, and right on time the party was arranged, complete with brand new evening gowns for Lynn, Janice and herself, all hand-made by Miss Jane. During our seven-year stay at the house on Adirondack Drive I had completed the basement. We had a very large family room, complete with bar, a playroom, a laundry room and even a small bedroom. The bar was well-stocked, Janice's piano was available and we had hi-fi music to back it up.

Jane decided on a catered affair for sixty-five guests and we had a professional photographer to record the entire scene for posterity. It was a fabulous bash and with some highly entertaining characters as guests it was a great party. All our close friends attended and many of them attended a repeat performance at our fiftieth anniversary. My associates at Computing Devices were there, as were many from the Hydrographic Office. The bar was supervised by a barman who came with the catering staff and he assuredly excelled himself.

For the record it may be advisable to name a few of our friends, particularly those who subsequently survived to attend our fiftieth. Most of the government types continued in their careers, and many are still around. Those of our guests who were executives with Computing Devices are either dead, or widely dispersed to foreign shores, some to the US and to South America, and some returned to Britain. The close friends we had over the years remained in Ottawa and we never lost contact: Ernie and Annalea Weeks; Mary Cook and husband Wally from Carlton Place; Sheena and George Blackwell; D'Arcy and Colleen Charles; Margaret and Jerry Cooper, to name but a few. Fate has conspired to allow us to grow old together.

However, during that earlier evening, whilst still upstairs, and with everyone sipping cocktails, the most glorious spread was displayed in the dining room with two handsome waitresses in attendance. Lynn, our young mother, was decked out in the latest finery, whilst Janice, just twelve, dodged about directing the assemblage into the various rooms. We have pictures of guests dining in the bedrooms, the sitting room, the study and even in the bathroom, whilst a small group decided to eat out on the front porch. With appetites satiated Ernie Weeks gathered the entire group into the sitting room, all squeezed together like herring in a barrel, with the odd squeal of protest occasionally overheard.

Dr Weeks provided us all with a long and very amusing speech, extolling the virtues of Scotland and the Scottish, and told some risqué stories that were well suited to the general air of inebriation. After a brief acknowledgment I invited them one and all to adjourn to the basement for fun and games. We have a very fine picture of a grandmother from England dancing with her grandson to the music of Benny Goodman to open the festivities. Before long 'the joint was really jumpin', as they say in the US, and a grand old time was had by all. Some of the pictures taken towards the end of the party do tell a story. Some are amusing and some a bit tragic. It is possible to identify couples who split up not long afterwards, and others who moved away and have never been heard from since.

There are several of the bold Miss Lynn draped over the bar, with brown eyes glazed and her young husband scarcely able to keep his eyes open. The final picture taken in a series of sixty-five was of the kitchen sink full of empty bottles, ashtrays and discarded fags. The clean-up was postponed till the following morning. We all had many subsequent conversations, and in retrospect it was a twenty-fifth anniversary party, but also a farewell party. However we were all consoled with the thought that we might be back.

Very shortly after that I had to attend a meeting at Bendix headquarters in Detroit, a meeting of various divisions, and I received an invitation to consider a vacancy in Bendix Field Engineering Division, in Baltimore, Maryland as Projects Director Marine Sciences. Within a few weeks, and after several visits to Baltimore, the die was cast and by the end of October I had severed my connection with Computing Devices of Canada and with the Decca Company. I was very satisfied with the very generous treatment from Bendix as they covered the entire move, transferred me immediately into their pension plan and even gave me a raise in salary.

Meanwhile Jane and I had to face up to another upheaval, and this time it meant separating from Lynn again. On the other hand Lynn had no desire to move to the United States and she appeared to be very happy to remain in Ottawa. Like most young mothers in the sixties she already had a job in a bank and little David trotted off quite happily to day-care. With the two salaries they seemed to be doing quite well. But we had a house to sell and Jane had her usual reservations in regard to how long it would take. I was more concerned with the procedures to achieve formal entry into the United States.

I had been assured by all my associates that there would be no trouble involved; just a matter of filling in a few forms, they said. I had no problems commuting to Washington/Baltimore to make arrangements at the other end. The passport was perfectly adequate identification. In fact to simplify the procedures of security clearance for participation in highly-classified US Navy projects both Jane and I had become Canadian citizens. Janice, of course, was born in Canada and was therefore an instant Canadian. Travelling to and fro across the border was absolutely no problem until we decided to move there. Before one could acquire a work permit it was necessary to become a registered alien.

To hasten the process I elected to go to Montreal rather than depend upon the mail. Documents were submitted and employment transfer details were explained, but awaiting final approval and receipt of the appropriate forms to cross the border with our personal effects was truly a nerve-wracking experience. As time kept marching on Jane grew more and more concerned. The house on Adirondack Drive was sold to the second person who came to view it, and for 27,000 dollars. The contract was signed and it was agreed that we would vacate the premises before 30 November. Arrangements had been made with Allied Van Lines to load our possessions on 24 November, then transfer them to storage in Baltimore at Bendix expense. With all these arrangements formalized there was still no final approval from Montreal.

In desperation I went back to Montreal and requested a meeting with the Consul himself. I sat for hours awaiting developments. Finally I was ushered into an office and found myself sitting across from a female, the Vice-Consul. She was very obviously displeased with my attempt to hasten the cumbersome processes to which she had dedicated her life. After much huffing and puffing she assured me that all was satisfactory, but because I had been a resident in Iraq for seven years from 1945 to 1952, and because Iraq was now on some peculiar Government black list of communist-dominated countries, it was necessary for me to produce a certificate, signed by the Iraqi Chief of Police, certifying that during my stay there I had never been convicted of a felony.

I was sorely tempted to laugh but happily I managed to refrain. The lady was in no mood to be amused. She was utterly serious. She merely shrugged when I explained to her that in 1958 young King Faisil, the Prime Minister and the Foreign Minister had been slaughtered like pigs by the mobs in the Baghdad bazaar. I went on to suggest to her that the chances of the Chief of Police being a survivor of the revolution were indeed remote. She did not bat an eyelid. I then asked her how I might accomplish this impossible task she had set for me, and she rose, shaking her head, saying nothing. I could see that the meeting was terminated. I left Montreal in a very despondent mood, wondering how on earth I could possibly explain the situation to Jane. It was getting close to our last night in the house and I don't believe that I slept a wink that night.

Next day I headed for the United States embassy in Ottawa to see if I might acquire some assistance, or at least some understanding of the position. At that time the embassy was located on Wellington Street and I remember pushing my way through a heavy door in the entranceway, and stepping rather gingerly into the hallway. I recall a massive staircase descending from the second floor and thinking how grossly out of place it looked. I hesitated, wondering where to turn next, when I heard someone call my name, 'Ian, Ian.' I looked up and there, descending the staircase in leaps and bounds, was a rather stoutish fellow in an obviously expensive suit, and I couldn't believe that he was calling to me.

Indeed he was and whilst he pumped my arm I could tell that he knew that I didn't recognize him. He laughed uproarously, then said, 'Basrah, 1950,' and suddenly I remembered. Wilbur Chase, US Consul from Ashar, in Iraq, was a very jolly fellow who worked very closely with us in the Basrah Port Directorate. After sixteen years it took a while to review old times and I remember he claimed that I had performed many a valued service for him in Iraq before he got around to asking me why I was there. I was led into a private office and given an opportunity to explain the situation. He left me after a while with newspapers and periodicals, and when he returned he provided me with a rolled parchment which was sealed with the embassy seal. I was instructed to call again at the

190

consulate in Montreal. Although I did not enquire I gathered that he was someone in authority like a first secretary.

When I returned to Montreal and waited in an endless queue to see the lady Vice-Consul, she expressed some surprise that I was back to bother her so soon. I passed the parchment across the desk without saying a word. When she read it she left the office rather hurriedly and returned some ten minutes later with my file and all the completed documents necessary to get me over the border at Thousand Islands. She actually went so far as to offer me her best wishes. I was never so glad to depart from a Government office in all of my life. I stopped at the nearest bar for a brief celebration then called the good news through to Jane.

We could hardly believe our good fortune and it was our last day at the house in Adirondack. Our goods and chattels were already packed aboard a great Allied Van Lines truck and our personal things were in the trunk of a very new, powder-blue, soft-top Pontiac Parisienne. We travelled to the Thousand Islands port of entry with the enormous truck trailing us, and much to our relief the Customs and Immigration people were most accommodating. A brief conversation, some documents to be stamped, and the big truck was on its way. A few minutes later, with their good wishes, Jane, Janice and I crossed the border into the state of New York. We were now 'Resident Aliens' in the United States of America. The date was 25 November 1966. We were off on a new voyage into a new life and we were, all three of us, very happy and cheerful about it.

PART V

CHAPTER XVI

US REGISTERED ALIEN – BALTIMORE, MARYLAND

We departed from the Thousand Islands area with considerable haste, as if to shed the aura of doom and gloom that had enshrouded our lives for the past few months. By the time we reached the expressway our mood had changed considerably for the better. Miss Janice was singing funny songs she had learned and kept her mother giggling with stories about her experiences at school. She had just turned twelve years old and she couldn't wait to get into high school. With a stop for petrol and a generous dinner at Howard Johnson's, we were hardly back on the road when she was sound asleep, stretched out on the back seat.

Although this provided us with an opportunity for discussion, both Jane and I were disinclined to talk. We were both just happy to watch the fading colours of autumn slide by the windows and to catch our breath in readiness for a brand new adventure. My personal dreams and ambitions were somewhat clouded, after all I was nearly forty-nine years old and I had learned from bitter experience how fickle the fates can be. When we pulled off the road and into a motel for the night, I felt quite despondent and a bit exhausted. It was the end of our first day as registered aliens.

Day two dawned bright and clear and after a cheerful breakfast we were on our way and in a mood to plan ahead. At that time, 1966, the ring road around Baltimore was well under way and long stretches of it were open to traffic. The personnel people in Bendix had booked us into a temporary furnished apartment in Pikesville, one of the many satellite towns already linked into the greater Baltimore plans for the future. Bendix Field Engineering Division was located at Owings Mills, another satellite only a few miles away. Even before we arrived Jane had spotted Loch Raven, the Baltimore reservoir, on the map and made up her mind to settle there. Typical Jane reasoning, 'I just had that feeling about the loch,' she said.

Meanwhile the furnished quarters were more than adequate and a brief reconnaissance of Pikesville and Owings Mills that same night convinced us that we should look further afield. It was not that there was anything wrong with these places, it was just that Miss Jane's feelings were not quite right. The next day I reported for local processing and then had a very pleasant lunch with my new associates. Art Pawling, Vice-President of Marketing, to whom I would report, suggested that I take some time to settle down, drive around, get acquainted, and then get ready for what he described as his pet project. The other executives to whom I spoke from time to time advised a serious look at Towson, about thirty minutes' drive from the plant and bordering upon Loch Raven.

Our first drive eastwards impressed both Jane and Janice. In particular, a massive shopping centre, bordering upon the ring road, took their fancy and we pulled in. A visit to Hutzler's Department Store in the mall convinced them that this was it, and this was Towson. Less than a mile outside the ring road, Hampton Gardens, a new community and an expensive one, welcomed us with open arms. It was absolutely beautiful, with brand new homes built on the side of a hill, dropping into a lovely valley with huge trees and orchards everywhere. Just beyond lay Loch Raven, shining like a jewel, and the view reminded us of our native Scotland. We checked out the schools for Janice and that was it. Hampton Gardens was to be our new home. Jane noted the phone number of Jett Construction, the developers, and we went home to rest and relax.

It was just as well we did as the next few days were hectic. December was closing in on us and thanks to Art Pawling who postponed his ambitious projects till January we had time to pursue Jane's negotiations. One visit to Jett and a guided tour by the President himself impressed Jane to a degree whereby she was ready to sign anything. She had located the house she wanted on Midmeadow, the last house on a dead-end avenue bordering upon a beautiful apple orchard. It stood on the crest of a hill with a curved driveway overlooking the entire area. It was her dreamhouse but it cost 47,000 dollars, and to us, at least to me, that was a small fortune.

However with the Canadian dollar worth more than one dollar and thirteen cents US, we had more than 20,000 dollars in our jeans. Jane felt wealthy, I guess, and she was wheeled around from the bank to the title company, to the mortgage company. The housing business was slow and the Jett boys didn't miss a trick. Within days Jane was ecstatic and Janice fit to be tied, whilst I became the nervous owner of 1408 Midmeadow, with the typical, large American mortgage. Whilst the house was absolutely stunning, and the front and rear landscaping quite well laid out, I could see that I had my work cut out for me for the next few years. In typical developer style, the half-acre garden at the rear was bereft of trees and the massive basement was absolutely bare. I did, nevertheless, join in the happy celebrations as we now had a home.

196

Moving-in day was scheduled for 22 December 1966. There had to be a frantic rush to get us in for Christmas. We were there at the house at dawn, scurrying about, planning and replanning. The huge Allied Van Lines truck arrived on time and the moving-in process went so smoothly it was almost unbelievable. The house was transformed, it was truly breathtaking. By 4.00 p.m. the truck pulled out of the driveway and we were alone. The first snowflakes had just started to fall. We thought the entire world looked beautiful and we slept the sleep of the just.

When we arose in the morning twenty-four inches of snow had fallen overnight and to our dismay we realized that we did not have a single item of food in the house. Driving was impossible. Snow clearing in Towson was vastly different to Ottawa, Canada. I do believe that the folks there just left it to the sun. However, we had to eat. Janice and I donned our winter gear and trudged through the two feet of snow, up through the next-door orchard, and on to a country road where we finally came upon a so-called corner store. Fortunately for us they stocked everything from soup to nuts, they sympathized with us as newcomers, and went out of their way to make us welcome. Getting the groceries home was a treacherous business, but we finally made it by following our own lonely tracks in the snow. We were absolutely alone.

That night we had real fun in the brand new kitchen cooking dinner and admiring the view through the French windows in the adjoining family room. There was a glorious brick fireplace but no logs to make a fire. Indeed, this was fortunate because Janice could hear some faint mewing coming from the open fireplace wherein there was an opening leading down through a cavity in the basement wall so that the ashes could be disposed of cleanly. Without doubt there was a cat in there. Janice opened the door to the verandah to retrieve the branch of a tree to help the cat escape. Being more daring I simply rammed my whole arm down the hole and dragged the poor shivering cat out by the tail. It was squealing like a young tigress and took off through the open verandah door like a rocket. It turned out to be the neighbour's cat and it had been missing for more than a week.

We assuredly enjoyed the first white Christmas that Baltimore had experienced in years, but it was early January before traffic was back to normal. Jane took the happy view that it was a real test of the sturdiness of the Jett construction. There were no leaks, no frozen pipes, no damage to the roof and she was delighted. All her positive feelings about the place were vindicated and even the experience with the cat was a sign of good luck. Apparently it was a black cat, or so she claimed. I was unable to verify that because the cat never ever returned to visit us. To her surprise and joy, Janice found that the house next door was home to a boy and a girl, both about her age. They went to school together.

By now I was familiar with the route to Owings Mills and winter driving, to a Canadian, was a piece of cake, even though the storm had brought Owings Mills to a standstill. Bendix Field Engineering Corporation, being dedicated to service, particularly as this related to support of NASA, the various space centres, tracking ships, worldwide observation stations, and general field services in support of Bendix equipment such as massive radar stations, avionic systems etc., required only a minimum of staff at their Owings Mills headquarters. Personnel management, public relations, accounts, marketing staff, and executive management were housed at these headquarters.

As always there was the typical American dedication to expansion and diversification, and leading this group was Art Pawling, Vice-President of Marketing. He had acquired approval and the appropriate corporate funding to pursue expansion into the field of marine sciences, the new frontier as he called it. The National Aeronautics and Space Administration, in support of which Bendix had a firm footing, something like 2,300 people at Cape Canaveral alone, was the goose that laid the golden egg. Outer space had been the name of the game, but according to Art it was now time to turn to inner space, the world's oceans, to harvest the new generation of lucrative service contracts. I was formally christened Projects Director Marine Sciences, and it was now my duty and responsibility to turn Art Pawling's pipe dreams into the kind of reality that directly and positively affected the bottom line.

It was agreed that we would concentrate our efforts on three separate projects: (1) Optimum Ship Routing in the commercial shipping field; (2) Marine Sciences Technical Education, through the Office of Education; (3) Technical Services to the offshore oil industry, always keeping in mind that, if necessary, diversification could be achieved through acquisition of small corporations. All this involved considerable travel with the relevant presentations. In addition, travel to headquarters in Detroit to report progress and justify expenditures was necessary. Much of the travel was on corporate aircraft, located at Friendship Airport in Baltimore. This all sounded very grand but in actual fact we used an old, beat-up B3 bomber, with a very limited altitude capability, and therefore a very uncomfortable ride.

I must confess I found it difficult to communicate with most of my associates, and particularly my superiors, because most of them had no earthly idea what marine science was all about. I had no choice but to follow Art Pawling's lead and emphasize the benefits to be derived in dollars and cents, downplay the scientific requirements and forget about the length of time it might take to achieve any real results. He always seemed to be delighted with all the glorious presentations I made and he maintained a remarkable sense of humour. He was also the supreme optimist and as time went on I realized that this was a very necessary characteristic of the real marketing man.

On my arrival home one week from a trip, I learned that we were all invited to a great garden crab-fest at a friend's house. It was a glorious fest indeed, several great tables were spread throughout the garden, and at the end of each table there was a great basket filled with crabs still in the shell. There was also an unlimited supply of cold beer. The tables were spread with newspapers, the traditional practice I was told, and thereon lay the necessary tools for pincing the crabs and extracting the delicacies. Everyone was digging in wholeheartedly and they were all in very high spirits, with the youngsters at separate tables, giggling and screaming like banshees. Jane disappeared and I wandered from table to table, concentrating on beer, and ignoring the crab. Shellfish is not my favourite food.

Then, to my horror, I found myself in a quandary. I didn't know what to do. There was an enormous Alsatian dog, a lovely old boy, but he was dancing about lifting his leg against every basket he could find. I couldn't believe my eyes. No one appeared to notice and I hated to bring it to anyone's attention in case I embarrassed the hostess. By the time I found Jane and brought it to her attention she was furious. Anyone might have thought it was my dog the way she went on. I backed off and stayed silent but I limited myself to the beer.

At the end of it all Janice was jumping up and down with excitement. She had just been to the basement to see some puppies, miniature poodles. She had fallen in love with the runt of the litter, a little black-eyed bundle that kept licking her hands. She wouldn't go home without it. We had a dog, Mitzie, and she became a very big part of our lives. She was very quickly house-trained, and every time I came home Jane or Janice would have some new performance by Mitzie to celebrate. There were parts of the house to which she was not permitted and she quickly learned to obey the rules. She was not allowed to get up on the family room settee without her special towel. This she would drag out from the closet with great pride. She was a great actress, Miss Mitzie, and a very lovable little dog.

The sliding glass doors from the family room to the patio looked out upon the apple orchard next door and there was neither fence nor hedge to obstruct the view. On many occasions I can remember Mitzie glaring out through the glass door and literally shivering with excitement. We all knew that she had spied a rabbit. Janice would open the door and Mitzie would take off like the wind, her ears flying. The rabbits all rather enjoyed the race and I feel sure they did it to torment her. She ran to the point of exhaustion, twisting and turning and skidding on her little behind in a vain attempt to catch one. She never ever managed to get closer than about three feet but she never stopped trying.

Back at Owings Mills Art Pawling's pet project was Optimum Ship Routing, and prior to my arrival he had established a rapport with an ocean sciences group in Long Island, New York. They had already signed a joint agreement in system development, and therein lies a tale. The several scientists involved were oceanographers and computer specialists at New York University, and at the same time consultants to a small but ambitious ocean sciences group. As was customary at the time, there were many engineering and scientific consultants promoting massive projects in the development of 'Inner Space' or 'Hydro-Space' as they liked to call it. In most cases their approach was top heavy with science, lean on good engineering and totally devoid of practical experience in the world's oceans. In many cases the marketing men were already selling systems that did not meet the stated requirement or were actually in the pre-production phase.

Nevertheless I was quite certain that the appropriate intelligence and experience could be bought and injected into the overall development before the product was ever marketed. On the understanding that the end project had to satisfy me, a mariner with extensive experience, I agreed to proceed. Bearing in mind that the financing came from Bendix, it was vital that controls be exercised and that each progressive step in the development justified the time and cost. Clearly, from my first visit to the developers, it was obvious that their initial drive was towards the development of an extensive scientific paper to be presented to the Society of Naval Architects' Annual Meeting in New York in the autumn of 1968.

It was agreed that the presentation of such a paper would represent the best advertising and probably the best marketing tool we could hope to have, provided the massive software package developed on a Univac 1108 really performed. Great emphasis was placed upon the detailed mathematics presented in the paper, with the formulation of the problem, the policy equation, the procedure for path calculation, the wave description procedures, the spectral wave growth and dissipation, the wave propagation followed by the ship system descriptions, based upon the various characteristics of those vessels likely to adopt such a system. Finally there was the 'Routing Algorithm', something the mariner might get his teeth into, but the successful route was dependant upon random atmospheric data and the subsequent build-up of the waves within the computer, based upon the scientist's mathematical equations.

Dealing with the entire North Atlantic, and providing a complete wave spectral analysis within a Univac 1108 of 1965 vintage appeared to me to be a horrendous problem. However, like the young Arab who wrecked the Cadillac in Bahrain, the computer specialists kept repeating, 'Don't worry about a thing, just a computer glitch. We can fix it.' As we drew nearer to the moment of truth, the first real test on real data, the scientists were preoccupied with duties at the university. The computer whiz, when finally cornered, showed us reams of computer output that was completely meaningless. But as Art Pawling kept saying, 'We're getting closer every day.' His system briefings took place over a two-martini lunch.

Meanwhile the project was supposed to move forward in accordance with the 'Pert Program' which advised Art of the various milestones in time that we were supposed to achieve. By early 1968 we were at the point of no return. We could not quit so we had to find a way of moving ahead. Fortunately I had hired a good team of meteorologists, shipmasters and data specialists in New York. Again for the sake of public relations, we had to start with a good address. We went first class. The staff were housed in a suite of well-furnished offices on the tenth floor of the Empire State Building, in the centre of New York City. Together we worked out a contingency plan. Ship routing services were to be provided to the containerized cargo fleet based upon computer-aided professional ship routing, taking maximum advantage of computer technology. The final goal would always remain, 'Automated Optimum Ship Routing'.

We produced some very excellent glossy brochures, which trumpeted our capability and then a carefully prepared general operations plan, followed by a very ambiguous set of operational procedures. The marketing was comparatively easy. We presented our service capability to the major shipping lines using a team consisting of shipmasters and meteorologists. We spoke the mariner's language and they understood how to save a dollar. Most of the executives were expatriate Scotsmen like myself. Containerized cargoes were the latest innovation and container ships were by far the most vulnerable to weather. The ship's captains needed all the advice they could get.

The glossy brochures opened with a reminder to the mariner of the treachery of the world's oceans. In one very appealing opening statement it was said that, 'The way of a ship upon the sea has always been strewn with danger and oftentimes with disaster as mariners guided their ships through formidable obstacles . . . for glory or for gold.' Obviously the problem of voyage planning has been with the seafarer since the beginning of time. In those days, that is 1968, we had cooperating international weather bureaux collecting and analysing copious quantities of weather data, and these, coupled to special data acquisition platforms as well as satellite sensors, were providing an information flow whereby automatic computer processing was critical to such operations. Surface pressure analysis, and marine weather forecasts, on a hemispheric basis were also available.

Optimum Ship Routing, the glossy brochure stated, is a methodology which assembles weather data through a worldwide communications centre and employs computerization with individual analyses checked by skilled professionals to direct ships on specific courses compatible with their destination and purpose. The routing is designed to minimize obstacles such as wave action, storms, ice and other weather phenomena. The modern voyage can be routed on the basis of computerized methodology, which not only includes the standard techniques of weather forecasting, but goes beyond this stage to deal exclusively with the hydrodynamics of the oceans and its relationship to the dynamic characteristics of the vessels.

And further, the ocean model, a matrix of grid points in the oceans, accepts input data in logical sequence. Internally the computer derives the wind fields over the oceans on the basis of surface pressure analysis and adjusts them by the additional input of observations reported by selected ships at sea. Surface pressure analyses, made upon polar stereographic projections and digitized, were fed into the ocean model in three-hour steps. The conversion of wind field to wave spectra at the grid points takes account of wind velocity, changing direction, and build-up of the sea resulting from such conditions.

The computer recognized the effect of previous conditions like wind fields, swell and sea generated from a distance, and the dissipation of energy with time. A coordinate transfer was also made from polar stereographic projection to Lambert Conformal, upon which the route solutions are run. Thus the wave field, described at each grid point in terms of fifteen frequencies and twelve directions, gives sea height and direction which can be interpreted in terms of ship reaction. Within the computer memory then there resides a detailed description of the dynamics of the oceans, so that isopleths of obstacle severity can be defined, almost like the contours on a topographic map. Permanent obstacles such as the Azores in the North Atlantic are simply given a permanent wave height in the model that would preclude the possibility of the route approach thereto. Without doubt, the brochures had significant appeal.

In the meantime, in addition to the New York project, there were many other responsibilities to take care of. By now I found myself serving as a panel member on the Ocean Sciences Technical Advisory Committee. Everyone was anxious to serve on these prestigious committees, but most of the time they failed to accomplish anything other than recommending various sets of standards to which no one ever bothered to adhere. Whilst Ocean Sciences was now the national buzzword, there was a growing interest in the development of the 'Great Society'. Industry was promptly saddled with the responsibility of doing something for the poor. Before long the marketing men were predicting that fortunes could be made out of poverty. They firmly believed that lucrative service contracts were soon to be had for slum clearance, educating the poor, training adolescents and expanding the prisons.

After many frustrating presentations to the Federal Office of Education, we did receive a contract for the development of curricula in the marine sciences technical categories to be introduced at technical college for the training of young men in specialized areas such as undersea welding, diving and other skills needed in the offshore development field. These responsibilities required considerable travel to Delmar Junior College in Corpus Christi, Texas, and for liaison with the Ocean Sciences Division of Southwest Research Institute in San Antonio, Texas. In addition it was necessary to cooperate with Blue Water Industries in Diving, and with the Bendix Marine divisions on the west coast.

I did have a social life to consider and old friendships to renew from my earlier travels. In addition, under Jane's supervision, I had to complete the large garden at the rear of the house. The basement, a yawning chasm each time I descended the stairs, was a constant invitation to 'do it yourself'. Jane's desire to have our relatives from Scotland visit us sealed the deal. Nobody could possibly come to the house with an unfinished basement. I never can remember how I found the time between travelling, commuting to New York City etc., but somehow the basement did take shape and it was much admired.

In addition to cold storage and a laundry room, we had a massive lounge complete with a leather-padded bar shaped like the bow of a ship and truly well stocked. In one corner a little bit of gay Paree with a sidewalk cafe was established. In the cement block wall, indented for the upstairs window, I painted a Scottish landscape in oils. With inside floodlighting and a lattice windowframe our guests were most impressed with the artistry. The remaining half of the basement became sleeping accommodation and all round the walls I painted great comic figures from the newspapers, like Andy Capp, and lots of animals for the kids. On some occasions with the beds pushed aside there were wild parties where everyone felt free to act like an idiot.

We also found time for family. Lynn and Rick visited from Canada, and Maureen and Donald, my niece and nephew, from New Jersey. Jane's Aunt Margaret and Uncle Bill came down from New Jersey and we were at their home in Midland Park quite often. By now the front of our house was a mass of yellow roses and the rock garden in the rear, created by yours truly, could be a blaze of colour. Janice and Jane just loved the place, the house, Towson, Maryland, Loch Raven, the weather, and above all the glorious colours of spring, with dogwood and azalea by the acre. Janice loved the school and had made many friends. Towson was a fun place to live and Jane took full advantage of it.

To provide mobility for Jane it was necessary to buy a second car. Believing that I was making the best choice for her I bought a bright yellow Corvair. At her request it was automatic and also brand new. Within a very short time it turned out to be my car as it was too difficult for her to steer. Meanwhile, quite quickly she became a local personality. She was very successful as President of the Towson Newcomers Association, and she still has a silver tray inscribed with appropriate acknowledgement of her valued service to the cause. In addition she was chairperson of a golf club, hosted wine and cheese parties and participated in a very prominent prayer group. She had hordes of friends, and among them, Virginia Detley. Virginia's husband was John Detley, a prominent Californian architect, now heading up an organization in the rapid transit business in Baltimore. He had, at one time, been married to Veronica Lake, my all time favourite film actress. John and I had many a humorous chat about Hollywood in the forties and fifties.

Miss Janice did really well at school and when she switched to high school some of her friends were friends with Spiro Agnew's kids. At that time he was convenor of the county and lived just down the road from us. Later, when he became Governor of Maryland, the kids were delighted to get an invitation to the Governor's mansion at Annapolis. At a later date I attended a luncheon whereat the then Vice-President Spiro Agnew was the guest speaker and he babbled on and on about the 'nattering nabobs' in the press. I was not at all surprised to read about his downfall and I understand he was lucky to escape a term in jail.

Meanwhile, bearing in mind my added commitment to identify those small, successful corporations in the marine sciences business which might become candidates for acquisition, I had an excellent excuse to entertain many of my old friends on a new expense account. One prominent scientist with whom I had had a warm relationship was Dr James Fitzgerald from Oshkosh, Wisconsin. He was more Irish than the Irish, a devotee of green beer on St Patrick's day, and drank nothing but Old Fitzgerald for the remainder of the year. He was acknowledged to be one of the foremost acousticians in the United States and a very successful one at that. He had a great deal of professional influence with the naval scientific community.

Just then he was a retiring president of a successful corporation, Chesapeake Instruments. It was rumoured that he was forced out by disgruntled shareholders, but he never discussed it with me nor did I ask for an explanation. I was more interested in his new ventures. He had a 'Dolphin Training' operation at Key West that was more fun than business and he started a new oceanographic research corporation, which he called Geraldine Laboratories. Most of the funding came from Texas. He had a research vessel of reasonable size with a capacity for several scientists. Bob Salin, one of my associates in Geonautics, had joined him and they had already acquired some good contracts.

Old Fitz liked the sound of the name Bendix; to him it spelled money. As a consequence we saw a lot of each other. Jane and I used to visit his beautiful home on Bay Ridge, near Annapolis and we spent many pleasant hours with him at Annapolis Yacht Club. His wife Mary was a fascinating lady and at that time they were supremely happy. Some time later, when James was overdoing the Old Fitzgerald, they separated and I heard no more, but it made me very sad for a while. One of the best parties we were ever at was a weekend with Jim and Mary and a large bash at the Yacht Club. A group of us spent the following evening at the film premiere of Sean Connery in *Dr No*. There wasn't a vacant seat in the house.

Through James Fitzgerald we met Mauricio Porraz, a Mexican scientist, who went deep-sea hyperbaric diving with Russ Carpenter, the astronaut, in the US Navy Deep-Sea Diving Experiment. Mauricio was president of his own development corporation in Mexico City, the Organization Submarina Mexicana, operating in the southern part of the Gulf of Mexico for 'Petrolios Mexicanos'. He and I became firm friends and we were involved in some business ventures together in Mexico City where I stayed at his home many times. Odd as it may seem, he had a large swimming pool on the second floor of his house. His wife Margarita was a doll, and Jane and she got along exceedingly well. These kinds of associations intrigued Art Pawling and he just loved to become involved with these kind of people. He would always talk about acquiring their corporations as though this was something one did over a quick lunch.

All this was at a time when the entire industry really believed that the US Government planned on spending billions on the development of hydro-space, as everyone now called it. Major corporations were talking wildly about dredging the oceans for manganese nodules worth millions per shipload. Others were discussing the 'Mohole', an experimental drilling program whereby a great, floating drill-ship would drill all the way into the bowels of the earth and acquire access to unlimited thermal energy. Offshore exploration people were talking about deep-sea development where hyperbaric divers would achieve sub-sea well completion using acoustics and having dolphins fetch and carry their tools. These were exciting days for the marketing men and they were not unpleasant for the project directors. Corporate headquarters were willing to invest in ideas, in technology, in the oceans, without exercising undue pressure to produce.

Back at the office in Owings Mills it was a much less glamorous experience. I was terribly disappointed with the office space. It was designed along the lines of a real estate office where space is always at a premium and each agent gets only a small desk and a telephone. However I was rarely there and I kept most of my files and my personal library at home. Jane's friends were far removed from the Bendix crowd and I made no attempt to socialize with the executives, other than one, Gerry Rossow, a very bright young lawyer from Bismarck, North Dakota. He was the corporate lawyer and therefore well aware of everything that was going on. He was a veritable fountain of good, sound business advice.

There were some interesting characters amongst our immediate neighbours. One young man had a very successful, and very lucrative, garbage collection business. His views on how the local Government should be run were nothing short of revolutionary. Another close by was a vice-president of the power company and absolutely crazy about football, as played by Johnny Unitas and the Baltimore Colts. He hosted a party in his basement for every game with unlimited supplies at the bar. In those days the Colts were a powerhouse and played the game like gladiators of old. The entire performance was truly something to behold. During summer, of course, the Baltimore Orioles were the weekend drawing card.

I must confess I never did become addicted to the weekend spectacles and whilst Jane was content with her golf tournaments I was preoccupied with the fascinating world of American business. It was not that I generated any burning desire to make a fortune, it was simply the excitement of that particular decade where it seemed to me that big business in the US was preoccupied with expansion and diversification, but without any clearly-defined goals. Focus on the future seemed to be entirely dependent upon rumours of massive funding from the Government for ill-defined objectives. I was grateful that in my role as Projects Director I knew precisely what my goals were and I could readily focus upon project milestones.

Through Bill Atwood, our President of Geonautics, I was back in touch with Robert Taggert of Falls Church, Virginia, a consultant naval architect, recently involved in CUSS I, the multi-million dollar experiment in the Pacific to determine the feasibility of 'Mohole'. He was a canny character and he and I had long conversations about the scientists involved in those exercises, most of which came to naught. We shared a common interest in the project in view of the need for hydro-dynamics expertise, as the massive drill-ship had to be maintained over a specific point on the ocean bed within very fine limits. It was the intention of the geologists to drill down through the earth's crust and through the mantle at its most vulnerable location to tap into the heat from the molten interior.

The experiment, CUSS I, whilst purely an exercise of technology, had been considered something of a triumph. Taggart was happy, as far as he was concerned they met the specs, and he was confident that as far as the ship positioning system was concerned they were now in a position to proceed with the project. The likely location was the Puerto Rican Trench where the drill-ship would have the advantage of the first 12,000 metres being salt water. Thereafter, the drill-stem and the drill-bit had to be guided into a prefabricated re-entry mounted over the drill hole to ensure recovery in the event of any temporary abandonment of the drilling operation. Position controls were to be achieved using acoustic beacons emplanted on the ocean bed with hydro-dynamic positioning controls activated by an onboard computer. On paper it was reduced almost to the level of a push-button operation. Fortunately for the sponsors the project was abandoned before any massive investments were made.

Meanwhile there were many less ambitious projects in hydro-space, funded by several Government agencies, and indeed about this time there were more Government agencies being created. There was now a large Department of Energy and an Environmental Protection Agency, all with unlimited funds the marketing men maintained. It was obvious then that the various scientific groups and institutions around the nation were anxious for a piece of the action. Wood's Hole on the east coast and Scripps Oceanographic Institution on the west coast tended to dominate. However additional groups of scientists managed to acquire funding from the National Science Foundation for marine environment studies. Beach Erosion on the east coast was one buzzword whilst erosion of the wetlands was the big thing in the Gulf of Mexico.

The competition for funding in marine sciences research did force some sort of discipline into the overall field and the need for reorganization became all too evident. Large groups of universities in specific regions, like the Gulf of Mexico, came to the sensible conclusion that to properly respond to the future demands for worthwhile results in marine sciences investigative projects they must enhance intercommunication and exchange of information. It was no longer feasible for individual marine scientists to potter about in their own laboratories. Marine technology companies began to realize how much they needed to communicate with the universities. Multi-Disciplinary Research became the popular buzzword, and the marketing men now discussed the 'International Decade of Ocean Exploration'.

In preparation for this promised explosion of activity in the field of hydro-space, several of the major universities in the five Gulf states bordering upon the Gulf of Mexico joined forces to form a non-profit organization called 'The Gulf Universities Research Consortium'. Within a very short time it grew to include all of the twenty-one major universities, plus the University of Mexico in Mexico City, and most of the major oil companies. The initial funding was derived from members' fees and thereafter from major grants from wealthy foundations. Quite quickly, small contracts were obtained from the National Science Foundation to sponsor various scientific workshops, and for the logistics and scientific planning of a Gulf Environmental Measurements Program.

In 1967 Bendix Field Engineering Corporation were advisory members of the GURC organization and Chuck Greenslit, the Vice-President of Engineering, was the appointed member. Shortly thereafter, as the organization had grown, I was elected to their Board of Directors. At that time too, a senior scientist I had met at the Southwest Research Centre in San Antonio, Texas took over as

President of GURC. The organization had big plans for the Gulf and the universities and the oil companies had more than a passing interest. In their view a massive study of the entire Gulf of Mexico was vital to the national interest as well as contributing greatly to the oil companies expertise in environmentally safe offshore drilling. Without doubt it was in the vital interest of the off shore development community to demonstrate to the nation that their activities were not harmful to the environment, thus enhancing the corporate image.

At that time, as a Director of GURC, I made many friends amongst the university group and I acquired visibility within the major oil companies thus projecting an image for Bendix in the marine field. GURC representatives were constantly in Washington DC, and I spent a good deal of time with them and with their Washington connections. This was all considered to be a very necessary part of corporate liaison and was greatly encouraged. It was time-consuming and sometimes frustrating because when operating as a member of such a team you find yourself sharing in all of their failures as well as participating in the benefits.

To occasionally get away from it all I spent time with an old friend in Falls Church, Virginia. Like me he had spent much of his life in peculiar places doing some very odd things. At one time just before the war he had been the personal pilot to an Indian maharajah, then during the war flew with General Chenault and his Flying Tigers. Even at that time Madame Chenault, the General's widow, resided in Washington DC. In the early post-war years he had devoted much of his time to General Chiang Kai-shek whilst holed up in Taiwan. He was obviously attached to the Central Intelligence Agency and even after retirement could not keep his nose out of their affairs. He also did a great deal of flying in Antarctica where a range of mountains bears his name, the Lassiter Range. He was a member of the very exclusive Explorer's Club in New York City and I had the pleasure of dining there with him on several occasions.

He was James Lassiter, a big, quiet man, who did everything on his own and for some strange reason always slept with a gun under his pillow. He was totally devoid of any real sense of humour but there was a strength about him that was noticeable everywhere. At this time he was running a corporation out of Falls Church supplying horizontal control services to the off-shore arm of the geo-physical survey corporations, and directly to the major oil companies, in the precise positioning of drill-rigs in remote parts of the world. Whilst the business was a moneymaker, he ran it out of his hip pocket. His field crews were recruited from London, England where an office was run out of someone's house. The equipment was warehoused in Las Palmas, Canary Islands to take advantage of the total lack of customs regulations.

208

Talking to Jim Lassiter was like spending an hour with a psychiatrist. He was the most totally laid-back man I had ever met. He had recently returned from a spell in Central Africa, in the Congo, just at the time when the natives were rebelling against the Belgians. What he was doing there was always a bit obscure, but whilst he was there he had recruited some very peculiar Englishmen who had been mercenaries for some years. The political situation had never been of any particular interest to them, their *raison d'etre* had been the opportunity it provided to blow up banks. They fought on any side with the wherewithall to pay them. A book had just been published by a Colonel Mike Hoare detailing his grizzly adventures as a mercenary in Africa. How he acquired the rank of colonel no one ever knew. He and Lassiter had been acquainted in Leopoldville for a brief period.

It is strange also to relate that a Belgian, Captain Pierre Dallemagne, was the Chief Hydrographer on the River Congo at that time. During his tenure there he had married an American girl, the Vice-Consul at the American embassy in Leopoldville. There came a time when they had to make a hurried escape from the revolution in the Congo through Kenya to Nairobi. The Belgian Government then sent him to Argentina with their blessing to assist in their agreed resettlement there with the Argentine Government. It was not long before he tired of the appointment and he came to work for me in the New York office of Optimum Shipping Routing. It is indeed a small world.

So by now it was the early summer of 1968. Jane was preparing to go off to Ottawa for her annual check-up at the Civic Hospital,and thereafter her happy vacation with Lynn and all her old friends. Janice was really enjoying her Towson High School and her girlfriends, but always found time to continue her piano studies. She had demonstrated unusual skills at some festival of music and the Principal advised us that she should try to qualify for the Peabody Institute in Baltimore. It was a nerve-wracking experience for all of us but she made it. She was extremely proud of herself as Peabody was nationally renowned.

We were all bubbling with joy about that time, the whole area was ablaze with colour, our back garden was a showplace and the front of the house was a mass of yellow roses. The basement was now complete and the neighbours came from far and wide to admire it. On top of all that our first visitors from Scotland, my sister Jean, her son Ian and his wife Betty were committed to arrival by air in September. I was commuting to New York Monday to Thursday. The drive was precisely 184 miles to the Holland Tunnel, then five minutes to the Port Authority to park my car, and then a cab ride to the Empire State Building. It was very pleasant there with the Steamboat restaurant on street level. I stayed at the Atlantic Sheraton just a stone's throw away.

Bob Raguso, a professional meteorologist, had been appointed Project

Manager there, with Pierre Dallemagne assisting, and supported by an excellent staff. The fact that the scientists kept throwing sand in the air or producing reams of useless computer printout did not phase us one bit. We did it our way and it worked out remarkably well. The scientists, headed by their Vice-President, dedicated themselves to their presentation for the Society of Naval Architects. It was their belief that without such holy water we could not survive. Fortunately shipowners and mariners have made their judgements based upon sound common sense for centuries and repeat business in the marine field is based exclusively upon success. We had the needed professionals on staff and they spoke the mariner's language.

With essential business taken care of, by the time September came around we were well prepared for our visitors. Jane had a large freezer stacked with her pre-cooked meals and friends and neighbours were all alerted in readiness for the big day. Detailed arrangements were made with immediate family for visits so that we avoided overcrowding. My holiday was arranged to coincide with their three-week stay. I drove alone to Kennedy Airport to meet them so that there would be plenty of room in the car. My sister, her son and his wife were so excited to be in America. They had visions of neon lights, traffic jams and hordes of crazy people everywhere. The trip lived up to their expectations, the lights, the highways, the traffic, the screaming police sirens, it was a vast difference from the quietness of Linlithgow, Scotland.

There had been a delay and I picked them up at midnight. The airport, the car parks, the struggle to get on the expressway, the bright lights, especially as we drove over the Tappanzee Bridge from where Manhattan could be seen ablaze with lights, left them in awe. Then suddenly we were in black darkness rolling down an expressway at high speed. They wondered why it took so long and they found it difficult to imagine someone driving two hundred miles to pick them up. It took them a little time to appreciate the vastness of America by comparison with the tight little country of Scotland, but they loved every bit of it, especially the Blue Ridge Parkway with its rolling hills and massive trees.

We picnicked, we partied and we behaved like real tourists. We covered every historical site and feature in Baltimore, and Washington, and attended whatever functions were available. Our neighbours put their swimming pool at their disposal and this helped to alleviate their daily physical exhaustion. My nephew Ian, a policeman, was enthralled for days at the Towson Police Station. My sister Jean, who loves to go about visiting, had to be taken to Linden, New Jersey and to Midland Park to visit relatives. It was the end of summer, the Parisienne was a soft-top and she loved to feel the wind in her hair, except that the six lanes of traffic, especially at intersections, made her a bit nervous. She had no alternative but close her eyes. On one occasion we had a front tyre blow-

210

out while passing a massive truck. It took her a couple of days to get over it.

The house seemed empty and quiet for a while when they left us to return home. However it was time for me to get back to work. By now Bendix had acquired United Geophysical Corporation in Pasadena, California. Whilst I must confess I wondered why, I spent time in California with them, and with marine advisers, and the Electro-Dynamics Division, and with Scripps. Their common interests at that time seemed to be centred around Project Mohole and the needed technological development in support of such projects. At this same time there was need for a contract extension negotiation with the National Aeronautics and Space Agency, so Art Pawling and I paid a visit to Cape Canaveral where we had hundreds of technical people.

By now the GURC operations were becoming more focused upon the acquisition of grants from the National Science Foundation in Washington and small contracts with some of the Government agencies headquartered there. I was able to work with them through liaison with Life Sciences Corporation headed by Joe Tyson, a liaison that became stronger as the GURC mission became more clearly defined. Tyson and I became good friends in addition to business associates and the information exchange was beneficial to both of us.

By the autumn of 1968 we were busy preparing for the Society of Naval Architects' November presentation. It turned out to be like most other seminars, an exercise in futility before a mutual admiration society. Whilst our science associates were delighted with themselves, I kept wondering what benefit our program was ever likely to derive from it. Here we were in the business of Optimum Ship Routing and I had yet to see a computer exercise that made any real sense to me. They were not yet ready to demonstrate on the basis of real data and unable to predict when such a state of readiness might be achieved.

Fortunately the professionals in our office were already providing conventional ship-routing, based upon weather forecasts, with several of the components of the system automated. The North Atlantic surface pressure prognostic charts were created from data reported by the US Weather Bureau and these were then analysed and converted into wind velocity charts. They were further modified by data from selected ships in the oceans and this provided the basis for route selection for individual vessels. The characteristics and the loading conditions of each vessel were considered in the selection of the optimum route.

It was reluctantly agreed that we proceed in this manner to provide time for the so-called experts to produce. Meanwhile various aspects of the data acquisition process were automated. An expensive digitizer, necessary to provide windfield input data on tape for input to the main computer, was also procured. Unfortunately, under these circumstances, the relationship between the OSR team, and the scientists, was rapidly deteriorating. Nevertheless we had no difficulty in convincing the North Atlantic cargo liners of the need for such a service and they were entirely satisfied with the results. The winter of 1968 convinced the executive that the project was successful and clearly demonstrated expansion potential. However relationships at home base were turning sour.

Without doubt it became obvious to those of us in contact with the OSR project that the major software delays created a bone of contention between the project engineers and the development scientists. Fortunately we were able to keep the market totally unaware of the technological deficiencies. Quite apart from the delays it became obvious that the principals in oceanics persisted in direct liaison with the BFEC executive. The fact that this was tolerated made the situation extremely difficult for me. It undermined my credibility with the staff in New York and the deteriorating situation grew worse.

Quite apart from all this the Field Engineering Corporation was no longer flying high, Government contracts were running out and overall business was not good. The pressure upon both marketing and engineering became noticeably greater. There were many internal disputes. The commercial projects, like Marine Sciences Technical Education, and Optimum Ship Routing, were subjected to undeserved critical reviews. Something had to be done. They were convinced that the solution lay in acquisitions, when what they really needed was a miracle. As a consequence I started to talk seriously to James Lassiter about the worth of his corporation.

While Lassiter went along with the discussion he admitted in the end that he had no desire to be acquired. He was honest enough to say that he was more interested in acquiring me as his Executive Vice-President to re-organize his entire operation. He had two corporations, Navigation Management in Falls Church, and Lab Navigation registered in the Bahamas. He had an equipment base in Las Palmas, Canary Islands, a personnel office in London, England, and an operations office in Singapore. His offer was very interesting but I had responsibilities with Bendix that would take almost a year to complete. We had an understanding, one that strengthened my hand in dealing with my associates in BFEC.

About this time massive changes were being undertaken in the city of Baltimore, particularly in the port area. The authorities there had realized that the containerized cargo concept had created a revolution in ship design and in the docking facilities necessary to handle them. The Port of Baltimore Authority were pioneers in the business and plans were already implemented in the creation of a very large container port. They succeeded in having the first International Containerized Cargo Symposium held right there in Baltimore. It was an international event and teams of interested port and shipping executives came from all over the world.

Jane became particularly interested in the whole affair as she became involved with the Scottish contingent from Clyde Port Authority in Glasgow, Scotland. We had some very grand parties with them and we sustained a correspondence for some time thereafter. There was absolutely no doubt left in anyone's mind, containers were the wave of the future, and this meant newly designed ships to carry them. International standards were discussed and as always there were complications and competition to consider. This was all very encouraging for Optimum Ship Routing, and all very much in line with the marketing men preaching their gospel of a 'Decade of International Exploration' in hydro-space.

These developments were also very much of interest to the Gulf Universities Research Consortium who considered all things in the oceans to be their territory. In the Gulf of Mexico marine operations were significant to the general welfare and the health of the environment was of grave concern. Indeed, with the mighty Mississippi running south through the middle of the continent and probably transporting the bulk of the nation's effluent they had a point. In addition, with the Texas and Louisiana Oil Patch, and commercial grains being exported from New Orleans, there was a vital need for their participation in environmental investigations. As a director I was kept in close touch with their developing ambitions. Our joint contract with the Office of Education kept me travelling to Houston, and Corpus Christi, and on occasions to Mexico City because of my association with Mauricio Porraz.

Mauricio and Margarita came to visit us in Baltimore and we had a fabulous time showing them around the city. We spent time at Annapolis with James Fitzgerald. Their interests merged to some degree but thus far they were limited to information exchange. The main reason for mentioning their visit at all was the impact it had upon our home life. Margarita, accustomed to her elaborate house in Mexico City with lots of servants, found it difficult to change her habits. Fortunately we had two large bathrooms because she practically lived in one of them. Even at bath time it was amusing and they behaved like honeymooners. Margarita insisted that Mauricio shower with her and the squeals and giggles could be heard all over the house. The entire bathroom was flooded with water when it was all over.

Janice was utterly awed by the whole performance and I can remember her breathing the information to her girlfriends all about the glamorous couple and their bathroom antics. I think that she maintained that she had most of the cleaning up to do. But she still thought that Mauricio was a good-looking man and Margarita was a star.

The spring of 1969 was gorgeous, blossoms and flowers everywhere, and by this time we were preparing for Jane's family to visit at the end of the summer. She planned on having her mother, her brother, his wife and their son. Two

213

grown-up daughters were to be left at home. Once more the ice-chest was loaded and final preparations completed before she took off for the annual trip to Ottawa. Janice was now fifteen and perfectly capable as a housekeeper. She had made some very close friendships and she and Mitzie were inseparable. I suspect that whilst her mother was in Ottawa, Mitzie was allowed to break all the rules and could be found reclining on Janice's bed. Many times as I drove up the driveway Mitzie was peering out of Janice's bedroom window.

Alas, when the time came for Jane to return I had to pick her up at Washington National Airport and I had to have a wheelchair for her. She had a ruptured disc and she was in extreme pain but she was doggedly determined not to permit her discomfort to affect her family holiday plans. A physiotherapist managed to get her back on her feet and to keep her going for some time. Surgery was inevitable but she made up her mind that it would be done after her family departed. She was anxious to impress her family so we went out to buy a new car, an Oldsmobile Delta, a beautiful shade of green.

Once again I found myself driving to Kennedy Airport to meet our visitors and once again there was a delay. The plane, low on fuel, was diverted to Montreal and finally arrived in New York well after midnight. Jane's mother's reaction to the car was amusing. She had never before enjoyed that level of automotive luxury and simply refused to believe that we had 200 miles to drive. Dawn was breaking as we approached Baltimore and the countryside was at its splendid best. The short drive into Towson, and then Hampton Gardens, was glorious at that time of year. The reunion was all that we could have possibly expected. Smiles and tears and the rapid-fire exchange of stories about family and friends took precedence over unpacking, or breakfast, or anything else. Mitzie went back to her bed in disgust.

We followed the previous year's itinerary more or less, with all the same visits to Washington DC, and the surrounding areas. The neighbours and friends really enjoyed these foreigners. They were surprised at how well they spoke English, although they did comment about the funny accent. Jane's brother, an avid golfer, had a fantastic time. We had the usual round of parties and entertainment, and visits from all the friends and relatives in Canada and the United States. Lynn was there to see her grandmother and proudly showed off young David who was now about five years old. He never did get along too well with Mitzie but other than that he was a very popular little boy.

Jane's nephew Stewart was about fourteen years old and he enjoyed every moment of his stay. His sisters back home were about twenty and twenty-two years old and I think he was delighted to be the only kid brought along. He loved the swimming pool, the Coke and the hamburgers, and I think he would have stayed. His mother, Chris, was a devotee of the sun and the swimming pool, whenever she could find the time, and quickly became as brown as a berry. We used to joke a lot about her being on her second honeymoon. As fate would have it she found herself pregnant shortly after her return to Scotland and a third daughter was born the following June.

Any telephone calls or correspondence we had during the pregnancy period, whilst serious to them no doubt, sometimes created a great deal of amusement for us. We were told that the older daughters were vehement in their criticism of their mother's condition. 'How could you, Daddy?' was part of a daily diatribe directed at poor Edwin. Poor Chris, rather foolishly we thought, was thoroughly embarrassed about the whole affair until Miss Nicola put in her appearance. Thereafter there was nothing but cooperation, congratulations, and sheer joy on all sides. To her delight, Jane was named Godmother, and the baby's name was Nicola Jane. As it turned out she was a truly beautiful child.

My return to duty at Owings Mills was not a pleasant experience. I had been having some real arguments with the executive about the scientists and their software and I questioned the relationship between the oceanics principals and my superiors. By now the entire BFEC operation was rocky and rumours were circulating that the President was on his way out. Meanwhile, Engineering in their wisdom had decided that what was needed was another engineer and this infuriated me. The individual appointed devoted his entire time to modifying the brand new digitizer, an instrument he knew nothing about. His basic knowledge of the required technology to accomplish fully automated ship routing was abysmal. I would have walked out right there except that I had obligations to the universities to fulfil my contractual commitments to the education project. The atmosphere was icy to say the least, but despite that conventional ship routing operations continued successfully for many years to my knowledge.

However Jane's surgery was scheduled for October. She had her operation in the sick children's hospital in Baltimore, a hospital with a splendid reputation. Her convalescence was agonizing but she finally did recover. Whilst she was there she was amazed at the number of great, tall basketball players brought in with the same problem. For a while at home she was almost crippled. I had to walk with her every night. It was not a pleasant time for us in view of the fact that I had to tell her that my position with Bendix was simply untenable. She took it well. She had faith in my ability to bounce back.

Bendix Field Engineering Corporation and I parted company in November 1969 without undue strain. They were in the process of a physical move from Owings Mills to the new city of Columbia, midway between Baltimore and Washington. In light of the obvious reorganization, and the likely downsizing, I was glad to go. I joined Navigation Management as Executive Vice-President almost immediately. The headquarters were in Falls Church, Virginia, seventy-

215

five miles away. I decided to commute for the sake of Janice's school year. Jane was quite happy to relax and remain amongst her friends in Towson till the following mid-summer.

As it turned out it was a convenient time to make the change from a contractual standpoint. I had managed to wrap up the Office of Education commitments, the Gulf Universities Research Consortium were totally unconcerned about my change of address and it did not affect my Director status with them. My liaison through Life Sciences continued and quite suddenly my whole life seemed to be a lot brighter.

CHAPTER XVII

McLEAN, VIRGINIA AND FALLS CHURCH

In preparation for my arrival at Falls Church, James Lassiter elected to move into more spacious quarters. It was obvious to me then that he was primarily concerned with corporate image and my duties as Executive Vice-President were to reorganize and to establish an image of experience, competency and fiscal soundness. No expense had been spared in the refurbishment of the office space and there was new furniture throughout. Both he and I had executive-style offices, lavishly furnished, and I acquired a very experienced private secretary. There were fewer than a dozen people at headquarters but this was entirely in line with the operations. The technical staff, providing professional services in the field, were widely dispersed throughout the world.

The seventy-five mile commute morning and evening sounds like hardship but I didn't mind. I was driving a brand new Oldsmobile and whilst it was the long way round the beltways were the fastest way to get there. In any case I spent a good deal of time travelling and much of my driving was to Friendship Airport. The technical base located in Las Palmas had to be checked out, and a Far Eastern technical base was in process of establishment in Singapore. The Personnel office in London, England had to be upgraded and an appropriate organizational structure established. The Lab Navigation Corporation in Bahamas was little more than an empty framework but useful to have available. Meanwhile extensive field operations were being conducted on the west coast of Australia, on the coast of West Africa and at several locations in Indonesia and Sumatra.

The technical equipment was US Government surplus, modified to suit the requirements of the offshore geophysical exploration companies. The field engineers had an edge over the competition as a result of high-gain pre-amplifiers developed by Lassiter personally, and the effective range of operations of the system was greatly enhanced. The modified system offered higher accuracy of position-fix, out to almost 300 miles from shore. With geophysical exploration ships being very expensive to run, it was obviously desirable to contract for horizontal control, so essential to position accuracy and position recovery, with dependable corporations having the best equipment. A success record and an

217

image of fiscal responsibility were essential to successful bidding. Nevertheless, much depended upon who you knew and both he and I were well known in the entire field of operations.

To assume responsibility and to take control it was vitally necessary to become totally immersed in company operations and to get to know the people upon whom field successes depended. The only way to do that was to travel and so armed with credit cards, telephone cards and airline cards, and sometimes carrying letters of credit, I did just that. London, Singapore, Sumatra, Australia, face to face contact was vital. Such contact often involved dealing with many of the wild mercenaries we had on the payroll. Our saving grace was the fact that nearly all of our operations were conducted in truly isolated areas where those characters simply could not get into trouble. Most of the time their carousing had to be limited to their final return to London when they had a pocketful of cash.

Meanwhile life went on at Hampton Gardens. Jane recovered slowly but surely and quite soon her residual complaint was no more than a numbness in one ankle. However we never did forget the warning by the Irish surgeon who did the operation. 'She will feel it when she grows older,' he warned, but just then we didn't care all that much about getting old. Janice's education was the all important consideration at the time. We had agreed that in the early summer of 1970, when the school closed for the holidays, we would move to the Washington area. During the spring, on those occasions when I was home, we did a good deal of reconnaissance and decided that we would like to live in McLean, Virginia where there was an excellent high school.

On those occasions when time permitted at the home office James Lassiter and I would talk, but getting down to the bare facts of the corporate beginnings was never easy. James just loved to sustain an aura of mystery and intrigue about his background and particularly about his sponsors. However, there came a time when it was necessary that his financial backers be identified in order that a brief corporate history be written to provide appropriate documentation.

He and I took a trip to New York City and we dined at the Explorer's Club. We spent the entire evening discussing his flying experiences in Antarctica. Next day we had a luncheon appointment in a very fine restaurant on Wall Street. Carl Mueller, Vice-President of Loeb Rhoades, the Wall Street financiers, was the host. Another guest was one of the principal shareholders in Sears. I thoroughly enjoyed the lunch and James Lassiter did all of the talking and most of it was about me. The two directors kept nodding sagely but said very little. We were invited to visit the Loeb Rhoades office and I remember being both amazed and amused. Close to the bottom of Wall Street there is a massive and very impressive stone building, and embedded in one wall at street level is a golden door. Mueller pushed some buttons and the door opened directly into an elevator which silently raised us to an upper floor.

The visit was brief, I signed some documents, we shook hands warmly and we left. Lassiter still spoke in vague terms about the relationship but from what I could gather he and they were associates of old and the basic funding for his corporation stemmed from Loeb Rhoades. I gained the impression that there were outfits like this around doing no more than providing cover for some off-shore information-gathering business. The relationship certainly made it easier for me to acquire map coordinates for survey monuments in remote territories from the military necessary for the temporary establishment of navigation systems. The only obligation was to secure such classified information, and the provision of any extensions of such classified information to the military upon completion of the project.

Under these conditions it was absolutely necessary to have a dependable secretary. The business was run almost exclusively on the telephone. Whilst travelling on planes I spent my time writing technical manuals and operational manuals for field systems as prior to my arrival there, there had been no such thing in existence. Ms Jacqueline Senier, my secretary, was a godsend. She typed accurately at high speed and she could read my scrawly writing. She and I got along famously and she rapidly became a true 'gal Friday'.

Each establishment of a system under contract, whether in Turkey, Trinidad, or Balikpapan, required an aircraft shipment of equipment and a field crew comprised of a supervisor and a crew of six or seven technicians. Thereafter, having established accurate coordinates for the shore stations, it was necessary to provide computer runs relevant to the desired position points necessary to the geo-physicists. Rushing to the Control Data Computer Centre in Falls Church with the software and the input data was only half the problem. The computer runs, after checking, had to be hand-carried to the ship to ensure delivery. Such ships might well be in South Korea, or the Black Sea, or off the coast of West Africa. Pressures of business left us with no option but elect Ms Senier as the courier.

Quite often she took off for far-off places in Turkey or Trinidad, to be met at the airport by an anxious supervisor just waiting to rush off to his ship, perhaps a helicopter ride away. Ms Senier would rest for a couple of days in the best hotel she could find and return loaded down with cherished mementoes. She became totally indispensable after a while and for her own amusement she kept threatening us with a second marriage. We all thought that she was joking about it, but the day I left the corporation she and a retired Air Force colonel tied the knot. They planned a happy retirement on a boat drifting around in the Caribbean. Like many more of my good friends and associates, she and I were but ships that pass in the night. I never heard from her again.

Nonetheless the work was most enjoyable and despite the constant pressures I really enjoyed it. Almost from day one the heat was on to reorganize, to expand and to generate an aura of competence and corporate stability. Within the first few weeks we established relationships with Computer Sciences Corporation, and with consulting specialists in computer modelling, wave hindcasting, marine biology and general oceanography. Corporate competency statements had to be prepared for issue to the offshore development industry, and proposals and bid-sets had to be produced.

Before the spring of 1970 was over Navigation Management was solidly in business and navigation systems were provided out of Singapore to service the Far East, Las Palmas to service Europe, the Middle East and South Africa, and from Freeport in the Bahamas to service Central and South America. Consulting, professional and technical services to the geo-physical, magnetic, electro-magnetic, gravity and seismic survey industry were available. Cartographic and computer software services, in association with recognized consultants, were available when necessary.

At that time we had operations underway for the leading geo-physical companies and oil companies throughout the world. During 1970 operations were in process in South Korea, Indonesia, Ghana, Trinidad and in the Bahamas. Internal development and the assembly of computer models resulted in cooperative experiments with a major oil company in the field of wave hindcasting, a technology they desperately needed. With developments extending further and further offshore and at the mercy of the elements it became essential that the structural design engineers concerned with hydro-dynamic conditions in the oceans must have access to design conditions based upon accurate wave spectral analysis.

The extent and the urgency of development in the North Sea at that time created the need for trips to London, England to deal with our clients and to acquire additional personnel. In addition there were a few glitches in the various operations which called for urgent visits. In every case time was of the essence and in most of my travels the only sleep I got was on aircraft. However, one of the real benefits of success is the resultant adrenalin flow. Somehow under these conditions, with exciting, profitable projects, fatigue simply does not exist. Waiting time at airports was spent on the telephone.

Our major problems were rarely of a technical nature. Most were due to the non-arrival of aircraft shipments or troubles with passports. We conducted operations in Israel, and thereafter, in those Arab countries boycotting Israel we dare not send personnel with an Israeli visa recorded in the passport. The only solution was duplicate passports and this was the kind of problem Lassiter could resolve. Indeed some of the troubleshooting work that he was able to do was peculiar to say the least of it but it paid off in contracts with seismic engineering corporations in some very unusual parts of the world.

There was an instance where one of the major seismic corporations had developed some very special drill-bits and the relevant support technology. These were anxiously desired by the Russians and the seismic corporation was keen to make the sale. Unhappily there were export controls imposed by the Department of Commerce and to acquire the special dispensation for such a sale to Russia required great skill on Lassiter's part. For reasons best known to himself he had no desire to be the front man. It therefore fell to me to visit the Russian embassy and deliver the documentation. Each visit I made was photographed from across the street above the Gaslight Club but I was never subjected to questioning. I developed a good rapport with a young Russian engineer and his wife, both from the University of Kiev. I understood that the exchange of information generated with the Scientific Institute in Moscow resulted in resolution of the problem. I did find it difficult though to figure out why I had to go to the Russian embassy at all. The young Russian engineer and his wife had an apartment in Silver Spring, Maryland. When I made the suggestion to Lassiter he replied that the tribal dance is always a necessary part of the negotiations.

Prior to the school holidays in Towson in the summer of 1970, Jane, Janice and I had decided that McLean was the place to stay, and this after widespread reconnaissance. Jane just loved the Washington Parkway, with its wealth of tall trees and the rolling countryside overlooking the Potomac. Janice opted for high school in McLean and was most anxious to register. She was told, in no uncertain terms, that first of all she must have an address in McLean. We elected to rent rather than buy, and we selected a beautiful townhouse on Montcalm Drive, just inside the ring road. The designs were unique and each had three stories. Entry from the street was directly into the middle storey, to a spacious hallway, dining room, sitting room and a large kitchen. The small garden at the rear was accessed from the basement level due to the slope of the ground. Downstairs, a great family room, guest bedroom with attached bathroom, and utility rooms. Upstairs there were three bedrooms, two bathrooms and all the necessary facilities. It was ideal and they liked dogs.

Jane's dreamhouse in Hampton Gardens, Towson was up for sale and it was sold quickly at a very handsome profit. We felt rich again and totally free of mortgages. It was a good feeling. Jane was well enough to handle all the moving arrangements by herself. For me there was absolutely nothing to do as the house was completely finished. The small gardens back and front were kept in immaculate order by a permanent staff. Janice found two girls of her own age just two doors down. They had a sort of instant girls' club and almost immediately

Janice knew everybody in the neighbourhood. Mitzie settled down without a murmur, but I think she missed the rabbits although there were many pleasant pathways to walk around the estate. On her walks Mitzie met a variety of other dogs which made life interesting for her and also for Jane.

Walking the dog brought Jane in contact with Senga Reid who lived only one street away and they became firm friends. Senga was Scottish and her husband was a second generation Scot who was a successful broker, and also President of the local St Andrew's Society. His name was James Wallace Reid and he was so proud of it that he had two full kilted outfits, one in the Reid tartan, and one in the Wallace tartan. They had a little black scotty called 'Haggis'. Our next door neighbour was an Air Force General, James Keck, and his wife Bobby. They and their delightful family were the most American Americans we ever met. For years afterwards we received a long letter at Christmas advising us of their family affairs after they were moved to the SAC base in Nebraska. On retirement there James Keck ran for the United States Senate but he did not quite make it. I always thought that it was truly a great pity as he obviously had so much to offer his fellow Americans.

Jane and Senga decided that they had too little to do at home and they needed an outside interest. Very shortly after they came to this conclusion, they were on the staff of Scotland House in Alexandria, about ten or twelve miles down Jane's favourite parkway. The place was owned by Anderson of Edinburgh and they thoroughly enjoyed themselves there. As a consequence I felt far less guilty when I took off on a trip. Jane was never lonely with Bobby Keck next door and further down the street Janice's girlfriends' mother, a young widow from Dallas, Texas who was Personal Assistant to Senator John Tower.

A very interesting elderly lady moved in across the street and her house was constantly illuminated with the curtains always left wide open. The house was luxuriously furnished and she threw a 'Getting-to-know-you Party', complete with hostesses, barman and a marvellous pianist strumming on a Steinway Grand in the basement. It was surely the most lavish affair the neighbourhood had ever experienced. She had recently sold her very large house in the older part of McLean where she had been next door neighbour to Robert and Ethel Kennedy and their large family. The ladies were all agog at the tales she had to tell. I was more interested in the gentleman she introduced as her boyfriend.

He always arrived in a Cadillac and he must have been close to ninety. No one ever said so but I feel sure that the lady was about the same age. He was a regular visitor and she used to sit on his knee in this luxurious sitting room, all done in red velvet with plush white carpet. A large brown and white spaniel always lay at their feet. They were the neighbourhood Darby and Joan and were loved by all of us. The lady liked to have candles burning all over the house and

Jane was terrified that the house might go up in flames. It never did. The romance still blossomed at the time we moved away.

Taking off on a trip for Navigation Management was either a last-minute dash for an aircraft or the result of a truly extensive plan. The plans never did work out but our travel agents did deserve some credit for lively imaginations. We were usually off to some remote destination beyond the scope of the average agent but they seldom admitted to being baffled. One trip I undertook is illustrative of the extent of the company's operations. I boarded a plane in Washington DC, bound for Anchorage, Alaska, via Seattle, to consult with an oil company about their plans for drilling in the arctic environment of the Beaufort Sea. Then on to Tokyo, and thence to Seoul, South Korea, for a consultation with the Hanoi Oil Company. Then by car to Inchon, South Korea, where we had a field crew preparing for a geo-physical survey offshore immediately south of the line of demarcation between North and South Korea.

There were some difficulties here as the US Army Map Service had control of the survey data necessary to the establishment of our shore stations. Lassiter's connections resolved the problem and thereafter the primary objective had to be to keep the geo-physical survey ship south of the magic line. They were shadowed everywhere by the North Korean Navy gunboats. With operations running smoothly, but dangerously, I took off for a pre-arranged meeting in Hong Kong for which I was already three days late. However my associates were waiting in the luxury of the Imperial Palace Hotel, in Kowloon, and no one could possibly get fed up with that. From there I was bound for Sydney, Australia via Manilla. During the stopover at Manilla we were at the airport at the same time as the Pope and during his arrival there someone tried to stab him. On arrival at Sydney, New South Wales I was disappointed to discover that my favourite horse racecourse, Randwick Park, was closed in favour of an outdoor service, and a massive altar and pulpit had been specially erected for the Pope. Nevertheless, a wily Australian advised me to take a trip to Canterbury Downs, accessible by electric railway, where a special day's racing had been arranged.

It was a beautiful day and my first few hours away from business affairs. Lady Luck not only smiled upon me that day but literally moved in with me. When I left the track I had money bulging out of every pocket. Sunday was a celebration in the King's Cross area of Sydney then back to business on Monday. We had several operations running on the west coast of Australia and the principals involved were headquartered in Sydney. Having made my peace with them by ironing out some finance problems I took off for the airport in a cab. My schedule was so hectic that in the confusion of haste I left my briefcase in the cab. When I realized what had happened my stomach moved up somewhere between my ears.

In the briefcase were several thousand dollars in cash, half a dozen plane tickets, several contracts and half a dozen reports ready for telephone transfer to Ms Senier. I called the cab company with a cock and bull story about the sensitive, classified contents of the case, and lo and behold the cab was back in less than an hour delivering the briefcase with a bill for the round trip. I was relieved and delighted. The cab driver couldn't believe his tip. I had the feeling that he would really have liked a peek into that briefcase.

And on to Perth, in West Australia, with a side trip up the coast, then a direct flight to Singapore to check out the new technical base and on to London, England to talk to more young men who wished to join in the venture. One last meeting with an American oil company regarding the location of offshore drilling platforms in the North Sea after which I managed to catch a night flight to Boston, then on to Washington. The entire adventure took less than three weeks but I suspect it knocked a few years off my earthly existence. It was not a simple matter to resolve the financial costs of such a trip. Travel and expenses had to be allocated to different contracts, and consulting fees charged to appropriate clients. Reports, usually written in aircraft, were transcribed, polished and published by Ms Senier, with elaborate drawings and accurate map projections prepared by our cartographer.

In parallel with my efforts to provide documentation including systems manuals, operations manuals and field supervisor's manuals, Lassiter was vigorously pursuing the possibilities of patent, and this was a complicated and expensive exercise. He acquired the services of well-known patent attorneys out of Oklahoma City, and a patent was finally filed in January 1971. There were times too when he organized some very pleasant outings on his powered yacht, the *Labnav*. He and I visited Dallas and Oklahoma City together to sustain relationships with the major clients. For a while he was unusually anxious for me to invite the young Russian engineer and his wife from the Russian embassy to join him on a weekend picnic. I discreetly avoided that issue altogether. I was a registered alien and already far too close to the various Government agencies one would normally avoid.

At different times our field supervisors, mostly Americans, and groups of field technicians, mostly British, appeared at Falls Church for a brief visit. Having completed one contract they had to make preparations for another. To avoid hefty hotel bills Lassiter had a couple of apartments rented on the fringe of the National Airport area where warehousing was available. There were occasions in the middle of the night when I might get calls to show up there to resolve some stupid conflict. The problems usually involved local females and it was wise for us to resolve such conflicts without recourse to the local constabulary. Ex-mercenaries and cops do not mix particularly well. However we managed to keep these escapades well away from the main office.

Meanwhile Jane, Janice and I managed to spend the odd day at Tyson's Corners, the fashionable shopping centre in McLean. A few miles further out there was a busy town, Fairfax, and beyond that a pretty spot called Vienna. Joe Tyson of Life Sciences, associates of GURC, lived there and I was able to sustain a close liaison with Dr Sharp, the President of GURC, through Joe. He and his family were all from Texas and it was obvious that they wanted to be back there. On the way home from such a drive we stopped to pick up the best pizza in the world right there in McLean.

During Jane's visits to a very prominent prayer group in Towson she had learned a good deal about Peter Marshall, the great Scottish Presbyterian minister, who had made his mark upon Washington DC. He lead the congregation in New York Avenue Presbyterian Church, and served there in the late thirties and through the war years. He died suddenly of a heart attack in 1949, whilst still a comparatively young man. In 1947 he had been appointed Chaplain to the United States Senate. His wife, Catherine, assured his everlasting fame when she published her book, *A Man Called Peter*, in 1951. As a consequence of reading this and other works, including the sermons of Peter Marshall, Jane was determined to become a member of the New York Avenue Presbyterian Church.

During our time there the Minister was another Scotsman by the name of Dr Dougherty, a man in his early sixties and a splendid preacher. Sunday, whenever I was home, was a big day with us. The drive down the Washington highway on a Sunday morning, with very few cars around, was inspiring enough but the hours within the four walls of the church sanctuary with Dougherty were truly an inspiration. He was a very friendly, outspoken man, anxious to make us welcome and proud that we were fellow Scots. He arranged for us to be guests at the Kirking of the Tartans in the impressive Washington Cathedral. It was the first time I had ever heard a full pipe band play within the confines of a church. We spent the afternoon having tea on the lawn at the Rector's house.

There were two separate incidents at the church which remain very clear in my mind and they are worthy of record. One Sunday morning, with the church full to overflowing, Dr Dougherty was in the pulpit and he had a harrowing tale to tell. Early that summer he and his wife of some thirty-odd years had travelled to Europe and whilst in Germany his wife had been stricken with terminal cancer and died very suddenly in the hospital there. To fulfil a promise made earlier, he had her body transported to Lossiemouth in the north of Scotland where she was laid to rest. During the telling of the story the good Doctor leaned over the pulpit and wept and many of his congregation wept with him. However, he recovered remarkably quickly and a few months later he was reported to have married the thirty-year old organist.

Again, during the Christmas season of 1970, we had a remarkable experience at the church. To appreciate the incident it is necessary to be aware of the church location. Whilst only a few blocks from the White House, it is located on New York Avenue, at about 13th Street on the very edge of the red light district. There are no extensive grounds surrounding the church and only at the east end was there a tiny garden surrounded by a privet hedge about four or five feet high. We were there for the Christmas Eve service and we joined the choir in the garden and sang carols. All kinds of weirdos, drunks, ladies of the night, pimps and panhandlers kept peering at us over the hedge. Suddenly, quite close to midnight, a whole gang of secret service men surrounded the church and we were hustled into the sanctuary.

As luck would have it we were ushered into the seat immediately behind the 'Lincoln Pew', preserved in its original state and we found ourselves staring at the backs of President Richard Nixon, his wife Pat, daughter Julie and David Eisenhower. I kept wondering what the secret service boys would do if they knew that those of us within reach of their President were all aliens.

In the early Spring of 1971 I was off on an expedition to Singapore and when I returned to McLean, Va. Jane was in hospital, attended by a specialist. He was an Italian, a very amusing guy, who gave me all kinds of good advice on staying home to look after my family. Fortunately, Bobby Keck had taken charge of everything and I fell heir to nothing more than the convalescence. Friends from Ottawa came to visit us and this relieved the situation considerably. It was a reminder that I was no longer young and the hectic life I had been leading might have a detrimental effect on my family. I did what I could to avoid travel for a month or so then the same pressures started again. Operations began in the Black Sea, then in Namibia, and the manpower situation became very difficult.

By now it was plain that Lassiter was ready to sell. He too was feeling the pressure from his principals in New York. They saw a possibility of recovery of their investment, and while the market in the offshore business was good, they encouraged our efforts. Lassiter kept reminding me that selling the corporation meant selling expertise and in his opinion that included me. I had reservations. I could not see myself moving to some place like Tulsa, Oklahoma and continuing to live on aircraft. In addition, competition was increasing and some of our own people broke away to form a company of their own. My own concerns about the emergence of highly accurate satellite navigation systems compelled me to think of other alternatives.

Whilst I had made no commitments it was made very clear to me that GURC operations were progressing and they too were in need of the practical experience that I had to offer. They were top-heavy with science, and the time had come for a serious entry into the environment along the continental shelf rather than the confines of university laboratories. Having been a Director for the past few years I felt at ease with those university 'Boffins' and Jane was willing to move to Houston, Texas if it meant a quieter life.

During a quick visit to Houston on related business I met Dr Sharp and his staff and they were already quite excited at the prospect of posting a sizeable contingent of scientists to the Mississippi test facility. This facility was the NASA Apollo engine testing facility at Baie St Louis, in Missippi. Some years previously this massive testing facility had been established there, in an area of swampland about 100,000 acres in extent. There they constructed an enormous tower and on selected occasions they tested Saturn-Apollo engines *in situ*. The engines never got off the ground but the scientists made the vital measurements of thrust, durability and stability etc. To provide office space for the hundreds of personnel involved a great high-rise building was erected and it also had a luxurious observation tower to impress the press. Alas, with the proven success of the engines, the usefulness of the facility was in jeopardy.

The lobbyists moved in, those who were concerned with the welfare of the State of Mississippi, and with John Stennis, a very powerful Senator from Mississippi in the lead, it was declared necessary that uses be found for this enormous facility. Within a very short time the facility Director, whom I met on all too many occasions, had lined up half a dozen Government agencies desirous of establishing extensions therein. Agencies in Washington with any claim at all to the marine environmental interests were signed on. Baie St Louis became a focal point for US Government research studies in the broad spectrum of marine sciences. An extensive computer facility, now idle, was placed at their disposal but still under the control of the original staff. There was serious talk again of an 'International Decade of Oceanography'. GURC, representing the major universities in the five Gulf states, with the declared intention of adopting the Gulf of Mexico as their private backyard, simply had to be a permanent member of such an elite fraternity.

Once again I had to carefully consider timing. By the summer of 1971 Janice would need one more year of high school before going on to university. It was imperative that she complete her year at McLean and then commence a final year somewhere in Texas. She was a bit disappointed at the thought of leaving because she already had plans to attend university in Maryland with her girlfriends. I agonized over the issue and finally decided to leave every thing to fate. Jane was confident that everything would work out all right and she was prepared to settle down in Texas for a while. At the same time she was always concerned about retaining her Canadian citizenship.

Joe Tyson advised me that he was about to abandon Life Sciences in favour of a return to Texas with GURC. He was firmly convinced that by mid-year the

GURC staff would have to be doubled. As he was leaving he claimed to be aware that I would be made an offer I could not refuse and he advised that I organize my affairs with Navigation Management with this prospect in mind. I gave it some serious thought whilst on my way to Europe. Meetings in London convinced me that a sale of the corporation was in the works. A geo-physical corporation in Dallas was rumoured to be the interested party. On my return to Washington James Lassiter confirmed that he was close to an agreement. The patent application was registered and the attorneys were confident of approval. We parted company without rancour.

Recognizing James Lassiter's penchant for mystery, I never did closely question him about his new arrangement. He was obviously disappointed that I was unwilling to be included in the sale as an integrated part of the corporate structure, but as always the imperturbable operator, he shrugged it off. The group supposedly ready to acquire would obviously scale back to best suit their own special needs, the best field crews would be selected and the remainder become redundant, a way of life in the field service business.

That same week the President of GURC, Dr James Sharp, in company with Dr Alan Lohse from the University of Houston, were in town for a presentation to the National Science Foundation in regard to a pilot program in the Gulf of Mexico. They presented me with a letter of offer from the consortium and the die was cast.

The fates decreed that the timing was perfect. Janice finished high school that same week. Our rental agreement in Montcalm was close to termination. Once again the Allied Van Lines truck showed up at the door but this time it was smooth sailing. We took off from McLean with light hearts heading south for the great state of Texas.

CHAPTER XVIII

HOUSTON, TEXAS

The journey to Houston was a pleasant experience for us. There was absolutely no sense of urgency and for the first time in a long while we all felt truly relaxed. Janice was delighted with the reports from her high school in McLean and her girlfriends had given her a glowing description of the schools in Texas. She had no qualms whatsoever about heading south. Jane was a bit sad at leaving all her friends behind but she was optimistic about Texas. She had feelings about it. I had turned fifty-three and had no illusions. I needed another good ten years before I could afford to quit and I was hoping I could achieve that with the Gulf Universities Research Consortium.

We stayed with the expressways and headed for Atlanta, Georgia where we stayed overnight, then on to Mobile, Alabama to link up with the new Route Ten West. The drive westwards through New Orleans was a nightmare of drenching rain, flooded roads and frightening thunderstorms. It was a real, dramatic introduction to the south. However when we reached St Charles, Louisiana the skies were clear again and our mood brightened considerably. Passing through Beaumont, Texas was something of a thrill for me as it was thirty-five years since my earlier visit. We made a point of driving by the San Jacinto monument to Sam Houston and down through the original oil fields of Texas, a depressing sight. I was conscious all the time of the changing looks of surprise, disappointment and sometimes amazement in the faces of my companions. When we reached Seabrook they brightened quite a bit.

At that time in mid-1971 the main office of GURC was located in Galveston, Texas. Even then it was obvious that a move to Houston was inevitable. As a consequence it made good sense for us to settle on the south side of the city of Houston. The Johnson Space Centre was located on the south side and quite quickly a satellite city, Clear Lake, had emerged. Immediately south of Clear Lake a very elegant district called Nassau Bay became the desirable place to live. Many of the astronauts lived either in Nassau Bay or Seabrook and both bordered upon Galveston Bay. Whilst the terrain was horrifyingly flat and a mere thirty feet above sea level, the man-made improvements made up for all that. The houses, the gardens, even the trees were luxurious, and the highways made the commuting easy.

It was not difficult for us to finalize a decision on where to live. Jane looked at a house in San Sebastian, Nassau Bay, and that was it. We drove to League City to inspect the high school for Janice, she approved and the die was cast. The house and garden, whilst gorgeous on the outside, turned out to be pretty grungy on the inside once the heavy curtains were properly opened up. As usual Jane made the decisions and I applied the paint, and very shortly we were settled in. Janice was delighted with her school, made friends very quickly and in no time at all was deeply immersed in music and drama. We had fun seeing her perform in *Fiddler on the Roof*. Lynn and her young sons came down from Canada on vacations.

The Tysons had settled in nearby Seabrook so he and I were able to share the driving to Galveston. The old city had changed a good deal from my earlier visits there in the thirties. Indeed it was now a very respectable holiday resort, complete with 'Sea World' and other delights for youngsters and miles of golden beaches for the grown-ups. It had its share of good restaurants and new hotels were springing up all along the beach. One very good hotel, built upon great concrete stilts out into the sea was the Flagship. Hordes of people came just to fish from its various piers. Jane loved the Flagship, mainly because of the elegant dinner dances they hosted, and also because of the excellent pepper steaks they had in the dining room.

The GURC Galveston office was located in a modern building on Tremont Street. The consortium was formed by seven original member institutions and one associate member in January 1965. It grew quickly to sixteen members and nineteen advisory members. With the addition of the University of Mexico in October 1967 GURC became an international organization. By 1970 every major university in the five Gulf states, Texas, Louisiana, Mississippi, Alabama, and Florida were members of the consortium. All of the major energy corporations were advisory members. Each member institution was represented by a senior faculty person or administrator designated by the member.

GURC was a non-profit corporation whose purposes were oriented to research, education and public service. I must confess that at that time in 1971, I was flattered to be a member of the board of directors, and I was very impressed by the calibre of board chairmen and members with whom I served. Dr Carey Croneis of Rice University in Houston was Chairman in 1965, Dr Grover Murray of Louisiana State University in 1967 and Dr Horace R. Byers of Texas A & M University in 1969 etc. The President was Dr James M. Sharp from the Southwest Research Institute in San Antonio, Texas. Funding support was derived from several sources: membership fees, contracts for services, grants and gifts. Major grants were made by the Moody Foundation of Galveston, the National Science Foundation and the National Council for Marine Sciences. Contract arrangements with the Corps of Engineers, the Federal Water Pollution Control Administration, the Environmental Sciences Services Administration and the General Electric Company were secured.

In the early days of corporate development several major conferences and symposia were organized. Workshops were held on such subjects as 'Law and the Coastal Margin', 'Data Management', 'Marine Geology', and 'Biology and Fisheries'. Several publications were issued covering these activities. Early efforts were made to involve more scientists in projects related to the Gulf of Mexico. These early efforts included placing eight scientists from GURC amongst those participating in trial dives of the submersible 'Aluminaut'. In addition, participation of GURC designated scientists in the diving program of the Westinghouse 'DeepStar 4000' in the Gulf of Mexico was arranged.

However, more recently the principal element of the GURC program was the launching of a comprehensive activity which would lead to a thorough understanding of the Gulf of Mexico and its problems. At that time the so-called 'International Decade of Exploration' called for a worldwide focus on the use of the oceans and their resources. The Gulf Environmental Measurements Program (G.E.P.) as proposed by GURC recommended a national and international focus upon the Gulf of Mexico. Without doubt the Gulf provided an ideal environment for concentrated studies in a model ocean context. It represented a pilot study for the world's oceans.

The economic impact of oil and gas exploration in the Gulf was at an all-time high. The Gulf was estimated to contain 60 per cent of US oil and gas reserves. Thirty per cent of the total US fish catch was landed in Gulf coastal states in 1968 yet we had not learned how to properly harvest these resources. A population growth of 40 per cent over sixteen years brought new industries to these coastlines adding to the problem. In the GURC recommendations seven key subjects were identified as necessary to implement the program. General circulation, air-sea interaction, man's effect on the Gulf, biology and fisheries, marine geology, tectonics, and man's use of the Gulf. The benefits in terms of return on investment were stressed. A completed study would provide the data necessary for lowered insurance rates, saving of lives and property through better weather predictions, renewal of fish stocks, determination of effects of geologic and other factors upon biomass and species diversity, and the relative rates of evolution of the Gulf biota.

My appointment to the GURC staff required that I occupy the position of Senior Engineer and Projects Coordinator, and in the longer term with emphasis on systems technology. At any of our seminars conducted on a variety of disciplines, we could gather 250 scientists without any trouble. However the processes of intercommunication, exchange of information and even the practical process of cooperation were at that time difficult to promote. Down-to-earth experience in the marine field, particularly on the outer continental shelf, was practically non-existent. Workshops were organized simply to encourage these exchanges and to foster the idea of multi-disciplinary research, so necessary to meet the challenge of the nineteen seventies, and to stimulate a revolution in technology, including data management, instrumentation and remote sensing systems.

The Mississippi test facility, dedicated to the testing of Saturn-Apollo rocket engines, was no longer needed. The facility Director, along with Senator John Stennis, lobbied the Government to sustain the facility for the purposes of ocean sciences research. Already several agencies had responded to the appeal and had established branch operations therein. In a very special situation such as this it is easy to imagine the level of competition within these premises for priority of space and the use of any special facilities within the buildings. At the same time it can be appreciated that the senior personnel had accepted positions there with the greatest reluctance. Baie St Louis, Mississippi and Slidell, Louisiana could hardly be compared to Washington DC. Many of them had wives who were unhappy to leave high-paying jobs in Washington only to sit idle in some unaccustomed surroundings. Local devastation from the last killer hurricane was a constant reminder of the annual threats to come, and who could forget Hurricane Camille of 1969?

Nonetheless, into this unhappy situation GURC had established a bridgehead and several universities had representative scientists posted there dedicated to the on-going development of a unique database management system. The team was headed by a very happy-go-lucky young German scientist with a Ph.D. in Archaeology. He had some very amusing tales to tell of his post-graduate studies of ancient Indian middens. He lived on a thirty-five foot sail-boat, berthed in Long Beach, and travelled back to his family in Houston by car each weekend. I was compelled to spend a good deal of time there analyzing the capability and the adaptability of the data system. Without doubt the basic system was unique, but because of the scientists' inclination to protect their developments there was already the beginnings of conflict with the personnel at the Univac 1108 Computer Centre. The staff, a holdover from the old NASA days, were determined to protect their turf at all costs.

On many occasions Dr Sharp and I visited the facility together and most of our effort was applied to trying to convince the facility Director of our honest ambition towards the development of a systems capability to the benefit of the entire community. The primary aim was the development of a complete computer software system capable of providing total access to non-computer knowledgeable scientists, thus creating the potential for publicly-credible, scientific analysis of multi-disciplinary databases. Suspicion of our motives prevailed. They were convinced that we were using their funds to further our own aims. The computer staff at the base were convinced that we planned their obsolescence. It was not a happy situation.

Within a very short time the relationship between our Project Manager and the facility Director became impossible. Rumours were rife in regard to his lifestyle and he had to be removed. I had no choice but to agree to take over. We had just completed an International Oceanographic Conference hosted by the University of Mexico in Mexico City. Jane and I spent at least a week there, and we thoroughly enjoyed the splendid entertainment. Jane saw enough of the conference and mixed with the delegates sufficiently to convince herself that GURC was emerging as a power in the ocean sciences field. There were discussions of joint contracts between the US Government and the Mexican Government supported by the major oil companies within the great Gulf of Mexico. These were exciting times, and the Gulf Environmental Program (G.E.P.) was the greatest thing since sliced bread.

Our San Sebastian house was put on the market and within two weeks we were offered 20 per cent more than we paid for it a year earlier. I had painted it outside and inside and the garden was a riot of colour. Again the gods smiled upon us and the timing was perfect. Janice had just completed her last year of high school at League City and she was now ready for the college adventure. She and two friends had decided that they would spend their first university year at the Stephen F. Austin, in Nacodoches, Texas. They were already enrolled and had accommodation arranged on campus. Jane and I were free to head east for Louisiana. She took one look at Slidell and I didn't have to ask her opinion, I could read it in her face. We stopped momentarily at Baie St Louis. We drove on through the hurricane wreckage of Long Beach and on to Gulfport, Mississippi.

We returned to a motel reasonably close to the test facility and thereafter Jane did most of the reconnaissance herself. At that time the motorway, Route 10, from Mobile to New Orleans, and on to Houston and El Paso, was under construction. The section from Gulfport to Baie St Louis was little more than a smooth sea of mud. However the old coast road was in good shape and not at all unpleasant to drive except for the constant reminders of hurricane damage. There was an excellent shopping centre in Gulfport, a beautiful marina and an excellent Sheraton Hotel. We spent an evening there on the top floor with Lou Rawls as the featured entertainer. Gulfport was undoubtedly the place to live. Jane's hairdresser, a Ms McArdle, was married to an expatriate Italian and was most friendly and helpful. Because of her policeman brother Jane was presented with a Mississippi driver's licence without bothering with the test, something that worried the life out of her. Lou Scardino, the husband, worked at the Navy base in Biloxi during the day and made saxophone music in a dance band by night.

This was an interesting friendship for us and in some odd way it helped me to retain my sanity in the midst of the appalling political scene at the test facility. The band with whom Scardino played specialized in real ballroom dancing. Their gigs were undertaken happily in a variety of places throughout southern Mississippi. Jane, Mitzie and I tagged along with the musicians and their wives and I believe we had more genuine fun with that group than with any we met who were attached in any way to the test facility. From the point of view of the Mississippi folks all the people at the test facility were foreigners. The original NASA crowd were mostly Europeans with a group of New Englanders supporting them. The new crowd came from distant points in the United States and they were loud and brash in their criticisms of the local way of life. Fortunately most of the newcomers chose to live in Slidell, and Gulfport was therefore able to retain its old-world Mississippi hospitality.

We finally settled on a brand new condominium in Gulfport, and as a consequence met some nice people and made many friends. I was appointed Chairman of the Board of this very new and very large condominium, much against my will, but they simply would not take no for an answer. In some ways it was Jane's introduction to the so-called seventies scene, where the ladies came of age all of a sudden and created the sexual revolution. It seemed that most of the condo owners were living with third wives, or in many cases simply living in sin. Some prominent citizens supported a condo to house a girlfriend in unaccustomed luxury and it was hinted many times that a variety of modern drugs were available. The developer, a handsome guy from Atlanta, maintained a variety of stewardess lady friends. The real estate people there with whom Jane became really friendly had so many mixed-up relationships it was tragically amusing. After a while it was difficult to know who was living with whom.

However at weekends Jane and I spent time in New Orleans, just sixty miles away. We visited all the fancy restaurants, breakfasted at Brennans, ate doughnuts at the Café du Monde and visited the Bourbon Street entertainment scene. The big names in those days were Al Hirt and his band, and Pete Fountain and his quartet. During our stay there, Pete Fountain, Al Hirt and Phil Harris opened a club in nearby Biloxi which really drew the crowds. On long weekends Janice rode the bus from Nacodoches to New Orleans. The bus station there used to frighten the life out of Miss Janice. I always had to stay with her till the very last moment and then wait till the bus actually pulled out of the station. The surrounding area was one of the worst dumps I have ever seen. On the other hand Gulfport was a real refuge to us and Mitzie just loved it there as all of our neighbours made a great fuss of her.

From my personal viewpoint Gulfport was a very pleasant experience. One of my good friends there was the Marine Superintendent for a large fruit company. He and his wife lived at the condominium. The company had several very modern ships running from Gulfport to Nicaragua and other central American countries carrying full loads of bananas. The cargo was transferred directly into boxcars at Gulfport and hauled at high speed all the way to Chicago. The ships were of British registry and Jane and I spent many pleasant hours aboard. The cocktail lounges and the meals they served were quite fantastic. Jane would have loved a trip or two to Managua but it was not to be.

Meanwhile the GURC team at the facility pressed on with their own development dreams and in their own quiet way made important progress. Henry Fleming, a biologist/entomologist, who had spent a good deal of time on expeditions to the Amazon sponsored by New York Botanical Gardens, was the team leader. He and Dr Appan, an East Indian biologist, had brought with them a unique data storage and retrieval module, ideally suited to the peculiar requirements of the taxonomist. They and their principal scientists at their respective universities were confident that this module, modified to include the flexibility demanded in marine sciences databases, could become the control module in a system providing full file content addressability. Elwyn Graham, a down-to-earth programmer, showed promise of becoming a worthy systems developer. Luis Herrera-Cantilo, an Argentinian from the University of Miami and an engineer who had specialized in cloud physics, became a computer whiz without equal.

The Univac 1108 computer system at the base was controlled by the original old hands from NASA and whilst they were committed to providing computer access and the relevant programming services, they were reluctant to cooperate with a team with a peculiar development that they failed to understand. They were constantly demanding access to the codes which were of no value to them in view of the changes being incorporated from time to time. They could not understand the scientists' attitude, and they in turn ignored them, so their queries went unanswered. At regular intervals a new Big Chief appeared with a firm promise of a complete reorganization but they too would fade into the woodwork somewhere and we would hear no more for a while.

Finally the original contract with the Mississippi test facility was running out in September 1973. There was no obligation upon us to produce anything so a decision was made to withdraw. The system development was such that GURC was convinced that we had assembled all the necessary elements of a system that could be integrated more readily at the computer centre at the University of Houston. Meanwhile at headquarters a decision had been made to establish a spacious office facility in Clear Lake City, and a head office in the city of Houston. The development team agreed to move physically to Clear Lake City and become staff members of GURC. We had several small contracts to keep us busy and I had commitments to the US Navy.

Once again this meant the transfer of our home. Jane had decorated our condominium so tastefully that we did not have to put it on the market. The developer, the big man from Atlanta, was delighted to buy it back. But we had an additional decision to make and that was truly an emotional one. Miss Mitzie, the cute little poodle, missed Janice terribly. She was inconsolable after each visit. However she found a substitute, two in fact, Elwyn Graham's two little daughters, about eight and ten years old. They just adored the little poodle and we felt that she would be happier with them, so she went off to live in Meridian, Mississippi. I am certain that she had a very happy old age because she was allowed to do exactly as she pleased and she slept with the children, just like a third sister. Jane and Janice were broken-hearted for a while but they had no doubt it was for the best.

Meanwhile an element of the Gulf Environmental Program entitled 'The Offshore Ecology Investigation', funded by the major oil companies, was under way off the coast of Louisiana and coordinated by Joe Tyson; the data management involved in that project was considerable. At the same time this provided our scientists with real data, controlled in time and space, and of an extent and diversity never before collected. To Henry Fleming this was a godsend. The various analyses required dictated the need for sophisticated processing modules. As a team they were now provided with specific goals to achieve and they thrived on it. Luis Herrera-Cantilo, the laid-back Castilian, arrived for work about 11.00 a.m., but he was often there till midnight. This became my first experiment with staff establishing their own hours and reacting only to time-specific goals. It worked. The performance was truly formidable.

Dr R. J. Menzies, from Florida State University, was the Chief Scientist on the OEI, and a short time after Jane had re-established our home in Nassau Bay he came to visit us. At the same time Jane had a visitor from Scotland, a niece. It was a delightful experience to take her around Texas. She marvelled at all the modern conveniences and she was wide-eyed at the way the great scientists she met could discard their inhibitions and behave like schoolboys at parties. Dr Menzies was returning from a visit to Costa Rica, his favourite place to relax. He brought with him a new wife, number three if I remember correctly. Jane's party was a howling success and we spent a great deal of time that evening toasting the success of the OEI project. Unfortunately he died shortly afterwards and was sorely missed.

Our quarters in Clear Lake City were totally satisfactory, and it was here that the Database Management System began to take shape. The data, accumulated from the organized synoptic expeditions at the mouth of the Mississippi River, was used to create dynamic data files for exercise by the scientists. Their demands for analysis provided the guidelines for refining the analytical routines developed by Fleming, Appan, and Cantilo. The contracts we had with other agencies were enhanced as a consequence of these internal developments. In particular we worked closely with scientists from the Oceanographic Office and with special experiment teams involved in anti-submarine warfare. One program, LORAP, a long range acoustic propagation project, was related to some degree to Project Caesar, wherein I had accumulated experience over a period of years.

The LORAP experiments, funded at a level of about thirteen million per annum, were a sort of support project for the Caesar arrays in the shore station analysis, and were funded by the Office of Naval Research. Such experiments required teams of scientists with different capabilities to work together with small groups from Government agencies, with the entire group managed by the Office of Naval Research. The experiments were organized to take place in a variety of locations within the oceans and required only small ships, moored sensors and buoy systems with strings of data sensors. The end product of such ventures then kept the scientists analysing data and writing reports for the rest of the year. I often heard unkind critics refer to the participants as the 'Beltway Bandits'. I often felt that the project managers behaved like 'Little Caesars', and the entire operation, on occasions, could have been better planned by Rube Goldberg. However my superiors reassured me by claiming that less than 10 per cent of Government-funded research is ever productive but that even such a low rate of success pays off.

Unhappily, in those days of 1973 and 1974, everyone in the computer business was peddling a new database management system. In fact there was a whole army of computer experts making a handsome living out of constantly analysing one such system against another. Within the Navy there was a variety of competing systems, each with some merit. They were naturally opposed to any outsider, and particularly opposed to a bunch of university scientists moving into their territory. The decision-makers unfortunately knew very little about computers and practically nothing about scientific data, but they did know about money. To avoid ever making the terrible mistake of rejecting a potential winner they were happy to fork out seed money, just enough to keep you coming back. We never did get anything more than seed money but they never knew quite what to expect from us, so the contract end items remained very vague. From our point of view their data and specifications provided useful exercises for our development team.

Our greatest difficulty in dealing with Government agencies was their failure to understand the system concept, and of course their view of our credibility. They simply refused to believe that university researchers were capable of such advanced development. These were the days of the massive Univac 1108 computers; there were no desktop or laptop computers then. The end product of a computer run was reams of paper output usually resulting from a special program written by a computer programmer to serve the customer's demands. It was difficult for people to accept the concept that major computer systems could be directly accessed by non-computer knowledgeable scientists, and special dynamic data files could be created at their command for purposes of analysis with the output automatically displayed on X & Y plotters.

To best describe the task facing our scientists it is necessary to describe the problem they faced in the Gulf of Mexico. The total Gulf system envisaged by the consortium extended upwards from the sediment at the bottom of the 'Sigsbee Deep' to the sea surface, through the air-sea interface, and upwards through the lower atmosphere affecting the continental climate. It extended from the deeps, up the slopes, on to the continental shelf and landwards towards the near-shore area, the land-sea interface, with its bays, its estuaries, its rivers, its marshes, and its estuarines. It included the mammoth inflow of tropical seawater through the Yucatan Channel, the Loop Current and its eddies meandering through the western Gulf, and the subsequent outflow that creates the beginning of the Gulf Stream. It considered the continuing tectonic upheaval, and it included the enormous run-off from the North American continent, in particular through the massive Mississippi River.

Within these boundaries, the energy exchange, the water budget, the sediment transport, the diurnal and seasonal changes, the surges, the catastrophic meteorological phenomena, the effects of man and his need for resources, all of these affect the all-important biomass, and the biotic potential for this life-giving, active system. Relatively speaking this Gulf system is not large, it has limited exchange with the world's oceans, yet it still receives the major portion of industrial, agricultural and municipal wastes from the United States and Mexico.

To make predictions for the Gulf's tolerance for these wastes without a general knowledge of the system circulation, its physical properties and processes and without a reasonable quantitative knowledge of the important components of the eco-system, was simply not possible. To understand the system, to accurately predict its motion in three dimensions in the sea and in the air, with a knowledge of the interactive processes, the interface processes on the shelf, at the near-shore and in the bays and estuaries was considered to be the first objective. To derive from this information the knowledge of how to induce beneficial change in the system itself was the second objective. To manage this complex system to ensure that man can derive maximum benefit was the final objective.

The consortium presented this program with the Offshore Ecology Investigation being a component capable of final integration. It was presented in a format suggesting the building block concept. Assuming that one can conceive of the Gulf system description emerging as a series of dynamic models, each interrelated, interfaced and interlocked, such models would in broad terms encompass the total system. In their own system, sub-system framework, a system of hierarchy of logical superiority and logical control would emerge. As knowledge increased it would be determined that the three-dimensional dynamic model of the sub-surface circulation, interfacing with the air-sea interaction model which provides accurate description of the sea surface, derived from the atmosphere and modified or amplified by the energy below, exercises the primary driving forces.

Within this general system and sub-system framework, all other eco-models, energy models, numerical and analytical models would be so constructed that while each may stand alone they must nevertheless be so scaled as to fit within the general framework, and so arranged that they can accept input from superior models, and produce output in a format that is understood as independent information, and at the same time be capable of acceptance as input to any other interfaced model. The relevant data was required to be accumulated in such a manner that the maximum amount of scientific information relevant to the system could be derived in the shortest possible timeframe.

An examination of the vertical boundary revealed that the disciplines, stacked from the bottom up, are tectonics, geology, biology, oceanography, and meteorology. The horizontal boundary at the sea surface extending from the deltas to the main inflow, outflow driving forces are oceanography, macrobiology, microbiology, geology etc. A systems overview of the total living system breaks down into major components, all interconnected and producing information and knowledge, the end product of which would define the logical priorities and finally determine the systems control and the systems interface with the public domain.

With the facilities available at the twenty-two member universities, and the array of scientists in all the necessary disciplines, it was not considered a problem beyond our capabilities. The Offshore Ecology Investigation clearly demonstrated our ability to organize multi-disciplinary expeditions capable of producing in accordance with fixed schedules. However, the driving force necessary to the resolution of these massive environmental problems is, and always will be, money. Proposals were submitted to Government agencies and institutions for pilot projects at a cost of several millions of dollars, but as was customary, approvals were always promised but rarely materialized. However, no doubt to avoid subsequent criticism, survival monies were grudgingly awarded. Our scientists wrote learned papers and our developers pressed on, enthused by their own accomplishments.

Meanwhile Janice moved from the Stephen F. Austin University in Nacadoches to the University of Texas at Austin. For her first year we were very happy to persuade her to settle for accommodation on the campus and we drove the 200 miles from Houston to Austin each weekend to ensure her welfare. There was a French bakery we used on the outskirts of Houston, run by Jean-Pierre, and we used to load up with all kinds of goodies for the girls. However, as one or two terms passed, Miss Janice insisted on switching to a co-ed residence where she was quickly made aware of the less glamorous facts of life like booze and marijuana. She begged us to get her out of there in a hurry and into an apartment which she shared with a very nice girl. Then with our welfare in mind she asked for a new car, and reversed the driving trend, so that she visited us at weekends in Houston.

Jane worried about her daughters a lot even if there was absolutely nothing to worry about. Janice was really doing well. She planned to graduate in languages and she had no plans beyond that other than a possible marriage, a preoccupation with all the young girls in Texas. Lynn came to visit us with her boys each year and Jane had her month vacation in Ottawa each July, along with her check-up. There was very little to bother her so Jane got bored and decided that she needed a fire-engine red Camaro to get around more. She was a blond at the time. There was not enough excitement in her life despite the hordes of friends so she took a job in a boutique, where she made more friends, and that meant more entertaining and more parties to attend.

The entire year of 1974 passed very quickly. The GURC executive, including yours truly, spent a good deal of time in Washington DC, in presentations, lobbying and technical discussions with the Energy Department, the Environment Department, the Central Intelligence Agency and with Scientists at Aberdeen Proving Ground, or the US Army, not far from Baltimore. Despite the fact that we never quite landed the big multi-million dollar contracts we did acquire several substantial contracts with enough to keep our lofty ambitions alive. As a result, many of our senior scientists were totally convinced that one day the entire GEP would be funded. The National Science Foundation and the Environmental Protection Agency were always reported to be swimming in money, but this was mere university gossip.

By the end of 1974 my group in the systems management business was ambling along, the cash flow was adequate without being overpowering, but the future always looked bright. Annual salaries were generous and the pension plan the envy of our peers. However, in certain quarters, there was evidence of delusions of grandeur. It was agreed at director level that the systems development potential was such that it was no longer an appropriate element of the consortium and might, at some point, jeopardize the non-profit status. With tongue in cheek, I and my associates had no option but to agree. As a consequence discussions were held with Daniel Industries of Houston, Texas regarding the possibility of the establishment of a commercial corporation to accommodate the systems development group.

The discussions were meaningful and serious. The President of GURC, Dr James Sharp, was obviously on good terms with the principals in Daniel Industries and they were quite deeply involved in the offshore Industry. Their main business was basically foundry work as this related to the production of massive castings for use in the undersea pipeline business, and these units were flow meters. There was very little competition in this area of business, they had a well-defined market that was obviously expanding and they had now generated a desire to expand and diversify. They already had a small computer group dedicated to the application of automated tanker loading systems. We could identify a common link between the two groups but the likelihood of potential cooperative effort was zero. They were in the hard-wire systems business and hopelessly remote from anything scientific.

Nevertheless it was decided by the powers that be to press on and I was required to prepare a business management plan for their review and approval. This document was about half an inch thick and projected our endeavours for the first year with a budget and a long dissertation on the data management system, its development status and its application. Current and projected contracts were included and GURC was naturally our biggest customer. The recipients were more interested in the market value of the system, its possibility of patent or copyright, and above all what it might contribute to their bottom line. It was very difficult to explain that development went hand in hand with operations and that whilst the core of the system and the analytical and display modules were available, it would not be wise to set anything in concrete pending final resolution of the overall requirement. Like our contract friends at LORAP they were mildly sceptical and were convinced we had something to hide.

Nonetheless the deal was done. By the spring of 1975 I was Executive Vice-President of Daniel Analytical Services Corporation, 'Danalyt' for short. The development staff, by now expanded considerably, found themselves to be employees of Danalyt. At a meeting arranged for this special purpose they were informed of the great benefits to be derived from such a move and were provided with a hearty vote of thanks from GURC. Fortunately we all had a hearty sense of humour and nothing changed except the name on the door. Our special personal interest lay in the success of the development as it related to science and to the universities. Henry Fleming and Appan had devoted much of their academic careers to the cause and Luis Cantilo was a brilliant scientist who cared little for anything other than science. The remainder of the staff were young, full of energy and delighted to participate in something they believed in. We were a happy group of dedicated people and we pressed on.

We had difficulties keeping our LORAP clients happy. Their primary objective appeared to be the creation of a mass of paperwork which could be used to justify their expenditures and avoid criticism from above. We rarely knew what they required from their funding and they were never able to appreciate the long-term potential as it applied to the oceanographic community. However we had an easier time dealing with the energy and environment groups. They were compelled to contemplate the big picture, and as a consequence they were willing to accept the system philosophy as it might apply to their portions of the overall environmental problem. Scientists in the US Army had specific problems to resolve and specific applications they could foresee for cooperative effort. The funding derived from these sources was more than adequate to sustain our existence through 1976 but this did not demonstrate the hoped-for potential to Daniel Industries.

They had to be convinced, they had to have a computer system to sell, they needed documents, and copyright, and a patent investigation, all the things that required a highly specialized staff and cost a lot of money. As a group we neither had the time nor the money so we had no choice but proceed on a do-it-yourself basis. It was not an easy task but we did document the entire system and copyrighted the relevant documents which were passed on to a patent attorney for perusal. Having been through the patent application process with Navigation Management I was well aware of the likely time-frame and the excessive cost. Patent attorneys do not come cheap. I convinced Daniel Industries that they should pick up the tab in view of their intense interest in the outcome.

It is difficult to compress several volumes into a few paragraphs of explanation but in order to appreciate what the so-called system was all about, I include a brief explanation. First of all one must understand what is meant by a Database. In our terminology, it is that data contained within the boundaries of the problem, relevant to cost-effective, publicly credible, scientifically supportable, problem resolution. We were concerned with an 'Integrated Database Analysis System', IDBAS, where, given a regional database and a team of scientists, the tools necessary for problem resolution were available. The system was comprised of a family of modularly inter-faced program packages where each self-contained module was designed to perform a specific task. A sequential application of a selected combination of modules accomplished the desired data processing function as requested by the scientists.

IDBAS was designed primarily to aid in comprehensive, regional environmental studies involving a coordinated team effort by multi-disciplinary scientific groups. Disparate, discipline-oriented, databases resulting from field operations could be consolidated for synoptic, inter-disciplinary synthesis, leading to interpretation of the dynamic eco-system behaviour and patterns of impact thereon. Alternatively, the objective might be the analysis and display of physical processes, and their impact upon long-range acoustic propagation.

Dynamically structured data-information files were derivatives of IDBAS. The primary module, Creatabase, had as its principal function the capabilities of: (1) Merging pertinent blocks of data from two or more scientific data banks, and generating multi-disciplinary data/information files appropriate to given temporal/spatial constraints; (2) Selectively retrieving data subsets pertinent to the resolution of a given environmental phenomenon, and feeding these subsets to the appropriate modularly interfaced software packages for transformation into graphic displays, numerical indices, statistical output etc. The modules included contours, X-Y plots, vertical profiles, vector diagrams, map plots, four-dimensional analysis, Shannon-Weaver species diversity index, Morosito-ono faunal affinity, statistical modules, arithmetic modules, report generators etc. All this was with complete flexibility, compression of data files, full file content addressability, and direct scientist/computer interface.

The contribution made by Luis Cantilo was very significant and highly sophisticated. In his four-dimensional analysis module the principles of operation were as follows: The environmental quantities to be measured, i.e. temperature, salinity, fluid velocity, and others derived from them, are physical fields continuous in space and time. The method most amenable to further processing is to store them in the form of arrays of values of each field at every point in a grid, covering the domain in which the observations were made. This is known as objective analysis and a technique was developed by which the fields are defined and stored as four-dimensional arrays, with the very important advantage that the inherent space-time continuity of the fields is embedded in the mathematical definition of the output arrays. The program interpolates in time and height (or depth), as well as in the other dimensions and is therefore no longer limited to the use of observations taken at standard times or levels, but employs all data gathered in the X, Y, Z or T, (space and time) domain explored.

The combination of Creatabase and this four-dimensional module permitted the construction, from independent observations of different variables, of a truly merged, four-dimensional file of environmental information. This permitted direct query, and on-line display of selected horizontal or vertical cross-sections. Output therefrom, in the three dimensions of space and the fourth dimension time, could then be entered as interpolated data into an appropriately structured and dimensioned file. Given data with spatial and temporal density commensurate with system parameter variabilities pertinent to the experimental objectives, a matrix of data corresponding to all grid points selected, and according to mission objectives, could be developed, the fields analysed and the four-dimensional file created.

The graphic package called 'EGO' was in some ways unique for the year 1976. In all cases the runstream necessary to the generation of the displays was simple, and understandable to a non-computer-knowledgeable scientist. The design philosophy was such that the computer generated its own instructions from the runstream, always permitting override by the user. In general this module provided the capability to generate more than thirty different types of display, including Standard Mercator Charts, Lambert Conformal Projections, or Polar Stereographic Projections, coupled with the coastline of any area selected. Such maps could include spatial density of desired data, symbol-coded (if desired) to project temporal density, scatter diagrams, functional relation diagrams, regression displays, vector displays etc.

All of the above software necessary to interface the science teams with the computer in a cybernetic mode was based solely upon computer logic. The analysis processes were all based upon approved mathematical equations written in Fortran, with all the necessary user controls embedded therein. The entire process of Integrated Database Analysis was an iterative one, involving scientists at every stage in the various processes, and every process applied, leading to database growth. The creation and analysis of the entire database was accomplished through a combination of techniques reduced to a methodology that provided total control to the scientists from program initiation to its logical end.

There was never any doubt about the positive interest of the university scientists, they enjoyed working with us and they participated in workshops, seminars and general training sessions through direct access by modem to the computer centre in the University of Houston. By early 1976 the consortium had made many extensive and comprehensive proposals to the various Government departments seeking funding for the Gulf Environmental Program. These were never rejected out of hand but shelved for some unspecified future date. However, in different ways, they would provide funding for some totally unrelated project. One such project of considerable magnitude had to do with geo-thermal energy studies within the boundaries of Texas. This involved geologists and geophysicists primarily, and again required the computer services from Danalyt. It meant much liaison with the Houston office, and some travel to

Washington DC.

On trips to Washington I was always able to arrange to complete my business by Friday afternoon and I then took the opportunity to catch a plane to Ottawa to spend the weekend with Lynn and her two growing sons. This often meant rather wild dinner parties in the better-class Hull restaurants with Lynn and her girlfriends. By this time Lynn had become a single mother, her own choice. Her friends were single mothers, it was the seventies and probably the result of the so-called sexual revolution of the sixties. However they were all remarkably cheerful about it and being a Dad I was accepted by all of them as a sort of confidante. Despite the problems they had with young children and errant husbands I have some very pleasant memories of some very jolly evenings with them.

On one occasion in the summer of 1976 when Jane happened to be in Ottawa for her check-up, I arrived to find Jane's niece Diane, from Edinburgh, Scotland. Here we were, Lynn, Diane, Jane and I, and the two boys, all in a two-bedroom apartment. On the Saturday night we had all wined and dined at a local restaurant, then carried on with the party at home. There was a good deal of reminiscing and catching up to do, and the night dragged on and on. In the morning, despite the sunshine, we all lay abed snoring, except for Master Justin, then about three years old. He was running about in the sitting room, stark naked, with Diane's jewellery and he then decided to take it out on to the balcony to watch it fall nine floors to the garden below. Diane was first up but her screams awoke the entire household.

As each of us appeared Diane repeated her hysterics, and momentarily one gained the impression that it was the greatest of tragedies. One might have thought it was the Crown Jewels emptied over the balcony but to Miss Diane each piece had enormous significance. Thinking it was about seven o'clock on a Sunday morning and that no one would be around Jane decided that I could go down with Justin to recover the stuff. 'There won't be anyone around,' she said. I was in scruffy pyjamas and Justin, all excited, was in his birthday suit. Just as the elevator arrived at our floor Miss Diane arrived to join us, still fuming, and dressed only in a flimsy nightdress. We stepped aboard the elevator and it seemed all of a sudden that the entire community was around, all dressed up and on their way to church.

We had no option but to brazen it out. Justin was jumping up and down with excitement. He had no clothes, I had no shoes and Diane had little of anything. Outside we were getting instructions shouted from the ninth-floor balcony whilst passing cars honked their horns in approval. Fortunately everything had landed on lush green grass and was easily spotted. Justin was hustled indoors and back up in an elevator at top speed. Diane was quite oblivious to the stares. I was never so thankful in my life to get back behind a friendly door. Any time anyone mentions costume jewellery to me now, I cringe.

That same day Diane departed for the west coast. She planned on a six-month stay in North America and she made it. By winter she had arrived at our place in Houston to stay for a couple of weeks, then off to friends in New Orleans and back to Edinburgh. She had been to Vancouver and all the way down the west coast to Mexico before turning east for Texas. She was truly a girl with the wanderlust. By the time I got back to Edinburgh in 1977 she was already in Belgium working for NATO in Brussels.

We had a really amusing time with Diane in Houston. We had hordes of friends many of whom threw parties to celebrate her visit. At cocktail hour, or happy hour as they called it at NASA, we all gathered at 'Jason's', a really smart nightclub, complete with disc jockey and dance floor. They served doubles for the price of singles and getting inebriated in those days was the thing to do. Many of our male friends were estranged husbands, or parents without partners was the term used, and the happy hour tended to dissolve inhibitions rather quickly. By the time we arrived back at someone's house, or out to dinner somewhere, the group might have changed completely.

There was always a solid core with whom we stayed pretty close. Jane had special friends like Dolores, who had been widowed, and on a second time round, divorced, and she was still full of life. Many of the folks in NASA were married for the second or even the third time and most did not have a care in the world, till the budget cuts caught up with them. Earlier, Jane had decided that the town house she had bought on our return from Mississippi was not quite up to standard. She decided we needed a California-style garden-house in Clear Lake City. All that showed on the street was the door of a two-car garage and a high gate leading into a garden. There were verandahs all round one side of the house and the bedrooms each had their own patio. A massive fireplace nearly reached the cathedral ceiling and I had to climb a ladder to water all the tropical plants on top of it.

The sale, the new purchase and the move went off without a hitch. We spent a lot of time and money at Finger's Wonderful Furniture Warehouse, and quite quickly we had a house worthy of a Good Housekeeping award. At this same time, just to complete the picture, Daniel Industries were issuing brand new automobiles to their executives like me. Janice just loved to come home from university at weekends. She had her own suite and revelled in the lap of luxury by comparison with the flat she shared with her girlfriend in Austin. Each time she drove down she brought her two budgies with her and the poor little things were exhausted when they arrived. They had no option but to cling on to their perch like grim death as Janice roared down the highway.

She brought her girlfriend with her on some occasions and on one weekend she had her boyfriend follow her in a truck. It was a very small truck, a Toyota, I think. She had decided that she needed her piano with her in Austin. She organized the loading whilst the boyfriend and I did all the work. I do remember advising that the piano should lie flat in the truck bed because of the small size of the truck. However, they knew best and the upright piano was indeed upright on the truck, but properly lashed down with ropes in really seamanlike fashion at my insistence. As the boyfriend drove off he had to make a sharp left turn at the end of the street, the piano remained upright on the truckbed but the truck heeled over like a sailing ship, and the right hand wheels rose about a foot off the road. He must have had quite a scare but we saw no more of him as he kept on going.

At this time, in the Spring of 1977, NASA was down sizing quite a bit. Many of the engineers there were being laid off. Surprisingly there were many Europeans among them and quite a few British. Most were enterprising characters and started businesses. Some went into insurance, or real estate, and a few just drifted away. Big houses in Nassau Bay and Seabrook stood bare and empty. It was not a happy sight. But in Houston the boom continued. Major oil industries moved their headquarters south out of high-priced New York. The Federal Government were concerned about Arab oil boycotts, underground storage in the salt domes of Louisiana became a big thing and the energy corporations were becoming ever more conscious of the possibility of massive oil spills. GURC and its associate members held meetings, workshops and seminars on the subject and these meetings were held in the Airport Hotel boardroom at the airport in Houston. This meant that it was easier for those from out of town to make such meetings in just one day. The meetings always terminated in happy hours where the discussions and sometimes the celebrations were intense.

We at Danalyt were always in attendance at such functions as by now the system capability was the cornerstone of all the scientific proposals. Bearing in mind the number of medical schools and medical centres within our university group, it was not surprising to find many of the doctors anxious to apply the system to epidemiology. They had no problem identifying the system utility to such problems, but here again it was a question of money and who would provide the necessary funding. We made many presentations to military medical installations interested in epidemiology, genetics and other problems. It was all very encouraging but it was also very difficult to convince Daniel Industries that we were little more than a blot on the computer landscape. Big contracts went to big corporations even if only for the personal security of the agency program managers.

In the summer of 1977 I was delighted to get a break from the constant turmoil. I left for Scotland to attend a major oceanographic conference in Aberdeen whereat anybody who was anybody in the North Sea oil business was in attendance. Daniel Industries had only recently acquired a subsidiary in Falkirk, Scotland to manufacture the flow-meters for the great pipelines being laid in the North Sea. They encouraged a visit to the plant as they could foresee a great future for their business there. I could scarcely imagine a less likely source of inspiration than a visit to a foundry. However, I was pleasantly surprised to find one or two truly bright young businessmen there.

Over a pint or two of real beer we had a happy old gossip about our principals. These men planned on having a hospitality suite at the conference. There was an amusing scene in the pub when a handsome woman of some forty summers appeared. She had to put up with a lot of ribbing as the men claimed that she was the girlfriend of one of the US executives. In addition, she handled the telephone exchange (they still had them in Falkirk) and as a consequence she supposedly knew everything that was going on. She related to me with much good humour stories about the opening of the plant the previous year. A grand Texas barbecue had been organized for outdoors by the American executives who came over for the occasion. The date was 6 June and believe it or not there was a violent snowstorm. It was not an auspicious day for a grand opening.

I spent a few days in Edinburgh with Jane's relatives and after a brief stop at Linlithgow I travelled on to Aberdeen where I met a goodly number of old friends. The oceanographic conference was a howling success and much enjoyed by everyone. At that time things were progressing well in the North Sea and Aberdeen, as a sea port, was rapidly becoming the main base of operations. Within a short space of time it became a little Texas. From there I toured the Silicon Valley of Scotland with an old friend and was amazed at the advances in technology to be found in the industrial parks at Glenrothes, Dunfermline and on through to Glasgow. Every major American corporation was represented there and it was a very prosperous community. I was sorry to leave.

Nevertheless, duty called and I returned to Houston to find myself in the middle of another massive proposal for an ungraded Gulf Environmental Program. Every university scientist was involved and in its preparation there was an army of scientists competing for sections and sub-sections of the investigations. Somewhere at the bottom of all this the Danalyt team was required to participate. With report writing, fulfilment of contractual obligations and on-going development there was very little time left for sharing in these futile proposal exercises and I regret to say relationships were beginning to show evidence of strain.

Towards the end of that year, 1977, it became obvious through second-hand reports that Daniel Industries principals were sorely disappointed with our apparent lack of success. As Executive Vice-President, supposedly responding to a Board of Directors who never met, I was more amused than annoyed by the information. In the original prospectus, and in the business plan, it was made abundantly clear as to where we were going and how we expected to get there. Our success was almost totally dependent upon the success of GURC. I could only conclude that they had never even bothered to read the documents. It was obvious that they did not have the faintest idea of what we were talking about. Considering the fact that they had not contributed one single dollar to our progress, their attitude did seem a little unjust. However it was expedient for us to make a joke out of it rather than to make a scene.

The GURC proposals, wherein we were always a very junior partner, but nevertheless the foundation stone upon which success or failure would depend, were now requesting funding from US Government agencies in scores of millions of dollars. With so much enthusiasm on the part of the senior scientists with national reputations at stake I could not but bow to their superior knowledge and remain convinced of a long-term future. Such success with GURC would have permitted us the luxury of additional senior staff and the funding necessary for procurement of more adequate equipment. The close relationship between Dr Sharp, the President of GURC, and Daniel Industries convinced me that I should keep my distance from their head office.

It was obvious at that time that their main business of supplying flow-meters was highly successful. They had just bought another small company in the pipeline connector business. Daniel Industries were in the process of moving their headquarters away from the outer fringe of the grubby manufacturing plant on the city outskirts to a downtown high-rise in a particularly lush area. They took a whole floor in the building and the entire headquarters, complete with boardroom, executive suites, private offices and reception area was furnished rather incongruously in French provincial. I can clearly remember how entirely out of place everyone looked when I was invited to visit. The private secretary to the President and Chairman of the Board, a delightful matron from somewhere out in the sticks, confided to me her discomfiture. She and I made quite a joke out of it.

The President and Vice-President, who were more or less inseparable, had just returned from an extended trip to the Persian Gulf where they had visited Saudi Arabia, Abu Dhabi and Kuwait. Their public relations jaunt had been a big success apparently and they were kind enough to invite Dr Sharp and me to a dinner party they hosted at the brand new Stoeffers Hotel in Houston. Fortunately Jane elected not to go. The conversation at this elegant dinner was devoted exclusively to the highlight of their visit to the Persian Gulf. For the first time in their lives they had discovered that the Arabs, being Muslims, did not use toilet paper, but instead carried a small vessel full of water with them to the toilet. This incredible bit of information was the source of continuous hilarity during the entire dinner. I was very relieved when the party came to an end.

It must have been obvious to Dr Sharp that the relationship was deteriorating rapidly but even then he was utterly enthused with the potential for success of the consortium. I gained the impression that he felt that he held the key and exercised control over the entire situation, including Daniel Industries. Indeed, I felt confident too that jointly we were about to achieve a considerable triumph and that his Daniel friends would then be happy to bask in the reflected glory. It was a feeling that kept us alive into the spring of 1978. Danalyt was still keeping its head above water but cracks were beginning to appear in the contract relationships.

We were making progress with the scientists at the Aberdeen Proving Ground and it was obvious that they were anxious to procure a system specific to their own purposes. However such an initial sale, creating a precedent in terms of price, became a bone of contention. At this point there were far too many fingers in the pie. At the same time the LORAP program managers became unusually upset at the non-delivery of their contract end-items. Such delivery being dependent upon our receipt of relevant data was again something beyond their understanding. But I do remember particularly the invective used by the program leader in his description of our efforts. He chose to demand that I be removed from management of his particular contract, something that amounted to peanuts. His description of our deficiencies was pitiful in its lack of comprehension of the basic principles embedded in the system.

Initially his complaints were treated with the contempt they deserved, but the record was later resurrected and as is always the case, entirely misconstrued. It was not until the official word came down from Washington that the massive GURC proposal was formally rejected for lack of funds that the future began to look very bleak and the front men began to run for cover. The principal scientists and their contributing proposals began to disappear from view. Most sought solace in their individual paper presentations for publication. Few if any continued their visits to GURC headquarters. Appeals were made to our oil industry friends for financial support, always believing that this was but another brief setback in the search for Shangri-La. The geo-thermal investigations were no longer as popular as they had been and GURC had no alternative but to downsize.

At Danalyt our downsizing took care of itself. The young scientists we had hired were quite happy to take off in their own selected directions as they looked upon their experience with us as a stepping stone in their careers. They were all graduates and there was no difficulty in finding jobs in their chosen professions. The key people remained. There was no need to regroup and we had enough work to keep us going so there was absolutely no panic. In fact we felt some relief that the situation with GURC was now resolved, we were on our own and we felt that we could survive and prosper. The relationship we had generated with the oil companies was in our favour and they had grave need to convince the Environmental Protection Agency that their offshore development did not add to the pollution problem.

We had encouragement from several Government agencies to submit proposals under our own letterhead for their consideration and that kept us so busy we had no thought of failure. We had visits from many hardware and software experts on the pretext of information exchange but as is usual in the industry information is a one-way street. Nevertheless there was much said that convinced us that we were on the right track. But how can one predict what is the right track? In those earlier days when the marketing men predicted a decade of oceanography there was absolutely no doubt that we were on the right track. But by now one wondered if funds would ever be made available for environmental studies. 'Who cares!' had become the attitude all of a sudden.

It was with this in mind that I was compelled to attend a meeting with the Daniel Industries executive. Not just the President and his ever loyal Vice-President but this time with a corporate lawyer and the president of GURC. It was in June, on a Friday, when I was due to join Jane in Ottawa where she was undergoing a very special check-up. I knew the moment I entered the French provincial boardroom that this was the moment of truth. I was invited to sit, but I chose to stand, much to the President's discomfiture. His planned broadside dwindled to a whine about our promise to conquer the world of scientific computing. The smirk on the little lawyer's face was particularly irritating to me.

I let them have it with a diatribe that left no doubt in their minds that from day one the success we predicted was predicated upon the success of the consortium ambitions in the field of environmental problem-solving in the Gulf of Mexico. The fact that they, the consortium, had failed was not in any way attributable to Danalyt. I made it plain that I had never wholly supported the consortium program ambitions in the scores of millions of dollars. I went so far as to suggest that the extent of the funding request was a direct function of the intensity of the happy hours in support of each planning session. I remember smiling faintly at the redness in their faces.

The good President was not prepared for this, he was looking for a whipping boy and had failed to find one. I could see that they were backing off from their original plan of hanging a scapegoat. I could feel my anger rising when I thought of how little any one of them had contributed to the effort, yet they claimed to control the end product. Fortunately I curbed my tongue and stared the President

251

down, eyeball to eyeball. 'We have no option but to make changes,' he said, 'just to preserve our existing contracts.' It was then that the LORAP situation was raised. The program manager there was another member of the club, an old friend of Dr Sharp.

They knew that if I were to walk out the entire house of cards would fall. However, I did agree to step down as Executive Vice-President and to stay on for a further six months as a consultant, thus losing the privilege of their limousine. By now the situation had become amusing to me as I knew that the little lawyer was afraid I might sue, a very common process in Texas. Danalyt was really an unregistered corporation and the dignity of the non-profit consortium, comprised of all the great universities, suddenly loomed large in his mind. They would surely love to avoid that kind of publicity. I was smiling when I walked out. The development team were not in the least upset; they knew I would see them through for the next six months and beyond. From an amusement standpoint, the icing on the cake came when headquarters sent a man to collect the limousine. I handed over the keys with considerable flourish and he drove off. On the Houston ring road, before the car was ever returned to Daniel Industries, it threw a piston and wrecked the engine.

Meanwhile I had made my trip to Ottawa to meet up with Jane. She took the news quite well. She reminded me that I was sixty years old and deserved a rest. We hadn't had a vacation in years. Back in Houston we quietly surveyed our entire position and decided to play it cool. As a consultant I did attend the office each day, and for the sake of Fleming, Appan and Cantilo I really went all out in the proposal route to acquire funding and I spent a good deal of time in Washington checking on the contractual climate. It was not encouraging.

Just about this time I had reason to recall the old Scottish saying, 'It never rains but it pours.' Here we were in the middle of a major family crisis and Miss Janice arrives from Austin to tell us that she is about to become engaged. She was very excited about this romance and she brought Whittington Hanks, a young MBA from the University of Texas to visit us. We had a very pleasant dinner party at Trader Vic's and Whit invited us to Austin to participate in the selection of rings for the occasion. We spent much of one weekend sitting in Tiffany's in Austin admiring some very expensive rings. Finally the choice was made and the date was set. There was the usual hurly-burly of exchange visits with family members and it was not easy for us to be constantly cheerful and full of the joys of spring.

We still had not made a decision on the move we would make on termination which worked out to be scheduled for just about Christmas. To cover Jane's concerns I promptly put the screws on GURC so that I could return to their payroll for two months taking me till March. By this time the relationship between

Danalyt and GURC was deteriorating rapidly. There was rarely anyone in the headquarters office at Clear Lake. They all spent their time at the Houston office riding out the remnants of the geo-thermal contract. Joe Tyson had already departed for greener pastures with the State Department of Texas and moved his home to Austin.

Jane, the mother of the bride-to-be, was persuaded by the Hanks family to permit the wedding to be held at Westminster Presbyterian Church in Austin. This way it made it easier for the extended Hanks family to gather from Texas and Alabama for the ceremony. After a while Jane began to regret her decision because she felt that she was losing control. However she hired a very active wedding consultant and things went off remarkably well considering that most of the instructions were passed by telephone.

Being compelled to think beyond the wedding date about plans for Jane and me, I took a trip to Ottawa to check out the job possibilities. At Danalyt we had no secrets from one another and as a matter of fact Henry Fleming saw me off at the airport bus. I learned later by telephone that immediately after he had waved goodbye to me Henry dropped dead on the pavement. The news saddened me greatly. He and I had been close friends and I had the greatest respect for his work as a scientist. Henry Fleming had been a tower of strength during our worst times. He had already turned sixty-five and he and his wife Mary had planned on retiring to their family home in Nyack, New York.

When I returned from Ottawa I was obliged to attend a GURC board meeting where there was a great deal of dispute about which corporation should pick up the tab for my trip. Considering that many of the attendees were senior faculty members in various universities, it seemed odd that they would gather at great expense to argue like clerks about the cost of an airline ticket. I noticed the little Daniel Industries lawyer sitting next to Dr Sharp. Apparently they were concerned that I might take the opportunity to vent my disgust at their atrocious behaviour towards the Danalyt staff. When the lawyer opened his mouth I silenced him with a cutting remark. I said only enough to let him know that I had learned from another attorney that he, Daniel Industries corporate lawyer, had been named in a Houston court case about a sugarcane swindle, as a non-indicted co-conspirator. I walked out of the meeting without further comment.

As Christmas approached there was the usual round of parties. So many of the people we knew were being laid off from NASA and from their major contractors. We quite quickly became a mutual sympathy society. Dolores, Jane's girlfriend, had recently been dumped from a job but had found a new appointment. She had something to celebrate. Some of the friends were moving out and I remember how unhappy they were about the depressed state of the housing market. It was then that Jane decided that our home would go up for sale immediately after Janice's wedding. One of her other friends, Patty Black, was much more upbeat than any of the others. She swore that the first person to walk in our door would promptly buy the place.

Patty Black and her husband Jack were neighbours of ours and they were a very interesting family. Jack was ex-Air Force and from a wealthy, landed family in Arizona. They appeared to have lots of money and Jack had a beautiful powerboat moored at Seabrook, capable of sleeping eight or ten people for weekend trips. Their family were young, teens and twenties, and truly adventurous. Two of the girls were ballet dancers out of the school in Des Moines, Iowa. An older son took off for Hawaii with a gorgeous new wife to manage a large restaurant there. Jack was busy creating a large restaurant in Clear Lake which he named simply 'Jack Black's'. He must have sunk close to half a million dollars into it. He had great signs erected on the highways and directions from the Houston to Galveston expressway. They were always an exciting group to be with and nothing ever seemed to bother them. The teenage son, Judson, was a real brain.

When the restaurant opened we were invited guests and everyone was amazed at the decor, at the massive fireplace and the distinctly different kitchen. I spent a good deal of time with Jack and his cheerful company went a long way towards keeping me sane in the midst of all our problems. He could identify humour in the most tragic of situations and I was given to understand later on that even when his great restaurant went bankrupt he was as cheerful as ever. He returned to his native Arizona.

Just before Christmas I abandoned the Danalyt office to its fate. By then I knew that Dr Appan had plans of his own, and Luis Cantilo, the computer whiz-kid, had accepted an offer as consultant at the US Army Rocket Centre in Huntsville, Alabama. I had to abandon my elegant Vice-Presidential suite in favour of a more humble abode in the consortium office at Clear Lake. By then there was no one around but a business manager and a secretary. Apart from being bombarded by telephone queries from every member university there was very little to do but organize luncheons with my associates from the various oil companies. On special occasions I attended meetings at the Houston office. At weekends we were busy with Janice in Austin. Actually I had very little to do with the wedding other than to chauffeur Jane around. There were questions of wedding dresses, receptions, accommodation, guest lists and getting Miss Lynn and her two boys down for the wedding.

Somehow everything got organized and the wedding went off without a hitch, but not before several minor crises were overcome. Jane was upset that she was persuaded to stay with Janice's in-laws. As is usual at wedding times the house was crowded with guests and at dressing time I could see that there were not enough bathrooms to go around. I could see that Miss Jane was seething about something and fortunately I managed to persuade her to take off alone with me to a cocktail bar downtown. After a couple of large margaritas she simmered down and we were able to sneak back in without disrupting the entire household. The reception never seemed to end and being father and mother of the bride we were obliged to hang on as co-hosts. Meanwhile Dolores and Lynn, and our other friends from Houston, took off to downtown Austin for a more boisterous celebration. The happy couple left for the Caribbean and I was relieved when we headed back to Houston.

The day we returned Jane put the house up for sale. On the day of the formal open house, advertised for 1.00 p.m. there was a ring at the doorbell at ten minutes to one. A young man in his mid-thirties apologized for being early then stepped inside. He spent only fifteen minutes or so with Jane, arranging to buy all the drapes, the matching bed-covers and several good pieces of furniture. Then his mother, a real estate agent holidaying from up north somewhere, arrived to join him. When our agent walked in they had an offer already prepared. The 'For Sale' sign was removed, the deal was done; we were to clear out by 11 March 1979.

There was an odd twist to the final deal. The sale went through and we happily collected all the money due to us, but the young man requested a couple of days grace to settle his deal with Jane for the furnishings. Mother, the real estate agent, left town to return to her home up north, and the new owner, the son, was left short of money. He persuaded Jane to leave all the stuff, made a great fuss of taking our address in Ottawa and assured us the cheque would be there before we were. The cheque never arrived. Jane wrote once but he didn't bother to respond.

I spent our last few days in Houston making absolutely sure that all of our documentation was in order. We were still registered aliens, still with Canadian citizenship and with a variety of interests in several different United States institutions. To be absolutely sure that there would be no border problems with the Allied Van liner, I went from one bureau to the next acquiring appropriate stamped approval. To be certain that I would not be hassled by the State and Federal tax men, I paid all taxes in full and in advance, and was provided with a formal statement to attest thereto.

We departed quietly one morning in Jane's red Camaro without goodbyes and with absolutely no regrets. We headed out towards Texarcana and on to Shreveport, Louisiana. We passed through Meridian, Mississippi and we thought a lot about Mitzie. In Washington DC we caught up with old friends, exchanged news, then pressed on for Canada. We made a point of re-entering through the Thousand Islands customs and immigration entry. Our Allied Van liner had already been cleared through for Ottawa. It was a beautiful clear night as we crossed the Thousand Islands bridge homeward bound. It was late evening on 15 March 1979. We were truly happy to be back in Canada and we hadn't a care in the world. We swung eastwards from Gananoque and less than thirty minutes later we were in one of the worst and most blinding snowstorms we had ever experienced. There were white-outs and the roads became treacherous. What a welcome home! It was near dawn before we finally made it to Ottawa and we both breathed great sighs of relief.

A couple of years later Elwyn Graham telephoned to tell me that Dr Sharp's wife had been killed in an automobile accident. I wrote a letter of condolence but received no acknowledgement so on one of my occasional visits to Texas I telephoned Dr Alan Lohse. His description of the final debacle of GURC at Houston was quite humorous but it was obvious that it was a situation everyone preferred to forget. The systems development was sold by Daniel Industries to a computer service corporation, with Elwyn Graham as part of the deal. Dr Sharp had quit the consortium and had moved into Daniel Industries as Director of Research, into the splendour of the French provincial head office. The consortium, with its non-profit status intact, prevailed. Such organizations are almost impossible to destroy.

PART VI

CHAPTER XIX

RETURN TO CANADA

Our return to Ottawa in mid-March 1979 was definitely low-key and we stayed with Lynn for a couple of weeks till we found temporary accommodation. It was not that we were anxious to get out from under Lynn's feet, as a matter of fact she made us most welcome and the boys were delighted that we were there. It was simply Jane's anxiety to have her own place again where she could be undisputed boss. Whilst the temporary move did help a bit she simply could not wait to settle and having her furniture stored somewhere on the east side of town seemed to keep her on edge. Being accustomed to such feverish activity, I left the search for permanent quarters entirely in her hands and she made up her mind quite quickly. She wanted a condominium in Ambleside Two and she wanted a view of the river and the Gatineau hills.

After several disappointing visits to available sites she had unexpected help from Colleen Charles. Colleen was aware that a widower on the fourth floor of Ambleside Two was about to remarry and his chosen lady had a large house which she refused to give up. All that was necessary was to convince this man to sell at once without benefit or rather the penalty of real estate agents. The negotiation was left entirely to Miss Jane and I felt sorry for the man who was really in no hurry at all to close a deal. He was persuaded nevertheless and literally hustled out in a very short time, leaving behind some very expensive curtains and other smaller luxuries that she convinced him he wouldn't need in this great new house to which he was moving. Jane wrote him a cheque for 40,000 dollars and the place was ours, a two-bedroom condominium with two balconies, a kitchen with a window (an absolute must) and an unrestricted view of the Ottawa River and the Gatineau Hills.

Once again our Allied Van liner arrived with the furniture and for a change, instead of having to go out and buy more, we had to give a good deal away. Lynn has always been happy to relieve her mother of any excess household goods and they very quickly agreed upon what should be transferred to Lynn's abode. For the first time in a long career of moves in North America it bugged me no end to have to pay for the transfer of our goods and chattels from Houston,

Texas to Ottawa, a bill for well over 5,000 dollars.

On several later occasions when Miss Jane decided to change the rooms or to redecorate, Miss Lynn fell heir to additional pieces. Jane was never entirely settled in one place for the long term, perhaps because of our long history of moves throughout the world. Without doubt, as the years have passed, Lynn has developed a taste for the better antiques and heirlooms, something she despised in her youth. It is a pleasure for me to see now how much she treasures her mother's needlework and some of the old family artwork. These are virtues her old Grannie Miller would endorse.

In view of Jane's regular annual visits to Ottawa throughout our American years, and my own irregular visits, there was no problem at all in the recovery of old friendships. Jane was back in the luncheon circuit in no time at all. Meanwhile I did the rounds of the Ottawa business circuit and thought a good deal about employment prospects. I was sixty-one years old with four more years to fill in before I could entertain the luxury of retirement. Indeed I was fortunate in the renewal of old associations and I received many hearty assurances of interest. Unhappily there were very few call-backs, but I refused to allow myself to get depressed about it and made up my mind that survival was all that was important. I had pensions due at sixty-five so we had very little to worry about.

However, one of Jane's friends, a very successful real estate agent, convinced me that my best bet was to go to Algonquin College and acquire a real estate licence, and thereafter I could practice the art at 'Rhodes' with whom she was associated. Actually the process of acquiring the licence was more fun than effort, the real trouble was that the moment I acquired the licence the bottom fell out of the housing market. The climate at the real estate office was grim and getting grimmer. The training course we had to go through there was designed for housewives but it did have some interesting points. If nothing else, we the newcomers got to know one another and all in all they were a very jolly crew.

The rewards were disappointing. We had heard all kinds of stories about the experts whom I never met who regularly made over a hundred thousand dollars a year. In fact the average was less than thirty thousand and to make that it was necessary to hustle about sixteen hours a day. I was not at all enthusiastic about either the rewards or the environment so I was always willing to accept whatever challenge might come my way. Around September of 1980 something new did crop up and I decided to take the risk. An experienced General Manager was sorely needed to take control of a sonar engineering corporation in Cornwall, Ontario, about sixty miles away. As it turned out what they really needed was a miracle but unfortunately no such miracle materialized.

However, the few months I spent there were both interesting and exciting.

Without doubt there was loads of talent and unique ideas around but as I had learned to my dismay in Texas, without adequate venture capital the chances of success are indeed remote. There was no way investors could be found, but the owners' natural instinct was to tighten belts and carry on and under these conditions a corporation dies a slow agonizing death. I had no choice but prepare them for the worst. Fate took a hand of course and I found myself dealing with an Austin, Texas-based sonar-development group with researchers at the University of Texas. Even this turned out to be another fruitless exercise in frustration.

At this same time the good principals at Daniel Industries had finally located me and I was able to clear up some neglected business affairs with them. They had finally sold Danalyt Corporation in Houston, Texas for three dollars a share. Oddly enough the total number of corporate shares issued was never divulged, yet as a director of their corporation they had no option but acquire my agreement and to solicit my letter of resignation from the Board. I could smile when I thought of the poor comptroller trying to keep the record straight and avoid any serious scrutiny from the tax man. Happily our exchange of correspondence and the formal parting of the 'brass rags' was limited to the Cornwall company fax machine and special delivery mail.

Meanwhile family life had become very important to us and Jane was happy to be seeing more of Lynn and her boys. By now she had become a fairly senior person in the Bank of Nova Scotia and she still had ambitions towards a more responsible position. On our return in 1979 she was a single mother (by her own choice), with one rather strong-willed son of fifteen years, and another still dependent at only six. Life was never the bed of roses for Miss Lynn that I had dreamed of and planned for her when she was small. But she had a peculiar knack for making the best of situations and always managed to retain an attitude of indestructible self-confidence which has served her well. For some reason, possibly her early schooling in Edinburgh, she projects an air of self-assurance and superiority.

David, Lynn's older son, was big and muscular and like most boys of his era went through some difficult years. To his credit, however, he never lost his love and respect for his mother and perhaps as a consequence, he settled down again and acquired a very necessary higher education. Justin, about nine years his junior, benefited to some degree from having an older brother. His instinct for rebellion in his late teens was much less in evidence, but in some ways this detracted from the normal adolescent drive to forge ahead. It was customary for years for the family to visit every Friday night for a special dinner and Justin to his great delight was allowed to stay. He and his Nana and I had loads of entertainment playing dominoes, scrabble or card games, and all kinds of stuff.

The other half of our family, Miss Janice, reported in by telephone at least once per week. She and her husband spent some very busy early years and like Jane and I seemed to be constantly on the move: Austin, Texas to Washington DC, to New York City, back to Austin, then off to Europe. I began to think that they too had the wanderlust. We looked forward so much to their phone calls and occasional visits, and at those times when Jane and I might be alone and counting the years, we could become very sad thinking about how we were separated from Lynn for so many years and now separated from Janice in exactly the same way. These are the sad problems likely to fall to the lot of the travelling man.

Janice and Whit had had a Caribbean honeymoon after their wedding and immediately thereafter Whit decided to discharge what he considered to be an obligation to a good Democratic Government. Being a subscriber to the National Democratic Party and a University of Texas graduate MBA with a passionate desire to run his own business, he felt compelled to serve his Government in Washington for the first year of his business life. Whether the Government felt the same level of enthusiasm for this generous contribution of his time is debatable. However he and Janice promptly moved to Washington DC and took up residence in the beautiful Watergate complex that had become famous as a result of Mr Nixon's brigands.

Jane and I visited this Washington abode for a long weekend now and again and besides catching up with old friends I was obliged to visit the 'Hill' with Master Whit. He had managed to get himself appointed as an aide to Senator Bentsen and then had a very difficult time elbowing his way into the general office space allocated to the Bentsen aides. Indeed there were many of them, all equally zealous and determined to serve whether they were needed or not. Eventually Whit managed to stake an undeniable claim to a converted clothes closet and from here he performed yeoman service for the Senator. I was fortunate enough to meet Senator Bentsen on several occasions and I must confess I have nothing but admiration for the way he sustained the undying loyalty and admiration of his very large staff. He had some gift for making each one of them believe that their feverish research on his behalf helped guide the Senate towards ever higher goals.

Meanwhile Miss Janice, not to be outdone, talked her way into the office of the Congressman from Texas, the well-loved Jake Pickle. In very short order she had managed to change the entire office philosophy and thereafter she became buddies with the IBM boys who brought the congressional offices into the computer age. She set up the first computerized filing system and headed the Capitol Hill 'Word-Processor User's Group' to improve communication between IBM and the ninety congressional offices. She just loved what she was doing and had nothing but admiration for the Congressman. Mr Pickle was surely the story-book Texan, a country gentleman at heart but one of the shrewdest politicians of his day. He became Chairman of the Banking Committee and as a consequence a real power on Capitol Hill.

Whilst the combined talents of Master Whit and Miss Janice may not have made an indelible mark upon the United States Government, their presence on the Hill did not pass unnoticed. It seems that Whit's maiden Aunt Mildred, a relative we had met several times in Austin, had been something of a genius in the real estate investment business. She died and left her considerable fortune to Whit, through his father Roger Hanks as executor. Included in the legacy there was a gorgeous Cadillac, chauffeur-driven, with scarcely a scratch on it and a very beautiful house in Austin. Whilst Whit was not at all excited about the house he was delighted with the Cadillac. Acquiring an official parking spot on the Hill for a Cadillac, and having a Watergate address, assured the young couple all of the privileges that go with obvious wealth in the United States. Janice loved the entire exercise.

But all good things come to an end. On completion of their year of commitment to the political arena they were ready to move. Fate took a hand and showed them the way. Whit's near ninety-year-old grandfather, who had divorced Whit's grandmother in the days when such a thing was unheard of, had later married a wealthy New York matron. He had been a widower for some time, with Whit as his only grandson. He died suddenly at his New York home, a large condominium at 19, East 72nd Street, and this he willed to Whit along with a life membership in the prestigious Union Club on 69th Street at Park Avenue. Under the terms of the will, Whit was obliged to occupy the condominium for at least one year.

At almost precisely the same time Whit was offered a golden opportunity with the Morgan Guaranty Trust. They were planning a program of special training on Wall Street in the fine art of financial management, and this to include young, promising members of the international banking community. He and Janice moved into the fully-furnished condo on 72nd Street just a few steps from 5th Avenue and Central Park, with Madison Avenue on the east side. To Miss Janice this was dreamland. She had five bathrooms in this residence, her own private elevator lobby and to add a little icing on the cake, the penthouse was occupied by the beautiful widow, Lady Oona Chapman and family.

With the training program in full swing they very quickly assembled a group of friends and life was a ball. With an admiring husband occasionally escorting her to Tiffany's, and an international set to entertain, our Miss Janice still found time to consider her own career. Quite promptly she was accepted as an account coordinator with Manning, Selvage and Lee on the 'I Love New York' campaign. She handled press relations to promote tourism on behalf of the State of New

York, wrote press releases and coordinated national news coverage. On occasions she led press trips throughout the State of New York. Jane and I made several trips to New York by car and we were most impressed. We enjoyed her friends immensely.

Christmas 1980 was a memorable one for us. The condominium was decorated to the ultimate, complete with a massive Christmas tree, and there were lots of visitors. Whit's folks came up from Texas to stay at the Union Club and we all went out to a church service at midnight on Christmas Eve. For the first time we met Sandy and Carol Dochin, also from Texas, old friends of Whit's from the Democratic Party days. Then there was Beat and Claudine, who had come from Switzerland to attend the Morgan training course. We saw more of them as the years went by.

In the spring of 1981 the training course was over, the international team of trainees dispersed and Master Whit was at another crossroads in his life. He was offered the beginnings of a very promising career with Morgan Guaranty Trust. Unfortunately he was to report to a female Vice-President, something not entirely to his liking, and in any case he still nursed a burning desire to run his own business. Janice was still on cloud nine and she left him to make his own decisions. She did call us nevertheless to let us know that the condominium was on the market at 9.00 a.m., and by 11.00 a.m. it was sold for $575,000.00. The die was cast and they returned to Austin, Texas. We were saddened at the thought as we had enjoyed New York so much. We were reassured, however, that we could stay at the Union Club any time we chose to do so.

Meanwhile, back in Ottawa, we lived a rather quiet life. After I wrapped up the work in Cornwall I had no trouble at all in returning to real estate. The market was still in the doldrums so I elected to sell new construction as this required very little effort. At the same time I kept myself busy and interested in the emerging technologies as a member of Associates Consulting Services. Jane had her friends and she had Lynn, and on Fridays we had Master Justin to keep us entertained. Whilst this was a major change from the rat race I had experienced south of the border it was relaxing even so. My sister Jean and her daughter Isabol came over from Scotland for a visit, a visit that was all too short. They left us with a keen desire to return to our 'ain folk'.

Janice and Whit had scarcely settled in Austin, in a neat little house on Laurel Lane, when Whit launched himself into the business of architectural antiques. Within weeks he had established his headquarters on Colorado Street in downtown Austin and with a series of buying sprees in New York he had a basic floor display. He just could not contain his enthusiasm for the business and by early summer he had assembled contacts and plans for an extensive buying trip to Europe. Janice's fluency in Spanish and French and her obvious capability in negotiation subscribed much to his confidence in a successful business venture. By mid-summer they were off to Paris where the contact turned out to be a vigorous French lady in her early eighties who had earned her stripes in the Resistance movement. Janice's tales of their hair-raising adventures whilst being driven around by this old lady in her tiny old car in the midst of the Paris traffic are truly hilarious. Apparently they drove together in the broken-down mini all the way to Belgium.

To complete the architectural antiques circuit in Europe they had included some independent trips to Spain and Portugal without benefit of contacts or guides. Whilst there they by-passed the tourist traps and spent some very pleasant days amongst the real mountainous countryside. Whit had purchased a brand new, top-of-the-line Peugeot to take home with him so they travelled in comparative luxury. All went extremely well till Miss Janice developed a very sore stomach problem and this aroused grave concern in view of the fact that she was then four months pregnant. Wisely they headed north for the English Channel ferries and on to Edinburgh, Scotland. The specialists in Edinburgh Royal Infirmary quickly identified the tropical parasite that had adopted her and in a very short time she was as energetic as ever.

By correspondence and telephone at the beginning of the European adventure Jane had arranged for them to occupy an apartment in Edinburgh, on Hanover Street, just off Princes Street, and with an unrestricted view of Edinburgh Castle. The apartment was attached to Jane's nephew's dental surgery and was on the fourth floor of a solid stone building. In Edinburgh such buildings do not have elevators and everyone dances up and down the stairs without the slightest hesitation. Janice felt that it was ideal exercise especially in her condition. It had been agreed that we, Jane and I, would join them for the month of August.

We arrived in Edinburgh in August 1981 and were mightily relieved to find Janice so undeniably healthy and full of vigour. Jane's niece Christine and her husband the dentist welcomed us to the holiday abode and we all had a very exciting time. The entire line of relatives on both sides of the family arrived on different occasions to pay their respects to the happy couple. Janice was in her element. She spent hours shopping on Princes Street, particularly at the very famous Jaegar shop, and on George street at the only butcher shop in the world with beautiful antique chandeliers hanging from the ceiling and the windows packed tight with haggis, steak pies and pheasant under glass. Whit was more interested in his Peugeot and the fact that the closest parking was about a mile away, and downhill, did not upset him in the slightest. He enjoyed climbing up the hill; kept him in shape, he claimed.

He and I went on several expeditions throughout the countryside, the primary objective always being antiques, but on many occasions we stopped at sheepdog trials, Highland Games and unique places of historical interest. He bought massive fireplaces, mahogany-panelled rooms and great oak doors, and arranged for their shipment by container directly to Houston, Texas. Without doubt he was developing real business acumen and had quite quickly developed the knack of pretending to walk away from a deal. However, I still felt that he was a bit naive and from personal experience in the Peugeot I could tell that he was not the best driver in the world. The car was rigged for the North American market so the steering wheel was on the wrong side for Scotland. With major roads with speed limits and intersections in the form of so-called roundabouts, there was an obvious need for discretion, something Whit lacked. He charged through the roundabouts without concern for the traffic speeding alongside him, then made some last minute lunge for his chosen exit amidst screaming tyres and honking horns. Without doubt, he bore a charmed life.

Indeed, he was undeniably naive. There was one interesting incident during our stay in Edinburgh which confirmed this view. He took off for the city of Glasgow on his own to track down some contact there who had been recommended by a man in the demolition business. Janice, her mother and I were delighted to be rid of him for a while as this gave us the opportunity to pursue our own interests. We took off for Linlithgow and had a grand old time with my sister and her friends at a pub lunch. By the time we got back to Edinburgh it was already late and the fact that Whit had not returned did not bother us in the least. We had a late supper while we watched the lights come on to floodlight the ancient castle atop its awesome, black rock, and with the lights in Princes Street gardens below it looked like something out of fairyland.

It was after 11.00 p.m. before Janice showed any sign of anxiety and close to midnight before the telephone finally rang. There was a brief, terse message from the Glasgow constabulary to say that Master Whit was in jail but about to be released on his own recognisance. Janice's face was a real study in emotions, first in anxiety, then amazement, and then suddenly brightened into a big smile. When she got off the telephone I thought she was about to have hysterics, but no, it was just that she thought that the situation was absolutely priceless and even hinted that a couple of nights in jail might do him good. We all went off to bed, relieved but more amused than saddened by Whit's misfortune. I looked forward to the story he would have to tell in the morning.

He showed up the following morning, a bit dishevelled and sorely in need of a shower. He was covered in some sort of powdery dust that looked like cement. We had to wait while he consumed a hearty Scottish breakfast before he related his experiences. It appears that the contact recommended was also a demolition man and claimed to be presently engaged in demolishing an elegant but ancient insurance building somewhere in the very heart of the City of Glasgow. Whit was invited to take an advance peek at some prize objects d'art in the process of removal prior to the arrival of the wreckers' ball. The prize piece, readily available he was assured, was an entire 'Boardroom' in elegant oak panelling, so thick that Whit drooled at the very thought of it.

In view of Whit's arrival from foreign parts, the demolition man advised that if he really wanted a good deal it would have to be cash on the barrel head and the job completed that very day. In addition, he just happened to have at hand six or seven of the best demolition men in the business, ready and able to whip the stuff off the walls and into a truck in short order. Whit, in his excitement at the thought of this lucrative deal, failed to notice that there wasn't another soul around in the entire neighbourhood. The demolition men were most obliging and cracked funny jokes about Texas. One of the seven was a fat, jolly fellow who gave the impression of being the boss. He did little else but smoke cigarettes and advise his cohorts to get the lead out. In retrospect Whit did realize later that the little fat guy was really the lookout but even as a lookout he failed miserably.

There was a sudden flurry of activity, a couple of blasts on a police whistle and the demolition men were off through the rear entrance and heading for the fence. Unhappily, a gap in the fence allowed the six to escape but the little, fat fellow just could not squeeze through. It was, as the policeman said as he climbed back on his bike, a fair cop. Whit had made no effort at all to escape and being arrested as a criminal stood him in good stead later on. The police sergeant at the station grew sympathetic after a while and Whit was finally able to convince him of his Texas roots. No doubt the credit cards made an excellent impression but also his demeanour, so obviously that of another foreigner taken for a ride, affected the outcome. However, to his everlasting credit, he had the guts to return the next day and to successfully negotiate the purchase of the boardroom through legitimate channels. It was later shipped to Austin and now adorns the walls in a beautiful home located there.

We said farewell regretfully to the wonderful Edinburgh Music Festival, and to Scotland, and we received a rousing send-off from the entire family. Janice and Whit were bound for Texas and we returned to Ottawa to a quieter life. But the quiet life did not prevail for long. Janice's first-born had arrived in early November and now back in the house on Laurel Lane she felt that she needed her mother. I put Jane on a plane in Montreal for Chicago and after a hair-raising plane change at O'Hare she was met in Austin by the proud father. As usual she took charge and quickly established a regimen whereby mother and son both progressed. Fortunately she had the good sense to depart after three weeks and left the young mother to cope by herself. The son and heir, a beautiful fair-haired boy, was duly christened Ian Hancock Edinburgh Hanks and I was intensely proud to have a grandson bearing my name.

I can remember Jane complaining about the house on Laurel Lane, most inadequate for babies, she claimed. Then, to her complete surprise, Janice mailed a newspaper clipping from the Austin daily paper. Whit's happy, bearded face graced the front page with the comment beneath stating that 'Whit Hanks saved the Mansion at 3215 Duval Street by entering a purchase agreement the previous day'. This was the end of January 1982. They had no sooner bought the house than Hospice Austin representatives approached them about using it for a designer showhouse. This meant that Austin interior designers would completely redecorate the house and show it off to the public for a few weeks as a fund-raiser for Hospice Austin. The timing was bad, Whit wanted to redecorate and move in as soon as possible. However Hospice Austin again offered complete redecoration by top designers for free some three years later. Janice and family were obliged to move out for three months to permit the process to proceed.

Jane and I had many pleasant vacations at 3215 Duval. It was indeed a mansion, with its grand ionic columns, standing in more than an acre of garden with many beautiful old trees. Over the separate garage there was a comfortable apartment and during our earliest visits there it was occupied by an enormous young man named Jeff Buffington, a university student from a very prominent New England family. Upon leaving Austin, he took off for the interior of China and that was the last we heard of him. He was a fascinating young man, athletic and handsome, and he worked in Whit's antiques showroom in his spare time. In the refurbishment of the massive three-storey house, complete with elevator, Whit had installed the very latest in burglar alarms and these were directly connected to the local police.

The bedroom suites were all on the second floor whilst the kitchen and the fridge were on the ground floor. In the early hours of the morning Miss Jane had occasion to rise, desperately in need of a cold drink. All that was necessary she thought was a quiet descent of the stairs and a few steps to the kitchen. No sooner had she placed her foot on the first step down than in a split second every light in the house came on, floodlights bathed the entire garden in brilliant colours and several sirens under the eaves commenced their appalling wail. By the time she reached the ground floor Jeff Buffington was running around in the garden in his jockey shorts and the throaty growl of the police cars could be heard in the distance. The entire family, bleary-eyed, stood gazing down from the second-floor balcony. I remember hoping that if there were robbers around they might refrain from pumping bullets in poor old Jeff's direction.

The policemen stepped out of their automobiles with drawn guns. We were all lectured on the need for care and attention to avoid false alarms. Jane was absolutely devastated, Janice was close to hysterics and Jeff Buffington was advised by the cops to stay in bed next time. Whit was delighted to find out that

268

his system really worked. Thereafter, when it came time to retire, no one moved and it was just like being in prison. Meanwhile the structure was designated an Austin historical landmark and the next year, 1983, the Hanks received an Austin Heritage Society award for their restoration efforts.

In August of that same year, 1983, Janice was blessed with a second son, another blond. He was christened Roger Cameron Linlithgow Hanks, Linlithgow being the ancient Scottish town where the Millers farmed for hundreds of years. By now, particularly with two young children, she needed a housekeeper in addition to the daily help, an attractive budding actress who arrived for work on a noisy motorcycle. Rosa joined the happy family as housekeeper, occupied the apartment over the garage and she has been inseparable from the family ever since. As time went by the boys glowed with good health and they had a wonderfully happy time playing with their friends in the garden. Hoses, rubber slides, swings, see-saws, bicycles, tricycles, they had everything a child could wish for.

Janice believed in friendships and she was the kind of girl who made friends easily and kept them forever. There were several young mothers from her university days and with the addition of children to strengthen the bonds of friendship amongst them it seemed to us that they were almost inseparable. There was Carol Nieman, Patsy Martin, Mary-Jane Dougherty, Marylyn and so on, and each of them were blessed with happy children. They even had arrangements amongst themselves so that in the event of any real disaster, one among them would assume responsibility for the other children.

Jane and I always arrived back in Ottawa exhausted after three weeks at the mansion. There was always a long list of stuff ready for me to do, things that only her daddy could do. Some of the fun things were teaching the boys to ride grown-up bikes, showing Janice how to plan a vegetable garden or being the chief cook for a roast beef dinner for a dozen or so. There was no such thing as idleness in the Hanks household. In the winter months the boys had to be entertained indoors, with tepees and tricycles in the hallways and all kinds of games out on the verandahs. One particular little friend they had was Victoria, Torrie for short, and she was a little doll, about Ian's age, the only daughter of another of Janice's friends, Robin, and thereby hangs a tale.

There was a time too when Janice and Whit and the boys visited us here in Ottawa. Unhappily they made the mistake of choosing the wintertime when the snow and the ice frightened the life out of the youngsters.

CHAPTER XX

RETIREMENT

By 1983 I had formally retired and made up my mind never to work again. This freedom provided me with the opportunity to pursue my favourite hobby, walking. Most weeks I walked fifty miles or more and thoroughly enjoyed it. I missed having a dog as the condominium rules do not permit pets. However, on nice bright days I would take off along the river parkway and walk the eight miles to downtown, eat a hearty lunch in Byward Market, then walk home again. Even in the harsh winter I could don the appropriate parka and trudge through the snow with a heavy, black hawthorn walking-stick I had bought in Achnasheen, a little town in the far north of Scotland. Retirement permitted us the liberty to visit Texas twice a year, in the spring and in the autumn, and when we were flush we took a trip to Scotland to sustain old family relationships.

With nothing but time on our hands and only two daughters and their offspring to worry about there was very little else for us to do but to concern ourselves with their affairs. At the end of 1984 we were alerted again about more exciting events in Austin. Hospice Austin had again offered to have the top interior designers redecorate their home for free, so they agreed. The day after Christmas Janice and family moved out and construction workers, designers, painters and carpenters moved in. It was agreed that all design proposals would be approved or vetoed by a committee that included Janice and Whit. Sixteen rooms, including porches and sun rooms, were radically changed, although the designers used as much of the Hanks furniture as possible as well as using antique pieces from the store.

The 'Designer Show House '85' at 3215 Duval was formally opened to the public from 27 April to 12 May 1985. The Austin Hospice Program is a non-profit corporation whose mission is to provide support and care for the terminally ill. Funding comes from generous people, foundations, corporations, and from the supporters of the designer showcase which contributes the majority of Hospice Austin's operating revenue. To complement the redecorated interior an antique rose garden, complete with sundial, was established and this could be admired from the screened porch, the sunroom and the balcony above. One very unique display in the upstairs hall was a three-dimensionally framed christening gown, well over a hundred years old, brought from Scotland for the christening of Janice's children. This pleased Jane very much as she had been christened in the same gown in a little church in Coldingham, Scotland.

For the four month period of redecoration Janice and family lived in the Hanks condominium in Woodstone Square, an exclusive condo development. The elder Hanks stayed out at the farm at Dripping Spring tending their pure-bred longhorns. Shortly before making the agreement with Hospice, Whit had planned to sell the house to find a home more suited to the needs of a young family. However by the time the house was ready for its grand opening to the public he had changed his plans and intended to stay. Thanks to the creativity of the decorators involved, the old 'Barker House' had become a truly beautiful, modernized mansion. It was claimed to be the most successful show house ever in terms of attendance and money raised. By the time we returned to Austin it was the autumn of 1985, the weather was glorious, the garden was at its best and the house was a home again.

On one occasion when Jane and I were there, we had a visit from Beat and Claudine from Switzerland. It was such a thrill to see them again after the enjoyable times we had had in New York. But there was a sad aspect to this visit too. Claudine was very early in her first pregnancy and had been advised by her doctors to seek rest and relaxation. Beat, a real athlete, was anxious to go off skiing so Claudine elected to stay in Austin while he went off to the mountains in Canada. Unfortunately she felt sick one night, and with Whit gone and the boys to look after, Jane and Janice had to stay so I escorted her to St David's Hospital. It was very difficult for us to communicate with the black nurse at the desk. With Claudine's French accent, my Scottish brogue and both of us aliens it was not easy to gain admittance. Finally Claudine was tucked into a hospital bed and the same nurse, who had mistaken me for the father, woke me up from a sound sleep in a waiting-room chair to tell me that Claudine had lost her baby.

I felt utterly sad and could not think of anything to say that might comfort her. She was so far from home and family. Nevertheless Claudine fully recovered and later in life had two healthy children. However her sad, wan smile when I last saw her in her hospital bed haunted me for days.

Meanwhile Janice had procured an old-fashioned rocking horse for Master Ian and this was kept on the upstairs balcony, a spacious, screened room full of over-stuffed toys. All of us had the most hilarious time watching him on this enormous old rocking horse. It was so slung with springs he could make it gallop and heave and roll like a real live horse. He could yell and holler like a cowboy and seemed to enjoy being the centre of attention. The burglar alarm was now adjusted such that our freedom of movement was no longer impaired and Jane learned the codes to punch into the control dials. We felt as if we were living in the lap of luxury and amidst lots of fun. Janice's young friends, all with young children, were always dropping by and they treated us like regular members of the group.

Very shortly after Whit had the urge to expand his business. Everything he bought in France, England and Spain was snapped up very quickly in view of the building boom throughout Texas. It seemed that everyone wanted a Whit Hanks door. There were doors in oak, in mahogany, panelled doors, doors with stained glass, doors with bevelled glass and doors that were decorative. Congressman Pickle went so far as to predict that there would be an even bigger housing boom because of Whit Hanks's antique store. 'All the women are seeing these doors and are going to buy houses to go around them,' he said at a Hanks Architectural Antiques grand opening party.

Whit organized successful auctions at those times when his warehouse was bursting with inventory, including doors, entry-ways, fireplaces; bevelled, etched, and stained glass; iron work, panelling, and flooring. There were entire panelled rooms, wrought-iron gates, railings, spiral staircases, copper lanterns, antique bars and numerous other massive pieces. In addition he carried carved mantels, gilded entry-ways, leaded-glass windows, and finely-painted glass panels. He had Lloyds of London Building Entry, a pressed steel balustrade from the London Insurance Company, a carved grey marble console, and a magnificent stained-glass sectional wall. He expanded in a very ambitious way.

Through real estate wheeling and dealing in the exchange of Trust property, with the help of his father, he opened a massive building on 6th Street, not far from the Governor's mansion, and thereafter the business was known as Whit Hanks at Treaty Oak. At the rear of the building an ancient oak tree bore mute testimony to the signing of a treaty in the previous century. In the years that followed, the building became a sort of artisan's mall with close to forty tenants involved in every aspect of the antique business from objects d'art to the cast-iron ornaments demanded by new architects in the creation of the modern monstrosities they call family homes. The second floor of the building housed interior decorators, architects and management staff. On many occasions this extensive antique centre hosted great parties and dances for charitable causes. As many as six hundred guests could be entertained in this treasure-filled palace, a masterful stroke of intelligent marketing.

Despite the young sons and the large home Miss Janice immersed herself in volunteer work, occupying publicity chairs in the school PTA and West Austin Youth Association. She served as chairperson of committees within the Junior League of Austin, and at times as a project consultant. In one publicity chair, 'A Christmas Affair', she coordinated advertising and publicity for an event that grossed over half a million dollars. She arranged interviews on local broadcast media and made many personal presentations to a wide variety of community-based organizations. She obtained first time coverage on the 'Home Show', a nationally distributed NBC production, and front page coverage in the Lifestyle Section of the Austin *American Statesman*. In addition she handled marketing and tenant relations for Whit Hanks at Treaty Oak, travelling frequently to markets in the United States and Europe to purchase products.

In addition to all of these activities they managed to produce a third child, our only granddaughter, born in February 1987. The beautiful christening gown was removed from its grand display once again. She was christened Louise Foster Coldingham Hanks, the Foster after her grandma Jane Foster Malcolm Miller, and Coldingham, her grandma Jane's birthplace.

Miss Louise quickly developed similar characteristics to her mother and her grandmother. She is indeed a 'Pistol', as they say in Texas, but she is the joy of our lives. Jane and I suffered through many crises with the boys and with the new baby. I walked up and down in the corridors of a hospital with Ian wriggling in my arms, screaming like a banshee, just waking up after a minor operation. I tended Roger like a dedicated nurse as he recovered from his circumcision. He too was born with lungs like blacksmith's bellows. Miss Louise is different. She manages to involve the entire community in the event of the slightest mishap. Everyone runs when Miss Louise lets go with a wail.

With a big business, a big house and a big family, Master Whit began to tire of 3215 Duval and decided that they needed a more suitable family home in the lush neighbourhood of Tarrytown, on the fringe of the city, with ease of access and escape in all directions. Duval was difficult to sell but finally a Doctor James Eggars, a very good friend, decided to marry and he felt that his young bride deserved such a mansion. Janice was delighted to move into 3308 Bowman at the end of 1987, with Louise only about eight months old and the boys about school age. The schools were better, the country club to which they belonged was closer and while the house was something of a disaster it was a very good deal according to Whit. However, within a few months they were reasonably well settled and we went down to Texas to visit. Whit's parents very kindly decided that Jane and I should occupy the condominium at Woodstone, only a few blocks away, so that we could get quiet nights away from the children. This arrangement worked exceedingly well and the elder Hanks stayed out at their farm at Dripping Springs.

We all felt better with the young Hanks family established in their new home. Ian just loved his new school and Roger could hardly wait to join him. Rosa had moved with the family and she surely lightened the burden on Janice who was already anxious to get back into career harness. Meanwhile Jane and I made trips to Scotland to be with her brother and his family, and my sister and her really grown-up family. We were able to enjoy the glorious Music Festival, we attended weddings and funerals, and visited Jane's elderly aunts and uncles down in the border country. Christine and Jim, the owners of the Edinburgh apartment we occupied, Janice's cousins, came to Texas to visit her.

Back in Ottawa we were enjoying visits from Lynn's number one son, David, by now twenty-six, six feet two, out of college and into the computer business. He had finally found for himself the love of his life, a pretty blond Dutch girl, Diane. He knew that we had never been particularly happy with any of the lady friends he had paraded before us, but he was obviously convinced that this time he had a real winner. His Nana approved and she was absolutely delighted to discover that she and he were now regular churchgoers. Indeed we were very proud to attend his confirmation. On the other hand, Justin at seventeen, still at high school, had reached the stage when adolescents know everything and adults are old fogies.

Miss Lynn, well-established at the Bank of Nova Scotia, together with Michel, her francophone partner of some ten years, became regular visitors too. Michel, one of Jane's favourite men, with Lynn and the two boys just loved to come by for lengthy happy hours followed by generous roast beef dinners. Jane was never happier than when she watched Michel and the boys polish off second helpings of everything. It was remarkable too how quickly they all took off for greener pastures after the dinner was gone. Life floated by with hardly a ripple upon the waters. I had the feeling that now, in my retirement, and at seventy-three years old, the storms in my life had all come and gone. From here on it would be smooth sailing, with trips to Texas, trips to Scotland, with nothing to worry about except the thought of growing old.

And there was icing on the cake. Early in 1991 Lynn decided that she and Janice would lay on a fiftieth wedding anniversary party. David had become engaged to Diane and they had made plans for a big wedding on the day following our fiftieth which fell on 14 June 1991. There was boundless excitement. Plans were laid, invitations were prepared for both the anniversary and the wedding. Gowns for the ladies, suits for the men so we went off on a buying spree. I have never seen our whole family so happy and constantly smiling.

As the month of June drew nearer the activity grew feverish, visiting Diane's family, buying wedding presents, organizing, planning, writing speeches, there was scarcely a moment to relax. There was but one minor sour note in the entire arrangement. Janice advised us by telephone that she would come to Ottawa alone. Master Whit would stay behind with the children. It was but a momentary disappointment.

The anniversary day, a Friday, dawned with nothing but blue skies and sunshine and these conditions promised to continue. Janice had arrived the previous day, happy and carefree, and kept us laughing with her stories about the children. Jane and I were ecstatic, we would all be together for the big day and we expected fifty guests, many of whom had been present at our twenty-fifth anniversary in 1966 when we lived at Adirondack Drive. The celebration was arranged in the condominium party room and the bar was stocked with the very best from Scotland. All of our old friends showed up and all in remarkably good health. Ernie Weeks was in good voice as well as good health; he kept the entire audience in fits of laughter with stories about our fifty years of married life. Lynn, the elder daughter, proposed the appropriate toasts and I was obliged to make a speech that included a word or two about everyone. A few warm words about the wedding on the following day and a few comments about my Texas grandchildren were well received.

Frank Miller and his wife Ruth, not relatives but very good friends, provided an excellent video of the entire affair. It was very cleverly edited so that it opened with shots of the anniversary cards, then a panorama of the bar, the decor and the entire group of guests. Frank had taken great care to ensure that he had excellent shots of the happy anniversary couple, the wedding couple and the two elegant daughters. Lynn was absolutely glowing in her Glen Urquhart finery and Miss Janice, demure as always, was in the latest of fashion. It concluded with a few shots that clearly indicated that time marches on for all of us. Attention was paid to the happy couple David and Diane preparing for their wedding the following day. All their young friends were in attendance, and as a consequence this provided a neat balance to the celebration. Jane and I felt that it was more a celebration of life than the customary dreary anniversary. After all, fifty years is something of a burden to bear in itself. To have this young vibrant couple about to launch themselves upon a similar voyage the next day lent an air of real celebration and a feeling of optimism that theirs might be smooth sailing.

The wedding day was a day to remember. The ceremony in the Calvin Christian Reformed Church was most impressive. The lighting of candles was a symbolic demonstration of the passing of the torch through the generations, very simple but tremendously expressive. Their vows were profound and binding and they both looked gloriously happy. The bride was beautiful and David, scarcely recognizable to me, cut a real figure in his wedding finery. They had organized a big bash at the Cedarhill Golf and Country Club and it turned out to be a worthy celebration. There were drinks, and dinners, and speeches followed by speeches in the early evening, then later hordes of their young friends joined in for a general free-for-all with dancing and drinks and a farewell supper party.

Jane and I met so many of Diane's family members that it was impossible to remember them all. David's father, Lynn's ex, joined in the entire ceremony and he too had a speech to make. We had the opportunity to meet so many of Lynn's friends, David's friends and old friends, and we even found time to renew our acquaintance with Lynn's ex and his new family. Janice thoroughly enjoyed the whole affair and during the course of the evening mixed with every group of guests. Each time I looked around to find her she was doing the rounds somewhere. So many of the folks there could not believe that she was the mother of three children. Seeing Lynn and Janice together it is difficult to believe that they are sisters. Lynn is a Miller from Scotland, and Janice a Malcolm from Texas.

With the young couple off on a honeymoon to Caesar's Pocono Palace in the mountains of Pennsylvania, and Janice on her way home to Texas, we were left with time to think. So many celebrations had been a bit exhausting for all of us and a long rest was recommended. However, with the summer drawing to a close and the glorious cool weather of the fall almost upon us we were quickly rejuvenated. We were making plans for Texas again when Janice called to advise of another celebration. This time it was Robin's wedding and little Torrie insisted we be there. We were delighted to go and looked forward so much to the wedding as Robin's romance had always been of intense interest to Jane from the first time we met her.

Robin, from Texas, had been in the Washington political scene at the same time as Janice and Whit and they had become firm friends. In 1981, when Janice was in Edinburgh, Robin was on a tour of Europe and dropped by for a couple of days. It seems that she had been madly in love with an Englishman she met in Washington and as a result of a breakdown in the relationship she returned to Austin, and little Miss Torrie had been the end result. Robin had been left a house there by her grandmother and she found a great job as a personal assistant to Mrs Lady Bird Johnson. Janice and Robin remained firm friends and Torrie was a constant companion to Ian and Roger. Many times Janice and her other girlfriends were invited with Robin to spend a long weekend at the Johnson ranch, a kind of grown-up sleep-over.

Jane could scarcely believe the good news. It appeared that Robin's original sweetheart had rediscovered his lost love after eight long years and was doing his level best to make amends. He and his pretty daughter hit it off exceedingly well and I remember how delighted Torrie was to have a Daddy. Janice's friends Carol, Patsy, Maralyn, and Mary-Anne were all thrilled with the whole idea. This kind of storybook romance had a real appeal for all of them. The wedding was a subdued but elegant affair and the reception to follow was held at Westwood Country Club. Ian and Roger, ten and eight years old, were dressed like little gentlemen, and Miss Louise was in a gorgeous gown in the very middle of everything. She and I had long conversations with Mrs Lady Bird Johnson, one of the honoured guests, and the three of us had our picture taken together. I must say I was most impressed with Mrs Johnson, she is quite a lady.

It was a great opportunity for me to renew my acquaintanceship with Robin's parents, who were from Houston. They had never been very sympathetic to Miss Robin's romance, both Juanita and Poppa Joe as Torrie called them, had always been a bit frosty to poor Robin, but the two of them absolutely adored Torrie. She, in turn, was devoted to Poppa Joe who was a real picture postcard cowboy, but a highly successful one. Robin and Torrie, now taking off for Washington, did nothing to improve the relationship as Juanita presupposed that henceforward she would see very little of them. I could see that the bridegroom was not anxious for a confrontation on the subject. Nevertheless, the celebration terminated without violence. The only casualty, if any, was Master Whit who had disappeared as soon as we got to the club and did not return. Jane thought it rather strange but assumed that he was more interested in his business than with the wedding.

Shortly after we arrived home in Ottawa, we left for a trip to Scotland, stayed at the Old Waverley Hotel on Princes Street and this way were able to entertain many of our family members. For the last half of the holiday we stayed at Linlithgow and to my surprise and delight a whole gang of Millers came up from England to see us. We had a splendid dinner party at 'Bonside', the original home of Sir Charles Wyville Thompson. Margaret, my eldest brother's only daughter, her husband, her daughter and her husband came from the Colchester area. Unfortunately, very shortly after, Margaret and her husband Peter took off for Hong Kong for a long-delayed second honeymoon and almost immediately upon arrival there she fell seriously ill. She had to be flown home by air ambulance. At the same time Alistair, second son of my third eldest brother, was there at Bonside with his wife, Gillian, and his three remarkably talented sons. It was a regular old home week for all of us at Linlithgow.

By the time we returned to Ottawa David had acquired his first house and with it the typical mortgage. Diane and he were so delighted with themselves it was a joy to be with them. The town house intrigued Miss Lynn so much that she found it difficult to wait till the following year to get a similar one. It was a real pleasure seeing them progress and participate in the so-called North American Dream. By now David was in the hardware end of the computer business and his mother, Lynn, was now an Assistant Manager with the Bank of Nova Scotia. There was still the problem of seeing Master Justin make his mark, but all in all we had little to complain about. Our life was great, everything was turning up roses until December 1993 when fate again took a hand and our world turned upside down.

CHAPTER XXI

REAWAKENING

That fateful day when the telephone rang I had an instinctive feeling of dread. Somehow I knew that it was bad news. It was Janice and she was utterly devastated. It was difficult to fully understand what she was saying as she did little more than whisper into the telephone. Jane and I were both on the line with hearts sinking into our boots. It finally became clear that after fifteen years of marriage Master Whit had suddenly decided that he didn't love her any more and that he planned on moving out without offering any explanation whatsoever. It is impossible for either Jane or I to remember how the conversation ended or what assurance we were able to offer. It seemed that she promised to call if there were any further developments and with tears at both ends of the line we hung up.

For four days we pondered the situation, discussed it, argued about it, but in no way resolved it. The problem simply would not go away. We were convinced that she and the children would not be abandoned or thrown out of the house. We waited and waited for the phone to ring but the silence was deafening. Jane could contain herself no longer so she called. It was Christmas Day. Whit answered the phone and abruptly advised her that Janice was not available, she was in hospital. He was brusque and hung up in the midst of her response. Next she called the hospital in a state of near hysteria and after discussion and argument at different levels she was finally connected to Janice's room where Janice merely sobbed and whimpered into the phone.

Fortunately her doctor came on the line and he was very patient and understanding when Jane identified herself as Janice's mother, 2,500 miles away. After making it clear to us that Janice was in the very depths of depression he emphatically stated that we should stay away. He advised that this was a situation whereby if Janice was to fully recover she must do it on her own. We had no alternative but accept the doctor's recommendation but now we were concerned with all the other problems – the children, the mortgage, the expenses and the unending list of responsibilities that go with a house and children.

Rosa, the housekeeper, had already moved in full-time and the children felt safe and happy, and even well fed. Her assurances in her Colombian accent were like a tonic to us. We breathed a lot more easily but the waiting was like an eternity. Jane, never patient, decided to call Janice's friends to gather whatever information might be available. Here again she was reassured. Carol Nieman and her husband were staunch friends and Carol assured us that she stayed abreast of the situation and would stay in touch. She and Carol Dochin reiterated the doctor's recommendation that we stay where we were and let Janice recover by herself, and this we did. Even so we had many sleepless nights. These kinds of anxieties cannot be easily cast aside and many a tear was shed.

Janice did recover quite quickly and on arrival home was at least assured that Master Whit would not abandon them. He agreed to continue covering the mortgage and provide the monthly housekeeping allowance. At this time he had decided, or been persuaded by a psychiatrist, that he should go to Montreal, Canada for a full month of treatment at an internationally-renowned clinic there. He claimed that this was necessary in order that he might find himself. For the first time in a long time I detected a little laugh in Janice's voice when she said that the fee for the clinic was 6,000 dollars. It was evident that Master Whit was generous to a fault with himself but positively miserly with his wife and children. We thought that the clinic idea was good news and that if anyone needed an army of shrinks to straighten him out, it was Whit.

By the time his month at the clinic in Montreal was over it was early February. During his period of incarceration there no phone calls were permitted. However at the end of it all, and supposedly having found himself, he persuaded Janice to fly to Montreal to join him and they would return to Austin together. The excitement in Janice's voice when she informed us of this development was obvious. We had high hopes of a reconciliation and for the first time in weeks we had a good night's rest. Again we waited for the phone calls and each weekend Janice did call to give us all the news of the children but appeared to be reticent about her relationship with Whit. Again we were concerned.

However, on a brighter note Janice called to advise us that Whit had persuaded her to attend the Montreal clinic for a month. His experience there had convinced him that she too deserved the joy of relaxation and the feeling of well-being. She was convinced that she should go. The children would be well cared for, the fees prepaid and the air travel was already arranged. She arrived in Montreal one day early, and Jane and I and she stayed overnight in a hotel at Dorval Airport. We drove down there, excited at the thought of seeing her again and she did not disappoint us. Janice was as dainty and as elegant and as self-confident as ever. The clinic limousine picked her up at the hotel entrance at ten in the morning.

There was lots of mother-daughter serious talk, but most of the time we were at least jovial and Janice appeared to be back to normal and displayed her customary sense of humour. As we drove back to Ottawa we felt quite reassured about the whole situation. Janice had brought pictures of herself and Whit at their reunion amidst the snow, with their arms wrapped around one another. The director of the clinic, a female, was included in some of the photographs and Janice had generated a good deal of respect for her. In the brief period she had been there to meet Whit, she and the Director had lengthy conversations and Janice was quite keen to see her again. We discussed all of this on the way home, but despite the reassurance there was still a nagging feeling of doubt.

We often spoke to the children by phone and they were happy to be with Rosa and their daddy, but were nervously awaiting the return of their mother. Whit came up to take her home and they went directly back to Austin. She called to say that all was well, the reconciliation was complete and the children were delighted to welcome her home. Jane and I breathed a heartfelt sigh of relief and we had a little celebration with Lynn and Michel. Indeed we were all at the point where we were making jokes and could readily identify the humour of the situation. Alas!, our joy was short-lived. It was exactly eight days later when Janice phoned to say, this time in a loud voice, 'He has done it again, Mother,' she cried. 'He is leaving me again.'

There may have been anxiety in her voice this time but there was no indication of depression. Apparently she had told him in no uncertain terms that if he was leaving then this time it was for good. He left with his clothes but nothing more. We offered to join her, but she refused reminding us that this was something she had to do alone. What she needed now was a good lawyer and the psychological support of her good friends. Fortunately they were there for her when she needed them. The children simply could not understand but there was no doubt in their minds that they were staying with mummy.

The next few months must have been absolute hell for Janice. She was there alone with three young children, Whit and his parents were as cold and distant as icebergs to her and on occasions were rude and unnecessarily cruel. But she was a very lucky girl in many other ways. She found the best lawyer in Austin and he was sympathetic to her cause. Without him I would have been afraid for her sanity. Almost immediately she had the assurance that the mortgage would be paid and the housekeeping allowance sustained. The greatest bugbear of all in the United States is insurance but this too was secured. By now Master Whit had also secured the services of a lawyer, a man not unlike himself, and the debate began. On those occasions when all parties would meet for negotiation of a settlement, Master Whit was getting tough and self-confident. There were times when Janice broke down on the phone to us and it was obvious that the strain was terrible.

They say that hell hath no fury like a woman scorned and there were times when I could detect a rising fury in Miss Janice's tone of voice. There was never a reason for Whit's leaving discussed, but there had never been any hint of philandering in Whit's past. Finally it was his continual smirk that got under Janice's skin and as a result she was convinced that there was something behind this whole affair, and she was bound and determined to find out about it. Her first clues as to where to begin an investigation arose from her visits to the support group she attended in Austin. This was a gathering of the local males and females who had spent time at the Montreal clinic. Most were young, educated, upper middle-class, and many were easy to talk to. Several suggested that she call the Director at the clinic.

In view of the group therapy sessions and the happy truth games they all played together at the clinic it was obvious that the notion of doctor/patient confidentiality went out of the door. One of the truth games involved each member of the group in a discussion on the root of their particular problem. Master Whit, during his spell in the hot seat, had described his dalliance with a member of his staff. As it turned out Janice, during her sojourn there, had become quite friendly with a gentleman from Philadelphia and they had exchanged phone numbers. When she called him he told her that his wife had been there ahead of him and her visit had coincided with Whit's. He called his wife to the telephone and the tête à tête began. Indeed it was true, Whit had confessed to a dalliance with a member of his staff, but no name was mentioned.

It was obvious that the lawyer would require a name and Janice puzzled about how she might find out. Some time previously she had had the responsibility for the personnel in the business and she had hired an exceedingly pretty married woman as Whit's secretary. Over time she and Janice had become quite friendly and as a consequence Janice felt that she might call her in confidence and ask if she knew what was going on. Such affairs were hardly suitable for telephone discussion during office hours so Janice decided to call this girl at home one evening. A man responded to the call and admitted to being the secretary's husband. He asked what he might do to help in the absence of his wife. Janice was hesitant about introducing the subject but the voice at the other end sounded helpful and sincere, even encouraging.

Finally she related the entire story to the voice and explained that she hoped that Whit's secretary might be aware of some office romance. To her complete surprise the voice grew suddenly harsh and almost venomous. Without hesitation he identified the guilty party as his wife and with this outright declaration their conversation became more animated, and the exchange of confidences provided Miss Janice with all of the necessary detail. With the name, the confirmation and with people willing to provide depositions regarding the group therapy sessions, the cat was well and truly out of the bag.

Lawyers are cagey characters and in due course, at one of the negotiation sessions necessary to establish an amicable divorce settlement he wiped the smirk from Master Whit's face even without divulging the full extent of the weapon at his disposal. From that moment on real progress was made. However when Whit finally was compelled to admit his infidelity and to make a deposition in this regard he was livid and made no secret of his displeasure. In so doing he admitted to several other cheap tricks he had played in the hope of relieving himself of his full financial responsibility to his family. Janice's visit to the Canadian clinic was no more than an excuse to get her out of the way so he could pursue his paramour, and at the same time video-tape every article of furniture and anything of value in the family home.

Obviously the family home would be sold and half of its value would go to Janice but he claimed that all of the items of furniture, silver and decor were antique, all were on his business inventory and therefore could not be divided. There was an offer on the house with a closing date in August yet he and his lawyer deliberately stretched out the negotiation to curtail any freedom of movement Janice might have. She was determined to remain in the same area for the sake of the children, their friends and their schools, but she didn't have the faintest idea how on earth she might manage it. I remember how she had visions of having to move into some cockroach-ridden apartment as it was obvious that the local houses were far too expensive for her. Once again fate took a hand. The elderly lady who lived next door was about to seek accommodation in a retirement residence and was considering putting her house on the market.

Miss Janice was almost feverish in her desire to acquire that house. It was the smallest and least expensive house on the block. It sat on the biggest and best lot and one would have thought that it was specially designed for Janice and her three children. She pursued every possible avenue and finally, with the benevolent lady fully acquainted with the detail of Janice's family disaster, a deal was struck, a deal that was a godsend for Janice. Her friend, a real estate expert, thought it was a fabulous deal and did all the work for her for free. With her share of the sale of the family home Janice could swing the deal and she was approved for a FHA 30-year mortgage at the lowest rate in years. It could be handled within her projected budget. She was so excited when she called that we thought she had won the lottery. The children just loved the house and they were all so excited about staying on in the area amongst their friends.

Whit was enraged when he heard about it and he declared that under no circumstances would he allow that family home sale to go through. Janice was devastated, the children were hysterical and the lawyers were at a loss to force anyone's hand. To secure the purchase of the house next door and accept the closing date, Janice needed 75,000 dollars in cash or an equivalent cashier's cheque. Finding money like that in her financial condition and with three kids was like looking for a needle in a haystack, or was it? Staunch friends came to the rescue. Carol Nieman, ever the concerned friend, and staying abreast of the situation took the matter up with her husband. A brief consultation with his mother about a family trust and within hours Janice had a valid cashier's cheque in the full amount.

At the settlement of the family home, when Master Whit announced that he would not sign the documents thereby depriving Janice of the necessary funds, he was crushed to discover that the Nieman family, well-known to his parents, had stepped into the breach thereby leaving him no option but to sign and walk away. It is difficult to estimate how he felt in view of the fact that only a few days earlier he had been boasting to the children that he would never allow them to get the house next door under any circumstances. Presumably he took off licking his wounds and in his absence Janice, aided and abetted by her friends, physically moved from 3308 Bowman to 3310. When she telephoned the news I gained the impression that they all felt as though they had moved into the enchanted forest.

From that moment on the negotiation towards a divorce settlement and its ratification was all downhill. In September, with the decree nisi in hand, and a satisfactory settlement formalized Miss Janice declared that she was now fully in charge of her life, not yet fully recovered from the psychological blow or the pain that goes with it, but at least ready for company. We were delighted to go. We were desperately anxious to see them and nervous about how they might be settled. We were surprised and delighted to discover a beautiful, comfortable home, the children had a massive trampoline at the bottom of the garden behind the house and on it they were truly jumping for joy.

The decree nisi defined the settlement and also provided schedules for the children's visits to their father and the details of his obligations in terms of country club dues, insurance, orthodontists, private schools etc. The lawyer had taken care of everything. He had even insisted that the entire settlement be insured. I was quite amused to discover that the State of Texas very wisely insists that the errant husband pays his alimony and child support to the State Treasurer, who in turn disburses the funds to the family through the County Treasurer's office. In addition, within the decree nisi there is a page of heavy type wherein the father is advised that failure to pay will earn him within thirty days, six months in jail, an admirable State law.

Janice, close to exhaustion, but in high spirits nevertheless, was preparing to renew her career and already had resumés in the post. She had contacts in Governor Ann Richards's campaign headquarters and was confident of making a fresh start in public relations. At the end of our vacation we departed with light hearts. The grandchildren had made a great fuss of us and they were so obviously happy that we were convinced that they were better off now that the decisions were made. They went off on their weekends when they were to stay with their father with little enthusiasm and always seemed to be delighted to get back home. In addition each of them was scheduled for sessions with Whit's favourite psychiatrist. Fortunately they treated the sessions with a considerable degree of scepticism and the good doctor finally gave up.

We had scarcely arrived home when Janice phoned to say that she was now in the public relations business in the Governor's campaign headquarters and was delighted to be back at work. Jane and I were very relieved and preparing for Christmas 1993. In addition we had plans to make for a trip to Scotland. Jane's niece and godchild, Nicola Jane Malcolm, was to be married on 7 May 1994. We knew that the wedding would bring relatives from all over the place so to avoid hassles we chose to reside in a very fancy guest house in Northumberland Street in Edinburgh. Mine host entertained us with his bagpipes at breakfast time. A rousing blast on the pipes went down very well with masses of bacon, sausages, haggis, eggs and tomatoes, with all the trimmings.

For an entire week we were entertained in different restaurants and pubs at parties in celebration of this great event. It was a relief when the wedding day finally dawned. The ancient church at Cramond really came to life that day. The sun shone and it was glorious, but bearing in mind it was Scotland, at the most inappropriate moment there was a brief shower of rain. Later, at a splendid reception at the Commodore on the banks of the Firth of Forth, the sky was beautiful, the water a dazzling blue, but a cold wind drifted gently in from the north. The ladies in their white suits and sunhats had to dance around to keep warm whilst the photographer fiddled about organizing different groups for his portraits.

The reception which went on past midnight was a unique celebration. We met, we gossiped and we tippled with relatives we had not seen in years. The young people, the bride, the groom, the bridesmaids and the young groomsmen were a fabulous group. It was a joy to be with them. For an all-too-brief spell we were amongst our 'ain folk'. Jane's brother Edwin was in his element and it was his kind of day. Chrissie, the mother of the bride, was gorgeous but in a constant state of panic. The bride's sisters, Christine and Diane, older by many years although they might stoutly deny it, and brother Stewart with his young wife Susan and their three small children were a handsome crew and a credit to the Malcolm clan. Each time I swallowed a nip of good Scotch whisky I thought for a brief moment of how John Malcolm, Jane's father and my old friend, would have enjoyed such a day.

We were able to mix Linlithgow visits even while staying in Edinburgh as there were so many obliging friends with cars. For the last half of our holiday we moved in with my sister at Linlithgow. Her son Ian and his wife, and daughter Kay and her husband were most attentive and to add to our joy her daughter Isabol came all the way from Australia to join us. We had a wonderful time together, so great a time that we were reluctant to leave. Since I was a small boy, Jean, my sister, and I have been close. We look alike and we think alike. I have always felt close to her children as I knew them so well when they were small. For decades we have kept in touch by correspondence and now that Isabol is in Australia she and I keep in touch by letter.

Strange as it may seem, although my sister has a son and two daughters there are no grandchildren. This became a topic of conversation on each of my visits as I am usually boasting about my grandchildren at every opportunity. However, on a recent occasion the conversation turned to more serious things. Many years earlier my sister had fallen heir to our mother's wedding china and it is by now close to a hundred years old. Her two girls convinced her that the china should go to Lynn, who has sons, and hopefully grandsons one day to whom it can be passed along. Lynn, with her passion for antiques, was more than anxious to get it and she made me promise to bring it back to Canada. I did not hesitate to agree as I assumed it was simply a case of telephoning Pickfords to come to pack it and ship it.

To my astonishment they advised me that the cost would be about 500 pounds sterling. Jane refused to believe it. I had made a promise to Lynn and I planned on keeping that promise. I decided to pack it and hand-carry it myself. I had a canvas carry-case with handles, so I acquired a stout cardboard box and cut it precisely to fit within the case. The china was carefully packed in crumpled newspaper and fitted tightly one piece into the other. The box took everything but the cake plates which were floated between Jane's silks and satins in a suitcase. The canvas carry-case sat between my knees tor the entire trip. Lynn was so delighted that she spent a fortune on a mahogany cabinet to house these treasures. So there is now a bit of the old Miller place to constantly remind Lynn of her forebears.

By November 1994 we were back in Texas. We had hoped to have a small part to play in Ann Richards's re-election as Governor of Texas but the fates decreed otherwise. Miss Janice, always alert to the voice of the people, foresaw a change in the State government and indeed she was right. George Bush's son won the election and Ann Richards was gracious in defeat. One can imagine the doom and gloom scenario in her campaign office where within days the staff would scatter to the four winds. Already Janice was working her tail off in 'Public Strategies', the largest of the political campaign management groups so prevalent in the United States. The hours were long and the travel involved left her with little time for the children, so rather wisely, she quit. This meant that she was totally free whilst we were there except for some extra work she was involved in with an old friend, Herb Reuben. This involved promotions and presentations and provided her with an opportunity to work within an area of special interest and with some very important local people.

However, she had to have a regular job, preferably part-time, to derive all the benefits of group insurance, so very necessary in the United States. Meanwhile she planned on spending Christmas at home with the children, then to seriously look for a job early in the New Year. Again fate was kind to her. She had a call from Washington DC advising her that Congressman Jake Pickle was retiring after something like forty years in the service of his Texas constituents. He planned on a return to Austin, opening an office and at the age of eighty-two continuing to pursue dedicated service to the State of Texas. He was welcomed home like the prodigal son. Every car on the highway had a bumper sticker reading 'Welcome home, Jake'.

Janice was overjoyed to be selected as his Administrative Assistant, and delighted to find out that he planned to restrict his hours to precisely what suited her. This meant that she could meet the two younger children at the school at 2.45 p.m. each day just like the other mothers did. Roger and Louise were delighted. Ian, of course at private school, leaving home about 7.30 a.m. each day and arriving back about 6.00 p.m., remained aloof from all the fuss. They were a family again. Janice could spend several evenings a week with Herb Reuben promoting and presenting their various activities.

On our return visit in April 1995 we gathered the impression that Miss Janice's world was back on an even keel. The children were happy and all straight 'A's at school. They went off on brief vacations with their father to places like Cancun, Mexico and Hawaii or whatever took his fancy. There was absolutely no doubt they were always delighted to get back home to mother. One day, whilst we were there, Jake Pickle dropped by for a visit. It was a memorable day for us as he is such a warm, easy guy to get along with. He had had an enviable career, is well-loved and admired by his constituents and greatly admired by his peers. Yet he was always a very gracious country gentleman with the heart of an old Texas country boy.

We stayed in Austin for Easter and Carol and Fred Nieman invited us to a family party at the Hyatt Regency Hotel on the riverbank. There was a delightful brunch served and the party occupied about three large round tables. One table took care of the children and they were happy to be on their own. Ian, Freddie and Roger must have been back for seconds about half a dozen times. Miss Louise was more of a young lady that day because of the influence of Freddie's younger sister Mary. After the party we were invited to the elder Mrs Nieman's home, a beautiful old mansion located in the prime area that had once been the heart of town. She lived alone, as a widow, but her son Fred and his wife Carol were very close and the grandchildren, Freddie and Mary were obviously very dear to her.

We left Austin for home and for the first time in a very long time we felt secure about Janice and her children. With her job, her house and her children, and with the staunch friends she has, we know that she is happy. She has been in the United States now for twenty-six years and twenty-three of these have been spent in Austin. Although she was born in Ottawa, in the Civic Hospital here, she now looks upon Austin as her home. We can but pray that the fates will be kind to her. As a consequence of this whole experience the children are developing character traits that will stand them in good stead in their future.

Here in Ottawa we feel settled again. Lynn has a lovely home and she is now a dedicated gardener. To her delight she was promoted to the status of Personal Banking Officer whereby she can now devote all of her time and talent to banking rather than to the supervision of personnel. I have the feeling that such a position is ideal for her. The experience gained in the financial management of other people's accounts should rub off and she can then apply her expertise to the development of her own portfolio.

Unfortunately when we returned home from Austin we discovered that she had damaged her back and X-rays and a catscan revealed that she had suffered a herniated disc. We worried about the possibility of a surgical operation but thanks to the skills of her physiotherapist she recovered sufficiently prior to seeing the neurosurgeon and it now appears that she should fully recover without benefit of surgery. Back problems have been the bane of Jane's existence since the day of her surgery in Baltimore, twenty-six years ago. On several occasions she has had appalling bouts of sciatica, one of the most painful complaints imaginable. Even as I write she is recovering from a devastating back problem. Meanwhile we receive letters from Scotland asking us when we plan on arriving there. The thought of six or seven hours on an aircraft is not a happy one for Miss Jane at the present time.

David is now a project engineer in the computer sciences business and he is very happy and successful at it. Diane is deeply involved in her nursing career and it is often difficult to get hold of the two of them together. They are both very ambitious and I have a feeling that they know what they are about and have very definite plans for their future. Justin has now flown the coop and is on his own in a cold, cruel world. His Nana worries a good deal about him, but at the same time she is confident that he will make his own way in his own time. As a small boy I can remember hearing my father say, 'You can lead a horse to water, but you canna make him drink'. This was his regular response to my mother's expressions of anxiety about her sons and their future.

And now their future is already in the past. All of the worry and the anxiety expressed by my mother is gone and forgotten, and I doubt if it ever had much influence upon the fate that was in store for each of us. All three of my brothers are now deceased. It seems like only yesterday when they were all alive and vibrant, each with a burning desire to control his own destiny. Yet it seems that circumstances played enough of a role to overwhelm their personal desires and they, and we, were but victims of our fate.

Very early in my career at sea I was presented with a copy of the Fitzgerald translation from the Arabic of the *Rubaiyat of Omar Khayyam*, a twelfth-century philosopher in Baghdad. It is comprised of seventy-five beautiful verses, and even considering Fitzgerald's brilliant translation the original must have been a masterpiece. Yet it was written before the days of Chaucer. The *Rubaiyat* outlines a philosophy of life that is difficult to dispute and many significant verses are retained in my memory. In 1964 Jane presented me with a brand new copy to replace my original which lies at the bottom of the Arctic Ocean amidst the wreckage of the MV *Cedarbank*. At those times in my life when tragedy strikes I am reminded of old Khayyam.

The verse that most often comes to mind is:

> Then to the rolling heav'n itself I cried,
> Asking, 'What lamp hath destiny to guide
> Her little children stumbling in the dark?'
> And – 'A blind understanding!' Heav'n replied.

And in my sadness I would remember when in my youth I had written a complete novel which I had titled 'Blind Understanding'. The original manuscript and the only copy I possessed were washed away in the terrible flood of the River Leader at Earlston in Scotland in 1948. At that time I had aspirations towards becoming a great writer but external circumstances took control of the destiny preordained for me and it is that which is recorded herein.

EPILOGUE

EPILOGUE

The summer of 1995 is on the wane, very soon we will batten down for the oncoming winter, and the cold arctic winds will remind us that another annual cycle has been completed. As I walk on the river bank in the dying light of day I can look into the heavens and still recognise the constellations and the stars that have guided mariners on their endless voyages for centuries. Old mother earth continues her ungainly orbit around a distant sun, providing us with our daylight and darkness, our summer and winter, and above all our sense of time. The constant repetition of the four seasons are the milestones by which our life is measured. The so-called three-score-and-ten is our allotted span and any years beyond are surely borrowed time.

It is now 183 years since my grandfather, the Auld Laird Miller, was born and there are times when I think I would like to see the full 200 years. But who knows what the fates have in store? Who knows when to terminate the memoirs? Perhaps it is best to prepare for today instead of trying to stare beyond tomorrow. Who knows? Perhaps a grandson will write a postscript. In our youth, in problem times, we referred to the light at the end of the tunnel, never believing that one day the light at the end of the tunnel would grow dim. Age catches up upon each of us in different ways and there will be a time when we will wonder what to do with the years.

Without doubt, if we are fortunate enough to be healthy, we will have time to remember, time to think, time to be more aware of the important things going on around us and perhaps time to be afraid. Even now I find myself remembering my grandfather McDiarmid and how he and I would march off to St Michael's Kirk on a Sunday without a thought for the weather. We were always half an hour early and I spent much of the time watching the changing light play upon the beautiful stained-glass windows. The Minister, the Reverend Doctor Coupar, glowered down upon us from his pulpit and his sermons were truly awesome to a small boy. Whilst I may have forgotten his message I have never forgotten the good Reverend Doctor.

Nevertheless his philosophy must have remained with me. During all of our travels throughout the world Jane and I have always been regular churchgoers, but without any real involvement in the work or support of the church. However Donald McDiarmid would be very happy to know that I finally became an elder of the church here, then as a member of the board I was persuaded to become more active and soon I was elected Chairman of the Finance Committee. The church is little more than seventy-five years old but the bricks and mortar here cannot compare to the massive stonework of St Michael's. Each year we face a financial crisis, we struggle against possible damage from the elements and against the threat of shortfall, but always praying for a miracle.

Witness and service to the church has now become an important part of our lives. It has greatly enhanced our social life, brought us closer to old friends, made new friends for us and has made us much more aware of the problems within our community. Above all it provides a sanctuary, a place of worship offering relaxation and peace of mind. The church, outside the sanctuary, is people and any group of people, anywhere, under any circumstances, means disputes, disagreements and resulting disorder. Finances generated by groups are the greatest problem of all, and they are never wholly adequate, so it is a constant struggle to survive. However, as always in life, it is tragedy and strife that brings out the best in people and in the end brings them closer together.

Within the church there are numerous small group ministries, some concerned with outreach and some dedicated to community activities. These give rise to social gatherings, all of which subscribe to the enjoyment of our leisure time. We have annual golf days, annual picnics and special celebrations. There are bi-weekly bridge parties, weekly youth groups, monthly men's clubs and monthly men's breakfasts.

Breakfasts don't sound all that exciting but with our group they are enjoyable, and a once-a-month dish of bacon and eggs can scarcely be harmful. It is the subsequent discussion that makes these meetings exciting. Those of us attending are retired, in the age range from sixty-five to nearly ninety, and the spectrum of professions represented provides a breadth of expertise in almost every topic of discussion. With our accumulation of years of experience in the fields of science and technology, military affairs and political affairs, coupled to the extent of our combined travel, entitles us to express an opinion on any subject.

Over the years these discussions have covered every conceivable political situation, every budgetary problem, every major crisis, every war, revolution or uprising, anywhere in the world. Whilst we do not always achieve unanimity of opinion, there is little doubt left in our minds regarding the likely outcome. All of us are alarmed at the prospect of a divided Canada, at the spreading of the war in the Balkans, at the obvious impotence of the United Nations, and indeed many of us are losing faith in the ability of any civilized nation to exhibit the leadership necessary to resolve these crises. The population explosion, increasing pollution, the wanton destruction of our dwindling resources, diminishing farm production, the rising level of starvation, and the horrifying spread of AIDS frightens us.

The awesome achievements of NASA in space exploration no longer impresses us. Their leadership in developing technologies, the breakthroughs in micro-electronics and the creation of virtual reality leaves us somewhat sceptical of their value to mankind. It appears to us that these technological advances are applied more to the advancement of weapons of war, or to the desktop computer industry to provide fun and games, rather than to the real benefit of mother earth. Vast sums are expended to apply these inventions to frivolity, to adapt the technology to the creation of ridiculous movies for the entertainment of an uneducated public, or to provide an Internet linking us all to useless information we do not need.

We are afraid that technology has outstripped our ability to educate. The rate of change of the rate of change in the emerging technologies is truly disturbing. The standards of education are hopelessly inadequate, the development and guidance of students is haphazard to say the least and everyone is now convinced that computer literacy is the key to success in any career. The arts and humanities are mostly ignored and emphasis is now centred upon the development of highly specialized skills. Young people are constantly bombarded with statements from our political leaders about the fearsome threat of global competition and the dire need to stay on top of the heap at any cost.

Without doubt the opportunities for success in the future will be limited to a chosen few. The rich will get richer and everyone else will remain in a highly stratified society where the vast majority will exist below the so-called poverty level. Computers coupled to machines, robots in other words, are replacing the skilled artisans, and their tireless, round-the-clock performance can quickly flood the market. Tradesmen and skilled workers will be relegated to the much-vaunted service industry where the rewards are less than satisfying. Rising dissatisfaction in the largest segment of the nation's workforce is not something that the politicians should ignore.

Even amongst the most advanced societies we see governments that are rife with corruption, countries that are living beyond their means and a constant charade played out by the politicians pretending to develop the legislation necessary to cure all the evils. Our newspapers are constantly reporting stories about revered public servants lining their pockets, civil servants padding their salary cheques and lobbyists influencing legislation that they know is for the benefit of their employers, and to the detriment of the taxpayer. We read about the ghastly array of chemical pesticides, and herbicides, freely used by our food producers, about train wrecks spilling poisonous chemicals and horrendous stories about pollution from massive hydro-carbon spills in our oceans. To add to the bad news we are treated to pictures and illustrations of the destruction of the Amazon rain forest, the one remaining, giant oxygen regenerator of our tainted atmosphere.

Under these circumstances, is it so surprising that nearly every developed country houses groups of religious fanatics and charlatans predicting the end of the world and willing to die for their peculiar cause? As we approach the end of this second millennium we have the evangelicals predicting the second coming of Christ. There are groups who describe the American Dream as a passport to Sodom and Gomorrah. We have television channels by the score, many with round-the-clock religion, but many others with an unending array of music videos that are utterly hideous. The music of the masters is rejected in favour of the bejewelled rap singer with his semi-nude chorus cavorting in the background. There is an unlimited supply of pornographic videos, and for a change of scene any young person of any age can lock into the Internet for an exchange of sexual images that distort the real intent of human nature.

Here, in 1995, in my declining years, at the age of seventy-seven, I have time to contemplate the state of the world. I am bombarded with news broadcasts, instant images of death, destruction, starvation, and out-and-out savagery. My world grows smaller by the day and I am assured from the television that it is ridden with suicide-bombers, horrifyingly destructive and deadly explosions, purveyors of poison gas, deadly drugs, and round-the-clock crime. However, I am advised how I can easily barricade my door against intruders, preserve my car from inevitable theft, and how to identify which one of my very few phone calls might be from a confidence man. To make life really worth living I am told that I can purchase lottery tickets that could make me an almost instant winner of millions.

For additional relaxation of course, I am provided with sports channels whereby I am privileged to watch multi-millionaires knock a golf ball around for a living. Others are batting little white balls or chasing footballs or hockey pucks for immense salaries, whilst the scores of thousands of spectators gladly hand over their hard-earned dollars for ridiculously expensive tickets to the game. The fact that some of the so-called stars may be throwing the game, or are high on cocaine, is of very little concern. I am always relieved to know that I am not involved in the traffic rat race following the game, particularly when the game might result in the award of a cup or a pennant and lead on to a parade.

Parades are supposedly ideal entertainment on television. National holidays, civic holidays, football cup finals, and anniversaries galore, like the Great Wars, the Victory Days, even Christmas, all provide an excuse for a parade. The truly massive parades, with military bands and all the pomp and ceremony that goes with them are generally dedicated to remembrance. Here we are treated to sombre spectacles where our fearless leaders, supported by the military brass, lay wreaths upon polished cenotaphs while pipe bands and brass bands march by with the aged, bemedalled survivors having their day in the sun. Following the 'Last Post' and the tearful faces remembering momentarily those who made the supreme sacrifice, the crowd drifts off in their shiny Japanese and German automobiles.

'Lest we forget' was the time-worn phrase used when I was a small boy remembering the millions of young men who were slaughtered in Flanders, in the war to end all wars. Today, on television, I can watch the crippled survivors of the Japanese death marches and the forced labour camps; and the thousands of so-called comfort women appealing for the courtesy of an apology and a pittance of compensation. Even after fifty long years their pathetic appeals fall upon deaf ears and no one cares. Who were the victors, and who the vanquished, we might ask?

With my television turned off and the satellite-directed images diverted elsewhere, there comes a time to remember, to contemplate, and reluctant though I may be to admit it, a time to be afraid. It is not a fear of living or even a fear of dying but a peculiar feeling of dread induced by thoughts of a final voyage into eternity. How can a man, looking up into the sky, into the vastness of the universe, not begin to wonder about that elusive but final destination. An ancient mariner like myself remains convinced that as always, when close to his destination, he picks up a pilot to guide him safely to his allotted berth.

Finally, at the voyage end, when the scrutiny of my records may induce recrimination and regret, I will once again remember my old friend Khayyam, who included these verses within his *Rubaiyat*:

> And the moving finger writes; and, having writ,
> Moves on; nor all thy piety nor wit
> Shall lure it back to cancel half a line,
> Nor all thy tears wash out a word of it.

> And that inverted bowl we call the sky,
> Whereunder crawling coop't we live and die
> Lift not thy hands to it for help –
> For it rolls impotently on as thou or I.

So we move on towards the end of this second millennium not knowing why or whence we came and still not knowing whither we are bound. An endless voyage shrouded in the fog of doubt and fear has always been the mariner's destiny. Today I heard a female voice on the radio singing, 'Is that all there is?' and I must confess I smiled remembering old Khayyam's philosophy of 'Come, fill the Cup'.

Without doubt these modern times bring with their affluence sets of options that confuse. Where do we go? What do we do? When do we do it? We have freedom of choice, freedom of movement and a selection of golden credit cards. Where our aged forebears merely wandered out into the face of a winter storm to ease the way to paradise, our generation are poised to wear themselves out before they even reach it.

Despite the television images of starvation, slaughter, disease and the threat of a population explosion, we are assured by our medical researchers that the aging process can be delayed and we can all live to be 130 years old. Another reminder that surely we must be God's chosen people, or are our medical breakthroughs and organ transplants to be available only to those who can afford them? The finance gurus ignore the happy scenarios promised by the medical researchers and they predict bankruptcy for Medicare and massive cut-backs for health plans. So what does the world really face? Will it be Shangri-La, or will it be the Apocalypse?

It is my firm conviction that I have been privileged to live out my life at the very peak of progress in our human society. It was for me a rare gift from Providence to have been born in Scotland, and as a consequence to have had ease of access to every other country in the world. Being aware of the dreadful conditions over much of the world it is a real privilege for us to spend our declining years in the vast, peaceful realm of Canada. Were it possible to ignore the ghastly problems that plague our planet, we could spend the rest of our days in happy contentment. However, as the pundits say, we now live in a global village and it is inevitable that we must share. The sharing of dwindling resources will certainly not lead to peace and tranquillity.

How I envy the Auld Laird and the lifestyle of his generation. As a successful man of advanced years with young sons he could foresee a future for them in a stable world that offered adventure with rewards for those with the courage to seek it. As the youngest son of his eldest son, I try to gauge the problems this global village will present to my grandsons and to their offspring but as always I am reminded that there is a veil through which we cannot see. The answer to our prayers for them will never be known to us. Their voyage upon the sea of life, like mine, will terminate at the edge of eternity.

APPENDIX

APPENDIX 1

THE MILLER FAMILY

Records are available at the Office of the Registrar in Linlithgow, Scotland. These can be easily verified where they are carved in stone in the graveyard of St Michael's Church, the Parish Church of Linlithgow, Scotland.

GRANDPARENTS

The Farmhouse,
Linlithgow Bridge,
Linlithgow.

The Auld Laird

William Miller	Born 1812	Died 1896	Aged 84 years
Married in 1866			
Jane Douglas Stewart	Born 1844	Died 1916	Aged 72 years

CHILDREN

1.	Annie	Born 1868	Died 1934
2.	William	Born 1870	Died 1935
3.	Robert	Born 1872	Died 1951
4.	James	Born 1874	Died 1959
5.	Barbara	Born 1878	Died 1879
6.	Alexander	Born 1882	Died 1953

1.   Annie   Married John Crawford – Settled on a large farm in Colchester, England.

Children 4 Sons 3 Daughters.
William, John, Hugh, Douglas, May, Annie, and Jeannie.

2. William Married Belle McDiarmid – Inherited The Farmhouse at Linlithgow Bridge.
Children: 4 Sons 4 Daughters.
William, Donald, Robert, Annie, Jean, Helen, Ian (yours truly) and Margaret.

3. Robert Remained a Bachelor.

4. James Married very late in life to his Housekeeper, Jennie Steele. Children: None.

5. Barbara Died in infancy.

6. Alexander Married very late in life to his Housekeeper, Mary. Children: None.

THE MILLER TRUST: was bequeathed to St Michael's Church in memory of the Auld Laird Miller by his sons and a brass plaque is embedded in one of the stone pillars of the church to commemorate it.

MATERNAL GRANDPARENTS

Donald McDiarmid Born 1844 Died 1937 Aged 93 years
Married
Annie Black Born 1850 Died 1917 Aged 67 years

CHILDREN

1. Jeannie Married Harry Candler, Customs & Excise.
Children: 1 Son 2 Daughters.
Nora, Nancy, and Harry.
Lived in Joppa, East of Edinburgh.

2.   Annie   Married Robert Crichton, Managing Director,
                   Scottish Oils Ltd.
                   Children: 2 Sons 2 Daughters.
                   Archie, Margaret, Anne, and Robert.
                   Lived at Castlepark, Philpstoun.

3.   Helen   Married Robert Forrester, Barrister.
                   Children: None.
                   Lived at Broxburn, West Lothian.

4.   Isabella   Married William Miller, Farmer.
                   Children: 4 Sons 4 Daughters.
                   William, Donald, Robert, Annie, Jean, Helen, Ian
                   (yours truly), Margaret.
                   Lived at The Farmhouse, Linlithgow Bridge.

5.   Margaret   Married Tom Trowsdale, Wholesale Grocer.
                   Children: None.
                   Lived in Darlington, England.

PARENTS
(At The Farmhouse)

William Miller	Born 1870	Died 1935	Aged 65 years
Married in 1903			
Isabella McDiarmid	Born 1881	Died 1973	Aged 93 years

CHILDREN

1. William	Born 1905	Died 1979	Married Letitia Greig. 2 Sons 1 Daughter. William, Margaret, Bruce.
2. Donald	Born 1907	Died 1966	Married Grace Wyllie. 2 Sons 1 Daughter. Gordon, Donald, Maureen.
3. Robert	Born 1908	Died 1967	Married Emma Marshall.

				1 Son, Robert. Widowed and remarried Gladys 1 Son, Alistair
4.	Annie	Born 1911	Died 1976	Married Ernest Schofield, Steeplejack. 1 adopted daughter, Joyce.
5.	Jean	Born 1914		Married John Morrison, Transport Manager. 1 Son 2 Daughters Ian, Isabol, Kay.
6.	Helen	Born 1916	Died 1928	Of rheumatic fever.
7.	Ian	Born 1918		Married Jane Malcolm. 2 Daughters. Lynn Anne, Janice Elaine
8.	Margaret	Born 1920	Died 1921	Of convulsions.

Notes: Cousins surviving as of 1995

Anne Crichton.	Spinster. Lives in Edinburgh.
Robert Crichton.	Married with 5 Children, and numerous grandchildren. Lives on a very large farm at Winchburgh, Scotland.
Annie Crawford.	Spinster. Lives in south of England.

NEPHEWS and NIECES

1.   William.

Son William, Ph.D. in Nuclear Physics.
Married twice, no children.
Lives in Kent, England.

Daughter Margaret, married Peter Hockin,
Construction Engineer.

Lives in Colchester, England.
2 Daughters, Shona and Wendy.

Son Bruce, married twice in Australia.
3 daughters, Monique, Venora, Martina.
Lived in Cairns and Brisbane Australia.
Died in December 1994.

2.   Donald.

Son Gordon, married twice in Australia.
1 Son, Ian Miller.

Son Donald, recently married for third time.
Several daughters. Lives in England but
sustains home in Canada.

Daughter Maureen, married, no children. Lives
in Flesherton, Ontario, Canada.

3.   Robert.

Son Robert, by first marriage.
Married, no children.
Lives in Stirling, Scotland, has own Electrical
Business.

Son Alistair, by second marriage.
Married Gillian, has 3 sons.
Lives in Pennicuik, near Edinburgh.
Head of Dept of Languages at High School.

4.   Annie.

One Daughter, adopted, Joyce.
Joyce is married and lives somewhere in the
north of England.

5.   Jean.

Son Ian is married, no children.
Lives in Haddington, Midlothian, Scotland.

Daughter Isabol, is married, no children.
Lives in Brisbane, Australia, and runs a Travel
Agency.

Daughter Kay, like her grandmother was a

Schoolteacher. Married no children.
Lives in Edinburgh, Scotland.

6.   Helen.   Died in adolescence.

7.   Ian.   Married Jane Malcolm, 2 Daughters.
                           See page 305.

8.   Margaret.   Died in infancy.

APPENDIX 2

THE MALCOLM FAMILY

John Malcolm	Born 1866	Died 1950
Annie S. Swan	Born 1872	Died 1952

CHILDREN

1.	Margaret	Married Frank Buckle – Lived in Duns, Scotland. 1 Son, Malcolm.
2.	John	Married Robina Wilson. 1 Son 1 Daughter. John Edwin, and Jane Foster.
3.	Nicol	Married. 1 Son 1 Daughter. Lived in southern Scotland.
4	Elizabeth	Married Wm Waite, Chief Constable. 2 Sons. Lived in Duns, Scotland.
5.	Joy	Married Peter Simpson, 3 Daughters. Lived in Duns, Scotland.
6.	Ena	Married Sam Walker. No children. Lives in Earlston, Scotland.

WIFE'S PARENTS

John Malcolm Married	Born 1896	Died 1962
Robina Wilson	Born 1896	Died 1979

CHILDREN

1. Jane Foster   Born 1920   In Coldingham, Scotland.
2. John Edwin   Born 1924   In Coldingham, Scotland.
    Married Christine Burke and has 4 children: 1
    Son   3 Daughters.
    Diane, Spinster, no children.
    Christine, married, no children.
    Stewart, married with 3 children.
    Nicola Jane, married, no children.

MARRIAGES

Ian Alexander Miller,   Jane Foster Malcolm
Born 10 January 1918   Born 19 June 1920
At Linlithgow, Scotland.   At Coldingham, Scotland.

Married on 14 June 1941
At North Merchiston Church,
Edinburgh, Scotland
By the Reverend John Penman.

CHILDREN

1. Lynn Anne   Born 11 August 1944 in Edinburgh, Scotland.

2. Janice Elaine   Born 3 November 1954 in Ottawa, Canada.

MARRIAGES

1. Lynn Anne   Married Richard Miskelly 1963. 2 Sons.
    Richard David   Born 1964
    Justin Francis   Born 1974.

2. Janice Elaine   Married Whit Hanks in Austin, Texas in 1979.
    2 Sons   1 Daughter.
    Ian Hancock Edinburgh Hanks. Born 1981

Roger Cameron Linlithgow Hanks. Born 1983
Louise Foster Coldingham Hanks. Born 1987.

MARRIAGE OF GRANDSON

Richard David Miskelly married Diane on 15 June 1991, in Ottawa, Canada.

BIBLIOGRAPHY

Much of the historical data contained in Chapter III was gleaned from a study of the following:

1. Wm. F. Hendrie, *LINLITHGOW, Six Hundred Years a Royal Burgh* (John Donald Ltd., Edinburgh BH3 5AA).
2. Bruce Jamieson, *The Church of St Michael of Linlithgow* (printed by Inglis Allen (Kirkcaldy) Ltd).
3. Mark N. Powell, *A Brief Architectural and Historical Guide* (Linlithgow Civic Trust).